Evening

PROMISES

90 Devotions to End the Day Well

JENNIFER GERELDS

DaySpring

LIVE YOUR FAITH

CONTENTS

TIME FOR REST

I t's hard for most of us to put a finger on it, really. *What is it* that makes us try so hard at (or in some cases avoid) the life we find set before us? As if on autopilot, we wake up each morning driven by the day's agenda, propelling us out of our beds and into action. We have work to accomplish. Schedules to keep. Church activities to attend. People to experience (and strive to please). *Life to live.* We're never certain what we will encounter in our unrelenting race, but we know one thing's for sure: unless something monumental stops us, we have to keep going. Keep pushing. Keep striving. If we don't, won't we miss out? Or worse, *won't things fall apart?* we subconsciously worry.

But what if our worst fears are *unfounded*, a cultural misconception that keeps us from truth? What if our pursuits are precisely the reason we're reeling from exhaustion and unable to experience the peace and security we crave? What if the best way to win at life's race is to rest instead of run harder?

Jesus says it is.

Time after time throughout all of Scripture, God invites, calls, and even commands His people to rest from their efforts to be God...to be still and remember something important, a reality we can't see when our minds and lives are filled with the clamor of constant activity: God alone is in charge and has a plan bigger and better than ours. He, the Sovereign One, is God... and we are not.

When we remember this fundamental truth, two miracles unfold. First, we find delightful freedom. It is amazing how light our hearts feel when we know that someone stronger and more capable than us shoulders our burdens. Then, as we witness His faithfulness and sufficiency in our struggles, we find our souls able to settle into true trust. Surrender to and trust in our more-than-capable and loving Father ushers us into lasting peace and promised rest.

Could you use a little R & R in your life right now— and always? *Evening Promises* is a ninety-day devotional sabbatical from the pull-yourself-up-by-the-bootstraps burden found everywhere else today. It invites you daily into the greater reality of God's goodness and provision already made for you. In His presence alone, your soul will find the perspective, hope, and peace you need for this day.

THE DIVINE DECREE

*By the seventh day God had finished
His work, and so He rested.*
GENESIS 2:2 CEV

Every time you round that corner in your house, you see him curled up in a ball on his favorite chair—the one that once served people but now has become a rather royal bed for your beloved cat. "Must be nice," you mutter, as you give him a quick stroke behind the ears. "How do you sleep all day?" For just a quick second, you ponder what it's like to be a cat. How would it feel to rest like that and not feel bad about it?

It isn't just our pets that give us a picture of rest. Every other kind of living creature does, too. Yet as humans, we feel exempt from this part of the created order. For sure, work is necessary—a God-ordained command and calling. But we have to wonder about our balance when we doze at traffic lights and yawn throughout our meetings. Our bodies are sending a signal that our kindhearted Creator wants us to hear:

we all need rest, from the tips of our toes to the depths of our souls.

The great news is that we can choose rest without guilt. Better still, God says we must rest—not only physically but also spiritually—if we want to really know Him. His divine permission unfolds in the first few pages of Scripture when He rested from His important work, and His call to follow suit fills the rest of His written Word. Only when we stop striving can we recharge our bodies and refocus our minds to the truth of who we are: humans fully dependent on God and designed to follow His lead in every way.

Then He said to them,
"The Sabbath was made for man,
not man for the Sabbath."
MARK 2:27 NIV

GREEN PASTURES
in the PRESENT

The LORD is my shepherd, I lack nothing.
He makes me lie down in green pastures,
He leads me beside quiet waters,
He refreshes my soul.
PSALM 23:1–3 NIV

That familiar feeling of panic is about to set in, and you feel it rising from the pit of your stomach straight to your head. As if on steroids, your mind races ahead of the emotion, rehearsing all the details that must fall into place before you can finally get a grip. In the moment (and it turns out there are many of these moments every day), it feels like so much is at stake if you fail. Fear grips you and threatens to sabotage your plans, your work—and ultimately your worth.

But as always, fear is a liar. If you are God's child, you are not on your own, struggling to pull all the necessary strings to make life work in your favor. With Jesus at your side, you lack nothing! His all-powerful hand leads you through life's twists and turns, always providing access to the calm, gentle streams of His indwelling spirit. No matter how crazy the day gets, God's presence with you in it is a verdant pasture of peace for your soul.

Today, if you feel panicked about an upcoming project or problem, don't let your mind race with all the what-ifs. Instead, put your mind and heart to rest by remembering that your God has this day—and your life—in His hands. Let the Shepherd lead you through each moment as you acknowledge His presence and goodness in it. Look to Him for guidance and lie down in His promised care.

> *The LORD makes firm the steps*
> *of the one who delights in Him;*
> *though he may stumble,*
> *he will not fall, for the LORD*
> *upholds him with His hand.*
> *I was young and now I am old,*
> *yet I have never seen*
> *the righteous forsaken or*
> *their children begging bread.*
> PSALM 37:23–25 NIV

TUCKED AWAY

They marched for three days after leaving
the mountain of the LORD,
with the Ark of the LORD's Covenant moving ahead of
them to show them where to stop and rest.
As they moved on each day,
the cloud of the LORD hovered over them.
NUMBERS 10:33–34 NLT

The room smelled of finger paint and playdough, the class of kindergarteners working steadily at their stations, when their teacher made the call: "Time to put up your work and get out your mats," she announced cheerfully. A few kids grumbled, resisting her assistance, but most went without incident to the mats designated for their daily rest. With lights off and mouths closed, the once-rowdy children soon drifted off to sleep, their tiny bodies refueling energy for all that lay ahead.

Like the teacher, people who know children understand the importance of rest for growing healthy young minds and bodies. In a similar way, God knows what His children need—even when we're convinced we need to keep going. He goes before us, providing pockets of time for needed rest tucked into each day when we can turn our minds and cares over to Him. But unlike the teacher, He doesn't force the issue. We must be willing to be still when the moment presents itself. Instead of turning on the radio, surfing the Web, or scrolling through social media whenever there's a lull, let your attention turn to God and His Word. Allow yourself time to rest in stillness, simply thinking about who He is and how He cares for you. At the end of the day, you will find that your time was never wasted. Instead, your mind and soul's rest today readies you for all God has in store for you tomorrow.

Your Father knows what you need before you ask Him.
MATTHEW 6:8 NIV

Storm Shelter

Whoever dwells in the shelter
of the Most High will rest
in the shadow of the Almighty.
PSALM 91:1 NIV

You can remember the moments like they were just yesterday—those chilling childhood memories when the terror of a night's dream or a clapping crash of thunder outside your window woke and worried you. Crouching low under the covers simply wouldn't cut it. Fear moved you out of your bedroom in search of a safer, more substantial place of shelter. Slipping silently between your parents even as they slept, your pounding heart quieted. Your panic stilled as your breathing fell in sync with theirs. Nestled next to them, you felt safe, surrounded by such powerful love.

As you grew up, though, so did your knowledge of the world. You learned: earthly parents—and people in general—aren't fail-proof. Real-life problems don't always disappear with the dawn. Fearful unknowns like insufficient finances, broken relationships, and failing health can leave you feeling like you did as a child, powerless to calm the mounting pressures all around you. Only this time, your problems are greater than any parent can solve...except your heavenly Father.

Child of God, you don't need to stay stuck in your fears, afraid of what is to come, wondering who can help. Leave the isolation of self-reliance and turn to God Almighty. He is a shield and source of comfort like no other. Not only is He right beside us, He is above us, below us, before us, and behind us! Better still, He put His Spirit *in* us so we can sleep, wake, and walk in total confidence that we remain always in His competent and constant care.

But as for me,
it is good to be near God.
I have made the Sovereign LORD my refuge.
PSALM 73:28 NIV

Be Carried

Then Jesus said, "Come to Me, all of you who are weary
and carry heavy burdens, and I will give you rest. Take My
yoke upon you. Let Me teach you, because I am humble and
gentle at heart, and you will find rest for your souls.

MATTHEW 11:28–29 NLT

It was supposed to be fun, according to the brochure. All you had to do to be certified to scuba dive was to complete a short training session, one that required you to swim the length of the pool and back a few times to demonstrate your ability. *No problem*, you think—until you step up to the pool's edge. "We have to put a weight belt around you to simulate diving conditions," they announce. A million arguments mount in your mind against the idea but they fasten the belt anyway, and you begin the now extremely difficult feat of swimming with all the extra weight. Before you've crossed the pool even once, exhaustion sets in and you start to think, *Maybe scuba diving isn't for me!*

Unfortunately, many people come to the same conclusion about their spiritual lives. They hear that a relationship with God is supposed to bring peace and joy, but they find that some of the religious leaders and even thoughts in their own mind are weighing them down with performance requirements too heavy to carry. *Being a Christian is just another burden,* they conclude.

But the truth brings blessed relief! Jesus beckons us to take on His yoke—His way of living—instead of the impossible burdens we find ourselves carrying on our own. Instead of weighing us down, His belt of truth actually buoys our spirits, filling our hearts with light, hope, and all the power we need to finish all the good works He has planned for us to do. Following Jesus His way frees us from all guilt and condemnation, fuels our hearts with unending love, and propels us toward our life purpose. And nothing's more fun than that!

But whatever were gains to me I now consider loss for the sake of Christ. What is more, I consider everything a loss because of the surpassing worth of knowing Christ Jesus my Lord, for whose sake I have lost all things. I consider them garbage, that I may gain Christ and be found in Him, not having a righteousness of my own that comes from the law, but that which is through faith in Christ——the righteousness that comes from God on the basis of faith.

PHILIPPIANS 3:7–9 NIV

PRICELESS REST

Is anyone thirsty?
Come and drink—even if you have no money!
Come, take your choice
of wine or milk—it's all free!
ISAIAH 55:1 NLT

Last month it was your turn. Your daughter got married and you pulled out all the stops to make it a wonderful memory. But the detailed planning and provision for the large event took quite a toll on your savings. *So much for retiring early*, you thought.

But today is different. You've been invited to someone else's party, and you don't have to prepare a thing. Upon arrival, you notice tables filled to overflowing with every kind of treat imaginable, with drinks all free for the taking as well. It doesn't take long for you to settle in, surround yourself with friends, and splurge on all the free goodness provided for you!

So guess what it's going to be like in heaven? The God of all creation has prepared a wedding feast for His people like no other party on our planet.

Everything we could wish for and then some will be provided at no cost to us—at all!

But God's celebration over His people doesn't start at some future time. It begins the very moment we decide to accept His invitation to come to Him. At no cost to us, God provides a feast of divine riches that are all ours for the taking because of our connection to Jesus. Are you out of wisdom? He's got that. Could you use a little joy? There's a fountain of it right here. Are you craving real and lasting relationship? You've come to the right place. The one thing He asks is that we leave our baggage with Him at the door. He knows just where to dispose of it. He's even got your party clothes covered, courtesy of Jesus, who already paid for it all.

They feast on the
abundance of Your house;
You give them drink from Your river of delights.
PSALM 36:8 NIV

FEAST *of* KINGS

You prepare a feast for me
in the presence of my enemies.
You honor me by anointing my head with oil.
My cup overflows with blessings.
Surely your goodness and unfailing love will pursue me
all the days of my life,
and I will live in the house of the LORD forever.
PSALM 23:5–6 NLT

At this moment, for different reasons, all your important relationships seem on the rocks. Your mother is frustrated with your infrequent visits. Your neighbors complain about how you keep your yard. Your kids get mouthy when you make them put away their phones, and your spouse said something sarcastic that sent your mind spinning with anger and worry. *They are not my enemies!* you mentally remind yourself as you try to keep your composure through all the relational interactions. But sometimes it feels as if they really are your enemies, leaving you feeling isolated and alone, your heart in utter unrest.

So picture this: All the people in your life who put different demands on you are standing in a circle around you. But in the center of it all, you're seated at a table overflowing with incredible food. Beside you sits Jesus, the King of all creation. He has prepared this feast before you and offers an exclusive opportunity for you to dine with Him—in perfect peace. Would you put everything else aside and focus on His favor, or would you continue to fret about everyone else around you?

Where we place our focus determines our level of peace in the present moment. Psalm 23 tells us that God does, in fact, prepare tables of delight right in front of our enemies, and He invites us to come and sit in the comfort of His company—no matter what mayhem swirls around us.

Today, will you turn your attention from all that seems wrong to see the Savior who faithfully stays by your side, supplying an abundance of goodness in the fellowship?

Look! I have been standing at the door, and I am constantly knocking. If anyone hears Me calling him and opens the door, I will come in and fellowship with him and he with Me.
REVELATION 3:20 TLB

PERFECT POSTURE

We have freedom now because Christ made us free.
So stand strong. Do not change and go back
into the slavery of the law.

GALATIANS 5:1 ICB

It's not that we don't know better. Oodles of times we've heard our parents, teachers, and physicians tell us, "You need to sit up straight." Posture is important! When we slump, our muscles fatigue and back pain inevitably ensues. And yet a curious phenomenon occurs as we drive long hours or sit at the computer. Slowly our shoulders start to sink, sometimes until they're almost in our laps! Gravity seems to take its toll despite our best intentions.

Spiritually speaking, God's people fight another similar dilemma even more damaging than poor posture: we slip out of alignment with the truth of God's grace. Though we know our salvation was a gift, we slowly start sinking back into a performance posture with God, trying to earn and keep His favor by our record. But like our parents and teachers, the apostle Paul warns us: *Watch your posture!* Don't let your minds slip back into a performance mentality. Jesus already finished the work of flawless living—followed by sacrificing His own life—that won God's favor on your behalf. You are now free to rest in God's unchanging affection, reaching your full potential through the power of Christ inside you.

Have you felt your spiritual posture slipping lately, sinking back into the wrong belief that God only loves you when you get it right? Our secure position in Christ and God's favor rests on God's incredible provision, not our performance. Confess the sin of self-reliance and sit up straight under the truth of God's grace, head held high with confidence as a chosen and beloved child of the King!

We who have believed are able to enter and have God's rest.
HEBREWS 4:3 ICB

The PEACE PARADOX

You, Lord, give true peace.
You give peace to those who depend on You.
You give peace to those who trust You....
Lord, all our success is because of what You have done.
So give us peace.

ISAIAH 26:3, 12 ICB

Before you even head out the door, you know by experience what's about to unfold. Months ago you agreed to volunteer at your church's VBS (thank the Lord you're not the one in charge). You simply agreed to show up and carry out whatever need they had...which turned out to be a class leader. Before you started to stress, though, the coordinator handed you the schedule, the script, and everything you needed to sail smoothly through the day. Though far from flawless, you still watched all the pieces fall into place with a small crowd of children knowing Jesus better in the end, a paradoxically exhausting and exhilarating experience.

Such is the mysterious nature of God, who calls us to work and rest in the same breath. Work to believe.

Rest because faith is a gift. Work out your salvation. Rest because God is the One really doing all the work in you. There is peace when we work in obedience, resting in God's provision—the paradox of true Christian living.

When Jesus invites His people to rest in His hope and peace, He isn't promising an easy or pain-free life. To the contrary, He guarantees that we will encounter trouble, a by-product of our broken, sinful world. The incredible news is that He has overcome the world and our problems in it. Like the VBS experience, He has already written the script and orchestrated every moment of history for His glory and the good of His people. Our part? We show up. We make ourselves available to do what only He can, what He chooses to do through us. We actively participate in God's work while our souls stay at rest, knowing He's in charge and has planned it all according to His purpose.

Jesus answered, "The work of God is this:
to believe in the one He has sent."
JOHN 6:29 NIV

INVITED *to* COME

Your spouse is turning fifty. Already he has mentioned, on more than one occasion, how much he'd like to reconnect with all his friends. So you begin to plan a party, one that will celebrate a life of special relationships. As you pull out all the stops, planning food, decorations, and places for everyone to sit, you ponder who to include. Invitations go out, and the waiting begins. After awhile a few RSVPs come back, but you can't help but feel a little nervous. What if no one comes? What if everyone you ask is already busy with work and kids and the other million calendar fillers that keep us all so disconnected?

What if that's a little taste of how God feels about us?

After all, He has planned not just a party but an entirely new life for every person who comes into His kingdom. He invites us to come and take part in the extravagance of His provision and love, connecting with other people who have chosen to come. But an invitation remains only that, if we don't respond. If we carry on with our worrisome ways, packing in even more activities in our hectic schedules, striving so hard for some semblance of the good life, but miss the spectacular opportunity that lies before us—what will we reap? Fleeting moments of happiness are a sad substitute for the life of eternal blessing and hope God has planned to last forever.

Today, don't turn down God's invitation to rest in His sovereign goodness. Turn from the temptation to plot your own life's course and pursue, instead, God's path to perfect peace through relationship with Jesus. Let the party begin!

Then he sent some more servants and said, "Tell those who have been invited that I have prepared my dinner: My oxen and fattened cattle have been butchered, and everything is ready. Come to the wedding banquet."
MATTHEW 22:4 NIV

REMEMBER WHO GOD IS

Do you not know? Have you not heard?...
Your Maker is your husband—
the LORD Almighty is His name—
the Holy One of Israel is your Redeemer;
He is called the God of all the earth.
ISAIAH 40:28, 54:5 NIV

You're starting to wonder if your entire family has a hearing problem. You feel certain you've asked the kids at least three times to clean up their mess, though it lingers still on the kitchen counter. And last time you checked, the very simple to-do list you left with your spouse is only halfway finished. It's hard, really hard, not to blow a gasket. But even under the simmering anger there's a more sinister fear lurking, though you work diligently to keep it suppressed. *Your control methods aren't working.* In fact, you can't get anyone to do anything that you want—that you desperately feel like you need. And if you're honest, at times you feel utterly helpless. Is there anyone reliable out there to come to your rescue?

Fortunately, the answer is yes! But you won't find your hero in your family or even your friends. The truth is, we don't just need clean counters and competent spouses to have peaceful hearts. We all need *saving*—including the people we secretly hope will make all of our anxieties and problems go away. Only one person on our planet, and in the entire universe, possesses the power to deliver us out of our current predicament, as well as position us for our eternal home in heaven, and it's Jesus. The One who created us calls Himself our Husband, sworn to uphold, protect, and provide for His people for as long as we both shall live...which is forever with Him. When we recognize that God is the very present help we need, we can rest assured that He will give us the grace, patience, and love we need to handle life's challenges well.

> The LORD is the everlasting God,
> the Creator of the ends of the earth.
> He will not grow tired or weary,
> and His understanding no one can fathom.
> ISAIAH 40:28 NIV

FAMILY BLESSING

Since you are God's children, God sent the Spirit of His Son into your hearts, and the Spirit cries out, "Father."
GALATIANS 4:6 NCV

It felt so foreign, this new life of love that she, a former orphan, was now feeling. Meetings had happened, papers were signed, transactions were finished. And now this young child was surrounded by new family and friends who loved her as if she had been there all along! Though she had not learned their language, their hearts spoke clearly through the hugs and smiles that encircled her. Her former life had been filled with pain. Now, she was finally home.

So it is with every person who places their trust in Jesus. When we enter into relationship with God, we step into a family bound by a love beyond our wildest dreams. Before time even began, before the first star began to shine, our triune God lived out the love that is His very nature. Father, Son, and Holy Spirit served One another in perfect unity, adding angels as witnesses to the wonderful bond. But as love always does, it expands. It grows. And God created people to share in the bliss of His perfect, beautiful, boundless love.

Today, let the love of God's forever family free you from your fears of abandonment. You will never walk another step without God right beside you, His Son covering you, and His Spirit filling you with the fruit of His incredible presence. You are a part of God's family blessing, and by our Father's grace you will bring that blessing to all you encounter this day.

So go and make followers
of all people in the world.
Baptize them in the name
of the Father and the Son and the Holy Spirit.
MATTHEW 28:19 NCV

HUNGRY SOULS

He proved He is real by showing kindness,
by giving you rain from heaven
and crops at the right times,
by giving you food and filling your hearts with joy.

ACTS 14:17 NCV

I f you could bottle the moment, it would sell for over a million dollars. Actually, it's priceless—this peace you feel—as your family sits gathered around the table, laughing and sharing the day's stories. Your soul stirs. *Something deep is happening here*, you realize, though you're not sure of the source. You simply know, *This is good. We were made for this.* And your heart overflows with thanks.

More than the food, we crave belonging. We crave connections that confirm we are not alone—and never will be. We long for confidence that the good will not only last but grow stronger as time goes on. It's an appetite for eternal love and community, the kind our hungry souls seek to have satisfied.

For many the search persists, with only momentary pleasures patching the deeper ache. What on earth are we to do with this raging need no place or person on earth can permanently ease?

The Father says to come. Sit at the table of eternal provision He offers through relationship with His Son. Breathe in His reality through His written Word, and rest from your wearying quest to satisfy the search elsewhere. With unlimited resources and riches, our Father stands ready to supply all that you need.

What worries you today? Are you afraid you can't make ends meet? That your future plans will fail? That you'll lose someone you love? Child of God, your Father knows...and He will fully satisfy the deepest needs of your body and soul.

So Abraham named that place The LORD Provides.
Even today people say,
"On the mountain of the LORD it will be provided."
GENESIS 22:14 NCV

COVERED *in* CONFIDENCE

My shield is God Most High,
who saves the upright in heart.
PSALM 7:10 NIV

When you were a kid, you didn't think twice about going outside to play. Blue summer skies beckoned you to build forts, ride bikes, and simply explore the outside world. You experienced endless hours of pure, unadulterated, worry-free fun in the sun—until scientists discovered the secret harm in some of the sun's rays. Diligent parents all over the planet began coating themselves and their kids in sunscreen so they could continue enjoying the sun's warmth without the skin cancer–causing side effects.

In a way, our souls experience a similar shift spiritually as we transition from the blissful innocence of childhood to the harsh realities of adult life. Painful past experiences magnify the potential for future disappointments, leaving you paralyzed with fear in the present. It can make you want to stay inside your own walled-up world so you don't have to risk getting hurt "out there." But when we withdraw, we don't really live.

So what is a fearful Christian supposed to do? You guessed it. Apply Son screen! It might sound silly—even childish—at first. But when you take the time to apply the truth of your redemption by Christ's blood, you can embrace life completely confident that you are covered in God's eternal favor. No accusation, condemnation, shame, guilt, or pain can ever harm who you are as a child of God. God's grace—His permanent presence in our lives—is our shield who empowers us to take the risk of really living by loving well. We were made to enjoy God and His world with childlike abandon, trusting Him to protect and lead us through life's every adventure.

After this, the word of the LORD
came to Abram in a vision:
"Do not be afraid, Abram.
I am your shield, your very great reward."
GENESIS 15:1 NIV

RISING UP

Guide me in Your truth and teach me,
for You are God my Savior,
and my hope is in You all day long.
PSALM 25:5 NIV

You didn't know it was coming. Maybe you heard warnings, but you didn't believe the forecasters when they showed the telltale mass of white clouds swirling like a pinwheel on their radars. You'd weathered hurricanes before. Why would this one be any different?

But then the floodwaters rose—not inch by inch, but foot by foot. You watched your home sink beneath its surge, you and your family climbing higher and higher trying to save yourselves. But the roof is all that's left, and you feel your home's foundation sway. You're in more trouble than you ever imagined. And you've never understood more intensely your need for saving.

Sometimes it takes desperate situations for our deepest needs to reach the surface of our understanding. Maybe we find ourselves caught up in a habit that's destroying our family. Maybe we've made a wreck of the relationships around us. Or maybe just the emptiness in our hearts starts aching too much to ignore and the realization dawns: we're in more trouble than we ever imagined...and nothing on earth can save us now.

But we have a God in heaven who will. It's in His name and it's who He is, Savior of the world. Whether we seek power for the present problem or eternal salvation for our souls, Jesus delivers what no one else on earth can: assurance. When we rest in Him, our rescue is guaranteed. In our utter weakness, we watch in awe and wonder at God's saving grace.

Our God is a God who saves;
from the Sovereign LORD comes escape from death.
PSALM 68:20 NIV

RELIABILITY RATING

Praise the LORD who has given rest to His people Israel, just as He promised. Not one word has failed of all the wonderful promises He gave through His servant Moses.
I KINGS 8:56 NLT

It's not my fault, you reason, explaining the uneasiness that urges you to keep checking up on everyone else's progress. Yes, you know your spouse is a capable and intelligent person. But you've learned from past experience that reliability wouldn't truthfully top his résumé. And your coworkers are no problem when they keep to their own projects. But joint ventures are just so stressful. You never know if others will actually pull through on their end, and you don't want to be left picking up the pieces. Micromanagement seems to be the only realistic option. It may make you—and others—miserable, but you want and feel like you need concrete resolution more.

But God offers another solution. You *do* have one Friend who is flawlessly faithful—not only to come through for you in a pinch but to provide the stability your uncertain soul craves. The Bible says God's faithfulness reaches to the heavens! Why not take a moment and look up at the sky to see how far that is?

Do you believe Him? God's ways are not like ours, and neither are His thoughts. He doesn't shift like shadows or turn His back when the going gets tough. Our God is faithful now and forever, His reliability rating higher than the universe itself.

Rest comes when we realize that our hope lies in our God, who literally cannot fail us. It would go against His very nature. So we *can* relax—even when others fall short. We have a God who always has our back.

The LORD passed in front of Moses, calling out,
"Yahweh! The LORD!
The God of compassion and mercy!
I am slow to anger
and filled with unfailing love and faithfulness."
EXODUS 34:6 NLT

THE GAME CHANGER

The LORD gave them rest on every side,
just as He had sworn to their ancestors.
Not one of their enemies withstood them;
the LORD gave all their enemies into their hands.

JOSHUA 21:44 NIV

You know it's just Little League. On the scale of eternity, this one baseball game doesn't even matter. But the other team is cutthroat, the little dribblers taking cheap shots at your child's teammates. When one of the biggest bullies shoves your child to the dirt, you're up from your seat in a millisecond screaming "Foul!" to the ref.

It may be just a game, but still it stirs something powerful deep within. *We want good to win.* It's why we grip our seats through thrilling movies where our hero fights against foe after foe—and we fear that all is lost. Yet in some twist of fate, he finds that one narrow path to victory and we can breathe again. As the credits roll, our souls rest for a brief moment and revel in the glory we feel is somehow our own.

And that's because it is. God won it for us through His only Son's sacrificial death and hell-defeating resurrection. As followers of Jesus, we will see the battle between good and evil unfolding on every front—from outside threats and lies to the sinister sin inside our own hearts. It may even, at times, feel like we've lost the fight and we're tempted to give up. But believer, take heart. Your God has overcome the world. Press on and fight the good fight, and you will, too. You're on the winning team!

You, LORD, have delivered me from death,
my eyes from tears,
my feet from stumbling,
that I may walk before the LORD
in the land of the living.
PSALM 116:8–9 NIV

CONSTANT
COMPANION

One who has unreliable friends soon comes to ruin,
but there is a friend who sticks closer than a brother.
PROVERBS 18:24 NIV

For a minute, you contemplate just chucking your phone out the car window. Thanks to technology, you no longer enjoy the natural boundary created by leaving the workplace. Now it follows you everywhere you go, along with the almost endless demands of not only bosses but other people you aim to please. You're not a negative person, but you are a perceptive one. And you're afraid if you fold or fail in any arena, you just might forfeit that relationship. People's loyalties just don't seem to last as long these days.

But then you arrive home, greeted by your ever-faithful furry friend. Excited circles, barks, and then almost manic kisses calm your fretful mind. You sit on the foyer floor, and instantly your dog rolls over, exposing his belly for better petting. To him, you can do no wrong. And as you let the day's worries melt away in his soft fur, your soul recalls the Source of such goodness.

God gives us glimpses of His heart through the comfort His creatures provide. Like your faithful companion, only infinitely better, God's affection for you never wavers. No matter how successful you are or how badly you fail, your heavenly Father never leaves your side. He never walks away, because our God is loyal like no other. Every confession is met with forgiveness, every concern resolved with compassion. Don't let the world's demands bring you down. Rest instead in the comfort of God's constant friendship, the God who never lets you go.

Return to your rest,
my soul, for the LORD has been good to you.
PSALM 116:7 NIV

FASHIONED
FOR ETERNITY

He has made everything beautiful in its time.
He has also set eternity in the human heart;
yet no one can fathom what God has done
from beginning to end.
ECCLESIASTES 3:11 NIV

The eighties are back. Just a simple stroll past each storefront window in your nearest shopping plaza will display the trend. High-waisted shorts with crop tops suit the mannequins just fine, but for someone who actually remembers when that fashion idea first started? Well, maybe those bell bottoms would be a better choice.

It's funny how adding a little age to your perspective alters what you perceive as important. What seemed so critical to you as a young kid (like winning that game or getting that toy) now ranks at utterly irrelevant compared to today's concerns. Much like fashion trends, what we worry about changes with our life's seasons. Hindsight tells us that much of the minutiae that drained our mental and physical energy didn't matter all that much in the end.

But we weren't made for insignificance. Believers in Jesus belong to a God who is eternal, and He has put that longing into our hearts. The frivolous life isn't for us anymore. God leads us through our longing to live for what lasts forever. When we walk in our destiny to receive and give God's love, we live every moment for His glory into eternity.

When you feel the floodwaters of stress rising around you, remember to add God's age to your perspective. The God who was and is and is to come is with you right now in this present moment. If you will surrender your plans and desires to His purpose and direction, your path, moment by moment, will take on eternal importance. Rest and realize that in God's hands, our ordinary lives wield extraordinary impact.

Trust in the LORD forever,
for the LORD, the LORD Himself,
is the Rock eternal.
ISAIAH 26:4 NIV

Shepherd

God, my shepherd!
I don't need a thing.
You have bedded me down in lush meadows,
You find me quiet pools to drink from.
True to Your word,
You let me catch my breath
and send me in the right direction.
Psalm 23:1–3 the message

It is early morning, and you secretly slip away from your sleeping spouse and children for some alone time on the dock. In the break of dawn, the warm sunrays reflect a sparkling gold on still, green water, inviting you down the well-worn path to the languid lake below. No boats or Jet Skis make a sound. Only the gentle wind rustles its way through leafy trees, the birds not yet awake from their slumber. Reaching the landing, you plop onto the waiting chair and breathe in deeply the earthy air.

Why do calm waters settle our soul? What is it in the sensation of stillness that sets our minds at ease?

Maybe in those moments we taste our rightful

place in God's created order. Surrounded by the simple beauty of what He has made, our souls drink in the truth of who He is. God is our Shepherd who leads us to still waters and restores our souls. In the stillness, we remember His grandeur. In the quiet, we hear His Spirit whisper words of refreshing life, the precious promise of His protective, paternal presence. We bask in His love.

But the sun rises higher, the day's activities ready to unfold. You also rise from your rest, though your soul stays seated in the comfort of your Shepherd's care. Your heart and mind are fixed on following His lead every step in this day, trusting His kindness to take you where you need to go, guiding you all the way.

I am the good shepherd.
The good shepherd lays down his life for the sheep.
JOHN 10:11 NIV

BLAZE *of* GLORY

There is no one holy like the LORD;
there is no one besides You;
there is no Rock like our God.
I SAMUEL 2:2 NIV

He was alone in the desert when he first encountered God's all-consuming fire. The blaze that burned no branch or leaf mesmerized Moses for a moment before the fearful reality dawned: *Who sees God's face and lives?* Surely he was doomed. And yet, by some strange mercy, Moses still stood, though his sandals were now removed in reverence. Here, by the Fire, his life purpose unfolded. "Set My people free!" God said.

And so the story unfolds, God's purposed salvation provided through a humble shepherd who obeyed because he saw God's glory. Later, the delivered people saw it too, when they gathered near Mt. Sinai to hear and learn the ways of God's holiness. To walk with Him, they must walk like Him—perfect to the core. Standing at a distance, the people watched the mountain quake, the fiery billows burn and churn around the mountain's peak. Creation crashed and flashed in awe of its Creator's presence. "It's too much for us!" they cried. They needed someone to stand between them and their God.

And we do, too. Even today, God's holy fire hasn't dimmed, despite the darkness of our world. To walk with a holy God we must be holy like Him—a fearful task, knowing our daily failures. Like the Israelites, we all need someone to stand between us and the flames. So God Himself forged a way.

Jesus became our holiness. Hidden in Him, we are invited to approach the mountain of God's holy presence, in fearful reverence but with hearts at rest. God welcomes us to fellowship with Him face-to-face through Jesus. Then, like Moses, we heed His call to go and set sin's captives free.

Speak to the entire assembly of Israel and say to them: "Be holy because I, the LORD your God, am holy."
LEVITICUS 19:2 NIV

SOVEREIGN

You have been my hope, Sovereign LORD,
my confidence since my youth.
PSALM 71:5 NIV

Her parents could barely breathe as they watched, their hearts pounding in their chests as if they were the ones up on that beam. Gracefully, the little girl-turned-teen moved nimbly across the narrow plank as if it were a valley wide. Back flip, front flip, with an occasional dance between breathtaking maneuvers, she kept her rhythm just as she had practiced thousands of times before. Serious, but with no sign of fear, she simply focused her eyes straight ahead at some invisible point on her mind's horizon. When she finished strong, the audience clapped hard—though her parents praised her the loudest.

Why is it so hard to watch our children struggle and risk? We love them so much it feels our hearts could break, and yet somehow we know that while the stretching and reaching is risky, it is good. Can we protect *and* propel them to reach their highest potential? Our power as parents is just so...limited.

But God's isn't. There isn't a single molecule in our universe that doesn't submit to His authority. Like our children, we too take every breath by the power of His grace. And so we train and work and risk life in motion, knowing that even when we fall (what athlete doesn't?), our Sovereign Lord holds our hand. We may fear the failure, but God is forging character that winning alone can't wield. We trust His process, like a gymnast with her coach. And we keep our eyes focused on the stabilizing point of His sovereign presence.

The LORD makes firm the steps
of the one who delights in Him;
though he may stumble, he will not fall,
for the LORD upholds him with His hand.
I was young and now I am old,
yet I have never seen the righteous forsaken
or their children begging bread.
PSALM 37:23–25 NIV

THE LOOK *of* LOVE

The LORD appeared to us
in the past, saying: "I have loved
you with an everlasting love;
I have drawn you with unfailing kindness."
JEREMIAH 31:3 NIV

It's the moment you've been waiting for, and you're not willing for a single disruption to interrupt its impact. From the very first time they met, you knew this man and woman were made for each other. And as the story unfolded, you witnessed countless diversions and distractions that kept them from their divine destiny together. *When will they see the secret love we've understood all along?* we wonder. And wait.

And when it comes, our hearts explode in unexplained joy. *It's just a movie,* we remind ourselves, embarrassed a little by our unrestrained emotion. How can just a look of love—a first embrace—stir our souls so strongly?

By the warmth of such soul connection, our walls of self-protection crumble. For a moment we feel our vulnerability, the hint of hidden hope peeking through the rubble. *Will we ever be loved that way?* we dare to wonder.

Better than the best romance story ever told, we have a date with destiny—love's full expression still unfolding. In the waiting, though, we don't have to wonder. Jesus, our betrothed groom, has been preparing our miracle moment to be unveiled in face-to-face union with Him in heaven. We don't have to wander around this life wondering whether we'll ever be loved or chosen or whisked away to some wonderful place with our beloved. We will! Our hope has no need for fortress walls. Be bold, bride of Christ, and let God's love free you to revel in His divine pursuit and eternal affection for you.

Whoever does not love does not know God,
because God is love.
1 JOHN 4:8 NIV

STORYTELLING

Philip said, "Lord, show us the Father.
That is all we need."
Jesus replied: "Philip,
I have been with you for a long time.
Don't you know who I am?
If you have seen Me, you have seen the Father.
How can you ask Me to show you the Father?"
JOHN 14:8–9 CEV

The children sat enthralled at the old man's feet. Occasionally his chair rocked back and forth as he waited for his last point to linger a little longer with his young listeners. Every story told blew their minds. And every week they gathered, eagerly awaiting the newest unveiling of intrigue. Full of unexpected twists and undeniable miracles, the old man painted his experiences in rural Uganda through truthful tales and vivid descriptions that sent their wildest imaginations soaring. There wasn't a child present who wasn't ready to go—right this minute—to experience the adventures for themselves.

And so is the nature of good storytelling. Unlike

facts told in cold, hard prose, stories unfold in ways that unite our experience with imagination. Stories take what we know and lift our understanding beyond conventional boundaries to the land of endless possibilities. It's one of the reasons Jesus taught people in parables. But His greatest story takes us even higher.

More epic than the universe in which we live, we have a heavenly Father who wants us to know Him. But how could He show us a Spirit we can't see, whose essence is so "other" than any earthly father we've ever known? God painted the hues of His heart through the person of Jesus, God the Father expressed through the life story of His Son, Jesus.

Today, don't let the Father feel distant from you. With the faith of a wide-eyed child, come sit at the feet of our amazing Savior and revel in the Father's love as you realize your role in the greatest love adventure ever told.

Surely You are still our Father!
Even if Abraham and Jacob would disown us,
Lord, You would still be our Father.
You are our Redeemer from ages past.
Isaiah 63:16 NLT

GUIDANCE COUNSELOR

For to us a child is born,
to us a Son is given,
and the government will be on His shoulders.
And He will be called
Wonderful Counselor, Mighty God,
Everlasting Father, Prince of Peace.

ISAIAH 9:6 NIV

She breathed in deeply and let out a sigh. With a touch of the screen, her phone conversation with her sister was over—for now. For years she had played the role of counselor, trying to bring calm to her sister's chaotic world. But her sister's impulsive choices and her endless stream of reckless relationships always sent her own emotions reeling. Like a stone in a rising river, she could feel the earth beneath her giving way. *How can I stay grounded when I'm always giving to others?* she wondered.

It's a question worth asking. After all, we have pressures of our own. Other people's problems simply compound the obvious issue: we need a helper. But who can handle—who even cares—about all the issues our hearts bear?

God.

The God who never sleeps or slumbers has His eyes on you and His heart toward you. As an ever-present Counselor, God's indwelling Spirit not only knows the way you work and think, but He sees into the hearts of the people you're trying to help. In amazing grace, He supplies the power and perspective we need to first receive God's grace and then to give it, time and time again.

Are you exhausted from your own servant heart, tired from the turmoil churning all around you? Don't grow weary in doing good, for you will reap a harvest if you don't give up. Instead, give in to the Spirit's counsel and let His power flow to others as your weakness forms the perfect channel for God's empowering grace.

The Advocate, the Holy Spirit,
whom the Father will send in My name,
will teach you all things
and will remind you of everything I have said to you.
JOHN 14:26 NIV

NINJA WARRIORS

Whom have I in heaven but You?
And earth has nothing I desire besides You.
My flesh and my heart may fail,
but God is the strength of my heart
and my portion forever.
PSALM 73:25–26 NIV

It's fascinating, watching the nimble athletes maneuver across the Ninja Warrior obstacle course. Conscious of the ticking timer, each person strategizes the best way to attack the present challenge. Determination and focus fuse into an all-out effort to finish the course with the fastest time. Typically, no one has trouble with the first few events. But as the intensity drags on, their strength drains. Will they have what it takes to make it to the end?

The crowd cheers on each athlete because we see a little bit of ourselves in those Ninja Warrior wannabes. We may never have worked an obstacle course, but life itself is complicated enough. Every day we battle the brokenness we find in ourselves and the relationships around us. Just when we make it over one hurdle, we find ourselves facing what seems an insurmountable wall. Will we have enough strength to finish the course? Or how about just the event in this moment?

It depends on our energy source. If we are working our way through life by our own willpower, pounding through every pressure in our own strength, we will get sapped. But we do have an endless source of strength in Jesus. Tap into the power of His Spirit by daily ingesting His words of life. Look to God in an attitude of constant prayer as you maneuver through your day. He alone has the strength and power to support you in the present life and the one to come. Plug into God's eternal strength, and He will make your path straight, your hands sure, your effort victorious.

It is God who arms me with strength
and keeps my way secure.
II Samuel 22:33 NIV

No Good

*Do not remember the sins of my youth
and my rebellious ways;
according to Your love remember me,
for You, LORD, are good.*

PSALM 25:7 NIV

You trusted him. Week after week you sat under his sermons, listening to your pastor pour out his heart along with powerful portions of God's Word. And even though he spoke of struggles, his admitted vulnerability only elevated him higher to "saint status" in your mind—until the story broke today, the headline alone breaking your heart. *How could he do that?* you gasp, as you read the scandalous report. Is there anyone good left in this world?

You don't have to wonder. Jesus already answered that question a long time ago. The man asking was a rich young ruler who wanted to know who qualified for heaven. "Have I been good enough?" he queried. Seeing into his soul, Jesus loved him AND pressed on his hidden problem to make the issue plain. Every person has a sin problem, except one. "No one is good—except God alone" (Mark 10:18 NIV). And, of course, He's right—because He's God.

As the body of Christ, we are called to work together for God's kingdom, but make no mistake: we still struggle with sin. Though God sees us as saints, covered by His Son, we still need our Savior every moment of the day. We wrestle with sin and rest in His grace together with others just like ourselves who need to know God's forgiveness and strength.

Don't let the misdeeds of others destroy your confidence in Christ. Instead, cling ever more closely to the only One who is truly good. He will give you the strength to stand and grace to catch you when you fall.

Dear friend, do not imitate what is evil but what is good.
Anyone who does what is good is from God.
Anyone who does what is evil has not seen God.
III JOHN 1:11 NIV

WHISTLE-BLOWING

*In fact, the reason I was born and
came into the world is to testify to the truth.
Everyone on the side of truth listens to Me.*
JOHN 18:37 NIV

On the outside it looked like madness, and honestly some of the teachers would have agreed. "Whoever decided Field Day was a good idea must have been crazy," one joked to another. As the teachers looked out from their vantage point, hundreds of elementary students milled around on the grass, talking and playing. But with one long blow from the head teacher's whistle, the chaos came to an end. Every head turned; every eye looked to the one at the lead. They knew that if they wanted to get to play in this day's games, they'd better listen and do as she said.

The same is true for God's saints. On the surface, it can seem as if we're just one with the rest of the world, our worries and work no different from each other's. Turn on talk-show radio or the news and the chaos grows even louder, the conflicting opinions on what works best never-ending. Like the teachers on Field Day, it's enough to make anyone want to escape. Except we know the one with the whistle. If we want our day—our lives—to work, we'd do well to listen when He calls and walk the way He leads.

Jesus calms our chaos by the very essence of His nature. He doesn't just know the way to the truth; He IS the truth. And the Way to the Life He offers is available only for those who hear and heed His call to follow.

Amid the noisy clamor of our culture, will you tune in to the only source of Truth? Follow His voice alone to lead you away from all the madness to a life of meaning and joy in Him.

Jesus answered, "I am the way and the truth and the life. No one comes to the Father except through Me."
JOHN 14:6 NIV

LIFE LIGHT

*Jesus said to her, "I am the resurrection and the life.
The one who believes in Me will live, even though they
die; and whoever lives by believing in Me will never die.
Do you believe this?" "Yes, Lord," she replied, "I believe
that You are the Messiah, the Son of God,
who is to come into the world."*

JOHN 11:25–27 NIV

They had sent for help long before Lazarus breathed his last breaths. The sisters watched their brother's life ebb away, wondering all the while, *Where is Jesus?*

Four days Lazarus lay in the grave, rotting. It was all ruined. It's no wonder Mary didn't come running when she heard her Lord had finally arrived in town. But Martha did, greeting him at the village gate. Full of questions, she stopped short at His. "I am the resurrection and the life," Jesus declared. "Do you believe this?"

Did she hear the Rabbi right? Did this man before her eyes really have the power to resurrect the dead? Though her mind answered in the affirmative, Jesus continued His path to her heart. "Show me where your hope died," He prompted. "If you believe, you'll see God's glory there."

Practical Martha protested. "He's too far gone now, Lord. The dead just stink too much!"

Her perception didn't fully estimate God's power. Pushing past the mourning people with tears of His own streaming down His face, Jesus looked at the sealed grave. Then He shouted, "Lazarus, come forth!" As Lazarus obeyed, hope was reborn, the now-empty tomb an unquestionable triumph. Seeing became true believing, and their hearts rejoiced with hope.

Believer, Jesus is our life, too. He calls us to come forth from our places of despair and witness the wonder of His power and love. Like Lazarus, we must come to the end of ourselves to see and believe in the resurrection power of God.

When Jesus spoke again to the people, He said, "I am the light of the world. Whoever follows Me will never walk in darkness, but will have the light of life."
JOHN 8:12 NIV

I AM ALWAYS

He said to me: "It is done.
I am the Alpha and the Omega, the Beginning
and the End. To the thirsty I will give water without cost
from the spring of the water of life."
REVELATION 21:6 NIV

Ma'am, do you know who's responsible for this?" asked a stern, concerned police officer, standing beside the broken wall and the wreck that is your car. You wish you could say, "No, I have no idea." Or at least point the finger in some other likely direction. But you were texting, and there really is no other explanation. "Yes, officer," you choke on the words. "I am." With two little words, the whole weight of the world seems to fall on your shoulders.

But what if the tables were turned? What if the officer said instead, "I am taking care of all this"? Would you not wonder at his generosity and grapple with such unexpected mercy? With a deep sigh of relief, you'd likely shower your hero with deep and heartfelt gratitude.

As unlikely as such a scenario seems, a similar

shift happens to us under the shadow of the Almighty. Culpable though we are, God offers to cover our offenses at all cost to Himself. In the exchange, our burdens are lifted onto the One whose shoulders are broad enough to bear them. The two little words "I AM" take on much more impact. For everything we owe and all that we need to carry on in this life and the next, God declares, "I am."

And He is. Our God is the great I Am who always was, still is, and forever will be. Rest as you realize, "I Am your righteousness. I Am your hope. I Am your peace. And I Am—always."

"Very truly I tell you,"
Jesus answered, "before Abraham was born, I am!"
JOHN 8:58 NIV

RICH REWARD

I say to myself, "The LORD is my portion;
therefore I will wait for Him."
LAMENTATIONS 3:24 NIV

The candles are burning low," the wedding director whispered to the young bride's mom. Since early that morning, the flowers had all been perfectly placed, the chairs lined up along the lake's shore. Prepared food filled the warming ovens, ready for the reception soon to take place—surely.

"Should we at least go ahead and start the music?" the bride's mom asked in return.

But the bride overheard and held her voice firm. "What good is a wedding without the groom? We will wait for him."

In any situation, waiting is work. In the interim between hope and fulfillment lie all the what-ifs: What if it doesn't work out? What if no one ever comes? What if I've been fooled? What if…

But what if the reward comes in portions greater than our grandest expectations? What if waiting only deepens our desire?

Believers, why do we insist on running ahead of our Savior? What can we work out ourselves without the Person whose presence is the very point of our existence? Let your fears go as you focus on the faithful One. Take time before the day's hurry begins and talk to your Father. Listen for His voice and praise Him for His promises. Though He may tarry, your groom will pull through—the power of His presence your richest reward for your wait.

Do not be afraid, Abram.
I am your shield,
your very great reward.
GENESIS 15:1 NIV

SHOWING UP

In your relationships with one another,
have the same mindset as Christ Jesus:
Who, being in very nature God,
did not consider equality with God
something to be used to His own advantage;
rather, He made Himself nothing
by taking the very nature of a servant.

PHILIPPIANS 2:5–7 NIV

A reality show currently airs on TV, featuring a different major-corporation CEO per episode. In each episode, the business owner ditches his white-collar suit to don the common laborer's clothes. No one announces anything to the workers. He simply shows up as one of them, seeking to learn the skills of their trade. Hidden cameras record the whole exchange, including the honest conversation that comes when working alongside one another. And it is brutally honest. In the interactions, disloyal and lazy attitudes often surface, while other employees reveal a strong work ethic. In the end, when the owner's true identity is revealed, each worker reaps what their attitudes earned, while the owner now runs his business with greater empathy for those who work under him.

Why does the trick work every time? Because no one expects the owner to appear as a common laborer. Yet God, creator, owner, and sustainer of the entire universe, came to earth—not for a simple show but to live a lifetime in our shoes. In astonishing humility, He even arrived in the poorest of places, not seeking to assert power and prestige but to learn obedience through service and suffering.

The humility of Christ helps us to rest. We have no need to put on airs because our Savior donned a servant's towel to wash dirty feet and show us a greater way.

He has shown you, O mortal, what is good.
And what does the LORD require of you?
To act justly and to love mercy and
to walk humbly with your God.
MICAH 6:8 NIV

DELIVERANCE

One of you routs a thousand, because the LORD your
God fights for you, just as He promised.
JOSHUA 23:10 NIV

Elisha's servant stood frozen in fear. Everywhere he and Elisha looked, they saw enemy soldiers encircling their city. "There must be thousands here," the servant said, starting to panic. But Elisha stood in perfect peace. What was the difference?

Elisha's perspective. The two men saw the same situation through very different lenses. So Elisha prayed for his servant—and God opened his eyes. More numerous than the enemy soldiers, God's mighty army surrounded Elisha and his servant for protection, blazing chariots included. The servant's quaking heart surged with confidence. Strangely, instead of using swords to fight, Elisha simply prayed that God would blind his enemies. Suddenly they didn't know where they were, and Elisha led them to a distant town!

It's just one of many victory stories the Bible records where God came to the rescue in the most unconventional way. In some of their conquests, they were required to circle Jericho for seven days in silence, shouting on the last day to bring the walls down. In another battle they smashed clay jars at God's command and startled their enemy into a self-killing frenzy. No matter which way God chose to deliver His people and no matter how small their numbers, God's people won every time they obeyed His commands.

The same God who worked wonders then still stands in command now. Heaven's armies are also at our disposal, ready to defeat our opposition as we fall in line with God's kingdom work. So what kind of foe opposes you today? How bleak does the outlook appear? Like Elisha, pray for clearer sight so you can see God's delivering power at work. When we trust God to fight our battles for us, we find the sweetest and most surprising victories.

> *The enemy took them as prisoners.*
> *And they won't let them go.*
> *But God is strong and will buy them back.*
> *His name is the Lord of heaven's armies.*
> *He will defend them with power*
> *so He can give rest to their land.*
> JEREMIAH 50:33–34 ICB

TALK IT OUT

Come now, let us reason together, says the LORD:
though your sins are like scarlet,
they shall be as white as snow;
though they are red like crimson,
they shall become like wool.

ISAIAH 1:18 ESV

She knew it was over for her the minute those blue swirling lights appeared in the driveway. The party had started calmly enough, just a few of her teenaged friends hanging out while parents were elsewhere. She wasn't even sure who brought whatever it was that she drank; she just knew that when the police arrived, she had no strength to run like many of the rest. When her parents came to take her home, she had no words to say.

But they did! When her mind finally cleared, they called her in to talk it out. Consequences would be doled out, but they were most concerned with her heart. Had she learned a lesson? Would she leave behind her careless, foolish ways?

With a similar tone, our heavenly Father wants

to work with us, wayward children that we often are. Far from the often-held image of fearful judge, God calls us to Himself as our loving, concerned Father. He wants to reason together: Are we really headed the way we want to go? Will we reconsider a better path that leads away from pain to peace?

When we surrender to our Father in repentance, our acts of aggression are covered in forgiveness. He doesn't hold grudges or keep long lists of grievances. God separates our sins from us as far as the east stays away from the west. In repentance, we find rest in the mercy of our gracious Father.

The Lord has mercy on those
who fear Him, as a father has mercy on his children.
PSALM 103:13 ICB

PAINTING GRACE

*He chose us in Him before the creation of the world
to be holy and blameless in His sight.
In love He predestined us for adoption to sonship through
Jesus Christ, in accordance with His pleasure and will.*

EPHESIANS 1:4–5 NIV

The artist surveyed his empty canvas. Though only white gesso coated the surface, the colors and shapes of a finished work formed solidly in his mind. And so he set to work, stroke after stroke, bleeding some colors and carving out others. While in process, the placement of hues and shapes seemed pointless. But at his completion, his plan for a beautiful portrait was perfectly clear.

It is amazing to watch a skilled artist at work. How does he get the image in his head to emerge with such dimension on a dull, flat board? We could ask our heavenly Father the same question. More skilled than any earthly artist, God has preplanned each of His children, choosing our shape and form, crafting us for our life's calling before He colored in a single stroke of our lives. With strategic precision, God plotted and framed the very family into which we were born. Using shadows and light, He shaped our personalities, minds, and physical features that we see with eyes that He made in just the right shade. No part of who we are or the lives we live unfold by accident. For those who love God, every part works together into the wonderful masterpiece our Author has planned.

When you look at yourself, do you like what you see? We find rest when we remember we are God's work in process. As we surrender to each stroke, we watch a supernatural creativity carve amazing depth and beauty into the canvas of our lives.

> *Listen to me, you islands;*
> *hear this, you distant nations:*
> *Before I was born the* LORD *called me;*
> *from my mother's womb*
> *He has spoken my name.*
> ISAIAH 49:1 NIV

SOUL SURGERY

He heals the brokenhearted and binds up their wounds.
PSALM 147:3 NIV

The procedure sounded terrifying. "It's just a simple cut across the surface of each eye," the ophthalmologist explained. "Then we just shine a laser light in for a few minutes and it'll all be done." The young patient calculated her options. Gut instinct told her to cut and run. How could razors and eyeballs ever be a good combination? But on the other hand, she could barely see without her glasses, and her dog always had a hankering for some good, expensive eyewear. On the front end, Lasik surgery seemed like so much risk. But in the end, she put her sight in the surgeon's hands—and her life has never been the same. "Everything looks so amazingly clear to me now!" she beams, beckoning others to experience the same healing for themselves.

And so it is with our Savior. We hear Him say, "Give up your life in exchange for Mine," and we worry about the risk. Maybe our broken, sin-sick lives aren't so bad after all, we hedge, hoping to avoid unwanted soul surgery. Perhaps we can get by with some self-applied bandages. But to resist His hand means to remain unhealed. Or as the Bible says: in keeping our life, we lose it. Our condition is far worse than simple sickness. Our spirits are dead and need a resurrection.

When we realize the gravity of our situation, our desperation drives us to the Healer. But take courage! He specializes in the brokenhearted and brings a clarity to our life's purpose we would have never thought possible.

> *"But if you can do anything,*
> *take pity on us and help us."*
> *"'If you can'?" said Jesus. "Everything*
> *is possible for one who believes."*
> *Immediately the boy's father*
> *exclaimed, "I do believe; help me*
> *overcome my unbelief!"*
> MARK 9:22–24 NIV

TRASH DAY

As far as the east is from the west,
so far has He removed our transgressions from us.
PSALM 103:12 NIV

As soon as she stepped inside the house, she could smell it. "What is that awful stench?" she called aloud, hoping in vain that her kids could give her a clue. So she began the sleuthing process, searching and sniffing the pantry, the laundry, and all the other places that could potentially put out such putrid fumes.

And then she found it.

Tucked away in the corner of her garage, something noxious was growing inside the large blue trash bin. "Thank the Lord tomorrow's trash day!" she mumbled to herself as she wheeled the bin to the curb. And when she awoke the next morning, no trace of her trash remained.

Do you treasure your trash service? Maybe you've never thought about it—at least until it fails to show up for some reason. When trash starts to pile up, we start to panic. "How do I get this stuff out of here?"

Strangely, trash day helps us picture our soul situation better. Without God's amazing grace, we're stuck in the growing stench of all our various sins. As they pile up, we start to worry, *Who else can smell the muck I live in?* If we want to rest and breathe easy, we just need to bring our junk out in the open where God will remove it, never to reach us again. Why wait another minute? The moment we turn to God in repentance, our sin's stench disappears.

If we confess our sins,
he is faithful and just and will forgive us our sins
and purify us from all unrighteousness.
I JOHN 1:9 NIV

SINGLED OUT

This is what the LORD says—
He who created you, Jacob,
He who formed you, Israel:
"Do not fear, for I have redeemed you;
I have summoned you by name; you are Mine....
Since you are precious
and honored in My sight,
and because I love you,
I will give people in exchange for you,
nations in exchange for your life."
ISAIAH 43:1, 4 NIV

Arriving early as usual, the young intern flipped the switch and lit up the small room full of office cubicles. Just the steady hum of the copier warming up broke the calm quiet as she rounded the corner to her small desk—the place where people higher up than her often dumped the tedious work they'd rather have her do.

But today was different. Paper stars cut out by hand lined her wall. Small streamers dangled from her cubby bin. And a flowing spray of fragrant flowers filled the space where her day's work usually went. Alongside it, a note said simply, "You are a sensational star on our team. Today, we celebrate you!"

She didn't know what to say. Somebody had taken the time to do this. Suddenly she felt seen. Known. And loved—exactly what they wanted her to feel.

At the heart of all good gifts lies a celebration of the one who's loved. Singled out from the masses, we feel important to someone.

You, child of God, have been singled out this day—and every day. As you make the rounds of your regular routine, do you see God's celebration? It's written in His Word and the way He calls you by name. It's painted in the skies at sunrise and shouted in the colorful clouds at dusk. Your God delights in you. He sees you, knows you, and sings over the sensational person He's made you to be. Don't miss the moment—or any of the daily reminders He tucks away in your day. Today, live as though you are loved because you are.

Give ear and come to Me; listen, that you may live.
I will make an everlasting covenant with you,
My faithful love promised to David.
ISAIAH 55:3 NIV

DRESSED FOR SUCCESS

May Your priests be clothed with Your righteousness;
may Your faithful people sing for joy.
PSALM 132:9 NIV

The moment she walked through the doorway, she knew she'd missed the memo. "Look at how everyone's dressed!" She elbowed her date, who had failed to relate the invitation details. Her favorite jeans and T-shirt, a suitable selection for other occasions, made her feel humiliated in front of everyone wearing floor-length gowns and black-tie tuxedos. Underdressed and overwhelmed, she simply wanted to leave. "We just don't fit in here," she hissed, pulling her apologetic date back out.

It's funny how something as simple as clothes affects our feelings of security. When we look smart or at least fit the part, we feel more like we belong.

Surprisingly, there's something deeper than social conventions in what could seem strictly superficial. Spiritually speaking, clothes do make the man— and woman. But not the kind with designer labels or intricate designs. From the days back in the Garden, we've all had a garment problem, trying to cover our inadequacies with whatever type of fig leaf we can find.

But God won't have it. His children dress in His royal best. So He provides the robes. Just as He clothed Adam and Eve with a more permanent covering, He clothes each child of God in the righteousness of His Son. We can't be a part of His family without it. But wrapped in God's favor and made right through our Savior, we are at home wherever His family gathers.

Do you feel "less than" when you're around certain others? Remember, you are clothed in God's permanent affection, and your presence is needed at the party!

I saw the Holy City, the new Jerusalem,
coming down out of heaven from God,
prepared as a bride beautifully dressed for her husband.
REVELATION 21:2 NIV

LIONHEART

The Spirit God gave us does not make us timid,
but gives us power, love and self-discipline.
II TIMOTHY 1:7 NIV

You could say she was a closet pray-er. Daily she prayed for her family, friends, and neighbors—especially the ones she knew hadn't yet surrendered to Jesus. On her knees in her bedroom, she was bold before the throne of God, asking for opportunities to share God's love with others.

But once she left the comfort of her own familiar quarters, she felt the battle begin. Out in the world where the people she prayed for lived, she felt less certain. For years she had simply blamed her inhibition on her temperament type. After all, the test profile proved that she was an introvert. So naturally, the way she avoided conversation, especially about her Christianity, was just a funny facet of the personality God had given her.

But no psychology test tells the full story for a believer. Ordinary inhibitions submit to God's supernatural power as we surrender to Him. No matter what our personality type may be, God gives us all a holy boldness when we seek His face first and fuel our faith with His truth and presence. Insecurities about our own abilities to carry out Jesus's Great Commission only open the door for God to do what we in our own strength can't.

Instead of cowering, cutting off the potential for spiritual conversation, trust God to make you brave and bold as a lion. As we pray, watch, and anticipate God moving, we can rest from our worries as we watch God make bold evangelists out of us all.

The wicked flee though
no one pursues,
but the righteous
are as bold as a lion.
PROVERBS 28:1 NIV

MIXED WITH LOVE

I am convinced that neither death nor life,
neither angels nor demons,
neither the present nor the future,
nor any powers, neither height nor depth,
nor anything else in all creation,
will be able to separate us from the love of God
that is in Christ Jesus our Lord.

ROMANS 8:38–39 NIV

As the porch swing gently swayed, the little girl looked up at her daddy's face, her own full of concern. "Daddy, will you ever stop loving me?" she wondered.

"No, honey, I'll always love you," he replied.

"But what if I do something really, really bad? Will you stop loving me then?" she tested.

He tipped his face in her direction. "Do me a favor," he said. "Would you please take your glass of lemonade and separate the ingredients? I want my lemons, sugar, and water separate."

Confused, she answered, "Well, I can't do that, Daddy. Once they're mixed, you can't unmix it!"

"And that's how it is with my love for you, little one." He smiled.

It's no wonder in our world today that we worry about our relationships. Sometimes the simplest conflicts can cause so much division that decades go by before any resolution is made. We often hide the truth of who we are inside for fear that those we love will leave us if they knew.

But God's love for us is far different from what we find in this world. Once God has added His love to the mix in our lives, we are an entirely new creation—one that can never go back to the life we knew before. No matter what our failures and frailties may be, our heavenly Father relentlessly loves us. Without any fear of present or future rejection, we are free to rest in real, authentic relationship with God.

"Though the mountains be shaken
and the hills be removed,
yet My unfailing love for you will not be shaken
nor my covenant of peace be removed,"
says the LORD, who has compassion on you.
ISAIAH 54:10 NIV

ALL THIS WAY

There is no fear in love. But perfect love drives out fear,
because fear has to do with punishment.
The one who fears is not made perfect in love.
We love because He first loved us.

I JOHN 4:18–19 NIV

He thought he was too late. A series of misunderstandings and missed opportunities had led their blooming love down different paths. Now she had flown away and settled on a far distant shore, certain he didn't care about her anymore...until she heard the knock. Opening her door, she gasped in amazement. *He came all this way!* His pursuit proved the love she longed for to be true. "Dreams really do come true," she whispered when they embraced.

And they do. Not just in the movies, but in the here and now. Deep within our souls, we feel the ache of separation caused by sin in this world. We want to feel unfettered affection, the kind that values us enough to push past our defenses to see us and love us for who we truly are. But does anyone actually do that?

God does. He loves us with an everlasting love. Though our sin has separated us and sent us to the farthest corners of our souls in opposition to His holiness, He has come after us. He left heaven to seek us out and even suffer a horrific death just to save our lives. Best of all, He's risen again and has promised to return one glorious day for all His people. We're never left to wonder whether our God still loves us. *He came all this way!* And He stands knocking on the door of our lives, waiting for us to let Him in and enjoy the eternal rest in His love.

I took you from the ends of the earth,
from its farthest corners I called you.
I said, "You are My servant";
I have chosen you and have not rejected you.
ISAIAH 41:9 NIV

Remembered

Can a mother forget the baby at her breast
and have no compassion on the child she has borne?
Though she may forget, I will not forget you!
See, I have engraved you on the palms of My hands;
your walls are ever before Me.
ISAIAH 49:15–16 NIV

"Can you take my picture?" she asked, wanting to be remembered as having attended the party. Her family members smiled and nodded, knowing her needs. For as long as anyone could remember, she had brought her camera everywhere. In fact, they often wondered whether she saw more of the world through her camera lens than with her own eyes. But she was driven to capture moments, haunted by the fear that one day she'd forget. Worse yet, that others would forget she'd been there.

After all, who wants to be forgotten? Don't we all work hard to build the kinds of connections that can keep that from ever happening? We spend all our money, effort, and time trying to make our time here matter, so maybe someone will notice—and remember. And even after all our efforts, we still worry and wonder whether it is enough.

But God puts our fears to rest. Knowing our need for assurance, He has taken the matter into His own hands quite literally, etching our names onto His eternal palms. He has captured us—in all our lives' earthly brevity—and bound us together with all the importance and power of His eternal presence. Our moments in life matter not because others remember what we've done, but because our loving God never forgets His children.

Today, take comfort in God's watchful care, knowing that your every move is on His loving mind. You matter to God, and He will direct your steps to work out His wonderful, meaningful, and eternal purpose for this day.

God—His way is perfect;
the word of the LORD *is pure.*
He is a shield to all
who take refuge in Him.
PSALM 18:30 CSB

DAILY DRILLS

Have you completely forgotten this word of encouragement
that addresses you as a father addresses his son?
It says, "My son, do not make light
of the Lord's discipline,
and do not lose heart when He rebukes you,
because the Lord disciplines the one He loves,
and He chastens everyone He accepts as His son."
HEBREWS 12:5–6 NIV

The young athlete's confusion soon turned to anger toward his coach. *I didn't sign up for this mess!* he thought as he recalled the week's practice out on the hot field. Even though he had been a top prospect for most of the country, he had chosen this program because he'd heard it was the best. But ever since he got there, the coach had seemed anything but kind. When he ran drills, the coach made him run farther, faster, and harder than anyone else on the team.

"What kind of treatment is this?" he finally complained to his coach.

The reply came quickly, "The kind I only give athletes with real potential!"

Good players know that without correction and driving discipline, they won't rise to the top of their game. But somehow Christians often lose the connection in the spiritual world. All of God's promises of love and peace get misperceived as guarantees against pain and suffering in this world. But Jesus corrects the judgment error. "You will have trouble in this world," He assures us. But we take heart because He has overcome it! (See John 16:33.)

Trials in this life become tools to sharpen us where we need skill training the most. When life doesn't go as planned or you find yourself in a place of suffering, don't wonder what you did wrong to deserve this treatment. Instead, submit your life to His loving leadership. Let His Spirit work in you the kind of character building that only comes from a good Father.

They disciplined us for a little while as they thought best;
but God disciplines us for our good,
in order that we may share in His holiness.
HEBREWS 12:10 NIV

ROYAL BLOOD

There is surely a future hope for you,
and your hope will not be cut off.
PROVERBS 23:18 NIV

To the young child, it was just another day of homeschool. Within the castle walls he learned to build with blocks, write the alphabet, and paint the kind of pictures typical for someone his age. So why were so many reporters clamoring in the hallway outside his classroom, commentating on his every action? Why was so much attention directed toward one child and his ordinary day?

He was no ordinary child. The young prince would one day become king. And everyone around him understood his destiny far better than he did. Even mundane activities took on greater meaning with his ultimate destiny in mind. They marveled at his royal training and wondered what it was like to be born into greatness.

Truth be told, angels could identify with those reporters. Created by God to guard His people, the

Bible says they watch and marvel as our lives unfold. *What must it be like to be adopted into God's royal family?* they wonder. *How must it feel to live so loved as God's precious children?* They long to understand the life of glory and affection we live.

Yet often we are like the young prince, unaware of our declared destiny. We go about our day as if it's like any other, not realizing the King of glory has planned every moment for our training and tutelage until we will one day reign with Jesus!

If you belong to Christ, your coronation day is coming. Keep your eyes on kingdom work and train well with eternal purpose, princes and princesses of the King!

> *As it is written:*
> *"What no eye has seen,*
> *what no ear has heard,*
> *and what no human mind*
> *has conceived"—*
> *the things God has prepared*
> *for those who love Him.*
> I Corinthians 2:9 NIV

TRAVEL PLANS

This is what the LORD says—
your Redeemer, who formed you in the womb:
I am the LORD, the Maker of all things,
who stretches out the heavens,
who spreads out the earth by Myself.
ISAIAH 44:24 NIV

It was just a pinprick in the distance, but you were delighted, knowing it was now only a short drive away. "Kids, it's time to wake up!" you called with enthusiasm. For months you had planned and plotted each point of interest you wanted your family to experience in Yellowstone National Park. And to ensure that everything went as smoothly as possible, you went ahead and assigned special tasks for each person. By working together as a team, everyone would get to eat, share the hiking-gear load, and enjoy time together at each spectacular point along the way.

In a similar way, our heavenly Father has planned the trip of a lifetime for each one of His kids, our final destination more spectacular than all the earthbound natural wonders combined. But reaching the end isn't the only objective. There's plenty of beauty to behold along the way—traveling as a team. We go as a family, working together to make travel lighter and paths clearer, and to help troubleshoot any obstacles we encounter along the way. In fact, our Father has crafted each of His kids with unique abilities perfectly designed to work best with all the others in order to experience the adventure of a lifetime.

Today, thank God for your special calling, and seek His wisdom to know it and walk in it. Rest from the temptation to carry out tasks assigned to other team members. Together, we will watch God's kingdom unfold in beautiful scenes of grace all along the path to glory.

We are God's handiwork,
created in Christ Jesus
to do good works,
which God prepared
in advance for us to do.
EPHESIANS 2:10 NIV

MAKING AMENDS

All of this is a gift from God, who brought us back to Himself through Christ. And God has given us this task of reconciling people to Him. For God was in Christ, reconciling the world to Himself, no longer counting people's sins against them. And He gave us this wonderful message of reconciliation. So we are Christ's ambassadors; God is making His appeal through us. We speak for Christ when we plead, "Come back to God!"

II CORINTHIANS 5:18–20 NLT

When the teen stormed off to her room and slammed the door, both parents looked at each other and sighed. "She can be so stubborn!" her mom said under her breath. But then she went to her daughter's door and knocked on it lightly anyway.

"Honey, can I talk to you?" she asked. She had no idea whether her words could help bring down her daughter's walls, but it was worth a shot. More than anything in this moment, her mom knew she needed friends who loved her—even if they were her parents!

Whether out in the world or inside our own homes, people of all ages feel the effects of sin—including the broken relationships and fractured hope rising from it. And Christians aren't immune, either. We all have an enemy whose primary aim is to divide and conquer, suffocating our hope and joy in the process. Polarizing political views, differing denominations, and dividing families are simply some of his favorite ways to tear us apart.

But we have a heavenly Father in the reconciliation business. As His children, we've taken up the trade as well. By His Spirit, we are called to keep reaching out in love, our intent to reconcile the lost with God. We don't give up and we don't give in to despair or hopeless thinking, because God's heart for reconciliation reigns with power within us.

Who today needs to hear His heart? Ask God to make your path plain and your conversation full of His Spirit.

When I bring you back, people will say,
"This former wasteland is now like the Garden of Eden!
The abandoned and ruined cities now have strong walls
and are filled with people!"
EZEKIEL 36:35 NLT

RISING UP

Now He uses us to spread the knowledge of
Christ everywhere, like a sweet perfume.
Our lives are a Christ-like fragrance rising up to God.
But this fragrance is perceived differently by those
who are being saved and by those who are perishing.
II CORINTHIANS 2:14–15 NLT

As she walked into the clothing store, she couldn't keep her eyes off the life-sized photos lining the wall. Every one of them depicted a beautiful (and of course skinny) girl with some gorgeous guy, laughing and living the good life. The room itself smelled like romance—and rich living. Mesmerized by every incoming sensation, she decided, *I want that! Why can't that be me?*

The marketing worked well by design. Our culture caters to our desire for connection, intimacy, and importance. If advertisers do their job well enough, we'll shell out whatever it takes to have their piece of promised happiness.

Only it's hollow. The pleasure it provides passes so quickly, we wonder what happened.

When the deception is realized, we reel with disappointment and disillusionment and, ultimately, a desire for more, mistakenly thinking that *this time* it will last. Deep within, we know it won't.

But God's marketing plan is markedly different. He doesn't post billboards about the abundant life He offers; He puts His Spirit inside His believers! As we walk around our homes, workplaces, and even favorite vacation spots, we emit the unusual fragrance of purpose and authenticity blended with love that lasts forever. As people see us spreading God's truth through acts of love, they smell the distinction between us and the world. The scent of God's Spirit always wields impact: to the rebellious, it repulses; but to the dying and desperate, it's the refreshing fragrance of renewal and hope.

Live a life filled with love,
following the example of Christ.
He loved us and offered Himself as a sacrifice for us,
a pleasing aroma to God.
Ephesians 5:2 NLT

REACHING OUT

God is able to bless you abundantly,
so that in all things at all times, having all that you need,
you will abound in every good work.
II CORINTHIANS 9:8 NIV

As she went to get her mail, the young lady looked wistfully down the street. A couple of doors down, her newly widowed neighbor stood peering into her own mailbox. Their eyes met. There was a pause. An awkward wave and a smile ensued, with the obligatory "Hello, how are you?" Retreating quickly inside, the young Christian woman chided herself the whole way. *I should reach out to her,* her mind scolded. *I should say something, do something—but...* And then a litany of rational reasons she should keep her distance dominated her good idea.

Unfortunately, our enemy uses two powerful weapons to prevent us from successful connection. First, he turns our focus on our inadequacies and past rejections. Adding insult to injury, he heaps on guilt when we fail to follow through, keeping the vicious cycle of fear and self-doubt repeating, instead of allowing us to reach out for meaningful relationships.

But God made us for so much more! We don't need to second-guess ourselves or strategize every ministry event. We simply surrender to God's Spirit inside us, knowing that He will not only guide us to every good work, but He'll supply the right words to say when we need them. Even as we walk toward opportunity, we rest knowing God will handle the results!

Today, ask God to open doors and make you brave to share with those around you. When you see the moment arise, sense God's Spirit surging inside you with His boldness and love. God will lead you and grow your faith in the following.

Pray for us, too, that God may
open a door for our message,
so that we may proclaim the mystery of Christ.
COLOSSIANS 4:3 NIV

CALMING WORDS

Have I not commanded you? Be strong and courageous.
Do not be afraid; do not be discouraged,
for the LORD your God will be with you wherever you go.

JOSHUA 1:9 NIV

She woke up with a feeling of dread. The day had finally arrived. No amount of planning or plotting could stall the inevitable any longer—and she wondered how she'd even make it out of bed, let alone face all that she knew lay ahead.

But as the early morning light slowly peeked through her shades, another thought dawned and she picked up her Bible beside the bed. There, in the pages of God's Word, she saw the promise. Written in red, Jesus's words proclaimed, "Surely I am with you always, to the very end of the age" (Matthew 28:20 NIV).

What a promise! No matter what kind of darkness threatens to undo us, we live with the promise that God never leaves us. As Jesus demonstrated to His disciples, He remains calm and completely in control of even the wildest storms. When we believe in God's goodness and power to save, our souls settle into rest with Him as we wait for His authoritative Word to have its way in our harrowing moments. Every turbulent time is an amazing opportunity to see how our Savior is mighty enough to save—*even in this*. Without the storm, we'd never experience His life-changing presence in its midst.

Instead of dreading your darkest hours or demanding that they end, draw closer to the Lord. Take pleasure in His presence and authority over your situation, and enter His rest knowing that you are safest by His side.

I have rescued you.
I have called you by name;
now you belong to Me.
When you cross deep rivers,
I will be with you,
and you won't drown.
When you walk through fire,
you won't be burned
or scorched by the flames.
I am the LORD, *your God,*
the Holy One of Israel,
the God who saves you.
ISAIAH 43:1–3 CEV

PURCHASE RECEIPT

He has identified us as His own by placing the Holy Spirit in our hearts as the first installment that guarantees everything He has promised us.

II CORINTHIANS 1:22 NLT

As she pushed her shopping cart slowly down the aisle, she scanned each shelf. So many variables factored into her thinking, but she wanted to get the best bang for her buck. Occasionally she'd find a better deal a little farther down and return her original choice to its spot. She proceeded this way throughout the store until she was finished, ready to make her final purchase, satisfied that she had selected well.

Sometimes, if we're honest, we harbor a secret fear inside. We see our position as Christians a little like those items the lady stored in her shopping cart. Sure, we're doing okay right now, but what if we screw something up or someone better comes along, and God puts us back? Just how certain can we be that we'll reach the final register to be purchased permanently?

Before we were even born, God knew the

insecurities that would lurk in our hearts. So He gave us a picture to adjust our thinking. Even though we haven't yet reached heaven, God provides a guarantee that His children will all get there. When we come to Jesus by faith, the purchase transaction is complete—and comes with a receipt. God's own Spirit fills our hearts, permanently planted in the new creation of who we are. He's not going anywhere without us. From now until we reach eternity's shore, we rest in the hope of all God's promises, proven by the presence of His Spirit in us.

The Spirit is God's guarantee that He will give us the inheritance He promised and that He has purchased us to be His own people. He did this so we would praise and glorify Him.
EPHESIANS 1:14 NLT

LOADED

I pray that the eyes of your heart may be enlightened
in order that you may know the hope to which
He has called you, the riches of
His glorious inheritance in His holy people,
and His incomparably great power for us who believe.
EPHESIANS 1:18–19 NIV

As the ladies sat eating lunch in the mall's food court, a famous celebrity sauntered in, apparently headed to shop in one of the common stores there.

"What on earth is she doing here?" gasped one of the ladies as the others craned their necks to see the source of the growing commotion near them. Instantly, they all recognized her.

"With all her money, why would she bother coming to a place like this?" they wondered. "She could buy the whole mall!"

No matter what our socioeconomic level may be in this life, we all understand the earthly benefits wealth brings. We don't expect the people endowed with it to waste their time searching for the best bargains when they're working with unlimited resources.

And yet, as believers, we often settle for the thrift-store goods when we've really been given the keys to the kingdom. In Christ, every spiritual blessing in the heavens belongs to us. We no longer need to scrounge through life merely hoping for some shred of peace, wisdom, purpose, or connection. We already have it all in Jesus. When we realize just how high we've been seated with Christ in the heavenly places, we begin to live here in a whole new light—like the rulers we are. We are no longer poor pawns of our enemy. We are endowed with all the wealth of heaven in order to walk in a manner worthy of our King and win the lost world back to Him.

If the inheritance depends on the law,
then it no longer depends on the promise;
but God in His grace gave it to Abraham
through a promise.
GALATIANS 3:18 NIV

CALLED OUT

You are a chosen people, a royal priesthood,
a holy nation, God's special possession,
that you may declare the praises of Him who called you out
of darkness into His wonderful light.

I PETER 2:9 NIV

She had never seen the airport more packed, apparently everyone wanting to fly out on the same day. Her own gate was stuffed to overflowing, people crowding around the walkway entrance wanting to ensure their spot on the plane. By all appearances, it would be overbooked.

Then the attendant called out over the loudspeaker: "Attention, please. All passengers in zone one may now board the plane." She checked her ticket. *That's me!* She smiled, and people parted to make room for her as she joined the other boarding passengers.

When we're worried about whether we'll make our flight, we feel such relief at being called out of the crowd to the front of the line. Even though it's just a plane trip, it feels oddly special to be a part of the privileged group, especially when our kind of ticket is the only defining difference.

As Christians, we too have been called out of our common culture into the most privileged position as kingdom children—the defining difference between us and the world stirring from the new heart God graciously gives us. Following in our Father's footsteps, we live and love with His kingdom in focus. Like Jesus, we work to see others restored without any worry about our place in line. We rest from the pressures of pleasing other people, listening instead to God's leading alone.

In short, we live lives of distinction—but not to assert a superior position. Instead, we set ourselves apart by the way that we love others, serving with purpose every place we go.

My prayer is not that you take them out of the world
but that You protect them from the evil one.
They are not of the world, even as I am not of it.
Sanctify them by the truth; Your word is truth.
JOHN 17:15–17 NIV

SUPPLY SURPLUS

In the beginning God created the heavens and the earth.
Now the earth was formless and empty,
darkness was over the surface of the deep,
and the Spirit of God was hovering over the waters.
And God said, "Let there be light," and there was light.
God saw that the light was good,
and He separated the light from the darkness.
GENESIS 1:1–4 NIV

Craving something sweet, she searched her pantry. Spying a bag of chocolate chips, she smiled. *I'll bake chocolate chip cookies!* she decided. Within a matter of minutes, she had lined her counter with bowls and beaters, adding ingredients as the recipe called for each...until it came to baking soda. And eggs. *Ugghh! Why didn't I make sure I had what I needed before I started?* She groaned.

Cooking works well when we have all the right ingredients to complete the project, but it's all stress when we lack what we need. The same goes for other areas in life, as well. Maybe we see bills piling up beyond our ability to pay or loved ones struggling with needs too great for us to meet. Demands at work and friction at home further divide our attention, drain our energy, and deplete our hope for a better tomorrow. We've opened the cupboard of our souls and found it empty.

Fortunately, God's supply for godly living never runs short. For whatever we lack, we simply ask the Lord in prayer. God says that when we humble ourselves and pray, He hears us. Even better, as we spend time in His presence, what we think we need begins to line up with His will. With His Spirit guiding our petition, our prayers change into beautiful trust and expectation. In the exchange we suddenly realize that our emptied reserves were no accident or oversight. They were ordained by God to drive us to Him.

In the past God spoke to our ancestors through the prophets at many times and in various ways, but in these last days He has spoken to us by His Son, whom He appointed heir of all things, and through whom also He made the universe.

HEBREWS 1:1–2 NIV

CHANGE *of* CLOTHES

*I counsel you to buy from Me gold refined in the fire,
so you can become rich; and white clothes to wear,
so you can cover your shameful nakedness;
and salve to put on your eyes, so you can see.*

REVELATION 3:18 NIV

She was so excited about her first day in kindergarten that she even helped her mom pick out her outfit the night before. Arriving early, she was enamored with the colorful classroom and the other wide-eyed children she saw. It was all so wonderful—until recess. Just as soon as she pulled up on the monkey bars, swinging her legs overhead, she heard her new friends burst into laughter. In all her excitement, she had forgotten about underwear. And now her secret was exposed. In utter shame she ran to the teacher, who quickly remedied the situation with some extra clothes she had brought—just in case.

Our hearts go out when we see others experience humiliation because we know all too well how deeply shame hurts. No matter how much we try to keep our flaws covered, we worry about exposure. We don't want others to know our secret past or present struggles.

But God sees, and like the teacher on the playground, He is more than prepared to cover our shame. When we place our trust in Jesus, an incredible exchange takes place. Every failure—past, present, and future—is placed on Christ, whose death nails our guilt and shame to the cross. He covers us up with His own righteous robe, clothing us with honor that lasts forever.

When you feel the weight of shame or nagging words of condemnation coming your way, remember that Jesus already covered it all. His blood silences our accusers and fills our lives with never-ending freedom.

Those who look to Him are radiant;
their faces are never covered with shame.
PSALM 34:5 NIV

The PARADISE PROGNOSIS

In all this you greatly rejoice, though now for a little while you may have had to suffer grief in all kinds of trials. These have come so that the proven genuineness of your faith—of greater worth than gold, which perishes even though refined by fire—may result in praise, glory and honor when Jesus Christ is revealed.

I PETER 1:6–7 NIV

It started out as just a tickle in her chest, causing her to cough on random occasions. After it persisted for a couple of months, she finally decided it was worth a closer look. And there it was on the scan—a preliminary explanation for her curious condition. Something was clearly growing in her lungs, but hearing the report, she felt something bigger growing in her soul: paralyzing fear. What did the future hold for her?

If she belongs to Jesus, the future holds perfect Paradise—eternity with her forever family, healthy and whole with her heavenly Father, no matter how much more time she has on this planet. Such knowledge brings perfect peace, even in scary moments like these.

While we fight for life and pray to bind Satan's schemes to steal, kill, and destroy, God's sovereign will stands supreme over all. Even in sickness and suffering, we find rest when we remember that our every breath comes from our Creator God, who not only called us into existence in the first place but fashioned our lives and the length of our days.

Remember, too, that He does not leave us to walk through life's shadows alone. Our good Shepherd stays with us through every moment. He has walked these painful places as a person Himself, and He knows how to carry us in our pain. Lean into Him, and let His love lift your worry. You and your loved ones are forever in His hands.

> *Your eyes saw my unformed body;*
> *all the days ordained for me*
> *were written in Your book*
> *before one of them came to be.*
> PSALM 139:16 NIV

BATTLE LINES

Then the fire of the LORD fell and burned up
the sacrifice, the wood, the stones and the soil,
and also licked up the water in the trench.
When all the people saw this, they fell prostrate
and cried, "The LORD—He is God! The LORD—
He is God!"

I KINGS 18:38–39 NIV

The battle lines were drawn. Baal's 450 prophets gathered on one side; Elisha—the one prophet of God—on the other, with all of Israel watching in the background. Before it began, Elisha issued this challenge:

"How long will you waver between two opinions?"

The people considered their options, choosing not to answer Elisha. The weight of popular opinion fell to the idols. *Who would want to risk alienation?* they must have errantly thought as they stayed straddling the middle ground. Then both sides built their altars. Both cried out for help. But only one God answered, His fire consuming every part of Elisha's altar.

Today, Elisha's challenge remains. Which side will

we choose? Pressure to conform to the world's way is strong, but it's God's way that always wins.

When we choose to stand with God, two things are sure to happen: First, we'll feel resistance and retaliation from a fallen culture that lives in darkness and despises God's ways. But in obedience, we find a real rest and a hope that is anchored in the only One who is true. We are no longer tumbled about by the restless waves of public opinion. Our eyes, hearts, and lives are fixed, strong and secure, on the One who sees us and saves our souls.

Today, tune out the jeers and sneers and take heart in God's truth instead. In time, God's glory will be known. And we are on the winning side!

To the one who is victorious,
I will give the right to sit
with Me on my throne,
just as I was victorious
and sat down with
My Father on His throne.
REVELATION 3:21 NIV

WAYMAKER

Strengthen the feeble hands, steady the knees
that give way; say to those with fearful hearts,
"Be strong, do not fear; your God will come...."
Water will gush forth in the wilderness
and streams in the desert.
The burning sand will become a pool,
the thirsty ground bubbling springs....
And a highway will be there;
it will be called the Way of Holiness;
it will be for those who walk on that Way.

ISAIAH 35:3–4, 6–8 NIV

It felt inevitable. For years, she and her husband had been at odds, the peculiar personality traits that once drew them together now driving them apart. Between work and the kids, they barely had any time together, but whenever they tried, their bitterness surfaced. As numbness set in, separation seemed the only answer, divorce and despair waiting around the corner.

They felt trapped—not unlike God's people so many years ago. The Israelites had left their homes in Egypt in hopes of finding a better life together—with God. But not long into the journey, their path ended at the Red Sea. Or so it seemed. Enemies pursued them, and certain doom awaited.

Except God had a plan all along, positioning them for a perfect miracle. As they cried out, God parted the waves. His people walked through safely, while their enemies were crushed.

Truly God has a flawless history of making a way when all hope is gone. Just look to the cross and see. Even the darkest hours give way to a new and lasting dawn in His presence. God's power raises the dead to life and opens up doors we thought were deadlocked forever.

What Red Sea roadblock are you facing today? Will you wilt in fear or turn your focus to your way-making God? Don't let your enemy convince you that all hope is lost. Every relationship and each situation in our lives serves to help us see God in a whole new light. Let your worries lead you to the God who saves, and He will light your way.

God is my strong fortress, and He makes my way perfect.
II SAMUEL 22:33 NLT

HEALING HOPE

Praise the LORD, my soul,
and forget not all His benefits—who forgives all your sins
and heals all your diseases, who redeems your life
from the pit and crowns you with love and compassion,
who satisfies your desires with good things
so that your youth is renewed like the eagle's.

PSALM 103:2–5 NIV

When the doctor removed her bandages, the patient paused in front of the mirror. With the tumor gone, she felt so much relief. But the surgical scars looked swollen, so unsightly. She hesitated to say anything, though her expression reflected her concern. *Will I ever fully heal?* she wondered.

We often ask the Lord the same question. We've all suffered from sin's effects in this world. Though we're grateful for God's saving grace, some wounds in our soul still seem to bear scars. Though we know in our minds we are healed, when we look in the mirror we still see someone broken. *How can God ever use me when my past prevents me from appearing whole?*

Like the woman looking at her reflection, in this

world we see as though peering into a darkened mirror. Often we can't make sense of the image we see and second-guess God's surgical performance.

But God sees us differently, our scars forming the seams where His light shines out the most. When we are willing to walk into our world with the message of God's grace, we no longer need to conceal our problems. Instead, we use them to point others to Christ and encourage those who hurt in the same way. Our experience and honesty may be the very key they need to unlock the door to their private pain and lead them to Jesus, who will save them, too.

> *He was pierced for our transgressions,*
> *He was crushed for our iniquities;*
> *the punishment that*
> *brought us peace was on Him,*
> *and by His wounds we are healed.*
> ISAIAH 53:5 NIV

LEADING LAMBS

He brought His people out like a flock;
He led them like sheep through the wilderness.
PSALM 78:52 NIV

When she read him the pregnancy results, her husband whooped. "I'm going to be a dad!" he shouted, and she smiled back in delight. With an embrace and a prayer of thanks, they beamed with the dreams of being perfect parents for this child and all the others God would bring into their family.

What they didn't imagine was how difficult the journey could be. As wonderful as kids are, at some point they grow—and wrestle to live with a mind of their own. Despite our best-laid plans and perfectly logical leadership, the same sweet souls we loved to cuddle when little now talk back and chart paths for their lives that we never intended. Earlier feelings of pleasure now melt into panic. *What do I do with these headstrong people?* we worry.

We look to the Lord, the same leader who led Israel out of bondage and is leading our own lives through life's long journey. Every day He delivers the power and wisdom we need to walk in His ways—but like His children, the Israelites, we must go out to seek Him. Gather the manna and ingest God's goodness daily. God promises to provide His life-giving presence when we seek Him with all our heart.

Surrender this day and your daily battles in prayer. Then rest as you hear the Shepherd's voice leading you—and your little ones—in the way you should go.

If from there you seek
the LORD *your God, you will*
find Him if you seek Him
with all your heart and
with all your soul.
DEUTERONOMY 4:29 NIV

UNDER HIS FEATHERS

They did not thirst when
He led them through the deserts;
He made water flow
for them from the rock;
He split the rock
and water gushed out.
ISAIAH 48:21 NIV

Normally, feathers repel water. They have a special coating that allows birds to stay dry even in a driving rain and enables them to float on water. The same holds true for the sandgrouse, a species of bird that lives in some of earth's driest places—except for the male's breast area. Sandgrouse parents build their homes miles away from water holes to protect their babies from the predators that lurk there. But to water its own young, the father makes a sacrificial flight every day, strategizing ways to soak its special underside without detection. When the feathers have absorbed enough water, the father flies home and lets his baby chicks "milk" their water straight from his chest.

While the sandgrouse story is simply amazing, the creativity of its design shouldn't surprise us. Our God has an awesome history of quenching thirst in the driest of deserts. Wandering through the wilderness, God's people witnessed water gushing spontaneously out of boulders with just a word from their leader. Later, Jesus came to quench our spiritual thirst for good.

Are you wandering through your days with a dryness of soul? Are you worried by your own lack of devotion or enthusiasm toward what could be your life's calling? Then come to the fountain of Living Water and let your soul soak up the nourishing love of your heavenly Father. Once you are refreshed, you'll feel free to fly, bringing God's life-giving water to others as well.

Whoever believes in Me,
as Scripture has said,
rivers of living water
will flow from within them.
JOHN 7:38 NIV

NEEDING
NOURISHMENT

*He humbled you, causing you to hunger
and then feeding you with manna, which neither you
nor your ancestors had known, to teach you that man does
not live on bread alone but on every word
that comes from the mouth of the LORD.*
DEUTERONOMY 8:3 NIV

She had worked hard since the break of dawn. Loads of laundry done, dishes cleaned, she then clocked in for paid work—right on time. Daily deadlines had driven her day and she simply kept on the go until she started up the stairs to the fourth-floor copy room. Suddenly, the room started spinning. Her legs felt weak. She wondered if she was about to faint. *Am I getting sick?* she thought at first, holding herself steady by the handrail. Then she remembered. *No! I haven't eaten a thing all day!* In her busyness, she had forgotten to refuel—and her body rebelled at the neglect.

As He often does, God uses the physical world to help us visualize intangible but important spiritual truths. Just as our bodies growl with hunger when we forget to feed them, our souls grow faint with fatigue and worry when we fail to nourish them with the fuel we need most: fellowship with Jesus.

Jesus, the Bread of Life, imparts all the power and love we need for life through His Spirit, a feeding process that takes place daily. We weren't designed to work without it. The longer we go without prayer or time in God's Word, the weaker we become, until we can't walk anymore. We don't need to wonder where our passion has gone. Our souls are just spiritually depleted! But why grow faint when we have access to our Father, where we can feed on His love through prayer and praise everywhere we go?

In their hunger
You gave them bread
from heaven.
NEHEMIAH 9:15 NIV

LOOKING *at* LIFE

Moses made a bronze snake and put it up on a pole.
Then when anyone was bitten by a snake
and looked at the bronze snake, they lived.
NUMBERS 21:9 NIV

S he was about to get started on the dishes in the sink when she noticed the long leafy tendrils from the bush right outside her kitchen window. Bothered by the sight, she left the sponge to work her hedge clippers. But as she was cutting away, a wasp nest jostled, and its swarm of soldiers stung her hand. Now the only thing she wanted was to escape their madness and make her pain go away.

God says that our sin is a lot like those wasps—except a single sting sends us to our death. God illustrated our dire situation through the true story that happened when the Israelites wandered in the wilderness. Because of their rebellion, venomous snakes slithered into the camp and began biting—and killing—people by the thousands. But God's cure was most curious. He had Moses make a golden snake on a pole and lift it high for all to see. If the bitten people simply looked at it, they were saved.

From the very beginning, faith has played a crucial role in God's plan of salvation. Even today, the world suffers from sin's deathly venom. It's coursing through everyone's veins. But trying to be a better person on your own only ensures death. God delivers the one who looks to His Son for salvation. Trying to save ourselves is not just pointless, it's poisonous. By faith we are healed in Jesus's name!

The sting of death is sin,
and the power of sin is the law.
But thanks be to God!
He gives us the victory through
our Lord Jesus Christ.
I CORINTHIANS 15:56–57 NIV

OUT *of the* TOMB

I was shown mercy so that in me, the worst of sinners,
Christ Jesus might display His immense patience
as an example for those who would believe in Him and
receive eternal life.
I TIMOTHY 1:16 NIV

As the convicted murderer stood to face his victims' families, he saw the hatred glaring from their tearstained eyes. And who could blame them? He had stolen their most precious loved ones and ruined their lives in the wake of his reckless actions. But a strange event happened in the years spent in his lonely prison cell. A chaplain met with him to share the gospel's Good News. Grateful, he received God's gift of grace. Though he knew his sins would send him to the electric chair, His Savior would pardon and receive him into Paradise. Looking out at the small crowd, he told them each how sorry he was. But who could forgive sins like that?

Our God can—and does every day. Nothing distinguishes our Father more than His amazing capacity to forgive even the most egregious sins and love people instead. To cover it all—the worst sins in the world—cost Him the life of His perfectly righteous Son. But when we surrender and receive God's free gift, sin's accusations are silenced. Murderers like Saul become world-changing Pauls in the grace-filled exchange. And the same miracle happens in our souls. Our failures fall away—as do all our self-righteous efforts. Even good works are worthless without Jesus Christ! But His blood covers it all when the broken and contrite repent from the heart and return to the Father who runs to receive us.

The Ninevites believed God. A fast was proclaimed, and all of them, from the greatest to the least, put on sackcloth.... When God saw what they did and how they turned from their evil ways, He relented and did not bring on them the destruction He had threatened.
JONAH 3:5, 10 NIV

The GOD WHO SEES

She gave this name to the LORD who spoke to her:
"You are the God who sees me," for she said,
"I have now seen the One who sees me."

GENESIS 16:13 NIV

She had been kicked beyond the proverbial curb to the hot desert sands outside of town. Hagar, along with her son, Ishmael, through no fault of her own, found herself on the wrong side of Sarah's favor. They weren't needed anymore since Sarah now had her own son, Isaac, the one God promised Sarah so long ago. Without a home and weak from wandering in a hot, barren wilderness, Hagar and Ishmael lost all hope.

But God was with them. They just didn't know it.

Though every human had forsaken them, God heard their cry for help. He saw their pain and cared about their problem. Best of all, He didn't simply solve it—He opened Hagar's eyes and *showed her Him*. Even out in no-man's-land, she never walked alone. "You are the God who sees me," she cried.

And He is. So many people walk this planet hiding

their private pain, alone and despairing despite the crowds around them. But we have a God who sees past our walls, deep into our hearts where we hurt the most, and He cares. He sits with us in our silent sadness, encircling us in His everlasting arms, collecting every tear in His bottle because they matter. We matter to Him. Let's ask Him to open our blind eyes and believe His promises.

When we do, He lifts us from our lonely places with a new outlook on life. The one who once was lonely grows strong in God's love and follows His lead, pursuing other lost people who need to know His salvation, too.

You keep track of all my sorrows.
You have collected all my tears in Your bottle.
You have recorded each one in Your book.
Psalm 56:8 NLT

DELIVERED GOODS

The weapons we fight with are not the weapons of the world. On the contrary, they have divine power to demolish strongholds. We demolish arguments and every pretension that sets itself up against the knowledge of God, and we take captive every thought to make it obedient to Christ.

II CORINTHIANS 10:4–5 NIV

She stared hard at her boss as he walked away from her desk, having just destroyed her day. Anger stirred within the young assistant at the injustice of it all. She worked hard to keep all the plates spinning that her boss set into motion, but if anything ever went wrong (which it rarely did) she alone bore the blame. It mirrored the frustration she often felt at home, too, where complaints were plenty but affirmation was so hard to find.

What she couldn't see were the invisible, evil forces circling around her like ugly vultures, filling her mind with fear-based filth: *Your work is worthless and you are too*, they whispered. She was listening, out on the battlefield with her sword and shield on the ground.

The Bible warns us that when we choose to follow Christ, we become Satan's worst enemy. When we've been wounded by others or are weakened by overwork and isolation, we are most vulnerable to his attacks. He plays to our secret insecurities, calling God's promises into question, drawing doubt about our true identity.

Whenever we begin to feel down and defeated, we need to take notice of what we're believing. Has our enemy snuck in to steal truth and joy in some sinister thought? Through repentance and returning to what God's Word says, we render every fiery dart powerless. Following our commanding officer, Jesus, we learn to walk in warrior ways as we take every thought captive and make it obedient to Him.

Sovereign LORD,
my strong deliverer,
You shield my head
in the day of battle.
PSALM 140:7 NIV

(Face) Planting Joy

Our mouths were filled with laughter, our tongues with songs of joy. Then it was said among the nations, "The Lord has done great things for them."
Psalm 126:2 niv

Everyone sat silently listening to the preacher that Sunday morning. She, however, was stressing out, secretly struggling to keep her children—two rows ahead—in line without attracting attention. She and her husband could both see them wiggling and occasionally whispering, when her husband's exasperation sent him over the top. Standing up in a huff, he stepped past each person to the main aisle, where he hoped to reach their row. Instead, he suddenly tripped over an unseen purse...and face-planted with a mighty *thud*—right in front of the preacher.

It was humbling...and it was hilarious.

And the wife was undone with belly-deep laughter, the scene so hysterical she had to fight for composure. The husband quickly rejoined her, laughing alongside her, the comic relief what they both needed most.

In pursuing perfection, they had felt tremendously burdened. In laughter's release, they found renewed focus and rest in remembering God's grace and affection for imperfect people—like their kids and them—in His church.

God, after all, gave us our sense of humor! As our Maker, He sings and smiles over us as His children, loving the pure laughter that rings from our souls when we're enjoying Him and the life He has given us. Instead of worrying about how well we perform or whether other people will judge our efforts, we are freed to relax, rest, and revel in the funny faith-builders God brings along the way. The joy of the Lord is our strength!

You shall go out in joy, and be led back in peace;
the mountains and the hills
before you shall burst into song,
and all the trees of the field shall clap their hands.
Isaiah 55:12 NRSV

FAITH FORWARD

Our children will also serve Him.
Future generations will hear about
the wonders of the Lord.
His righteous acts will be told to those not yet born.
They will hear about everything He has done.
PSALM 22:30–31 NLT

He had thought he was an anomaly when he prayed to receive Christ. As far as he knew, he was the first in his whole family to make that life-changing decision. And it seemed surreal, all the steps leading up to his conversion—like some unseen hand had put all the right pieces into place.

Then the phone rang. His aunt, who lived on the other side of the country, had come across an old journal in her attic, handwritten by his great-grandfather. When it arrived in the mail and he read it, he wept. Generations before he had ever been born, his great-grandfather had been praying for him—and all the other descendants down the line, asking for their salvation. His new life in Christ was the answer to the old man's faithful, visionary prayer.

We serve a mighty God who is unbound by time constraints. When we cry out to Him for our children, grandchildren, and distant future generations, God hears and moves in times and places we may never see. Our worries about wayward generations fade as faith in God's unlimited power grows. Through prayer today, we can make an impact on people's lives all over the globe for generations to come. Let's not waste another moment, wishing times now were like they were in the past. Instead, press into God and ask Him to deliver the hope we need now and for our children's children.

The LORD who made you and helps you says:
Do not be afraid, O Jacob, My servant,
O dear Israel, My chosen one.
For I will pour out water
to quench your thirst and
to irrigate your parched fields.
And I will pour out My Spirit on your descendants,
and My blessing on your children.
ISAIAH 44:2–3 NLT

FINISHED WORK

*I am certain that God, who began
the good work within you, will continue
His work until it is finally finished
on the day when Christ Jesus returns.*
PHILIPPIANS 1:6 NLT

With one hand on her hip, the other gripped her phone as she stared hard at its screen in disbelief. The man who was supposed to be helping her build her backyard deck had decided he didn't want to work on it anymore. Apparently he had been offered a more lucrative project he couldn't turn down. With half her money gone and only a half-finished deck to show for it, she sat down on the boards that would have been her steps and sighed.

When the people we rely on—even pay—to keep their promises fail us, our hope in humanity dims just a little. Why can't people just do what they say and finish whatever it was that they started in the first place? Unfortunately, people just aren't perfect. But we know the Carpenter who is! Better still, every project God begins ends in perfection every time—even when that work is us!

Jesus, the Author and Perfecter of our faith, began a good work in us the day we surrendered our lives to Him. Through the power of His unseen Spirit and His written Word, He chisels away all the waste and works in the character of Christ, building from the foundation up. Whether we one day die and go home to heaven or our Lord returns here to earth first, we can be sure of one thing: Jesus will finish what He started in each of us, presenting us to our Father without a single fault—and full of His glory.

Now all glory to God,
who is able to keep you
from falling away and will bring you with great joy
into His glorious presence without a single fault.
JUDE 24 NLT

SON SHINE

Turn us again to Yourself, O God.
Make Your face shine down upon us.
Only then will we be saved.
PSALM 80:3 NLT

As the budding young artist applied more and more paint to the paper on her plastic easel, she felt proud of her picture. Though each paint container held its own color, her creativity blended them all, using one brush for trunks, treetops, and flowery fields. She wondered if anyone else in her kindergarten class was watching her wonderful masterpiece unfold. As she turned around to find an audience, she found her teacher right behind her, beaming with pleasure. The child was elated! With more energy than ever, she returned to her work.

It's amazing what we can accomplish when the people we love believe in us. Often just a simple word of encouragement or even acknowledgment of our efforts can make all the difference in whether or not we forge ahead with our ideas. It's one of the reasons the apostle Paul prayed so hard for the people who had put their faith in Christ. "God, help them see just how high and deep and wide Your love for them all actually is!" he prayed.

When we belong to Jesus, we no longer have to wonder what God thinks about us. His favor doesn't fluctuate based on how well we're drawing our picture! He's delighted that we've picked up the brush and begun applying the paint He's providing. Trust His heart, and rest with confidence in His declared love for you. This world needs to see the work of art your unique personality brings to it, treasured by God every stroke along the way.

> The Lord appeared to us
> in the past, saying:
> "I have loved you with
> an everlasting love;
> I have drawn you with
> unfailing kindness."
> JEREMIAH 31:3 NIV

BABY FAITH

Our LORD, You will always rule,
but nations will vanish
from the earth.
You listen to the longings
of those who suffer.
You offer them hope,
and You pay attention
to their cries for help.

PSALM 10:16–17 CEV

It was the third time that morning she had to change her youngest son's diaper. Meanwhile, her two other toddlers ran like tornadoes across the room, enjoying their tired mom's distraction with other duties. Setting the baby back down to join the other two, she picked out a book she thought they'd all enjoy—at least for a few minutes. But two pages in, she was nodding off, the words jumbling together in a partial dream.

She needed more energy. Truth be told, she could use some help. But her husband was out of town and her mom six states away. So she downed another cup of coffee and tried to keep the whirlwinds contained.

But in her stupor, she missed her unseen Friend, a supernatural source of hope whose strength outperforms all the caffeine in the world! Jesus is our ever-present help in times of need, whether we are seeking to survive parenthood or to simply find a parking space so we won't be late. No need is too great or too small for our Savior's concern or capacity to solve, but He does want one small step of faith from us: instead of pulling up our bootstraps to make the best of our situation, He invites us to turn to Him for help. In the asking, we're believing that God really is involved in every detail of our day. Even diaper changes develop our faith as we find God to be a most faithful listener, helper, and friend.

We are certain that God will hear our prayers
when we ask for what pleases Him.
And if we know that God listens when we pray,
we are sure that our prayers have already been answered.
I JOHN 5:14–15 CEV

GOD RESTORES
and BRINGS JOY

*It seemed like a dream when the L*ORD *brought us back*
to the city of Zion. We celebrated with laughter
and joyful songs. In foreign nations it was said,
*"The L*ORD *has worked miracles for His people."*
*And so we celebrated because the L*ORD
had indeed worked miracles for us.

PSALM 126:1–3 CEV

As she watched her husband being baptized, she knew she was witnessing a miracle. Tears streamed down her face as her thoughts reflected on the long, hard road that led him here. Enduring years of his alcohol and work addiction, she had spent so much time alone, tending to their children and talking to God. When she was fearful about finances or their children's future, she leaned into the Lord even harder, looking to Him for the leadership she lacked at home, praying and believing that one day her husband would step into his God-given role.

Twenty years later, her husband's heart changed, and now he stood humbled and submitted to God's

Spirit like never before. But he wasn't the only one.

In the painfully long struggle, she had experienced God's tender mercies and saving grace, day by day. Her dependence on His Spirit had grown so strong that her heart sang no matter what situation she faced. By experience, she knew her Savior was near, and she was safe.

We, too, can rest in hope regardless of our current circumstances when we realize God's goodness. He is God with us, our peace amid unpleasant realities. Today, draw closer to Him and pour out your heart's cry. Though we weep for a season, we rest knowing that with the Lord, unspeakable joy comes with the morning.

The whole earth is filled
with awe at Your wonders; where
morning dawns, where evening fades,
You call forth songs of joy.
PSALM 65:8 NIV

LIVING HOPE

Jesus said to her, "I am the resurrection and the life.
The one who believes in Me will live,
even though they die."
JOHN 11:25 NIV

At the funeral service, the parents were numb, their sudden shock and pain at their son's passing still unfolding. Others tried to encourage, but everyone was at a loss, wondering why God would take someone so young, so kind—such a strong Christian—home so soon. Didn't God know they needed him here more?

Whenever we lose a loved one, regardless of age, we grieve at the separation. The truth is, we weren't created to die, but humanity's sinful state seals each fate, and our souls suffer an agonizing ache in the wake of severed community. We imagine how it could have been for our loved ones and us if their lives had kept going. How can Christians cope with hope in the midst of such sadness?

Without Jesus, it would truly be the end of our story here on earth, our exit here leading to judgment and pain forever on the other side. But God, by His incredible resurrection power, has removed death's sting by opening a door to a whole new level of living hope. For the believer, passing from this life releases us from all pain and sorrow and places us immediately in Jesus's presence, where we will live for the rest of eternity. Though it grieves us to lose friends and family now, our pain is limited to our remaining time on earth. Time and friends help heal the wound, but heaven solves the problem for good. When we, too, pass into glory, all tears will be wiped away. All will be new, and God's family will reunite in one glorious wedding celebration with Jesus.

Good people pass away;
the godly often die before their time.
But no one seems to care or wonder why.
No one seems to understand that God
is protecting them from the evil to come.
For those who follow godly paths
will rest in peace when they die.
ISAIAH 57:1–2 NLT

WORDS THAT WORK

It is the same with My word.
I send it out, and it always produces fruit.
It will accomplish all I want it to,
and it will prosper everywhere I send it.
ISAIAH 55:11 NLT

The young gardener was impatient. "Mom, it has been weeks since we planted the seeds," she explained matter-of-factly. "And look! Nothing! Nothing is coming up at all," she complained, a secret worry brewing that all their efforts were actually wasted.

"If the seed and soil are good, it will happen. We just have to wait," the mom answered. And she was right. Just a few days later, tender shoots sprang up from the barren earth, and the young girl gushed with excitement and hope.

Even as adults, we also get impatient, wanting God to cause immediate growth in us or others. In our unbelieving children or friends, we want to see signs of faith. In ourselves, we want to stop slipping into the same kinds of sin. We're seeking change and wrestling with the worry that it won't come.

But God has promised: His Word works. His truth packs so much power that it produces fruit every single time He sends it out. When we learn what God's Word says and pray that Scripture back to Him with eager expectation for His answer, God moves. It may take days, weeks, months, or even years before we see the first sign of spring, but we will. God's Word, spoken through prayer or seasoning our conversation, releases God's Spirit to work in supernatural ways and reaps results that last into eternity.

Where do you want to see growth most? Commit it to prayer, persistently applying God's Word. Study and speak out loud the truth you learn. Then watch what God will do!

The Son is the radiance
of God's glory and the exact representation of His being,
sustaining all things by His powerful word.
HEBREWS 1:3 NIV

THE GREAT REWARD

This is what the LORD says:
"Restrain your voice from weeping
and your eyes from tears,
for your work will be rewarded,"
declares the LORD.

JEREMIAH 31:16 NIV

Every Sunday she shows up, first for the service, and then to serve the children. Each week she plans ahead for the little Bible lesson she'll share and strategizes creative ways to make it fun and keep their attention while sowing God's Word into their fertile minds and hearts. Week in, week out, she works while few people see the effort and enthusiasm she puts into her time with the children. But there is only One whose audience she seeks, and He smiles at what He sees.

As believers, we no longer need to worry about our standing before Christ. We are made righteous through faith, and His grace won't fail us when we stand before our Father on Judgment Day. But God holds even more fun in store for those who will inherit heaven. Along with the wonder of living forever with God, we each will be rewarded according to what we did on earth.

What kind of rewards will heaven bring? God doesn't give us details, just directions to concentrate our efforts on building heavenly riches instead of earthly ones. Every smile of encouragement, every prayer for the saints, every good deed we do counts for glory because our God sees, smiles, and saves His very best rewards for heaven's grand celebration.

When we are weary of doing good day in and day out, we would do well to remember who's watching. Our good Father seeks to support us in our efforts and faithfully rewards us with the richness of His presence, both now and into eternity.

The eyes of the LORD range throughout the earth to strengthen those whose hearts are fully committed to Him.
II CHRONICLES 16:9 NIV

DOWN *and* UP

*God has delivered me from going
down to the pit, and I shall live
to enjoy the light of life.*
JOB 33:28 NIV

Everyone else at church seemed so happy, but she couldn't find the strength to even fake a smile. Simply getting out of bed and brushing her teeth was struggle enough. Being awake meant facing certain thoughts and feeling the pain that wouldn't go away, no matter how many prayers she prayed or praise songs she sang. She felt forever stuck in her depression and wondered why she couldn't find her way out.

These days, more light has been shed on depression's darkness than ever before. Throughout history, though, even the godliest people have grappled with it, sometimes struggling their entire lives long. As with all other illnesses we encounter in this broken world, both physical and spiritual factors have an effect. While many times prayer, praise, and Scripture study can steady our fear-filled minds, in other instances the battle trenches must be dug even deeper. God can bring amazing healing through different medicines that restore the mind's chemical balance, while time-tested therapies and counseling can work wonders alongside.

Sometimes we find supernatural healing. But God calls some people to find peace in the struggle, to seek the strength needed each moment from Him and to surround themselves with people who are standing in a stronger place and can pray for them when they can't find the words.

When you find yourself or a loved one fumbling in the darkness, don't give in to despair or dismiss the pain. Recognize the many avenues of relief, and rest in the comfort of God's never-ending care. He cradles you in the dark and has destined you for future glory.

> *The LORD protects those of childlike faith;*
> *I was facing death, and He saved me.*
> *Let my soul be at rest again, for the LORD has been good*
> *to me. He has saved me from death,*
> *my eyes from tears, my feet from stumbling.*
> *And so I walk in the LORD's presence*
> *as I live here on earth!*
> PSALM 116:6–9 NLT

PUZZLE PIECES

It's in Christ that we find out who we are and what we are living for. Long before we first heard of Christ and got our hopes up, He had His eye on us, had designs on us for glorious living, part of the overall purpose He is working out in everything and everyone.

EPHESIANS 1:11–12 THE MESSAGE

She always started with the edges and then moved her way in. Her lips tight in concentration, she worked each puzzle piece, looking for its place in the grand design. She enjoyed the challenge, knowing that no matter how many pieces were in the box, persistent work would pay off in the end. And it always did, the rectangular art matching the image on the box lid.

Puzzles bring pleasure because they are solvable problems. If we try hard enough and long enough, we can work them out. And we often approach life the same way. As difficulties arise, we go to great lengths to decipher the purpose behind them. We sort out the colors and edges and work with all our might to make sense of it all. Only sometimes we simply can't. And we start to question whether all the right pieces were put in the box to begin with.

Yet life with God is not flat, nor are the edges predictably straight. God's design is far more dynamic with a vibrant, living, and multidirectional dimension far beyond our limited understanding. Rest assured that if we love Him, God promises that every moment of our lives packs eternal significance, every piece with a place. Though we find joy whenever we see how some fit together, we find lasting rest when we trust that God knows what He's doing. He's shaping history—and His people in the process—for His glory and our blessing.

You intended to harm me,
but God intended it all for good.
He brought me to this position
so I could save the lives
of many people.
GENESIS 50:20 NLT

GAZING AND BLAZING

*And we all, who with unveiled faces contemplate
the Lord's glory, are being transformed into
His image with ever-increasing glory,
which comes from the Lord, who is the Spirit.*

II CORINTHIANS 3:18 NIV

Just imagine it. When Moses led the Israelites along God's winding wilderness way, he wasn't left alone to guess where to go or what to do. God Himself met with Moses, often more than a month at a time, imparting His heart so Moses, the mediator, could teach God's people. And something visibly miraculous resulted from the intimate exchange: Moses's face glowed with God's glory. It was such an unsettling sight when he returned to camp that the Israelites asked him to cover it with a cloth. To them, a glowing human was just too...supernatural.

Now picture this: God still brings His glory into earthly temples in the same dramatic way! Even though our bodies may be aging or our appearance may be "nothing to see," something supernatural happens when we sit at God's feet and soak in His glory. As we allow our thoughts to dwell on His goodness, power, provision, and love, our lives begin to glow with inexplicable peace and purpose. The dark world around us may wonder or wince at its brightness, but we don't need to cover God's brilliance. As the little child's song says, we change the world when we let God's light shine.

Today, let us make time to marvel at God's majesty, drawing close to Him in silent reverence as we listen for what He has to say and how He reveals His heart. As we do, His Spirit inside us renews our strength, fills us with hope, and sets our whole life ablaze with His passion and glory.

We do not lose heart.
Though outwardly we are wasting away,
yet inwardly we are being renewed day by day.
II CORINTHIANS 4:16 NIV

THE WAY OUT

So then, since we have a great High Priest who has entered heaven, Jesus the Son of God, let us hold firmly to what we believe. This High Priest of ours understands our weaknesses, for He faced all of the same testings we do, yet He did not sin. So let us come boldly to the throne of our gracious God. There we will receive His mercy, and we will find grace to help us when we need it most.

HEBREWS 4:14–16 NLT

The audience watched in fearful anticipation. What the magician attempted to do seemed doomed to disaster. Shackled by thick chains around his feet and his hands tied behind his back, he was supposed to escape the small, clear box where he stood—even as it was filling with water. Soon it was over his head, and everyone held their breath while they waited to see what would happen.

Watching escape tricks can be fun and entertaining, but wrestling with real-life temptations and traps feels more traumatic. We wonder if we have the will or wits to make it out of the situation alive.

But God is the One waiting for us to wake up and

realize He's handed us the key that unlocks our chains. No matter what difficulty or daunting temptation we face, we walk away free when we go to God for help in the middle of it. Jesus Himself understands our issues because He experienced life on this earth just like we do—only He did it without sin. When we feel doomed to repeat our same sinful behavior, we have a way out. It's Jesus Himself, who comes to our aid when we call out to Him as the water is rising.

Where or when do you feel destined to failure? Is it when you walk to the fridge? When you turn on the computer? When you enter into conversation with those people? Recognize the rut for what it is and run to the One who will show you the way out.

No temptation has overtaken you except
what is common to mankind.
And God is faithful; He will not let you be tempted
beyond what you can bear.
But when you are tempted,
He will also provide a way out so that you can endure it.
I CORINTHIANS 10:13 NIV

GOD'S NATURE

Look to the LORD and His strength;
seek His face always.
I CHRONICLES 16:11 NIV

It was his little girl's favorite game. Every time they went on family walks through the woods, the dad would issue his challenge: a nickel for every neat nature surprise she could find, but a whole quarter for the coolest discoveries (think lizards, frogs, snakes—anything living). She loved it! Every walk became an amazing adventure, her senses fine-tuned and focused on every unusual motion, color, or sound that could potentially score more reward. In the end, she cashed in her points at the ice cream shop, where she and her dad remembered together all the wonderful scenes they had experienced.

But God doesn't want the adventure game to end as we grow up. As our loving Father, He continues to lead each one of us daily on the wildest journey of our lives. When we learn to pay attention to how God is working all around us, a whole new world of wonder and awe unfolds before our eyes. Suddenly our conversation with the cashier becomes a life-changing encounter. The wildflower springing up from the cracked sidewalk is a sign—that God's loving nature is seen everywhere we go. As we keep our eyes peeled for God's purpose—even in the mundane moments—we find a million beautiful miracles right around us. Joy and peace and purpose are ours every step of the way as we watch with anticipation to see God's goodness in all its glorious forms and then celebrate what we see in sweet praise to Him.

They celebrate Your
abundant goodness and joyfully
sing of Your righteousness.
PSALM 145:7 NIV

HOLDING OUT

The LORD God is our sun and our shield.
He gives us grace and glory.
The LORD will withhold no good thing
from those who do what is right.

PSALM 84:11 NLT

As he offered excuses, she stared at him, completely stunned by this turn of events. He was the perfect Christian guy, and she had given so much of her time and effort to the relationship. She had prayed for God's direction and felt so much peace pursuing this path. It just seemed perfect. Except now it wasn't, because he was backing out. Anger invaded her thoughts, followed by bitterness—aimed first at her ex-boyfriend but later at God. She felt tricked, mistreated. *If God loved me, why would He let this happen?* she let her mind wonder.

We all have to watch our hearts and minds when life doesn't work out the way we planned. Our enemy is ready and eager to sow seeds of discontent and distrust as we question what God is doing. Like Eve in the Garden when the serpent second-guessed God's goodness, we're tempted to believe that God is holding out on us.

But God invites us to walk away from that temptation into a place of utter trust. When we can't figure out why God has blocked our path, we can lean even harder on His leading; let go of our demanding; allow the Spirit to change our thinking while healing our wounded hearts. When we keep our hands open to God, we experience deeper rest. In the resting, we realize God's plan—always drawing us closer to His presence—was far better than what we imagined in the first place.

So if you sinful people know
how to give good gifts
to your children, how much more
will your heavenly Father give
good gifts to those who ask Him.
MATTHEW 7:11 NLT

REST RESTORED

The Spirit of the Sovereign LORD is on me, because the LORD has anointed me to proclaim good news to the poor. He has sent me to bind up the brokenhearted, to proclaim freedom for the captives and release from darkness for the prisoners...to bestow on them a crown of beauty instead of ashes, the oil of joy instead of mourning, and a garment of praise instead of a spirit of despair. They will be called oaks of righteousness, a planting of the LORD for the display of His splendor.
ISAIAH 61:1, 3 NIV

Her daughter had a wonderful idea to plant a garden. So the two took a trip to the local nursery, picked out pots and seeds, shovels and fertilizer, then formed a plan about who would do what as they weeded, prepped, and planted their garden. They worked at it for hours in the hot spring sun, digging holes and putting in seeds until darkness took over.

But in the morning, they both woke up to disappointment. Apparently intrigued by all the activity, their dog had dug up all they had planted. The yard was a ruined mess, the destruction seemingly beyond repair.

Sometimes we experience life like that garden. We put in the hard work of parenting or preparing for a long-held dream, only to wake up years down the road feeling like either we or someone else has ruined our plans, utterly destroying our hope.

But in Jesus, hope always grows. Though our garden may no longer spring up in the pattern we planned, God's Word promises to bear fruit—even in the unlikeliest places—when we stay surrendered to Him. Wayward children often return home and dreams rerouted by devastating roadblocks wind up working out after all under God's sovereign plan.

When reflections on the past bring regret, remember that God restores ALL things. Nothing remains broken in His hands. He is the master Gardener who tills our souls' soil and sends the rain for our nourishment, though we'd rather it stay sunny all the time. Waiting and trusting in His way, we'll witness the growth of a richer faith—with roots winding deeper into His love.

I will restore to you the years that the swarming locust has eaten....
You shall eat in plenty and be satisfied, and praise the name of the
Lord your God, who has dealt wondrously with you.

JOEL 2:25–26 ESV

CARRIED

The horse is made ready
for the day of battle,
but victory rests with the LORD.
PROVERBS 21:31 NIV

When she awoke, she didn't need to check her calendar. She knew what day it was. For over a month she had been prepping her home and scouring every place to find empty moving boxes. Yesterday they were finally all filled with her family's belongings. Now she just needed the movers to arrive. Without their help, she'd be up a creek—without any of her stuff. She was a smart and strong woman, but she knew her limitations. When the load was too much for her, she let someone stronger take over and handle the rest.

It's a great strategy, the very kind our Savior says works in His kingdom, when we strike the right balance. Whenever God calls us to move from where we are, we may feel uncertain at first. How can we know God's will, and what's the best way to get there? Certainly anxieties often lessen with a semblance of order, so putting a good plan in place may be the perfect solution for some of the stress!

But the secret to real rest lies in relying on who's strongest. While God has given us physical bodies to think and brainstorm, plan and plot, He alone has the understanding and strength we need for life to work. More than that, He infuses our earthly efforts with supernatural power, wielding impact beyond this life into eternity.

Today, don't wear yourself out, trying to wing it on your own. Let your Father do the heavy lifting as you lay your needs before Him in prayer.

It does not, therefore,
depend on human desire
or effort, but on God's mercy.
ROMANS 9:16 NIV

ANCIENT WAYS

This is what the LORD says:
"Stand at the crossroads and look;
ask for the ancient paths,
ask where the good way is,
and walk in it, and
you will find rest for your souls."
JEREMIAH 6:16 NIV

Her granddaughter looked up at her in earnest, eyes twinkling with eagerness.

"I don't know, honey," the grandmother answered, uncertain, eyeing the bike she was supposed to get on and ride. "I haven't done that in many years." But love for her granddaughter compelled her, so she gathered her wits and all the energy she had and hopped on the bike.

As they rode down the sidewalk, wind in their hair, the woman's mind flooded with memories. She remembered what it felt like to be adventurous and fun, free from the worries the adult world brought with it. Her feet pedaled faster and her hands steered with skill just as they did when she was younger, the rhythm and joy of childhood returning to her heart.

Some things in life just feel right. They settle in our souls like *This is how it should be.*

We need to listen. The One who whispers behind us which way we should go in life sounds louder when we return to the simplicity of childlike faith. And Jesus says, *Come. Return to the place where you once knew grace and love and forgiveness.* The fountain of joy and peace still flows there, the Lord of all eager for you to experience Him again like when your faith first began.

Life in this world can slowly lead our hearts astray until our souls feel hard and dry. When we wonder what went wrong, God says to return to the ancient paths. Place your trust again in the only One who's proven true, and you will find your way.

Start children off on the way they should go,
and even when they are old they will not turn from it.
PROVERBS 22:6 NIV

FIRE POWER

Fear of the LORD leads to life,
bringing security and protection from harm.
PROVERBS 19:23 NLT

The young boy watched his father tend the fire. Flames billowed and sparks shot up into the night sky whenever he carefully moved the logs to allow more oxygen to fuel it. It was beautifully warm, mesmerizing...magical. So when the father went around their tent to gather more wood, the boy eased closer to play with the glowing embers. But in stirring them, the heat surged up and sparks flew out, singeing his face and hands. Suddenly he knew a new level of respect for fire's power.

God, the Creator of fire, uses the common energy to help us understand Him better, too. His call to come and circle around His presence warms our hearts and souls, and we grow comfortable with who we think He is.

But He is far greater.

Though His love, forgiveness, and mercy are certain, God is supernatural. Our finite minds can't contain all He is, His power and wisdom so far stronger and higher than our own. We warm ourselves in His love and draw comfort from His grace, but our knees drop down in reverence when we reflect on who He really is.

What an awesome privilege we have to walk with our Maker! The Great I AM who blazed before Moses on God's holy mountain beckons us to come closer this day. Let us draw near to our Father in full assurance of His love. And let us live in reverence, following His ways, as our fear of the Lord leads us to true worship and wisdom.

I listen carefully to what God the LORD *is saying,*
for He speaks peace to His faithful people.
But let them not return to their foolish ways.
Surely His salvation is near to those who fear Him,
so our land will be filled with His glory.
PSALM 85:8–9 NLT

PRAY *for* WISDOM

If you need wisdom, ask our generous God,
and He will give it to you.
He will not rebuke you for asking.

JAMES 1:5 NLT

The storm raged all around the passenger plane, despite the pilot's efforts to avoid it. Lightning bolts split the sky outside as the passengers tightly gripped their seats, many sending up prayers for protection. Dark and menacing clouds veiled outside vision, so the pilot radioed the tower for assistance. The ground's radar capabilities could track his course in a reliable way and reroute him to a better path. As he listened for directions, he dodged the worst parts of the storm and eventually landed the plane in safety.

In life, we often feel like the pilot of that plane. We're supposed to be in charge of our families, our careers, even planning for the future, but we can't see past the windshield, which is a problem no matter what kind of weather is outside.

But we always have a strong tower to call on

who helps us find our way. None of us here on this planet have the perspective we need to navigate life well on our own—we were designed to radio for help! God's Spirit and His Word are true, both working in tandem to impart the wisdom we lack.

Whenever you find yourself fearing the unknown and trying to find your way through dark places, run to the tower for wisdom and guidance. God promises to give you all that you need as He gently steers you toward deeper trust in Him.

The name of the LORD
is a strong tower;
the righteous man runs
into it and is safe.
PROVERBS 18:10 ESV

HOPE SINGS

Why am I discouraged?
Why is my heart so sad? I will put my hope in God!
I will praise Him again—my Savior and my God!
Now I am deeply discouraged, but I will remember you—
even from distant Mount Hermon, the source of the
Jordan, from the land of Mount Mizar. I hear the
tumult of the raging seas as your waves and surging
tides sweep over me. But each day the LORD pours His
unfailing love upon me, and through each night I sing His
songs, praying to God who gives me life.

PSALM 42:5–8 NLT

A s she swept the floor (for the umpteenth time this week), her mind wandered with a wide range of thoughts. Sometimes she felt angry at all the junk left on counters and floors, her family failing to notice the toll their negligence took on her and her work. But just then she saw an old toy tucked into a corner, and warmer sentiments filled her.

Like a seesaw in her mind, her emotions rose and fell depending on her focus, both positive and negative fighting for the high seat. The fight in her head sapped more strength than the sweeping! Even in solitude, she needed some peace! So she turned on some praise music. And that move made all the difference.

We may not understand why music moves us in ways nothing else can, but we know by experience that it does. But music that lifts up our Lord's name in praise does even more, taking our thoughts to a whole new level and transforming our minds to make them like His. As we listen to truth and agree in song, our souls are soothed in God's all-encompassing goodness. Petty grievances and task-driven agendas give way to repentance, and declaring God's greatness brings light to our darkness. In His presence, our minds change and our souls are moved to work in sync with the Spirit. Praise is God's secret weapon that silences distraction and focuses our hearts where they belong—at home with our Lord.

> *Praise the* LORD! *How good*
> *to sing praises to our God!*
> *How delightful and how fitting!*
> PSALM 147:1 NLT

BELIEVING BETTER

*"You will not succeed by your own strength
or by your own power. The power will come
from my Spirit," says the Lord of heaven's armies.*

ZECHARIAH 4:6 ICB

The longer she sat in her class, the more her stomach turned and twisted. *How am I ever going to get this done?* she worried as she scanned her calendar, calculating all the assignments she'd been given for the week. The mounting pressure surged like a rising tsunami. She felt certain she would drown. *How are humans supposed to survive so much stress?* she silently wondered.

By nature, we worry when pressures rise. It seems like our hearts can't help but buckle under the heavy loads we bear, and we labor hard to either tackle and tame every towering challenge or take a leave of absence from any effort at all.

But Jesus invites us to a better way—one that requires work, but lighter than the kind we've grown accustomed to do. He says, "Believe."

When we fear that we're going to fail, we can believe that He's with us and will keep us from stumbling. When we question our future, we keep our eyes on Him because He's already there. And when we're tired from faith's fight, His name is our refuge. We find peace in God's unfailing promises—when we fully believe He's as good as His Word.

And what if we find ourselves failing in belief? By faith, move forward in obedience anyway. As we follow Christ's directions to come to Him for relief, we find our belief grows stronger—and our Savior was right, after all. His yoke is easy and His burden is light. In our unbelief, we can ask for more faith. No matter what our feelings, our Father remains faithful.

Now we who have believed enter that rest, just as God has said, "So I declared on oath in My anger, 'They shall never enter My rest.'" And yet His works have been finished since the creation of the world.
HEBREWS 4:3 NIV

STEADY STRENGTH

Therefore everyone who hears these words
of Mine and puts them into practice is like
a wise man who built his house on the rock.

MATTHEW 7:24 NIV

It took everything within you just to get inside the gym. Now you're sitting on the bench press, wondering if it also works for short naps. *I don't think I can do this,* you mumble under your breath, hating the heaviness of the weights now in your hands. Spurred on by the sleek physiques that seem to encircle you, you press on, repeating the count until the set is complete. *Excruciating,* you conclude. But tomorrow, you know you'll try again. Getting back in shape is simply hard work. But every day, your courage and conviction for a healthier you grows, and you can feel yourself growing stronger.

The same is true for the spirit inside us. Even if we feel instinctively weak spiritually, by God's grace we will grow stronger with each act of obedience. Instead of heavy lifting, we daily lay our weights down through prayer, developing a greater dependence on God's guidance and resources. As we press through passages in God's Word, His Spirit works understanding and reverence into our soul. And as we remember and reflect on what God says, our ability and desire to do life God's way grows each day.

Scripture warns us that trials will come our way, but if we've trained our minds to stick to God's truth, we'll stand through the storms. Obstacles become only opportunities for God to display His amazing faithfulness. As we press on, others will see our strength and seek to know the God who empowers us to stay so steady.

Surely My arm will strengthen him.
The enemy will not get the better of him;
the wicked will not oppress him.
PSALM 89:21–22 NIV

THE PERFECT PLACE

*Let the peace of Christ rule in your hearts,
since as members of one body you were called to peace.
And be thankful.*

COLOSSIANS 3:15 NIV

It was late afternoon, and she had a little time on her hands before beginning dinner. Sitting down at her computer, she started to surf. Pop-up messages reminded her of people she hadn't seen in years, and before she knew it, she was scrolling through photo after perfect photo, looking at all the fun and fellowship everyone else seemed to be having. Even as she clicked "Like," she couldn't help wanting… wishing…wondering if her life (with all her worries) would ever be that good.

Then she went outside. The sun was setting behind the trees, brilliant streaks of pink and gold gilding a faint blue sky. A light breeze blew as the summer cicadas stirred in evening celebration. She sank onto her patio chair to enjoy the show, God's glory cast through chorus and color. In her pleasure, she felt

God's presence. In His nearness, she gave thanks, her gratitude for all God's goodness washing away the discontent.

In giving thanks, we find our rightful place in this world and rest for our searching souls. We are the recipients of God's extraordinary grace, the object of His undeserved favor. In all the moments of our lives—the fun and the fearful, the successes and the failures—we live loved. All of eternity, beginning even before our birth, has been purchased for us at the highest price, our future secured by our loving Savior. The beauty of creation sings with worship and wonder at such extravagant love, lavished on us, God's beloved children. Let us join in with the song!

Rejoice in the Lord always. I will say it again: Rejoice! Let your gentleness be evident to all. The Lord is near. Do not be anxious about anything, but in every situation, by prayer and petition, with thanksgiving, present your requests to God. And the peace of God, which transcends all understanding, will guard your hearts and your minds in Christ Jesus.

PHILIPPIANS 4:4–7 NIV

TO:

_____

FROM:

_____

DATE:

_____

Morning
PROMISES

90 Devotions to Start the Day
Knowing You Are Loved

JENNIFER GERELDS

DaySpring
LIVE YOUR FAITH

Morning and Evening Promises Flip Book
© 2019 DaySpring. All rights reserved.
First Edition, October 2019

Published by:

P.O. Box 1010
Siloam Springs, AR 72761
dayspring.com

Scripture quotations marked HCSB are taken from the Holman Christian Standard Bible®. © 1999, 2000, 2002, 2003 by Holman Bible Publishers. Used by permission.

Scripture quotations marked NASB are taken from the NEW AMERICAN STANDARD BIBLE®, Copyright © 1960, 1962, 1963, 1968, 1971, 1972, 1973, 1975, 1977, 1995 by The Lockman Foundation. Used by permission.

Scripture quotations marked NKJV are taken from the New King James Version®. Copyright © 1982 by Thomas Nelson. Used by permission. All rights reserved.

Scripture quotations marked GNT are from the Good News Translation in Today's English Version- Second Edition Copyright © 1992 by American Bible Society. Used by Permission.

Scripture quotations marked CEV are taken from the Contemporary English Version Copyright © 1991, 1992, 1995 by American Bible Society, Used by Permission.

Scripture quotations marked NCV are taken from the New Century Version®. Copyright © 2005 by Thomas Nelson, Inc. Used by permission. All rights reserved.

Scripture quotations marked NLT are taken from the Holy Bible, New Living Translation, copyright © 1996, 2004, 2007 by Tyndale House Foundation. Used by permission of Tyndale House Publishers, Inc., Carol Stream, Illinois 60188. All rights reserved.

Scripture quotations marked TLB are taken from The Living Bible copyright © 1971. Used by permission of Tyndale House Publishers, Inc., Carol Stream, Illinois 60188. All rights reserved.

Scriptures quotations marked NIV are taken from the Holy Bible, New International Version®, NIV®. Copyright © 1973, 1978, 1984, 2011 by Biblica, Inc.® Used by permission of Zondervan. All rights reserved worldwide. www.zondervan.com. The "NIV" and "New International Version" are trademarks registered in the United States Patent and Trademark Office by Biblica, Inc.®

Scripture quotations marked NRSV are taken from the New Revised Standard Version of the Bible, © 1989. Division of Christian Education, National Council of Churches. Used by permission of Zondervan Publishing House, Licensee.

Scripture quotations marked KJV are taken from the Holy Bible, King James Version.

Scripture quotations marked THE MESSAGE are taken from THE MESSAGE, copyright © 1993, 1994, 1995, 1996, 2000, 2001, 2002 by Eugene H. Peterson. Used by permission of NavPress. All rights reserved. Represented by Tyndale House Publishers, Inc.

Scripture quotations marked AMP are taken from the Amplified Bible, Copyright © 2015 by The Lockman Foundation. Used by permission.

Scripture quotations marked ICB are taken from the International Children's Bible®. Copyright © 1986, 1988, 1999 by Thomas Nelson. Used by permission. All rights reserved.

Scripture quotations marked ESV are taken from the ESV Bible® (The Holy Bible, English Standard Version®) copyright ©2001 by Crossway Bibles, a publishing ministry of Good News Publishers. Used by permission. All rights reserved.

Scripture quotations marked CSB®, are taken from the Christian Standard Bible®, Copyright © 2017 by Holman Bible Publishers. Used by permission. Christian Standard Bible®, and CSB® are federally registered trademarks of Holman Bible Publishers.

Printed in China
Prime: 89894
ISBN: 978-1-68408-622-1

CONTENTS

DAWN'S EARLY LIGHT

The LORD's lovingkindnesses indeed never cease,
for His compassions never fail.
They are new every morning;
great is Your faithfulness.
LAMENTATIONS 3:22–23 NASB

The darkness is giving way. Rays of light from a yet-unseen sun have already colored the morning sky with pale pink and glimmers of gold. A new day is literally on the horizon, the sun its herald, inviting you to wake up to experience all that God has planned for you on this day.

But waking up isn't always easy. There are a lot of unknowns that lie outside that bedroom door, and it's tempting to not get out of bed at all. Or if you do, you may simply be going through the motions or getting sucked into everything that seems so urgent in the moment. If you're not careful, the day gets spent (along with your energy), without any real investment being made into what you know matters most.

So how do you greet the sunrise with more intention, hope, and expectation? It begins by waking up to grace—the beautiful reality that your Creator knows you intimately, loves you passionately, and promises to stay with you relentlessly throughout every moment of your life. When you begin each day reflecting on His grace and refreshing your soul with the life-giving power of His Spirit, you can tackle whatever comes your way with a deeper sense of confidence and divine purpose.

Morning Promises is your daily invitation to greet God each morning. May you gain precious insight from each devotional and divine inspiration as you meditate on each Scripture. Together may they help you wake up to each new morning with joy and hope, relishing His great love, reveling in His mercies, and receiving the power you need to live each day to its fullest.

*It is already the hour
for you to wake up from sleep,
for now our salvation is nearer
than when we first believed.*

ROMANS 13:11 HCSB

THE FORECAST
for TODAY

"Come, let us discuss this," says the LORD. *"Though your sins are like scarlet, they will be as white as snow."*
ISAIAH 1:18 HCSB

You heard the weather report, but you weren't sure it would pan out. It wouldn't be the first time you'd awakened in the morning hoping to find snow on the ground, only to see a soggy mess instead. But today was different. The light shining through the cracks in the blinds seemed brighter than before. So you tugged the shade's cord and pulled open the view to a brand-new world. All the dreary browns and grays of winter had vanished; in their place, pristine snow glistened against a brilliant blue sky. Nestled on tree branches, streets, cars, and everything in between, the weather miracle transformed the bleak world you'd known into a scene of magic, mystery, and undeniable beauty.

Better than any forecaster, God has issued a

prediction for your day—no matter what the physical weather outside your doors. If you are trusting Him to make the landscape of your life brighter and better than before, you will wake up each day discovering a truth better than transient snow. God wipes your slate perfectly clean each new morning. The failures and regrets of yesterday are completely covered by His love and forgiveness. You are free to enjoy the beauty of all He is as you discover the treasures He has hidden for you in this day.

Unlike the weather, God's miracle of grace never changes, never fades away. You are forever forgiven, simply through faith in Him. Praise God for His mysterious, permanent, and undeniably beautiful gift of daily grace!

Purify me with hyssop, and I will be clean; wash me, and I will be whiter than snow.
PSALM 51:7 HCSB

HIDE *and* SEEK

He who comes to God must believe that He is, and that
He is a rewarder of those who diligently seek Him.
HEBREWS 11:6 NKJV

The stadium is packed, cheers from the crowd roaring. The game has already started, and you know your friend who invited you is somewhere in that sea of faces waiting for you to join him. But the scene seems quite daunting. How will you ever find the one you are looking for in the midst of all those people? Determined, you start scanning, row by row, the faces in the crowd. Up and across, up and across— you search until your eyes lock. This whole time, your friend has been watching you, waiting for you to notice the waves and smile beaming your way that say, "Come up here and join me!"

When you walk out your door this morning, it might seem like just an ordinary day full of responsibilities to fill. But you have one friend who has invited you to experience it and enjoy it with Him. God is hidden in the details of your day, watching you and waiting to reward you with the pleasure of His presence.

Will He be in the quiet moments you spend studying His Word? In the tender touch of your child's hand? In the conversations you have at school or work? In the car ride to get there? In your thoughts as you consider how to handle this day? The answer is yes! God is hidden in every moment of your life. Seek His face today, and enjoy the reward of His presence with you everywhere you go.

Seek the LORD while He may be found,
call upon Him while He is near.
Isaiah 55:6 NKJV

Always

Jesus Christ is the same yesterday, today, and forever.
HEBREWS 13:8 GNT

For a time, people believed the earth was flat. After all, knowledgeable scientists confirmed it, and anyone who could see the horizon could draw a straight line with their finger, tracing the fixed edge of earth against sky. Yep, flat all right. Except that it isn't. And when technology and math advanced far enough ahead, a better perspective emerged. Of course now, with all the outer-space flights and cameras and irrefutable documentation declaring the earth to be round—just like all the other planets—it's hard to imagine we could have ever been that far off.

Life is like that too. We are convinced that something is true or right, and then over time as changes happen, our perspective shifts. In fact, life brings so much change that we can find ourselves desperate for solid ground, some place or truth that stays the same.

He is here, that One you seek—the One who is the same today as He was yesterday and a thousand years before. And He will remain the same forever. As you wake up to face a myriad of uncertainties today, may it calm your soul to remember that God is the solid ground beneath your feet and Jesus is the irrefutable proof of His love for you. His spoken Word and promises are more rooted in reality than the challenges you will face today. Draw near to Him this morning, and thank Him for always loving, protecting, guiding, and forgiving. His faithful friendship is our constant in an ever-changing world.

The eternal God of Israel isn't a human being.
He doesn't tell lies or change His mind.
1 SAMUEL 15:29 CEV

STORM SHELTER

The LORD is like a strong tower,
where the righteous can go and be safe.

PROVERBS 18:10 GNT

Though you've slept for hours, you feel like your head just hit the pillow. Already your mind is swirling with thoughts for the day. Of course, there's the usual getting ready, making coffee, facing traffic. But there's more weighing on your mind than the daily grind. That conversation you had with your spouse the other night just didn't sit right, and you're worried you're drifting apart. Your child's project due today is only half finished, and you question your parenting as well as his future. There's a boss to please and laundry to fold, bills to pay and church to attend. You want to do everything well, but you start to feel like you should just hide somewhere and hope everything works out.

Sometimes, escape seems like the most logical conclusion when faced with the overwhelming circumstances of life. After all, modern psychology tells us we are programmed for either fight or flight when perceived trouble rolls around. Right? The question is: without adequate strength to fight, will you run to the only refuge on this earth with power great enough to protect you and keep you safe forever?

God says His name is a strong tower, and the righteous run to it and find safety. He assures us that no one who comes to Him for protection will be turned away. He is our fortress, our secret place where we can hide, and He Himself will fight the big and small battles we face each day. There is no better place to go today than to the only One with the power to save you in this moment, and your lifetime.

You have been my protection, like a strong tower against my enemies.
PSALM 61:3 NCV

Growing Up

When I was a child, I spoke like a child,
I thought like a child, I reasoned like a child.
When I became a man, I put aside childish things.
1 Corinthians 13:11 HCSB

If you've ever dropped off your young toddler at a nursery, you've likely seen it happen: unbridled fear and anxiety. Sobs quickly erupt as the little one realizes she can't see her parents. She remains inconsolable until they return and take her back into their arms. Fortunately, as children mature, they gain a greater understanding of their parents' reliability and deep commitment to them, and they walk free of their earlier fears.

The same is true in our relationship with God. Before we really know Him and His character well, we fear that He has already abandoned us or will if we make the wrong move. It's the mind-set of an infant who doesn't understand the situation. As His beloved children, we are never on the brink of abandonment, despite what our feelings tell us. In fact, even though we feel like God has left and He's out of our sight—especially when we veer off His prescribed path—His sovereign hand is still holding us. Before the world was even created, God devised a plan through faith in His Son that would pave a permanent path back to Him no matter what problem besets us.

We can let the panic, shame, misunderstanding, and fear of our younger years go. We are being held, right in this moment. We have a loving Father, our heavenly Daddy, who has made a way for us to belong to Him forever, and He will never leave us, nor will He forsake us.

I pray that you,
being rooted and firmly established in love,
may be able to comprehend with all the saints what is
the length and width, height and depth of God's love.
EPHESIANS 3:17–18 HCSB

THE RIGHT FIT

The LORD is my shepherd; I have everything I need.
PSALM 23:1 GNT

As you open the door to your closet, you pause. *What should I wear today?* Factoring in the latest trends you've seen at work, school, church, and on social media, you immediately know which options are out. So you search until you find the right ensemble to look presentable and fit in with the people you know will see you today.

It isn't easy to keep up appearances, staying on top of the trends and keeping up a "successful" image. And it isn't just about clothes. It's job performance at work. The parenting or relational prowess at home. For some, it's the size of the house, the type of car, the right neighborhood, or the best school. Whatever it takes to declare to the world, "I have arrived. I've got it together. I, for one, know where I'm going."

But God knows us better. It helps if we just pay attention to Him. He says that people are like sheep—

they tend to go in circles when following cues from each other. If we want to know where to go, however, we have to follow the Shepherd.

When you get ready to meet your day today, let your mind look past the pressure of fitting in to following the only One with a real plan for your life. It might not look like everyone else's plan. It might not even seem like a path to success. But in surrender to God's lead, you will find yourself on the right path and in the sweetest of care.

You had wandered away like sheep.
Now you have returned to the one
who is your shepherd and protector.
I PETER 2:25 CEV

GOOD MORNING, SUNSHINE

For you that honor My name,
victory will shine like the sun
with healing in its rays.
MALACHI 4:2 CEV

You had hopes of sleeping in this Saturday after a long week at work. The sun isn't even up, though, when you feel the bedsheets ruffle. Soon, you feel two little hands patting your arm. "Lift me up!" your young child whispers in the dark. Trying to stay as asleep as possible, you reach over and pull your little guy up next to you. He snuggles in under the covers, his warm, small body now breathing in sync with your own. As he drifts off to sleep, you have plans to do the same, but suddenly it hits you: this is a sacred moment of amazing grace. Though the sun still hides below the horizon, an even greater light has risen in your heart.

God has created this tiny, living, growing person who trusts, loves, and looks up to you for everything he needs. He didn't come with a manual, yet you've watched God guide you as a parent who works to meet his every need. In this moment of rest and total trust, you reach to feel his hand. It is small in your own, and you wonder if that's how God feels as He's holding onto you.

Just like you always welcome your child when he comes to you, your heavenly Father will always welcome you anytime you say, "Lift me up!" With delight and affection deeper than that of any earthly parent, He pulls you up into the warmth of His embrace and invites you to rest under the cover of His grace.

He will cover you with His feathers,
and under His wings you can hide.
PSALM 91:4 NCV

PIECE *of* CAKE

Taste and see that the LORD is good;
blessed is the man who trusts in Him!
PSALM 34:8 NKJV

You're unusually excited this morning. The alarm didn't even have to sound for your eyes to open wide, your feet ready to hit the floor. In your mind, you know it's silly, maybe even a little unhealthy. But you saved the last piece of cake for your morning breakfast, and now nothing stands in your way as you relish the idea of one of life's little indulgences.

Cup of coffee in one hand, fork in the other, the moment does not disappoint. The moist, rich chocolate lights up your taste buds and fills your mind with delight. *God, how can anything be so good?* you wonder, silently giving thanks to the One who created a world with such deliciousness.

There it is: the sweetest truth of all. God, in His incredible kindness, gave us taste buds. Not only did He give us the ability to taste and smell, but He created all kinds of foods with a myriad of flavors to add mystery, variety, and, most of all, pleasure to life. It's just one more evidence that God, our Creator, is good and kind and generous. And it's a reminder that He has invited us to taste and see just how good He is. It's written all through His Word, and it shines all through His world. This morning, enjoy the food and drink God has given you. And let the pleasure drive your thoughts, and your thanks, to the One who made you smile.

Listen carefully to Me, and eat what is good, and let your soul delight itself in abundance.
ISAIAH 55:2 NKJV

GETTING SCHOOLED

My children, we should love people not only with words and talk, but by our actions and true caring.
I JOHN 3:18 NCV

Want to know what's really awesome these days? Online school. Yes, you can stay right in your PJs and stumble from your bed to the computer. Class begins when you log yourself in. Before you know it, you've heard a qualified professor explain the topic on your syllabus and gotten your assignment, which you will both research and turn in online.

But even the best online classes require application in the real world. You can't just study for a master's degree in counseling. At some point you have to engage in real person-to-person contact. You can't just get a degree in vet tech. You have to go to a vet clinic and help with real animals. Education without application has no impact in the real world.

The same is true when we learn about God. When the alarm sounds, we're free to roll over and pick up our Bibles and study books to begin our day. It's an incredible necessity and blessing to do so. We can also go online and research topics, hear sermons, and consider the opinions of people across the world. But when God sent Jesus to our world, He showed us what real-life application looks like. It is one thing to think about doing something grand; it's quite another to make it happen. What has God taught you lately through your experiences, studies, or work? This morning, ask Him to show you how to translate His truth into concrete ways to apply your faith.

I will give to the peoples purified lips,
that all of them may call
on the name of the LORD,
to serve Him shoulder to shoulder.
ZEPHANIAH 3:9 NASB

Soul Care

I, the Lord, *am your healer.*
Exodus 15:26 NASB

You can still feel it if you think about it hard enough: the searing pain that shocked your senses the first time you fell off your bike. Knees and elbows scraped down several layers of skin, and the wounds seemed too big to heal. Tears streamed down your face as your mom tried to ease the hurt with bandages. Stiff for a few days, you had difficulty bending in places near the injury, the scabs limiting mobility. But in time, a new patch of pink, shiny skin stretched over the place of past trauma.

It happens so naturally that you might just miss the miracle. God, who made your body, created a system to heal your wounds. You don't even have to understand how it works. Your body just gets busy patching you back together whenever foreign invaders or injuries happen. But what about soul wounds—those injuries to your heart that leave you feeling torn and reeling in pain? The kind that can haunt you the moment you wake up. Aren't those too big to heal? Not in God's care.

The One who created your body to self-heal packs a supernatural power to restore your soul. Just like with your body, it's a process that takes time. Instead of a bandage, you apply the truth of God's love, protection, and provision for you, choosing belief instead of doubt. As you allow God's love to wrap around your hurt, a miracle happens. New life begins to grow where old wounds once were. God seals those places with His grace, healing you by His love and freeing you to face whatever may come your way today.

He restores my soul.
PSALM 23:3 NKJV

The GREAT REVEAL

He reveals things that are deep and secret;
he knows what is hidden in darkness,
and he himself is surrounded by light.
DANIEL 2:22 GNT

You're sitting in your seat, just a few rows back from the stage. Your eyes are glued to the magician as he taps on the transparent box before you, urging you to understand, "There's nothing inside!" To underscore his point, he drags his arm above, below, beside, and behind so that you can clearly see there's nothing around the box except the magician. The fabric drapes down, obscuring your view for just a second (it shouldn't matter anyway because you can see all around it), but then *whoosh*! He whisks back the cover to reveal something inside the box, a girl who seems as surprised as you are by the exchange.

Magicians practice countless hours to perfect their timing and ability to manipulate perceptions. Their goal is to capture the great reveal. It's impressive, but the magician is only capable of creating an illusion.

Our God, however, is no illusionist. He lets us discover His truth in the same exciting way, but unlike the magician, His great reveals are all they're cracked up to be. He hides the keys to a successful, purpose-filled life in His Word. You keep your eyes focused as you read the same Bible story for the umpteenth time. Then suddenly a new facet of His character or your own looms into view. *How did I not see that before?* you wonder. The secret is God's Spirit. He is the one who reveals what you need to know when you need to know it.

This morning, don't settle for an illusion. Instead, fix your eyes on the Great Revealer. Ask Him to help you see and understand His direction for your life as you read His Word. Prepare to be amazed!

There is a God in heaven who reveals secrets.
DANIEL 2:28 NKJV

NIGHT LIGHT

I am the light of the world.
If you follow Me, you won't have to walk in darkness,
because you will have the light that leads to life.
JOHN 8:12 NLT

The alarm clock sounds, but your bedroom is pitch dark. You're trying your best not to wake your spouse, who is still sleeping soundly under the covers. Hands outstretched, you feel your way to the dresser, then wall, door frame, doorknob. Then, there it is: the bathroom light switch! Now you can stop fumbling and start a smooth transition into your new day. Of course, if you have to go back for clothes, you use the flashlight on your phone to undertake a stealthy search for all you need, returning to the place where light can shine freely on your day.

Light makes a difference! Whether it's in our morning moments or the darkest nights, our bodies work best when we operate in the light. We're just designed to see better that way. Isn't it incredible, then, that light was the very first thing on God's creation "to-do" list? God spoke and created light before the sun or moon even came into play. How? God's light is different from the kind we see with our physical eyes even though the physical light illustrates the spiritual picture of what God provides.

God tells us in the Bible that He is the Light of the World. The truth we find in Him and what He tells us in His Word sheds the brightest light into the darkest places of our souls. It illuminates where we need to confess and repent, while also lighting our world with all the colors of His grace and forgiveness. God's light ends our fumbling through darkness and sets us free to see His incredible love throughout this day and for the rest of our lives.

God is the LORD, and He has given us light.
PSALM 118:27 NKJV

THIRST QUENCHER

Is anyone thirsty? Come and drink—
even if you have no money!
Come, take your choice of wine or milk—it's all free!
ISAIAH 55:1 NLT

You're finally rounding the last stretch of sidewalk before you reach home, your daily exercise nearly complete. Accelerated heart rate, beads of sweat, and panting breath all confirm that today, you got a good workout. But you're parched. Before you head for the shower, you grab a glass from the kitchen and fill it with clean, cool water. As you drink, you instantly feel life and energy returning to your fatigued body. Always hits the spot, you think.

Did you know that more than half of your body is made up of water? It's no wonder you need it, even crave it, throughout your day. But God tells us our souls are no different. He explains the idea in the Bible. Jesus meets a woman at the well where she has gone to draw water. He strikes up a conversation that goes like this, "Those who drink the water you draw from this well will get thirsty again, but those who drink the water I give will never be thirsty again. The water I give them will be like a spring welling up inside them giving them eternal life." Then Jesus explains to her that the water He gives is "living water." It's not of this world. It comes from God's own Spirit, filling every child of God.

When God floods our lives with His forgiveness and grace, our thirst for redemption is filled forever. And the invitation to drink from His refreshing and replenishing store of love and hope repeats daily. When you get up this morning, have a satisfying drink of water. As it fills you, let your heart also be filled with the truth of God's everlasting power, forgiveness, and love.

The Scriptures declare that rivers
of living water shall flow
from the inmost being of anyone who believes in Me.
JOHN 7:38 TLB

LOVE LETTERS

What God has planned for people who love Him is
more than eyes have seen or ears have heard.
It has never even entered our minds!
I CORINTHIANS 2:9 CEV

I t's a new day, and you're already hard at work. Your "to-do" list is halfway done, but the pace hasn't slowed and there are miles to go before you sleep. When the workday ends, you head home to face the onslaught of duties that await you. On your way in, though, you stop at the mailbox to get the day's allotment of bills and miscellaneous junk. As you rifle through the contents, though, one small envelope catches your eye. You scan the return address and realize it's from your closest childhood friend, someone you haven't heard from in years! You drop all the other mail on the counter as you plop down in the nearest chair to peruse your newfound treasure. When you're finished, you hold it near your heart. What an encouragement to know you're loved and remembered.

With all the e-mails and text messages today, it's easy to forget the power of a handwritten letter. Unlike all other communications, it speaks of intentionality, value, and time spent crafting it. It is something special.

This morning, there is a treasured communication waiting for you from your best friend. It was written with all the purpose and passion a letter can wield, and it is probably sitting right next to you. God has written about His love and affection for you throughout the Bible—a handwritten letter bearing the history and heart of a God who longs to reconnect with His people. Your God has written you a love letter! Open it—and your heart—to receive it today.

God blesses the one who reads the words of this prophecy to the church, and He blesses all who listen to its message and obey what it says.
Revelation 1:3 NLT

COMFORTING TRUTH

Praise be to the God and Father of
our Lord Jesus Christ,
the Father of compassion and the God of all comfort,
who comforts us in all our troubles.
II CORINTHIANS 1:3–4 NIV

It's cold outside, but snuggling deep under the comforter on your bed this morning, you are toasty warm. So at the sound of the alarm, you stick a toe out to assess the likelihood that you will be getting up. *Nope, not gonna happen*, you decide as you pull back your toe. *They call this thing a comforter. Boy, they got that right*, you muse as you snuggle down deeper, shutting out any opportunity for cold to seep in. It just feels too good to be surrounded by warmth and softness to even consider facing the cold, hard reality of the day.

This morning as you revel in the warmth of your bed, let it remind you of another Comforter who envelops you beyond just the morning. God, who walked this earth and experienced the same hard roads of life we all travel, knows all about your worries, your dreams, and your life. Because He knows and is powerful enough to help you, His Spirit in you can comfort you in the very moment you need it most.

Whenever you feel the coldness of this world pressing in on you, wrap your fearful, shelter-seeking heart up tight in the comfort of God's presence. Remember, He not only sees and understands, but He also waits to envelop you in the warmth of His promise never to leave your side. Your God will go with you to comfort and protect you in all you face today and every day. You are able to brave the cold outside, because His love will keep you warm.

The LORD says, "I am the one who comforts you."
ISAIAH 51:12 NCV

The AUTHOR

All my days were written in Your book and planned before a single one of them began.
PSALM 139:16 HCSB

You just wanted to buy an encouraging book for a friend, and maybe pick up a good read for yourself while you're there. But the moment you open the door to your favorite bookstore, your senses are overwhelmed by colors, titles, and topics. It seems like everyone in the world has written something, and it's up to you to search until you find that one selection perfect for the occasion. So you begin the hunt, but you suddenly find yourself engrossed in book after book, the back cover teasers leading you into the stories contained in those pages. Though there is a sea of options, each book has a different and captivating angle on life that broadens your thinking and piques your interest. Each book is an unexpected adventure.

But adventure doesn't just happen in novels. It's happening in and through your life this very moment.

Today is not just another day. It's a pivotal page in the story God is writing in and through your life. Today is an integral part of the plot He's weaving to lead you closer to Himself and use you for purposes higher than you can imagine. He is inviting you to trust Him because when you do—when you follow His prompts instead of trying to make your day fit your expectations—the plot thickens, and the threads connect in unpredictably delightful ways.

This morning, hand the pen to God, and ask Him to write His story through your life. With Him in control, you'll know you've made the perfect selection.

Only I can tell you the future before it even happens.
Everything I plan will come to pass,
for I do whatever I wish.
ISAIAH 46:10 NLT

COUNTING *on* JOY

The angel said to them, "Do not be afraid; for see—I am bringing you good news of great joy for all the people."
LUKE 2:10 NRSV

You've spent months planning for this moment, the one where family gathers around the tree for this year's Christmas Day. There is a spark of excitement in the air as the pajama-clad kids file in, hair still tousled from sleep, waiting for the signal to begin. Once videos are rolling, the magic unfolds, and you watch for the one thing you've worked so hard to see: joy. You scan the faces of each person opening their gifts and hope to see happiness over the thoughtfulness, pleasure in the gift, and gratitude for the giver. Surely hugs are in order, yes?

Inevitably, though, the magic comes to an end. People pack up their gifts and head back to the reality that is life. It's the inevitable valley after pleasure's peak that reminds us real paradise is still lost, at least here on earth. All the money in the world can't purchase lasting peace and joy. But riches from heaven can. God's gift to us is not an object we can open but a relationship we can embrace.

Unwrap and revel today in the grace of God that goes everywhere you do. His grace fills you with infinite joy, blesses your life with every good thing, and promises perfect peace as you trust in Him through every earthly moment. Best of all, God's gift of grace never goes away. Don't settle for temporary treasures. Today, take hold of all God's goodness and celebrate a life lived eternally in His love.

You bestow on him blessings forever;
You make him glad with the joy of Your presence.
PSALM 21:6 NRSV

LET FREEDOM RING

He has sent me to proclaim liberty to the captives and recovery of sight to the blind, to set free the oppressed.
LUKE 4:18 GNT

For twelve years, you went through the paces. Put in the work. Endured the drama—especially in junior high and even some in high school. But at last the day came when all the blood, sweat, tears, and triumphs that were your school experience were completed. Wearing cap and gown, you walked across that stage, accepted your diploma, and walked toward a whole new life of freedom—that place inside your soul that says no matter what lies behind, you have the power to choose where you go from here, and no one can take that away from you.

God tells us that we were born to live in freedom. Every day when you wake up, God hands you the keys to your soul emancipation, the kind that frees you from everything that lies in your yesterdays and gives you a fresh start on your tomorrows. Today is a new day, and you get to choose what you do with this day.

But what about the hurts you carry from the past? Or the ongoing crisis that threatens to remain no matter what you do? Today you have the choice to lay them at God's feet and feel the power of forgiveness and healing. Today you have God's invitation to cast your cares on Him, because He cares for you. You have the choice to entrust your deepest heart cries to His expertise. The key to real freedom is not found in a diploma, job offer, or any life situation. Through repentance, obedience, and trust in God, you are released to stride across the stage of life with all the hope of heaven in your heart and hands.

*Where the Spirit of the Lord is present,
there is freedom.*
II Corinthians 3:17 GNT

Signs *of* Spring

Behold, I will do a new thing;
now it shall spring forth; shall ye not know it?
I will even make a way in the wilderness,
and rivers in the desert.
Isaiah 43:19 KJV

Everywhere you look, buds are bursting out on tree branches. The grass is getting greener, the days becoming warmer. Fragrant, colorful flowers fill in the landscape, followed by the larger, spectacular displays in the trees and shrubs. Birds and crickets and frogs and cicadas have come out of hiding and are calling for spring to come. And indeed, spring has sprung. You couldn't be happier. While the snow and stark vestiges of winter have a beauty and charm of their own, there's something special about spring and the new hope it brings. The world is just a bit brighter and your breathing lighter, as if with just the change of weather, the weight of the world has lifted a little.

No matter what the season is, let the signs and reminders of spring grow hope in your heart today. It is no coincidence that the dead of winter gives way to such spectacular growth. God's same goodness grows in you and your life circumstances. Though situations may seem bleak in certain seasons of your life, God's love and purpose never lie dormant. He is effecting the greatest transformation you can imagine, setting the stage for your growth to bloom for His glory.

If you wake up this morning to find yourself in a season of waiting, then set your eyes on God and settle in for the upcoming show. In His time, you'll see, as will we all, the telltale signs of spring. It's then that we will celebrate the growth only God can bring.

Weeping may go on all night,
but in the morning there is joy.
PSALM 30:5 TLB

WANTING WISDOM

*If any of you needs wisdom, you should ask God for it.
He is generous to everyone and will give you wisdom
without criticizing you.*

JAMES 1:5 NCV

Your daughter is at a crossroads. With just a few more months of high school, she's wondering which college? What career? Where should she live? How will she pay for it all? These are just a few of the questions coursing through her mind on a daily basis. But it doesn't end there. She'll need to know where to move once she has her degree. If and who she should marry. Children or no children? Natural or adoption? Be a stay-at-home mom or stay in the workplace? And it seems it's not just the young men and women who are lost for direction. The older we get, the more we come to realize just how many choices come with each new day.

Fortunately, we know Someone who has the answers we need and the divine perspective we lack.

God, who knows the end of the story from the very beginning, sees exactly what is best for our lives. Every ounce of wisdom we need for today can be found in Him and His Word. In fact, God invites us to bring it on. No matter what we've done in the past, God promises not to judge us when we come to Him asking for help. Instead, He pours His wisdom—the divine kind that comes from heaven—into our lives whenever we ask Him to.

Life may throw us a thousand curve balls, but God is the expert on hitting each one out of the park with His eternal perspective and insight. This morning, ask Him to give you the wisdom you need to know and follow His path today

Getting wisdom is the wisest thing you can do!
And whatever else you do, develop good judgment.
PROVERBS 4:7 NLT

LET IT RAIN

Let my words fall like rain on tender grass,
like gentle showers on young plants.
DEUTERONOMY 32:2 NLT

It starts as an occasional *plunk* on the windowpane. Soon, though, the sound shifts to a steady, dull roar not too unlike the sound machine that lulls you to sleep each night. So you climb out of bed and pull back the shades to confirm what your senses have already declared: it's raining. The dark clouds and gentle noise beckon you to climb back in bed for as long as your schedule will allow. It's the perfect moment for a little more rest and maybe some reading. Isn't that why God gave us rainy days?

Maybe. God gives us all kinds of invitations to slow down and rest—not necessarily in bed every time, but to rest in Him and His presence. Just like plants grow hot and tired under the sun's heat, as beautiful and needed as those rays may be, so we dry out and wilt when we fail to slow down and hydrate our souls. God is waiting to pour out His life-giving water into your morning through the nourishing power of prayer and reading His Word. When we take a few moments at the start of each day to soak in His goodness, we are refreshed and empowered to handle the day's tasks in God's strength instead of our own. As we are properly nourished, God produces in us lasting fruit, the kind that blesses and strengthens those He puts around us.

Whether it's rainy or sunny outside your window this morning, take a few minutes before the crazy pace of the day begins. Quiet your soul before God and let the truth of His love pour into and out of your life today.

I lift my hands to You in prayer.
I thirst for You as parched land thirsts for rain.
PSALM 143:6 NLT

BECOMING ONE

My beloved said to me,
"Rise up, my love, my fair one, and come away."
SONG OF SOLOMON 2:10 TLB

He nervously pulls at the bottom of his coat as the bridesmaids slowly file into their places. Then the music changes, and his attention fixes on the place where the one he loves steps into view. His heart seems to stop, and tears begin to flow down his face as he watches his future walk toward him, the life partner and friend God has given him. As she nears, he sees the same look of wonder and joy in her own tear-stained eyes. They are just now beginning to understand the amazing miracle of two becoming one.

Marriage, the way God intended, creates the incredible portrait of intimacy and love every soul longs for. Yet in real life, couples often find that their earthly relationships never fully satisfy their longing or hope for unbreakable connection. Tempers flare, communication crumbles, and the tyranny of life in a broken world takes over. They find themselves struggling to preserve their lifelong commitment.

Yet where our earthly relationships may fall short, our faithful God never does. Calling us His Bride, God invites us into a permanent love commitment that knows no bounds. He leads us to a place where we are free to let down our guard and revel in His delight over us. Whether you are married or not, you have a Husband who pursues, cares for, protects, and cherishes you like no other. It is out of this love God has first given to us that we learn how to love one another.

Draw close to your first love this morning, and marvel at the magnitude of God's amazing grace. Invite His Spirit to strengthen your earthly relationships as He pours His love into and through you.

I have loved you with an everlasting love;
therefore I have continued My faithfulness to you.
JEREMIAH 31:3 NRSV

HUES *of* HOPE

He woke up and rebuked the wind,
and said to the sea, "Peace!
Be still!" Then the wind ceased,
and there was a dead calm.

MARK 4:39 NRSV

T he storm's severity caught you off guard. Though you could see the dark clouds looming ahead as you drove across town, you had no idea how fast and hard the rain could fall. So you pulled off to the side of the road, deciding to wait it out. As suddenly as it started, it stopped. The clouds pushed past, and the sun came streaming down through crystal-blue skies. But before you could start back out on the road, curiosity caused you to turn and look. There it was! A rainbow was shining brighter than the sun's rays on rain-soaked streets, painting the dark sky behind with an amazing palette of color.

Is it any wonder that God chose a rainbow to promise hope to Noah and his family after such a horrific flood? Rainbows are God's colorful reminders that there is no storm in our lives too strong or too dark that God can't create something beautiful out of it.

As you wake up today, what storms—if any—loom on the horizon? Even if one takes you by surprise, you do not need to be afraid. Just as Jesus stilled the waves and calmed the storms for His disciples, so God has the power to carry you through whatever the day brings. The light of His presence packs a remarkable power to shine through our moments and reveal a beauty we never thought possible. Storms are simply our invitation to trust Him as He works miracles into every moment.

When the rainbow appears in the cloud,
I'll see it and remember the eternal covenant
between God and everything living,
every last living creature on Earth.
GENESIS 9:16 THE MESSAGE

COLORING LOVE

God looked over everything He had made;
it was so good, so very good!
GENESIS 1:31 THE MESSAGE

D o you remember the first time you opened a box of crayons? The smell of wax and paper tightly wrapped around each beautiful color arrested your senses and set your imagination to flight. In an instant you were an artist, transforming the ordinary white sheet of paper before you into lines and shapes and patterns that rendered your inner world awash with color right before your eyes. What were stick figures and circular flowers to older, less-sensitive souls were your early masterpieces, your version of Eden.

But what if instead of a full spectrum of differing hues, your box had only one color? It may have entertained you for a moment but certainly wouldn't have held your attention. There's beauty in diversity and pleasure in harmony. We witness the same miracle every time we open our eyes and really see the world around us. God did not make our world a monochromatic experience. Brilliant color fills the skies, the trees, and the land. Eyes and skin and cars and houses and flowers and oceans all treat our eyes to a feast of festive colors that turn the entire world into an extraordinary work of art.

As you rise and shine this morning, recapture the wonder of color as you get ready for the day. Notice the hues in everything your hands touch and all your eyes see. Then give thanks to the One who prized you enough to color your world with His creativity and love, making your brilliant, beautiful life into an integral part of His magnificent masterpiece.

Oh yes—God takes pleasure in your pleasure!
Dress festively every morning.
Don't skimp on colors and scarves.
Ecclesiastes 9:7 THE MESSAGE

KEYS *to* FREEDOM

Forgive us for our sins,
because we forgive everyone who has done wrong to us.
LUKE 11:4 NCV

Your mind keeps wandering back to the person you trusted—the one who turned on you. Your stomach tightens. Though the trespass happened long ago, the wound feels fresh. You may deny it, stuff it, and do your best to push it away, but experience warns you to build up walls around your heart to protect it from future pain. Relationships just aren't worth the risk, your wary and weary heart concludes. And so the chains that bind you to the past and keep you from feeling the full pleasure of today grow ever tighter. You need a different kind of Savior.

Thank God you have one who knows your hurts and cares deeply about the wounds in your soul. He invites you to come close and washes you clean. He tends to your heart with whispers of true and lasting love. Drawing near, light floods the darkness, and you can see the key to freedom dangling in front of you. But to use it will change the course of your life forever. Freedom happens through forgiveness— God forgiving you, and you forgiving those who have hurt you. Forgiveness doesn't mean condoning the offense. Instead it means setting yourself free. In miraculous exchange, as we set the captives of our anger and bitterness free, our hearts break forth in glorious freedom.

This morning, take a moment to ask God to search your heart for any traces of bitterness that are still holding you captive. As He reveals your soul's secret wounds, pray that God will heal those places with His love and empower you to forgive on your path to freedom.

Whoever has a complaint against anyone;
just as the Lord forgave you, so also should you.
Colossians 3:13 NASB

PUPPY LOVE

You will show me the path of life;
in Your presence is fullness of joy;
at Your right hand are pleasures forevermore
PSALM 16:11 NKJV

You are sitting at your computer desk, trying to make heads or tails of the stack of bills lying beside your keyboard. "How on earth did we spend that much money eating out?" you ponder aloud as you stare at your online checking account. Already, you can feel the throb of stress starting to build in the front region of your head.

Then you hear the bark. Not a mean one, just a questioning little yip from your small but ever-so-loyal dog sitting at your feet looking up at you and begging to be in your lap. So you acquiesce, reaching down to pull up the soft, furry ball of love. Licking on arms and hands immediately commences, but eventually he settles in for a nap, sleeping soundly without a care in the world. As you stroke the soft fur between your fingers, you can't help but smile. Without a word, this small creature—by his mere presence—has eased away some of life's load. And you wonder, *Is this why God made pets?*

Truth is, pets are just one of the delightful ways God shows His love and concern for us. He didn't have to give us dogs with soft fur and tender tongues, cats that purr when petted, and a host of other domesticated creatures people welcome into their homes. God intended animals to not only showcase His creativity and power but also to give us pleasure. As you love on your furry family member this morning, thank God for His soft reminders that He always has your best interests at heart.

GOD's not finished.
He's waiting around to be gracious to you.
He's gathering strength to show mercy to you.
ISAIAH 30:18 THE MESSAGE

GOOD NIGHT KISSES

At day's end I'm ready for sound sleep,
for You, GOD, have put my life back together.
PSALM 4:8 THE MESSAGE

Your phone's alarm sounds through the darkness of your bedroom. As you fumble to find it and shut off the most unwelcome noise, you sleepily consider possible options for delaying the day. You could call in sick, you think for a moment. No, lying's no good. But then the thought, *Just hit snooze!* But in the blink of an eye, the alarm is sounding again.

The struggle is real, and getting up seems unavoidable. Then it hits you—it's Saturday! You can sleep in! The hectic pace of your regular week can wait for another day. Today you can rest and savor the simple pleasure of extra sleep. So you put your phone on airplane mode and settle back in for a long, relaxing morning.

Sleep—the good, sound, rejuvenating kind—is a sweet kiss from our heavenly Father. It's comforting to know that He doesn't make the same driving demands we find virtually everywhere else. No, our God invites us to rest, and often. He encourages us to rest from our attempts to earn His favor, because we already have it. Rest from the need to control our lives and those around us, because He is the only one with that kind of power and has promised to work everything out for our good. Rest from the maddening pursuit of pleasing everyone else. He simply offers Himself as a quiet place for us to lay down our burdens and relax in His care. When we take Him up on the offer, our souls rejuvenate. Having rested in His love, we are ready for that alarm in the morning and all the adventure that awaits.

Come to Me, all who are weary and heavy-laden, and I will give you rest.
MATTHEW 11:28 NASB

Sunrise Surprise

His coming is as certain as the morning sun;
he will refresh us like rain renewing the earth
in the springtime.

HOSEA 6:3 CEV

It is still, quiet, and dark outside. In the wee hours of the cool summer morning, you wrap yourself in your warmest robe and venture into the dark, just far enough to find your favorite outdoor chair. Wiping off the dew, you sit and wait. Slowly, your eyes adjust to the darkness, but the trees and shrubs nearby seem whitewashed silhouettes in a lonely, gray world.

Then it happens. The first rays of light peek over the horizon. Sky and hills, branches and blades of grass catch the energy, and color pours out onto every lighted surface. Like magic, light dispels the darkness, and animals respond on cue, chattering and chirping, their call to greet the morning. As pink and orange hues paint the pale blue sky, you soak up the beauty, the miracle of this morning's sunrise. And your heart joins in their song, the celebration of the sunrise's Creator.

If you rise early enough each day, you will see this blessing again and again. Each day God brings our earth back around for the sun to shine on our lives once more, initiating beauty from the very beginning. It begs us to begin our day mindful of a Master Painter, Sustainer, and the source of all we call beautiful. Our hearts burst with praise and worship for the only One who can transform darkness into a magnificent, light-filled world of future promise. He is here in this sacred moment. Here where light chases away the darkness. Here where He reminds us day after day that His goodness rises to greet us and the sweetness of His morning touch lingers for the rest of our day.

The heavens are telling of the glory of God;
and the expanse [of heaven] is declaring
the work of His hands.
PSALM 19:1 AMP

CONNECTION

Let us have confidence, then,
and approach God's throne, where there is grace.
There we will receive mercy and find grace
to help us just when we need it.

HEBREWS 4:16 GNT

Not that long ago, cell phones didn't exist. Land lines were tethered by stretchy, spiraling cords that kept communication limited to the places where the cords could reach. If you were stuck in traffic and needed to tell your appointment how late you'd be, you simply had to make your excuse in person once you finally arrived. There was no such thing as checking e-mail or social media or surfing the Internet to make purchases, locate maps, or look up menu choices.

But today, communication is virtually instant all the way across the world. Technology has bridged the gap that existed between people in different places throughout the ages. When you stop to think about it, the cell phones in everyone's hands may be annoying at times, but they're also a communication miracle.

But an even greater miracle than cell phones has happened. And that miracle took place long before telephone lines were even a developing thought. When Jesus paid for our sins on the cross, He reconnected the lines of communication between us and God. His provision paved the way for instant access to the Father anytime, anywhere we are. Whether we choose to talk out loud or pray in our minds, God hears every word we say. And He answers, sometimes even while we're speaking—the connection is that strong.

This morning, before you pick up your phone to check the latest everything, make that most important connection with God. Commit your day, your words, and your life to Him. And thank God that His reception works wonderfully everywhere you go.

We have also obtained access through Him
by faith into this grace
in which we stand, and we rejoice in
the hope of the glory of God.
ROMANS 5:2 HCSB

MORNING SONG

Sing to the LORD a new song;
sing to the LORD, all the earth.
PSALM 96:1 NASB

If you are still, you will see it. And if you listen, you can hear a symphony playing right outside your door. Don't bother looking for a bassoon or clarinet, a cello or a trumpet. No man-made instruments are needed in God's performance hall. Instead, living creatures contribute their sound of praise to the Creator, with pitch and rhythm unique to their kind. Tree frogs chirp from secret hiding places. Bullfrogs bellow in low, steady calls. Cicadas and crickets sound like maracas, and birds are the woodwinds, their melodies sweetening the sound.

Are you delighted by the free concert outside your door, day after day? God certainly is! He created all of His creatures to declare His praise in ways only they can. Something about music soothes our souls. It reminds us of a beauty greater, a power stronger, and a purpose eternal that exists beyond ourselves. Music, in all its forms, can lead us to worship when we remember the One who put the song in our hearts in the first place. Perhaps that's why God chooses to live in the praises of His people. When we join in with all of creation, singing God's praise from grateful and thankful hearts, our lives join creation's symphony of praise, and we are music to God's ears.

Whether you put on a praise CD, play worship music from your computer, or simply sing in your heart to God this morning, let this day begin with a heart that stands in awe of His beauty and love. Let His greatness inspire your heart and lips to declare His praise today.

It is good to sing praises to our God;
for it is pleasant and praise is becoming.
Psalm 147:1 NASB

COMING HOME

God is not ashamed for them to call Him their God,
because He has prepared a city for them.
HEBREWS 11:16 GNT

Your children are grown, each working hard to make their own way in the world. And you are proud. Thankful. Always eager to answer the phone whenever one calls with a need. Though the day-to-day labor of raising children has ceased, your love and prayers certainly have not.

So when the holidays roll around and your children announce that they all will be coming home this year to celebrate with you, your heart stretches wide with the same giddiness you remembered from Christmases long ago. The music, the laughter, crackling fires, and fragrance of pine and cinnamon add to the festivities, but you know you don't need a gift under the tree. There is nothing more precious to you than the presence of your family. It is the present. You thank God for the blessing that they are all coming home.

Coming home. It's the heart call inside every one of God's kids. Every reunion, each Christmas or Thanksgiving gathering, is simply a foretaste of the moment we finally reach that permanent place where joy and love and peace never cease. That place where we know we are safe, richly blessed, and bound together to celebrate God's great love forever.

This morning, thank God for your home and family here on earth and the wonderful times you have when all of you are under one roof. Then celebrate with God in advance for your future home with Him and all of His huge family!

Happy are those who are strong in the Lord,
who want above all else to follow your steps.
PSALM 84:5 TLB

ROOTS

Keep your roots deep in Him, build your lives on Him,
and become stronger in your faith.
COLOSSIANS 2:7 GNT

There it is, sticking up like a stealthy intruder right in the middle of your garden bed. You walk over and bend down to pull up the errant oak tree seedling that has sprouted in the middle of your tomatoes. But much to your surprise, the short seedling seems to have hidden strength. So you wedge the weight of your body against the tree's resistance, and slowly you feel its root system give way. With the sound of a garment being torn, the roots break and release their grip in the ground, with long tendrils of underground anchorage slipping to the surface. Once fully uprooted, the small seedling looks several feet in length. How could so much be happening underground with so little to show up top? you wonder.

It's funny how the small things can have that kind of impact in our lives. A little negative comment here, a white lie there, can suddenly take root in our souls. Left unchecked, bitterness and apathy spread out with tenacious tendrils, burrowing deeper into our hearts and minds, choking out the love and life that once dominated. On the surface, others may only see a small discontent. But inside, anger has taken hold with a viselike grip. To uproot it requires the full weight of your entire person, leaning in the opposite direction, with reliance upon God's great mercy. But once it's removed, the seeds of God's love and forgiveness are freed to grow and bear the kind of fruit you want to see in your life.

This morning, ask God to uproot any bitterness, complacency, or dishonesty lurking in your soul. Ask Him to plant in their place a harvest of love, joy, and peace.

May your roots go down deep
into the soil of God's marvelous love.
EPHESIANS 3:17 TLB

WINDS *of* CHANGE

Just as you can hear the wind
but can't tell where it comes from or where it will go next,
so it is with the Spirit.

JOHN 3:8 TLB

It's summer, and the stagnant heat of the day is taking its toll on your tired body. You stop walking and lean forward with locked arms braced against your knees as you try to catch your breath. *Why did I think it would be a good idea to go hiking in the woods today?* you wonder. Truth be told, you thought the trees' shade would be adequate cover to keep you cool. But you hadn't factored in how stifling heat can be without any breeze to cool you off. Then suddenly, as if on cue, a cool, refreshing wind blows through the trees, bending their branches and bathing you in a literal breath of fresh air. Smiling at God's invisible refreshment, you find the strength to finish your course.

Isn't it amazing how something we can't even see can have the power to bend (and at times, even topple) tall trees and lower our temperature? We may not even understand where the wind came from, but we enjoy the benefits and marvel at its power. God says His Holy Spirit moves in the same way. We can't see Him with our eyes, and we don't understand fully how He does it, but He blows into our lives, refreshing our dry and weary souls and filling us with the supernatural power we need to keep walking with God.

If you woke up this morning in need of refreshment from the sapping, dry heat that life often brings, ask God to cause His blessed wind to blow into your soul. His soothing love can cool your frustration and fill you with energy.

Awake, north wind. Come, south wind.
Blow on my garden, and let its sweet smells flow out.
SONG OF SOLOMON 4:16 NCV

DIVE IN

Trust the LORD with all your heart,
and don't depend on your own understanding.
Remember the LORD in all you do,
and He will give you success.

PROVERBS 3:5–6 NCV

I'm too old for this, you think as you fidget with your vest. *Planes are meant for flying, not jumping out of.* Your thoughts quickly escalate, as does the churning in your stomach. Then it's time. Your much-more-experienced partner attaches himself to you, covering your back and ushering you toward that gaping opening in the plane. Before you even have time to think, though, you are free-falling, wind rushing up as your body plummets. Utter terror combines with excitement, all of it heightened by the stunning beauty of the world below you and an entirely new vantage point. As the parachute deploys, the wonder of it all sinks in. Life seems different now that you have experienced a beauty you had never known before. Grateful for the ground and the thrill of a lifetime, you vow never to forget the moments you soared above it all.

For many of us, skydiving seems like a reckless or pointless endeavor. But those whose lives have been changed by it understand the attraction. Something sacred and sensational happens when you jump into the unknown, trusting that you will be held as you enjoy the ride.

Today, as you get up to face what lies ahead, realize that you aren't alone. Your much-more-experienced partner—God—has got your back covered, and His powerful presence is tethered tightly to your life. If He leads you into unexpected places, embrace the adventure and let your fears settle in the knowledge that He has everything under His control. See the world from His vantage point, and marvel at the beauty of a life lived trusting in Him.

This is my command—be strong and courageous!
Do not be afraid or discouraged.
For the LORD your God is with you wherever you go.
JOSHUA 1:9 NLT

The PURSUIT

Nothing can ever separate us from His love.
Death can't, and life can't. The angels won't,
and all the powers of hell itself
cannot keep God's love away.

ROMANS 8:38 TLB

What is it about romance movies that keeps us coming back for more? Each one is simply a story about two people, but the intrigue of connection and the mystery of how it happens arrests our hearts, minds, and souls every time. We sit riveted, waiting to catch the flicker in his eyes and the lingering look into hers as they pass each other in the crowded marketplace. We worry uncomfortably as twists and turns seem to throw them off course for the love we hope they're destined for. And of course, when the obstacles fade and they at last embrace, a rush of hope and excitement fills our hearts even though we know it's just a movie. The beauty of pursuit, of being discovered, loved, and held, satisfies—if only for a moment—that deep soul desire we feel in real life.

But romance isn't just a Hollywood fabrication. You have a lover, a pursuer, a soul mate who desires to lavish you with love. To look at you in utter delight and declare your beauty and infinite worth. To embrace you with a love that will never let you go.

The twist is that it isn't your earthly partner. God, the Author of romance, is the only one who loves us in this pure and noble way. He left everything He had in heaven just to make you His own. He loves you in spite of your flaws, transforming you into a treasure of true beauty. His is a love story like no other, ending with an actual "happy ever after."

Will you come to rest in the warmth of His embrace? Choose, this morning, how you want to see the story end and watch how real passion begins.

*The Son of man is come to seek
and to save that which was lost.*
LUKE 19:10 KJV

SHINE ON

Don't hide your light! Let it shine for all;
let your good deeds glow for all to see,
so that they will praise your heavenly Father.
MATTHEW 5:16 TLB

You're hungry, and even though you've been trying to stay away from fast food, the tyranny of the day takes over and you steer into the drive-thru and place your order. As you pull up to the window, you fumble for some cash or a card to cover the small expense. And then you get the news. "It's okay, you're paid up," the cashier says, smiling. "The person ahead of you in line paid for your meal." "What?" you ask, incredulous that someone who doesn't even know you would be so kind.

As the impact of this simple gesture sinks in, you drive to the next window and pick up your food. Suddenly, the rushing, hectic pace of this demand-driven day comes to a halt. Unexpected love and favor have altered the scene, giving you a taste of something far better than the hamburger you hold in your hands. It's the savory sensation of being noticed, and being loved for no other reason than the one who blessed you simply chose to do so.

Random acts of kindness get our attention because they so rarely happen in a me-centered world. They are like rays of light breaking through a darkness that shrouds the world we live in. As God's child, you possess that life-changing light inside you. When you notice others' needs and take action to meet them, your life is like a star shining out in a dark universe. How will you let God's light shine through you today?

Those who put others on the right path to life will glow like stars forever.
DANIEL 12:3 THE MESSAGE

DRINK UP

I am calm and quiet, like a baby with its mother.
I am at peace, like a baby with its mother.
PSALM 131:2 NCV

In the middle of church, you can hear the discontent build. Piercing people's quiet concentration, a baby starts to fuss, with short groans and grunts of discomfort. You hear the nervous mother rustling for pacifiers, whispering words of comfort to her little one. But he will not have it! Soon the short cries stretch into all-out shrieks of what sounds like intense agony. Heads start to turn as the young mom works her way quickly up the aisle, baby siren blaring in her arms. Only one thing can satisfy his tiny little soul, and she knows it—her body is already responding to the sound, readying itself for the feeding. And so she does, in the quiet of the nursing room. Holding him tightly to herself, her own life supplies the nourishment that his body demands. Once he's satisfied and content, she slips back up the aisle and into her seat.

Babies are often our greatest teachers. In them, we see our own helplessness, our basest needs demanding satisfaction. How beautiful that God would create such a portrait of how He meets those needs. How He holds us close and pours out His own life into ours so that we can be fed and filled. Because of His love and care, we grow up into the people we were created to be.

Is your soul unsettled this morning? Do you find yourself irritable or restless, unable to find anything on earth that can pacify your needs? Turn to the Source of life, hope, and love, and drink your fill from the God who cares for you. He will hold you close this day and every day.

The humble will eat and be satisfied;
those who seek the LORD will praise Him.
PSALM 22:26 HCSB

It Is Finished

I am sure that God, who began this good work in you,
will carry it on until it is finished
on the Day of Christ Jesus.
PHILIPPIANS 1:6 GNT

For weeks, months even, you have labored for this moment. It began with an idea, an inspiration to create a work of art you hoped would fill that space in your home perfectly. Then you shopped in stores and online, searching for the right tools and materials to make your vision come to life. Over time, piece connected to piece, and your idea became reality. Now, at long last, your creation is complete, ready to take its place on the wall you reserved for it. Standing back, you smile in deepest satisfaction. The finished piece is your reward, confirming your efforts were worth it all.

Finishing tasks, even the smallest ones like vacuuming a room or loading the dishwasher, brings a level of satisfaction. It's a reclaiming of order, if only for a moment, a restorative accomplishment in the middle of mundane details. But the projects that take longer to complete, even lifetimes, bring the greatest reward of all. These are the achievements worth standing ovations, the prize yielding the most glory.

You, child of God, are a great work of art in process. Before you were born, He planned exactly where He would place you in this world, unfolding beauty and boldness as only you can. If you wake up this morning frustrated by your failures, remember that your life is not yet complete. The Master Designer is strategically crafting every moment of your life, shaping your character into one that matches the perfection in His mind. So do not worry. He has promised to finish the work He has begun, yielding His glory through you all along the way. Your task today is to surrender to His plan as He finishes His perfect work in you.

We are His workmanship,
created in Christ Jesus unto good works.
Ephesians 2:10 KJV

POWER SOURCE

We now have this light shining in our hearts....
This makes it clear that our great power is from God,
not from ourselves.

II CORINTHIANS 4:7 NLT

You tested the lights before you began stringing the tree. You even purchased new ones to ensure the greatest quality and success. It took an hour of struggle, but you wound them in place so that tiny white lights could brighten up every branch. So why aren't they all working? you wonder, moaning as you retrace the wires. You stare dumbfounded at the one, rebellious strand that refuses to light. Finally, you find it! As you tugged around the tree, one of the plugs had pulled away from its power source. You smile as you quickly reconnect the cords. Voilà!

Some things just require connection to function. We are like that. We need love and support from other people, kind of like all the other lights on our life strand. But without a power source, we can't shine.

Without an outside energy surging through our souls, we end up strung out without a purpose. God tells us, though, that He made us with the purpose to shine for Him. We make the world a more beautiful place when we're living as we were designed.

But when we stand back and take a look at our lives, do we see vibrant light pouring out or sparsely lit bulbs due to the strain and pull of our daily lives? If we want to live with power, we have to check our Source. Are we connected in heart, mind, and soul to the One who made us? Are we relying on Him to fill us with His supernatural energy, or are we trying to wind through life on our own? This morning, take time to reconnect with God, who alone can give you the charge you need to shine brightly for this new day.

I am the vine, ye are the branches:
he that abideth in Me, and I in him,
the same bringeth forth much fruit.
JOHN 15:5 KJV

The VERDICT

Through Christ Jesus the law of the Spirit who gives life
has set you free from the law of sin and death.
ROMANS 8:2 NIV

The media has been abuzz for weeks following what appears to be a cut-and-dried case. The defendant was caught red-handed in the middle of an unspeakable crime. Everyone who heard about it was outraged at the evil. And everyone waited on the edge of their seats, eyes glued to the TV as the jury read the verdict. "Not Guilty!" the jury foreman declared. A pause of unbelief. Then the uproar. Cries of anger and disbelief poured out from every corner of the courtroom, except the one where the defendant stood speechless, marveling at the mercy verdict.

Our desire to see justice prevail comes from our Father's heart, who tirelessly defends the downtrodden. But from the same heart flow rivers of mercy for tired souls destined for destruction without His saving grace. In every sense, we are all criminals caught in acts of egregious sin against a holy God. But our cases are not lost because we have a representative who pleads for us. Better still, He paid the price for the life-debt we owed. Miracle of all miracles, we as former prisoners to sin now walk free as the prized and beloved children of God, no matter how much murmuring you hear from the crowd or even your own mind. Your case has been tried and the verdict is in. You have been found not guilty, cleared of all guilt by the only begotten Son of God.

As you rise to freely enjoy the day, remember that your freedom came at the highest cost to God. May His unmerited mercy on your behalf fill you with the assurance of His love and the determination to show that love to all, including those who deserve it the least.

The wages of sin is death, but the gift of God
is eternal life in Christ Jesus our Lord.
ROMANS 6:23 HCSB

STRONG BREW

You prepare a table before me
in the presence of my enemies...
my cup overflows.
PSALM 23:5 HCSB

It's early in the morning, and you know the routine. Climbing out of bed, you make your way to the coffee pot. Rinse. Fill. Pour. Liner in. Spout turned. Lid closed. Push the button. Wait for the magic to happen. Actually, you rarely sit and wait for the coffee pot to fill because you're busy making the breakfast to go with your brew. And slowly, drop by drop, the pot fills up until it's ready—you're ready—to grab your favorite mug and sit down for a few sacred moments before the din of the day takes over.

It's funny how something as simple as a coffee pot, simply doing its job, can give us a life lesson along with a jolt of caffeine. It reminds us that whatever we put into our relationship with God determines what comes out and how strong it is in our lives. But just like that pot of coffee, a full and rich relationship with God doesn't happen instantly. It builds, one moment at a time, each time you choose to talk to Him in prayer, read what's on His heart from His Word, listen to and sing songs of worship, spend your time wisely, and view every part of life as under His control. Every thought you think and moment you spend is another drop, either filling you with more of Him or more of whatever it is you're choosing over Him.

This morning, choose to fill up on the joy of God's presence. Ask Him to pour out His Spirit on your day and help you to live every moment in His grace. And enjoy your coffee!

May the God of hope fill you with all joy and peace as you believe in Him so that you may overflow with hope by the power of the Holy Spirit.
ROMANS 15:13 HCSB

FALLING UP

The LORD will hold your hand,
and if you stumble, you still won't fall.
PSALM 37:24 CEV

A rm upstretched, she slipped her tiny hand into the strong grip of her daddy's as they began walking together down the sidewalk. His every stride confident and sure, her small legs working hard to match his pace. The world around her shone bright, beautiful, and full of intrigue. Suddenly, just as her eye caught a jogger headed their direction, her foot slipped off the edge of the sidewalk. The bend of her ankle buckled her knee and she felt the weight of her body start to give way.

But she didn't fall. Instead, her father's grip grew tighter, the strength of all he was held her, even lifted her, suspended for a few seconds in air. Dangling there by her father's brute strength, she knew what it was to be held. Loved. Protected. And the two continued walking on their way.

Just like that little child, you have an opportunity to reach up to your heavenly Daddy this morning and put your hand in His. You are His pride and joy, the apple of His eye. He will keep you close beside Him as you go about your day. Linked to your Creator, you are free to explore all that this day has to offer without fear. Be bold in your witness. Curious in your study. Generous in your giving. Risk the adventure of walking with God with a heart wide open. It's not that you won't ever trip up. It's that when you do, God will hold you up with His mighty right hand.

Because you are sons,
God has sent the Spirit of His Son
into our hearts, crying, "Abba, Father!"
GALATIANS 4:6 HCSB

PARTY TIME

They shall celebrate the fame of Your abundant goodness,
and shall sing aloud of Your righteousness.
PSALM 145:7 NRSV

You've been planning for months, Pinterest pinned too many times to count. And now that the day is here, the whole family can feel the excitement as you launch final preparations. House cleaned? Check. Balloons inflated? Yes. So now there's just tablecloths to be pressed, centerpieces to be arranged, food to be cooked, candles lit, music selected, and family members prepped for their roles in helping you pull off this party. As the guests arrive, everything falls into place. Soon, you're able to relax and enjoy the fruit of all the effort—the point of all the planning.

Did you know that parties are God's idea? In the Old Testament, we read about several different festivals God designed for His people to celebrate at different times throughout the year. In the New Testament, Jesus explained how the heavenly host celebrates every time a lost soul repents and returns to God. Best of all, He tells us about the all-out, no-holes-barred, literally out-of-this-world celebration He has planned for all His kids when we join Him in heaven. God is planning the party of all parties to celebrate His people joining Him forever.

Parties—the fun of planning and participating—all point to the joy and love flowing from our Father's heart. On top of being holy, righteous, all-powerful, and all-knowing, God is also fun. And He invites you to get excited. He's got surprises in store for you today and something spectacular waiting for you in the future. Can you feel the anticipation rising in your soul? Then look for ways to help set the stage, preparing the way for a day, a life, an eternity celebrating God's goodness.

The people of Israel, the priests and the Levites,
and the rest of the returned exiles,
celebrated the dedication of this house of God with joy.
EZRA 6:16 NRSV

Name Calling

I am doing this—I, the Lord, the God of Israel,
the one who calls you by your name.
Isaiah 45:3 TLB

I t's date night, and you're out at your favorite restaurant, savoring the food and some much-needed fellowship. The hum of conversation happening all around you is a soothing white noise, a pleasant backdrop to your own dialogue unfolding across the dinner table. But suddenly you stop talking. "Did you hear someone say my name?" you ask. A moment of silence follows, and you both tune your ears to the topics at the other tables. Yes! It's that couple over there, you determine, hearing your name spoken again. But it's clear you've never met them before and conclude they must be talking about someone else.

Isn't it strange how hearing our names can penetrate through all the noise in our lives? It's as if our minds have a special radar solely for detecting someone in the great big universe who actually knows who we are and wants to make a connection. Really, it's a God thing. Our Creator, the One who has a name for every single star, has also named you. You are His child, His treasure, His chosen friend for all eternity. And He calls for connection as you work at your desk, interact with your family at home, drive alone in your car, or sit in a crowded restaurant. If you tune your ears to His heart, you can hear God whisper your name, inviting you to share that moment with Him, to know you are known and loved.

It isn't your imagination. God is beckoning you to come spend time with Him. Tune in to His tender voice this morning and discover a closer connection with Him than you have ever dreamed possible.

He has decided the number of the stars and calls each one by name.
PSALM 147:4 GNT

INTERMISSION

They that wait upon the LORD
shall renew their strength.
ISAIAH 40:31 KJV

Warm breezes chased thin white clouds across an azure sky. Golden dandelions danced in the sun as the wind rustled through the tall green grass. What a perfect day it's been, you muse, seated on a hill overlooking the valley not far from your campsite. As you sit and watch the world around you, colors shift to deeper hues. On the horizon, the sun sinks low, painting clouds with deep pinks and oranges as the shadows stretch long on the earth beneath. Even in the changing, the ending, you see an unsung beauty. The world has entered an intermission, the brilliance of day demanding a break until dawn. There is both a sadness and a satisfaction in the day that's been and anticipation for what's yet to come.

Sunsets color more than the skies. They fire our imagination and fill our souls with hope for a beauty that lasts beyond the day. They beckon us to be still, to embrace the necessity of endings to prepare for new beginnings. As much as we resist change and the uncertainty it brings, we see God painting promise for tomorrow every time the sun sets. In His hands, endings are only the temporary pause allowing us rest before even better blessings begin.

Are you nearing a season of change as you rise to greet this new day? Cast your cares on the One who commands the night and ushers in the dawn. Rest in the quiet, and trust God to shine the light on His purpose and plan when the time is right.

*What a stack of blessing You have piled up
for those who worship You.*
PSALM 31:19 THE MESSAGE

SOILED AGAIN

Our light affliction, which is but for a moment,
worketh for us a far more exceeding
and eternal weight of glory.
II CORINTHIANS 4:17 KJV

It was only yesterday that the floor had been neatly swept and mopped. But this morning, appearing as if by magic, pawprints of dirt line the floor like a railroad track, recording every filthy footstep your dog made after his trip outside. You groan in frustration as you get the mop, mumbling under your breath about everything that seems to complicate your life, not the least of which is your almost daily battle with the dirt. If only it would just go away, you wish, as you finish up and finally sit down outside to enjoy your morning coffee with some fresh air.

As you relax, you notice God's grand creation— the towering pines and delicate dogwoods; the azaleas and crepe myrtles; even the grass beneath your feet. And a new thought dawns: Dirt anchors all the beauty we see growing above! What seems like a nuisance, a life complication, is really the substance that sustains life's growth. Without dirt, foliage has no foundation. Plants have little source for nutrients. The world as we know it would cease to exist. Dirt is nature's hero.

The same is true for the trials in our lives. Just like dirt, on the surface, our struggles seem intrusive, out of order, something we work hard to sweep out of our lives as soon as possible. But God invites us to see life's circumstances through His eyes. When we do, we see how hard times drive us closer to God, as we lean on Him for strength and support. Our spiritual roots grow deeper and stronger into truth when we respond rightly to the trauma of the day. Far from being pointless, our pain provides the surface from which we sink down deeper into God's sustaining grace.

Consider yourselves fortunate
when all kinds of trials come your way,
for you know that when your faith
succeeds in facing such trials,
the result is the ability to endure.
JAMES 1:2–3 GNT

FALLING *for* YOU

God saw all that He had made, and it was very good.
Evening came and then morning: the sixth day.
GENESIS 1:31 HCSB

You felt it the second you stepped out your door this morning: a crisp, cool breeze blew against your skin. The sky overhead seemed a darker blue, the white of the clouds higher and thinner than before. Autumn has arrived, you realize, letting the reality of shifting seasons settle in your mind.

Already you can picture in your mind what lies ahead in the unfolding months. The green foliage of today will give way to dazzling golds and reds, painting the landscape outside your door with royal color. As you recall past fall beauty, you can almost smell the scents of the season, just the thought of spiced apple cider and savory cinnamon making your mouth water in anticipation. And then there's the football games, the roar of the cheers, the comfort of friends gathered around, and the crackle of fire in the fireplace. You've fallen in love with fall. You smile as you savor the moment and then make your way toward your car.

But before the busyness of the day sets in, let your imagination walk one step closer to the Father who brings you the beautiful fall season. The sweep of color and crunch of leaves underfoot are the sights and sounds of God's creative genius, His magnificent painting designed for your pleasure. Like a lover who brings roses to your door, God brings beauty and laughter and life together to demonstrate the depth of His love for you. As you rise this morning, receive life's beauty as His personal gift to you, His invitation to enjoy life in Him, with Him, this day and every day.

I remembered the old days, went over all You've done,
pondered the ways You've worked.
PSALM 143:5 THE MESSAGE

OCEANS DEEP

This hope we have as an anchor of the soul,
both sure and steadfast,
and which enters the Presence behind the veil.

HEBREWS 6:19 NKJV

It seemed like a fun idea when your friend talked you into it. "Deep sea fishing is amazing. You'll love it!" he promised. As the small charter boat pulled away from the dock into still bay water, familiar sights of seagulls, pelicans, and people lining the shore helped settle your nerves. Soon, though, the scenery changed. Smooth, still water surged in medium-sized swells, rocking the boat left and right as it plunged ahead into what looked like another world entirely.

As you look out in all directions, the dark, deep blue of the ocean and the pale day sky seals the world in a far-out circle around the tiny boat. Suddenly, the thought dawns: I'm trapped in the middle of an incredibly deep ocean, with no land for safety anywhere in sight. Panic sets in as you nervously peer over the boat's edge to see what creatures may be lurking beneath you. But you paid money for this adventure, and you don't want worry to win. So you bait your hook and drop your line, trusting the friend with you that fun is on its way.

This morning, you may find yourself in the middle of a moment, an event that rocks your world and sends you searching for solid ground. Remember God's promise that everywhere you go, no matter how foreign it feels, God is already there. He made the world, and He made this day for you to trust Him as He calls you into the deeper waters of faith and obedience. Don't let the panic win. Set your soul's anchor in your Father's unfailing love, the only solid ground in life's turbulent waters. And wait with anticipation for today's fun, the catch of the day God has ready for you when you drop your line in trust.

When you pass through deep waters,
I will be with you.
ISAIAH 43:2 GNT

Soak It In

Eye has not seen, nor ear heard,
nor have entered into the heart of man the things
which God has prepared for those who love Him.
I Corinthians 2:9 NKJV

You've made it! All your hard work and planning have landed you in this spot, plopped down on your beach chair, toes digging into cool, wet sand as the playful surf stretches toward them. Your body responds with a deep breath in, the salt and warmth washing over your weary body. Nature's sights and sounds arrest your senses, and you are struck with wonder: *How can a world so beautiful, so comforting, so soothing, be so real? And why can't this moment last forever?* you wish.

Your heavenly Father smiles at the longing. After all, He spoke the suds and sun into being. He marked the shore's line and sets the seagulls to flight. All that your eyes see and body enjoys are simply a sample from your Father's hand to comfort you now and point you toward an even greater place of permanent joy ahead for you—a place He has been planning and preparing from the beginning of time. God's promised grace now and forever sounds and feels too good to be real. But just like the grains of sand that spread farther than your eyes can see and mind conceive, greater still is the number of thoughts God has of you, His most highly prized creation. His plans to prosper His people are so great you can't even imagine it if you tried, He promises us in His Word.

So today, soak in the warmth of the world of beauty and joy this life affords. And let it well up into an offering of thanks for the forever goodness and grace of God that follows you all the days of your life into greater worlds of love yet to come.

How precious also are Your thoughts to me, O God!
How vast is the sum of them! If I should count them,
they would outnumber the sand.
PSALM 139:17–18 NASB

CROWN *of* GLORY

We do not lose heart,
but though our outer man is decaying,
yet our inner man is being renewed day by day.
II CORINTHIANS 4:16 NASB

Your morning had been going like clockwork. Speeding along, your shower's complete, clothes arranged, and you lean in toward the sink to brush your teeth when you notice a new patch of gray sprouting along your crown line. You're not feeling very royal about it. Taking a step back, you look at the image you see before you in the mirror. Oh, it's not the worst, you try to console yourself. But it's not as good as it used to be, the more realistic part of you concedes.

Growing old can be a pain—literally. Nuisances like graying hairs and handles you don't love at all are one thing. But add to it the wrinkles, the aches and pains, even the eyesight giving way and you can't help but complain at least a little. Why doesn't beauty last? Why hasn't science figured out how to reverse the aging process for good? The good news is that God does have a reverse process happening inside you. Though the outside is "wasting away," as the Bible puts it, God is steadily at work in our hearts, changing our minds and shaping our souls into His beautiful image. Though it may not feel like it, in God's eyes we are becoming more beautiful with every passing day.

As for that body that can be such a bother at times, don't let it get to you. Remember that you get to exchange it for a perfect one that never grows old when you get to heaven. But for now, your sags and soreness can just be your signal that you're one day closer to perfection and fully loved by God in the process.

Bless the LORD, O my soul...
who satisfies your years with good things,
so that your youth is renewed like the eagle.
PSALM 103:2–5 NASB

As *by* Fire

Endure trials for the sake of discipline.
God is treating you as children;
for what child is there whom a parent does not discipline?
HEBREWS 12:7 NRSV

From the base of the trunk, you can barely see to the top. Like mammoth spears plunged into the ground, thousands of ruddy, rough trunks line up across the landscape and shoot straight up into the sky. Foliage found way above blocks out much of the sunlight, casting cool shadows on the forest floor far below. It's a magical feel in the forest of Redwood National Park. Home to the world's tallest trees, it's easy to feel small, even insignificant, surrounded by such overarching beauty.

But beside one of the trees you can also find a sign explaining the growth process. As these trees grow, so do the weeds and underbrush that threaten to steal much-needed nutrients from the soil. Left unchecked, the underbrush becomes the great redwood's undoing.

But as God would have it, lightning periodically ignites fires that burn through the forest. The stronger redwoods withstand the heat, though the blazes often leave scars. But the undergrowth doesn't burn away, and the redwood is free to reach even higher toward heaven.

In a similar way, God allows the right kind of fires in our lives. These fires are perfectly designed to burn up the weeds that are choking out our love for Him. Maybe we lose a job or a home. Maybe our kids rebel in ways we never thought they would. Maybe our marriage falls apart, or we get a bad diagnosis. These fires are always painful. But through them we grow stronger and closer to God if we stay rooted in His love, trusting His eternal purpose.

See to it that no one fails to obtain the grace of God;
that no root of bitterness springs up and causes trouble.
HEBREWS 12:15 NRSV

Riding Roller Coasters

When we were children,
we thought and reasoned as children do.
But when we grew up, we quit our childish ways.
I Corinthians 13:11 CEV

Before you even find your seat, your heart is already racing in anticipation. Inside, you pull the harness down tight. You worry as you feel a little give in the lock. But you don't have time to analyze because the ride has started, and you know there's no going back. Jerking you into alignment, the cars make the telltale click as they slowly climb what seems to be straight up into the air. At long last, you teeter at the top for just a second. Suddenly, the cars pull you straight down into certain death (or so it feels) as your stomach and head revolt against such madness. Strangely, at the same time as all the terror, a silly smile lines your face. This is terrible and tremendous, tragic and terrific, all at the same time!

And so it goes, not only on roller coasters, but also in life. The highs and lows even in a single day can send your heart racing, emotions surging from anger to ecstasy in a matter of minutes. Thank God for the emotions! Emotions are a gift that helps connect us to God and others. They let us know we're human, and very much alive. But they aren't reliable drivers in the ride.

When we acknowledge that God alone directs our course and stay connected to Him—just as roller-coaster cars always keep on track—we can stay anchored even through the rises and falls of life. The twists and turns in life can be scary and exhilarating, nerve-wracking and incredible, unpredictable and delightful. Through it all, we can smile, knowing we're held all the while by the strong, certain, and unbreakable grip of God. So today, sit back and enjoy the ride!

He will order His angels to protect you wherever you go.
They will hold you up with their hands
so you won't even hurt your foot on a stone.
PSALM 91:11–12 NLT

STAR *of* WONDER

God saw that the light was good.
Then He separated the light from the darkness.
GENESIS 1:4 NLT

Have you ever wondered what it's like where the stars live? Not the celebrity kind, but the celestial sort—those curious, gleaming beams of light we see shining through the darkness of our night? Can you imagine getting closer? The brightness and burning would be so intense that you couldn't describe it. A ball of surging power, radiating a glory as it sits alone, suspended in space. Though deepest darkness lies all around, its light shines greater, sending energy in waves countless light-years away.

What a miracle each star is! What a wonder that God would compare us to each of these. Yet He did. When we look up at the night sky, we witness God's picture of His people, lives filled with the glory of His incredible power and brilliance. Burning with a supernatural passion for real beauty and truth, we stand out in the darkness of this world. And for some who come near, our fire is too bright, too intense for them. With no light of their own, the lost often prefer the darkness. But don't be discouraged. Starlight also illuminates our world and lights the way for those who recognize their need.

Today, as you rise up for the occasion of life, fuel up on the power of God's Word. Invite His Spirit inside you to chase away any shadows of self or the darkness of doubt, and let His love wash over the world around you and illuminate it with His wonderful light.

Live clean, innocent lives as children of God,
shining like bright lights
in a world full of crooked and perverse people.
PHILIPPIANS 2:15 NLT

WRAPPED UP

Take away my sin, and I will be clean.
Wash me, and I will be whiter than snow.
PSALM 51:7 NCV

It has been a long, hard day. It feels like you've literally walked miles to and from the millions of errands you take care of for home and work, your pedometer confirming your suspicions. All you want to do now is take a shower, put on your PJs, and climb into bed, in that order. And you do just that. Only you have a pleasant surprise waiting for you as you pull back the covers: clean sheets. How could something so simple feel so spectacular? Sliding in, your body embraces the cool, silky sensation, and you can't help but rub your legs back and forth across the smooth surface. With cleanness all around, it's easy to unwind and usher in the sleep you so desperately need.

There's just something special about being clean and wrapped up in it. It feels right. Maybe even what we're born—and destined—for. In the Bible, John relays the vision he saw in heaven, that of a vast sea of people praising God and waving palm branches. The angel next to John explained that those people were God's family, all those who have trusted in Jesus to wash their souls white as snow. And now, standing before the very throne of Almighty God, they were given robes, washed perfectly white with God's own righteousness. They were all clean and wrapped up in their robes, thanks to God's glorious grace.

As you get up this morning, meditate on your destiny. One day you will stand spotless and perfectly clean before God's throne if you have put your faith in Jesus. You are destined for perfection and will revel and rest in the Savior's cleansing sensation.

The LORD rewarded me because I did what was right, because I did what the LORD said was right.
PSALM 18:24 NCV

BURNING LOVE

Let's not get tired of doing what is good.
At just the right time we will reap a harvest of blessing
if we don't give up.

GALATIANS 6:9 NLT

It may be cold outside, but in here, snuggled on the couch with a cozy blanket and a crackling fire in the fireplace, it's toasty warm and oh-so-comfortable! So you pull out your favorite book and begin to read, reveling in the relaxation and comfort the moment affords. Before too long, though, you notice a bit more of a chill in the air. Looking up from the page, you notice the fire has died down, now curling quietly over the last remaining logs. You wrap the blanket around you a little tighter and plunge ahead in the plot, the most intense part just a chapter or two away. But before you get there, the fire goes out altogether. Suddenly, the room seems far less romantic, far colder, and clearly in some serious need of attention if you want the heart- and body-warming ambience to continue.

The same is true for our relationships. Like the fire in the fireplace, they only produce heat and warmth when you put the necessary work into them. But they are not static. Neglected, they are destined to diminish. Ignore them long enough, and they will die out completely. So God urges you to keep the fire burning in your relationships—with Him, your spouse, and everyone God has put in your life to love and serve. Resist the temptation to let life coast along or become too distracted by the day's drama, and you will reap great rewards in your soul and life.

This morning, ask God to give you creativity, perseverance, and determination to keep up the good work of cultivating strong relationships with others.

Love never gives up, never loses faith, is always hopeful, and endures through every circumstance.
I CORINTHIANS 13:7 NLT

BREATHE IN

This is what God the LORD says—
the Creator of the heavens...
who gives breath to its people,
and life to those who walk on it.
ISAIAH 42:5 NIV

Take a deep breath in, the doctor instructs. You comply as she readjusts her stethoscope to hear different places around your lungs. "Now breathe out." You exhale, waiting to hear about any discoveries she may have made while the oxygen exchange was taking place. It's important to make sure the lungs are functioning properly. The quality and amount of oxygen you process with every breath in has a direct impact on the way the rest of your body functions.

When you stop to think about it, breathing itself is its own miracle—one that happens anywhere from 17,000 to 30,000 times a day, depending on your age! In order to keep on living, laughing, talking, and loving, we have to keep on breathing. It's the way God designed for us to get the energy from the outside to the inside of us, fueling our bodies as needed. It's a second-by-second reminder of our critical reliance upon the divine breath of God who brings us life in the first place. Should He want to, God could withdraw His breath from His creatures, and all life would instantly cease. Fortunately, He wants the opposite: to fill His people with His breath of life—not only to keep your physical heart pumping and body running, but also to fill you with His Spirit so you can live this life to its fullest.

When you breathe in deeply by reading and believing His Word, you are filled with supernatural energy, joy, and power to exhale God's amazing grace into the world around you. This morning, take a deep breath, drawing on God's incredible goodness and love for you. Then look for all the ways God brings you today to breathe out His grace everywhere you go.

The heavens were made by the word of the LORD,
and all the stars, by the breath of His mouth.
PSALM 33:6 HCSB

CENTER STAGE

For you that honor my name,
victory will shine like the sun with healing in its rays.
MALACHI 4:2 CEV

When you awoke this morning, it was peeking through your windows. Once you are outside, though, all formalities are gone. The sun bears down, casting its rays full force onto you and everything around you. It's so bright that you involuntarily shield your eyes, hand cupped over forehead, as you look at all the beauty lit up by its brilliance. It's going to be another gorgeous day, and you can't wait to get going in it.

But before you do, take a moment to soak up a powerful truth along with the sun's rays. God, who made this reliable source of energy for all the Earth's needs, didn't place our planet in the center for the sun to circle around us. Instead, the sun takes center stage, and we spin precariously through space at just the right distance to receive blessing instead of burns from the sun's massive output of energy.

Likewise, God has also given us His Son, Jesus, the source of energy for all things, including stars and planets. We do not demand that God cater to us, orbiting around our small worlds, insisting that everything happen the way we please. No, we understand our rightful place when our lives are orbiting around the Son of God. With proper perspective of Who's in the center, we find ourselves poised at every angle to reap the healing warmth and power of His love.

Today, do you need to realign your thinking to become more God-centered than self-centered? If so, confess it to God and ask Him for wisdom from above. Let the light of His love shine down full force into your soul to keep your life anchored in orbit around Him.

From east to west, the powerful LORD God has been calling together everyone on earth.
PSALM 50:1 CEV

REFLECTIONS

In returning and rest you shall be saved;
in quietness and in trust shall be your strength.
ISAIAH 30:15 NRSV

Not a breeze is blowing. Only the sound of crickets stirs the thick summer air as you step up to the sandy lake shore. Looking out, you almost lose your breath. Languid water and hazy blue sky pose as mirrors, the image and colors of the heavens reflecting so perfectly on the stillness below that you can't even discern where one ends and the other begins. It's just a palette of blues in differing hues, dotted by clouds. But as fish break the surface and ripples roll across the lake, the illusion is lost and the unyielding sky wins.

The truth is, reflections are seen best in the stillness. It is why God calls out to His very busy creatures to "be still, and know that I am God." While we carry on the frantic pace of our lives, we miss the beauty of all that is above. We worry, we stress, we plan, we manipulate, we labor long to make life work the way we think it should when all along we'd be better off being still and reflecting the beauty of the heavens.

Today, take time to be still. Sit in silence before the God who made you and knows you. Listen for the still, small voice that tells you what your heart really needs to know for this day. When you take time to sit still in God's glorious presence, you take on His image—a work of beauty that will take the world's breath away.

> *Be still, and know that I am God!*
> *I am exalted among the nations,*
> *I am exalted in the earth.*
> PSALM 46:10 NRSV

MORNING MIRACLES

In him we live, and move, and have our being;
as certain also of your own poets have said,
For we are also his offspring.
ACTS 17:28 KJV

It's a miracle if you get out of bed this morning, not because you're desperately wanting to sleep longer, either. Marvel, for just a moment, about how God has wired your body. Without as much as a conscious thought, your heart has continued beating and your lungs breathing all throughout the night and carries on even as you read your morning devotional. In order to pick up this book, the bones in your body worked in tandem with muscles perfectly connected to make motion happen. Nerve endings and sense of touch and sight sent signals to your brain which almost instantaneously assessed the data and reacted with a command for your hand to open, close, and retrieve the book you wanted to read.

And so it goes with everything we see, say, and

do. We are living, breathing, miraculous acts of God. And as Paul explained it, we live and move and have our being in God. The source of all this magnificent biological technology that we most often take for granted is our Creator, who designed us perfectly to live this life in grateful devotion to the One who sustains our every moment.

So take a deep breath. Wriggle your toes. Notice the fine prints on every finger. And realize that this day—and your life in it—is a miraculous gift from God, not to be taken lightly. Thank Him for creating you exactly as He did, and for His amazing grace that keeps you going day after day. Then ask Him to fill you so that He can use your physical frame, as well as your heart, mind, and soul, to bring Him the glory He is due this day.

You protect me with your saving shield.
You support me with your right hand.
You have stooped to make me great.
PSALM 18:35 NCV

TRAINING DAY

*No day will pass without its reward as you mature in
your experience of our Master Jesus.*
II PETER 1:8 THE MESSAGE

Anyone would have been impressed, the way that
that dog on stage followed its owner's every command
on cue. Pet owners know that training of that caliber
doesn't come easy. Time, repetition, consistency,
and relevant rewards for right behavior are crucial
for training success. But what about us? What is the
motivation for making right decisions? We don't have
people around us popping treats in our mouths every
time we choose to behave in a God-honoring way.
What is the motivation today to do what is right?

The same God who wired animal brains designed
ours in a similar, though higher-functioning fashion.
We, too, can train our minds to think and respond
according to our Master's commands, the process
developing through a system of rewards. Only the
rewards don't come out of a store-bought bag. They

come from God's presence in our lives. God tells us in His Word that when we seek after Him with all of our hearts, He rewards us with a richer, deeper, stronger relationship. Generous gifts sown toward His kingdom reap lasting pleasure as we discover our God-given purpose in this world while storing up riches in heaven. Suddenly, to act in ways against God's nature just seems empty. Pointless. Offensive even. We begin to live for the reward we know is surely coming. God is giving us more of Himself every time we choose to follow Him.

Today, as you walk out onto the stage of your life, will you surrender to the Master as He trains your soul in righteousness? He wants to retrain your brain to obey the One who brings the richest rewards.

If you do what is right,
you are certain to be rewarded.
PROVERBS 11:18 GNT

TOUCHED *by* LOVE

The one with human likeness touched me again
and strengthened me.
DANIEL 10:18 HCSB

You were able to hold it together up until this point. Though sadness had seeped deep into your soul, you steeled yourself to keep all appearances steady. But your friend blew your cover with the simple, caring touch of her hand. Seeing the tears welling in your eyes, she hugged you hard and firm, the softness of her concern shattering the dam holding back the emotional torrent now surging through your entire body. How can a single touch yield such tremendous power? How can a hug demolish all defenses?

When we feel loved, when we tangibly sense the touch of another person, connection happens. Not just the kind between giver and receiver, but a sense of your heavenly Father's deepest affection flows through the current, healing both souls. For whatever reason, God has chosen people, His people, to be the physical vessels through which His Spirit pours, the literal hands and feet of God's own body to serve and save the world. When we reach out to those who are hurting, we are living conduits of God's grace and love. And when we receive hands laid on us for prayer, encouragement, and support, we receive the embrace of God.

Do you ever wonder if God loves you? Do you ever wish He'd just appear and prove His love is real? Remember, God sent His Son so we could see in human form what real love is. Then He sent His Spirit to live inside His children, so we can feel, receive, and give that love to others. As you prepare for your day, ask yourself who in your life could use God's touch of love today. Then make it happen.

Jesus came up, touched them, and said,
"Get up; don't be afraid."
MATTHEW 17:7 HCSB

ARTISTIC LICENSE

*God gives us many kinds of special abilities,
but it is the same Holy Spirit
who is the source of them all.*
I CORINTHIANS 12:4 TLB

The art teacher stood in front of the class, satisfied that she had given her students all the directions they needed. The living model was sitting as still as possible in full view of all. "My objective for this assignment is to see your perspective," she concluded. After time passed, the teacher slowly walked down each aisle and surveyed each student's work. *What a pleasant surprise*, she thought. No one had drawn the entire man. Instead, each student accentuated a different part, with some adding imaginative twists all their own. The resulting amalgam of artistic license took the teacher's breath away. One single model had inspired an entire world of creativity.

Such creative genius isn't just for the artistically inclined. Each of us offers a unique perspective, a delightfully different personality through which the love and grace of God can flow. The idea that all Christians should look and act the same way is as boring a thought as a duplicate art piece. The wonder and beauty of creativity stems from the Creator who gives it to us. When we approach the people and circumstances of life confident in who God created us specifically to be, we usher breathtaking beauty and perspective into this world.

As you enjoy the beauty of this fresh, new morning, thank God for wiring you exactly the way He did. Ask Him to help you be yourself, filled with His Spirit, inspired by His creativity, ready to paint your world with the creative perspective that only you can give.

He has made many parts for our bodies
and has put each part just where He wants it.
I Corinthians 12:18 TLB

LOST *in* TRANSLATION

May our Lord Jesus Christ…
comfort your hearts with all comfort,
and help you in every good thing you say and do.
II THESSALONIANS 2:16–17 TLB

You've had it happen before and swore you wouldn't repeat the mistake. At the moment, it seemed like texting your thoughts would simplify the situation. After all, you had time to think and craft your words before pressing "send." But seeing the reply, you sensed a signal got crossed. Words meant for explanation wounded the recipient instead. Strangely, you could feel the tension, even through the text. Immediately you choose to switch modes, clicking the call button instead. Real conversation ensues, and the miscommunications get sorted out. Tragedy averted. Relationship restored.

Good communication can be tricky no matter what mode we use. But words are not the only part of communication people choose to read. How we say what we say and the hidden motivation behind our comments carry even deeper meaning. God calls His kids to be strong communicators for His kingdom's sake. He reminds us throughout His Word that the world is watching—and reading—our lives. Any discrepancy between how we talk and how we live speaks volumes. Do we say we love God but fail to help those in need? Do we like our church but sit out when they request help? Do we tell others we'll pray for them but not with them in the moment? Though we may not mean for it to happen, the reality of God's love and presence gets lost in our contradicting translation.

This morning, ask God to help you sync the story of your mouth with the plot of your life. Be the salt and light God has called you to be, leading others closer to Him in every kind of conversation.

Little children, let us stop just saying we love people; let us really love them, and show it by our actions.
I JOHN 3:18 TLB

BORN *to* BE BEAUTIFUL

While the king is on his couch,
my perfume releases its fragrance.
SONG OF SOLOMON 1:12 HCSB

He had it hidden behind his back so you couldn't see. Still, you smelled a sweetness even while he stood at your door. Then, with a smile on his face and outstretched arm, he revealed his hidden treasure: a dozen red roses wrapped tightly at the stems, bow flowing down. Instinctively, you bent over and breathed in the scent, even before accepting the beautiful offering. Flattered and humbled, you couldn't help but blush as you brought the bouquet inside.

Isn't it amazing how something as simple as flowers can bring the world such beauty and joy? What starts out as a tiny seed planted deep in the dirt simply grows over time. Sun, water, and soil work a mysterious magic, splitting the hull and sending shoots straight toward the sky. In time, the tall green of the stems yields to the crowning bud, where color and fragrance infuse delicate petals, soft and curled around each other with stunning precision.

In a similar way, God is growing each of His people up into unimaginable beauty that makes this world a better and brighter place. Every day that we soak up the rich nutrients of His love and truth, our roots grow deeper, stems stronger as we grow up in Him. And as we grow, a deeper mystery unfolds. Our lives soften. Our thoughts and words and actions grow sweeter. And we become the very fragrance of Christ, God's beautiful gift of love to the world He wants to win over.

Today, don't grow impatient with yourself or your circumstances. Instead, understand that God's growing beauty in you is in process. Stay rooted in Him, and you can be sure that your life, God's gift, will bless the world around you.

God uses us to make the knowledge about Christ spread everywhere like a sweet fragrance.
II Corinthians 2:14 GNT

The RIGHT MIX

It is pleasant to see plans develop.
PROVERBS 13:19 TLB

I t tasted so good at the party, you knew you'd have to try baking it yourself at home. But now that your friend has sent over the recipe, you're a little dumbfounded. Staples like sugar and flour you certainly recognize. But some of the spice requirements stop you in your tracks. Heading to the most gourmet grocery near you, you scan the spice rack until you find the special ingredients your recipe calls for. Back at home, you begin measuring, mixing, blending, noting that even the order of instructions seems counterintuitive to your cooking experience. Yet you stick to the script, following directions, trusting that in the end you will produce the same delicious dessert you first tasted at the party. In the end, you are delighted with the results.

Life is like a big mixing bowl filled with very different ingredients. Part of the mix is sweet. But other events and circumstances can add quite a bitter edge. It's hard not to question some of the trials and challenges God incorporates into the lump of dough that is your life. The ingredients and the process often seem out of order and completely counterintuitive to how you would have written the recipe. But if we want to taste the heavenly delight in the end, we need to stick to God's script. Keep living according to His Word, trusting that He will work both the sweet and the unsavory into one complete dish worth serving to the world and pleasing to Him.

Today, as you taste different foods throughout your day, remember that God's goodness and control bring purpose to the process. He is bringing exactly the right mix of people and circumstances needed to make you the person He created you to be.

Take firm hold of instruction,
do not let go; keep her, for she is your life.
PROVERBS 4:13 NKJV

FOREVER FAMILY

*God decided in advance to adopt us into his own family
by bringing us to himself through Jesus Christ.*
EPHESIANS 1:5 NLT

For years they had waited, hoped, prayed, and spent money, time, and countless tears as they wrestled through mountains of paperwork and jumped through every government-required hoop. As months turned into years, faith mingled with fear: fear of the country closing adoptions, fear that the child they loved sight unseen would never make it home. But then it came in the mail. It was only a single photo of their child with a short description beside it, but to the couple it was their hope reborn. Yet even that moment paled in comparison to the one when they finally met, face to face, eye to eye. At last, they were family.

All the struggle, cost, and completed joy adoption brings helps us see our Father's heart. We were spiritual orphans, desperately needing a home. He could have ignored us, made us slaves or even guests, but He didn't.

He wanted more. God wanted a family—children with whom He could share His love and home. Though sin had separated us from Him, God relentlessly labored to bring His children home, the cost He paid in Jesus infinitely higher than any earthly fee.

This morning as you prepare for the day, consider all the preparations God made so you could be His own child. You are no outsider to His love, affection, power, and riches. Everything He has and all He is was given to you the moment you accepted His invitation to life with Him. Joined together with every believer, we now celebrate the largest family of brothers and sisters this world has ever seen. And we will never be separated again.

You are citizens with everyone else who belongs to the family of God.
EPHESIANS 2:19 CEV

CUTTING EDGE

Faithful are the wounds of a friend.
PROVERBS 27:6 NKJV

Y ou couldn't believe it. You had been carrying on, laughing and joking like you usually do. But then your friend called you out. Even worse, she admitted she had given thought, even prayer, to the problem. Dumbfounded, you listened long enough to learn that she actually believed you had sin in your soul, a blind spot that surfaced whenever you spoke about a particular person you both know. Her words cut like a knife, and you recoiled from the wound. Thoughts flooded your mind as you mentally mounted a strong defense against her accusation. "I do not gossip! I'm only telling the truth," you rebutted. Then you thought, *And who is she to tell me I talk badly about others?* But then her smile disrupted your mental tirade before the words escaped your lips. "You know I love you, right?" she asked. And on second thought, you remembered that she indeed did. That she actually was kind. And maybe, just maybe, she was right.

As painful as it may be at times, God often corrects His kids through others. Left to our own devices, we simply tend to gloss over our weaknesses. But God loves us and the world around us too much to let us inhibit our spiritual growth. So He gives us spouses, teachers, and close friends who will risk telling us the truth, people who are willing to navigate the turbulent waters of our tempers so we can be free.

And freedom is the result of a blind spot surrendered. Once it is seen, we can confess and be cleansed, bound no longer by that secret sin's power. This day, ask God to help you receive His correction, in whatever form it comes, with a humble and listening heart.

No chastening seems to be joyful for the present, but painful; nevertheless, afterward it yields the peaceable fruit of righteousness.
HEBREWS 12:11 NKJV

Sakura Blooms

The grass withers, and its flower falls away,
but the word of the LORD endures forever.
I PETER 1:24–25 NKJV

It's early April, and already the delicate pink blooms of the sakura, Japanese cherry trees, have burst into billowy color. Tens of thousands of tourists have converged on the nation's capital, eager to see the softness of willowy beauty amid somber stone memorials. The landscape does not disappoint. For a brief couple of weeks, the city grounds are awash in pastel glory, the cherry blossoms accentuating the noble and heroic feats of all the lives lived and lost for a cause greater than themselves.

And then, just like that, the glory fades. The petals fall, and the world moves on. The transient display of the beautiful sakura trees tell a story just as profound as the words and historical scenes that populate the city: Even the greatest leaders do not lead forever. Soldiers, prisoners, civilians, politicians flourish or flounder in the brevity of their lives. They, like all of us, are here today, but gone tomorrow. Those who lived for something greater than themselves, however, left a lasting legacy for those coming behind. A life lived with the joy of heaven in mind brings lasting impact here on earth. God's Word alone will stand the test of time, as will all those who base their faith and actions on it.

This morning, may the sobering thought of life's inevitable brevity make you bold. There's no time to waste. Live life to its fullest with God and His eternal riches in view as you ask Him to establish His order for your day.

> *Lay up for yourselves treasures in heaven,*
> *where neither moth nor rust destroys and*
> *where thieves do not break in and steal.*
> MATTHEW 6:20 NKJV

GREATER

If our conscience condemns us,
we know that God is greater than our conscience
and that He knows everything.
I JOHN 3:20 GNT

Unable to sleep, you decide to walk off dinner and the normal jitters you feel when you travel. At the short boardwalk over the dunes, you ditch your shoes and soon sink your toes into the now cool, soft sand, the golden glow of day now washed in night grays. Silence settles in, except for the gentle rhythmic lapping of the shoreline at your feet. Alone, the quiet calms your soul, and you breathe in the bigness of it all: black night sky and deep, dark ocean accentuate the smallness of your frame. All the important matters of the day, of your life, seem lost in the vastness of the universe above and around you. In the grand scheme of all that is, you wonder why you even matter, how your life can possibly make a difference in this overwhelming cosmos.

But in the stillness, a small voice with the power of a thousand suns reminds you of a young boy's lunch given long ago. A small meal surrendered into the Master's hands became life and nourishment for an entire multitude. He was only a child. It was just one meal. But in the surrender, God made a miracle of eternal impact. On your own, your life may very well be a simple drop in the ocean. But when that drop is surrendered to God's almighty presence and power within you, He brings eternal purpose to even the smallest acts of love you do.

Today, as you face the enormity of all that comes your way, remember that God is so much bigger. He will empower you to make the difference you are destined to make for this day.

He has spoken to us through his Son.
He is the one through whom God created the universe.
HEBREWS 1:2 GNT

LOVE SONGS

The LORD your God is in your midst....
He will exult over you with joy,
He will be quiet in His love.
ZEPHANIAH 3:17 NASB

The second it comes on the radio, your heart soars—it's your all-time, hands-down favorite love song. Without a second thought, you crank it up in your car loud enough to be heard from outside, but inside you've let the music and melody take you to that special place in your mind it always does. Through those notes and lyrics, you imagine another place and time where you reveled in the affection and attraction of some other, a place where you are free to not only be yourself, but to be fully loved as the quirky and unique person you are. For the three minutes the song plays, you are in your perfect paradise. Of course, when the song ends, the day's realities resume.

Romantic notions of hope and deep connection get shelved for another day, perhaps another song. In real life, your experience tells you that even the best, most enduring loves might not last, at least not with the unbridled passion of youth. In real life you have to settle for a love that's more, well, down to earth. Or do you?

Maybe that's exactly the problem with an earth-bound love. We were made for more. We were designed to know and be known on the deepest levels of our souls. Did you know that the God who created you sings love songs over you as well? His attraction and commitment to you rivals none. He alone can satisfy our aching souls with the kind of connection we all truly crave. Unlike love songs on the radio, God's singing for you started before He made the world, and His delight in you doesn't fade away. It welcomes you to stay in His presence and revel in His love now and forever.

To those who are the called, beloved in God the Father, and kept for Jesus Christ: May mercy and peace and love be multiplied to you.
JUDE 1–2 NASB

CHOSEN

GOD judges persons differently than humans do.
Men and women look at the face;
GOD looks into the heart.

I SAMUEL 16:7 THE MESSAGE

The team captains stood in front of the PE class, surveying the assortment of gym-shorts clad potentials before them. Those who were confident in their athletic reputation simply wondered if they'd be picked first. But the others, those who knew their talents lay elsewhere, just dreaded the process. Of course they wouldn't be picked—at least not until everyone better had been snatched up. For some of them, it was the story of their lives. Being the one chosen simply never happened. Not in PE, not ever.

Fearing rejection follows us far beyond the travails of childhood. Even into our golden years, it's hard to grasp our true value and worth with all the ways the world has to bring us down. Yet God surveys the playing field quite differently. Far from the team captain who chooses the one who is smartest, fastest, and brightest, God often chooses the weakest, the neediest, the ones desperate for His divine help to live and achieve His purposes. Over every asset our culture deems important, God chooses the humble.

This morning, if you find yourself feeling too weak and too inadequate for what lies ahead, you are in the perfect place to be snatched up by the team captain and placed in the starting lineup. Take your need to the only One who can give you the power and strength you need. Humbly submit to His Spirit's coaching, and you can be certain He will choose you to be on His team, ready to win the world to Him by His mighty power.

Your servant is in the midst of
Your people whom You have chosen,
a great people, too numerous to be numbered or counted.
I KINGS 3:8 NKJV

FULL FORCE

*There is now no condemnation awaiting those
who belong to Christ Jesus.*
ROMANS 8:1 TLB

You open the drawer and let out a deep sigh as you reach for sweatpants again. After all the festivities and food from the holidays, it's just expected, you rationalize. But it doesn't make the New Year's leaf any easier to turn over. You know what it's going to take to get back into your better-looking wardrobe: a lot of work. So you set your mind to the goal and begin anew. For a week, you stick to your plan, but week two is another story. It seems like every temptation possible is testing your resolve. Before long your resolution melts away instead of the weight you intended to lose. *Why are the simple things so hard to do?* you wonder.

The apostle Paul says we're in a fight. He probably didn't have a scale in mind, but he did know that our bodies are often at odds with our hearts. We desire to do well physically, emotionally, and spiritually, but another part of our person seems to have other plans. When we fail, it's so easy to want to give up. But God, through the words of Paul, sets us free. Even when our own hearts condemn us, God does not. He has declared His people to be perfect in His sight, simply because we belong to Him. So we stay in the fight— the fight to believe God's power to declare us perfect and the fight to fend off the fleshly desires that would keep us from becoming all God created us to be.

As you start your day, remember that you are perfectly loved and sustained by God's grace. Then pray for His power to fight off everything that hinders you from feeling its full force

I have fought a good fight,
I have finished my course,
I have kept the faith.
II TIMOTHY 4:7 KJV

BEAUTIFUL SOLES

The Scriptures say,
"How beautiful are the feet of messengers
who bring good news!"
ROMANS 10:15 NLT

You probably hardly ever notice them, but they're with you everywhere you go. Every stair you climb. Every trip you take. There, at the end of your legs, are the two most important tools for your personal transportation. Whether you're walking, jogging, jumping, or simply standing, your own two feet have to toe the line every time. And when they don't—when injury or illness impairs—life takes on a whole new level of difficulty. You and I—we all need our feet!

In fact, God says our feet are beautiful. They take us to the people who need to hear about hope. They walk us away from our comfort zones to those places of need where others won't go. God gives us feet so we can carry His blessing beyond our own borders into the waiting world beyond. Best of all, God promises to direct our steps to those very places and people where we need to go. God could have chosen to keep Jesus here on earth ministering from village to village as He did while on earth. But God had bigger plans. In fact, Jesus told His followers that it was best that He return to heaven so that His Spirit could come and fill all believers with His presence. Now He works through us, physically and practically bringing God's hope, joy, and love into every life we touch, every hand we hold, every hug we give.

God is calling you, this morning, to go for a walk! Let His Spirit lead you into all the ways He has planned for you to minister to others in His name. You are God's expression of love for others, and it is beautiful!

Shapely and graceful your sandaled feet....
Your limbs are lithe and elegant,
the work of a master artist.
SONG OF SOLOMON 7:1 THE MESSAGE

GARDEN GROWTH

The seed that fell on good soil represents
those who truly hear and understand God's word
and produce a harvest of thirty, sixty,
or even a hundred times as much as had been planted!
MATTHEW 13:23 NLT

She led you through the halls of her humble home until she reached the back door where she welcomed you to walk ahead. As you pushed open the door, it took a moment for your eyes to take in the beautiful scene that spread before you. Nestled inside the old brick fence lining the perimeter of her property grew the most spectacular garden you had ever seen. A graceful weeping willow kept the corner guard, with dozens of daffodils standing at attention, all swaying slightly in the warm spring breeze. Brilliant pink and red peonies, encore azaleas, and a variety of ferns and tall grasses lined the pebbled pathway through the hand-wrought paradise. It was obvious the owner was proud of her handiwork. "What's your secret?" you wondered aloud as you inhaled the varied fragrances.

Smiling, she answered, "The secret's in the soil."

Before she ever planted a single bulb, she had tilled the soil and tested the quality. Much of it required additional nutrients before the conditions were ripe for planting. But rooted in the right soil, beautiful growth was inevitable. Our hearts are much like our gardens. We may all hear the message of truth about God's grace and forgiveness, but only hearts that are tilled with humility and repentance are seasoned properly to receive those spiritual seeds. When we are open to receive God's grace, acknowledging our desperate need for Him, the light of His Son streams down, the richness of truth fills up, and our lives sprout up in beautiful display of His magnificent handiwork.

This morning, ask God to tend to the soil of your soul. Then watch in wonder the beautiful growth God will bring to your life.

It was already planted in good soil and had plenty of water so it could grow into a splendid vine and produce rich leaves and luscious fruit.
EZEKIEL 17:8 NLT

Seasoned

Your speech should always be gracious,
seasoned with salt, so that you may know
how you should answer each person.
Colossians 4:6 HCSB

You've been working on the stew for hours and have followed the recipe exactly as prescribed. But as you dip the spoon into the promising liquid and take a sip, you're taken aback. Despite the vivid color and even aroma, the soup base itself is far too bland for your liking. So you break out even more spices, adding some fresh-cut basil, ground cumin, and a little curry for good measure. Then you cap off your seasoning frenzy with a healthy dose of salt and black pepper. Swirling it into the liquid, you hope for the best and give it another taste. *Ah...perfection!* You smile. Now the look, smell, and taste all work together to make your stew a hall-of-fame winner for your family.

God says that more than just good soups need seasoning. Our lives require even more. It's one thing to say we are Christians and give the appearance of being good, moral, upstanding people. But without a real relationship with the Creator, our lives are bland, watered down, and without the power needed to please God or give others a taste of what He's like. So God uses trials and difficulties to season our souls, enriching the depth of our life's flavor as we learn to depend solely on Him for strength, forgiveness, righteousness, and hope. His spice blend is different for each of us, but it always produces His desired effect.

When you yield to the Master Chef, your life—struggles and triumphs—will produce a depth of character that can truly feed and nourish others with God's goodness. As you prepare for the day, ask God to season your conversations with His grace and deepen your taste and experience of His love.

You are the salt of the earth.
But if the salt should lose its taste,
how can it be made salty?
MATTHEW 5:13 HCSB

FLYING HIGH

[God] sent from above, He took me,
He drew me out of many waters....
He brought me forth also into a large place;
He delivered me, because He delighted in me.
PSALM 18:16,19 KJV

At least you don't panic at the thought of flying. But now that you're thousands of feet in the air in the middle of a violent thunderstorm, there's a knot in your stomach. Instinctively you tighten your seatbelt and peer out your small porthole window, willing the plane to land safely. Instead, you're amazed by the density of thick, dark clouds whirling past your window at breakneck speed. You understand there's nothing you can do to save yourself. You'll have to trust the pilot you can't see and the plane with mechanisms you can't fully understand. After a series of tumultuous turns and sudden drops, you catch the faint sight of blue and yellow runway lights. Then you hear the landing gear engage. Before you know it, the plane has touched down and come to a stop. At last you can exhale, giving thanks to the pilot and God for His grace.

It's uncanny how similar our lives are to airplane rides. We may think we're in control of where we're going and how we get there, but there are some serious limits to what God enables us to do. As the true Pilot, He directs our course and keeps us safe. He can see into the dark places and turbulent air masses with ease. No matter how scary it may seem and how many surprise bumps we experience, we can still soar through life with true peace when our lives are completely in His loving, capable hands.

This morning, don't let panic steal your joy. Remember that if you have chosen God as your Pilot, you will reach His destination for you safely. You are free to enjoy the view and comfort those around you who don't yet fly with God's higher perspective.

People may make plans in their minds,
but the LORD decides what they will do.
PROVERBS 16:9 NCV

SUN-KISSED SOULS

In the heavens God has pitched a tent for the sun....
It rises at one end of the heavens and makes its circuit
to the other; nothing is deprived of its warmth.

PSALM 19:4–6 NIV

It looks to be a blustery day today as you head outside, determined to take a morning walk. Dressed in gloves and what you thought would be warm pants, you quickly acknowledge the miscalculation. Coldness like liquid seeps through your clothes, chilling your skin, sending shivers all over. Goosebumps spring up on your arms and legs despite your determined pace. Eventually, even your bones revolt as a cold-induced rigor mortis starts to set in. Defeated, you start to turn around when a miracle happens. Like the waters of the Red Sea, overhead clouds blow apart, revealing beautiful blue skies beyond. Better yet, the sun in all its golden glory steps out of hiding and showers your body with unbelievable warmth. The painful chill melts under its glow, and your clothes and skin absorb the welcome warmth. Turning back in the right direction, you resume your pace, grateful for the gift that is God's sun.

Can you imagine what our world would be like without warmth? It's one of those wonders we can't live without yet often overlook in our day-to-day lives. Love functions in a similar way. The pleasure of true fellowship and communion with others fills our hearts with life-giving warmth. But even our earthly relationships are rays of hope sent from above. The true source of love and light and eternal warmth comes from the Author of it all. His presence in and through us brings meaning, hope, and the energy needed to persevere through whatever He lays before us.

This morning, soak in God's presence and love for you. Let it wash you in a warmth that you can share with everyone God brings across your path today.

When we arrived in Jerusalem,
the believers welcomed us warmly.
ACTS 21:17 GNT

EXPRESSIONS

The LORD make His face shine on you,
and be gracious to you; the LORD lift up
His countenance on you, and give you peace.
NUMBERS 6:25–26 NASB

You're already nervous. Though you feel confident about your resume and your ability to do the job, you just didn't have a good feeling about the first round of interviews. You sat up straight and tall, but the interviewer rarely looked up from the paper. When you attempted to answer questions, his arms remained crossed, face flat—stern even. The whole affair seemed so tense you were shocked when they called you back for a second interview. Then the CEO walked in with a strong stride and serious expression. You sensed your doom approaching. But suddenly, a great big smile stretched across his face, and he reached out his hand in greeting. "I know you," he said with a grin, and then explained that he had grown up in the same class as your dad. His tone was casual, his expressions positive, and you could feel the pressure ease. It was okay to be yourself, to communicate clearly and confidently without fear of rejection.

For some people, approaching God in prayer is like an uncomfortable interview. They picture Him stark and angry, brows furrowed, presence demanding. No wonder they reserve prayer for emergency situations. But God is not that way. He declares every ounce of anger toward sin stopped at the cross of Christ. He knows us, His beloved children. We are not only forgiven but also cherished. God's expression toward us is full of light and love; the depths of who we are always meets with His smile.

When you talk to God this morning, imagine the best expression of joy you've ever seen. Then multiply the effect in your mind, and marvel that God's face shines on you today!

The eyes of the Lord are over the righteous, and His ears are open unto their prayers.
I PETER 3:12 KJV

ANCHORS AWAY

Stay grounded and steady in that bond of trust,
constantly tuned in to the Message,
careful not to be distracted or diverted.
COLOSSIANS 1:22 THE MESSAGE

The skies were the deepest blue, but the crystal-clear ocean waters gleamed aquamarine in the warm sunlight. Sitting atop your small boat, you can clearly see the brilliant colors in the coral reef below, the promise of exotic fish and maybe a sea turtle or two tempting you to dive beneath the surface. Slipping into the cool water, you secure your mask and snorkel, ensuring a tight fit. Then you take off, slowly paddling as you float on the surface looking into all the beauty around and below you. Curiosity beckons you forward, but after a while, the thought dawns: *Did I drop anchor?* In a slight panic, you look upward in search of your boat. Finally you see it far in the distance. Switching gears, you swim freestyle and full throttle to the one place you never meant to veer far from.

Experienced snorkelers and scuba divers know the importance of dropping anchor and always staying within sight of the boat. And God's children would do well to apply the same principle in the spiritual realm. The world around us often shines brightly with beautiful attractions. Many of them are given for us to explore, but when we let them lure us away from the foundational truth of God and His Word, we discover danger in what once seemed benign or even beautiful. God repeats the theme throughout His Word: We are to keep our relationship with Him anchored in His Word. Only then can we safely navigate the life-waters of this world.

Where do you stand this morning? Are you anchored securely in God, your relationship rightly tied to His saving grace? Or have you drifted away from center? Without delay, ask God to direct you toward His love and truth this day.

Do not let me wander from Your commandments.
Your word I have treasured in my heart.
PSALM 119:10–11 NASB

BATTLE CRY

Let petitions and praises shape your worries into prayers,
letting God know your concerns.
PHILIPPIANS 4:6 THE MESSAGE

Cup of coffee in one hand, plate of buttered toast and egg in the other, you sit down at the table for an early morning breakfast and a quick look at the news. You grab the remote and flip to the channel where you usually find reliable information, only to discover yet another "Breaking News" banner trailing across the screen. As you listen for details behind the latest horrifying story, the spirit inside you recoils at the tragedy. There's so much trouble and heartache in the world, you muse, your sunshine-filled morning now veiled in sadness. With a troubled heart, you press the remote and turn off the TV.

We often feel powerless when we learn of the tremendous pain experienced by people across the world. But God's people aren't powerless. God has given each of us the most potent weapon in the entire world: prayer. Not the simple "saying grace" kind of conversation with God we relegate to meals, but meaty, heartfelt, down-in-the-trenches intercession for our loved ones and all the lost people we've never even met. Down on your knees lifting up others' needs for healing, salvation, and restoration, you access all of heaven's power and pour it out on people and places only God can touch. You are a mighty warrior, valiantly fighting against all the unseen forces of evil in the world, and effecting greater change kneeling beside your couch than you ever could do outside your doors.

This morning, don't despair over evil in the world. Instead, fight with all your energy through the powerful gift of prayer. Our God hears our cry, and He is mighty to save.

*I'm standing my ground, G*OD*,*
shouting for help, at my prayers
every morning, on my knees each daybreak.
PSALM 88:13 THE MESSAGE

GOLDEN GOODNESS

How sweet your words taste to me;
they are sweeter than honey.
PSALM 119:103 NLT

Would you travel 55,000 miles for a pound of honey? Probably not. But a nest of foraging honey bees would put in that kind of work to produce the sweet treat. Each forager bee leaves the hive daily to collect nectar from at least one hundred flowers before returning home. As they suck out the nectar from each flower, they safely store it in a separate stomach—the one reserved just for honey. With their honey tummies full, they fly back to the hive and deposit their golden goodness into hexagonal-shaped honeycomb chambers, capping them with a layer of wax when full. In this way, they have plenty of food stored up for future seasons when winter looms and blooms are scarce. Altogether, it takes more than five hundred bees visiting more than two million flowers to create one pound of honey.

Would you ever have imagined how much work went into that tiny teaspoon of honey you dab on your toast or swirl in your tea? But put it straight on your tongue and you know it's a true golden treasure, the kind of treat only God could mastermind.

It's no wonder, then, that the Psalmist compares God's Word to the sweetness of honey. The Bible you hold in your hands is no ordinary book. It is a miracle of God, the single sweet message of saving grace spoken by God through the pens of ordinary people through the course of more than a thousand years. His labor of love satisfies our souls in a way no other earthly pleasure ever could. This morning, savor the sweetness of God's truth and love, and thank Him for all the extravagant measures He took to bring the truth to your heart.

The laws of the LORD are true;...
They are sweeter than honey,
even honey dripping from the comb.
PSALM 19:9–10 NLT

JUMP IN

The God of old is your dwelling place,
and underneath are the everlasting arms.
DEUTERONOMY 33:27 HCSB

The toddler stood precariously near the edge of the pool, wistfully looking at her father just a few feet away. His arms outstretched, he beckoned his child to jump into his arms. Eyes darted from father to the ever-so-deep water in which he stood. One miscalculation and she might drown, she worried. Growing desperate, she reached out her own arms, leaning forward, hoping he would pick her up off the edge. But it wasn't his plan. Instead, he called her by name. Encouraged her to trust him. And then he patiently waited...until she jumped straight into his arms. Heart beating wildly, the little girl found herself instantly against his chest. The waters around her were indeed deep, but he was taller, stronger. She was safe and warm, right where she wanted to be.

As one observing the situation, it's easy to

understand the girl's fears but also the father's heart. Though she felt her world was on the brink of extinction, he knew far better. He was teaching her to trust. And so it is when God calls us to Himself. Though our trials in life seem inevitably devastating, He invites us to trust and jump into His arms. He is not satisfied with simple half-hearted assent or theoretical trust. He wants full heart, mind, and body trust with complete abandon into His reliable grace and goodness. When we finally leap, we find there is no place better than His warm and certain embrace.

Today, which areas in your life are keeping you sidelined on the edge of full trust? Talk to God in prayer, and take a leap into His loving arms. Discover the place of peace where you've always wanted to be.

You will feel safe because there is hope;
you will look around and rest in safety.
JOB 11:18 NCV

MEMORY MARKERS

Don't forget the things you have seen.
Don't forget them as long as you live,
but teach them to your children and grandchildren.

DEUTERONOMY 4:9 NCV

It's raining outside, and your calendar is clear. Unused to finding empty time on your hands, you are wondering what to do with your day. Then your eyes rest on the bookshelf in the corner, the one where you keep your family's treasures—the trinkets and photos that tell stories of love and laughter throughout the years. *I haven't looked at these albums in ages*, you muse as you wander over and select one from the shelf. Sitting down, you slowly turn the pages and with it the hands of time as your mind remembers the moments. Hours go by. Lost in remembrance, your soul has found shelter in the world of grace in which you and your family have grown.

It's so easy to lose sight of the gifts in the middle of the day's madness, but hindsight paints the picture of purpose and beauty you couldn't always catch in the moment. God knows our propensity to overlook or even forget His tiny gifts of love tucked into day-to-day busyness. It's why He instructed the people of Israel to set up memorial stones by the Jordan River, so they could remember all the mercies that had led them across. And He loves it when His children do the same, taking time to sit still and reflect on God's amazing faithfulness before the next obligation overtakes them. And be encouraged to record your memories on paper, stones, or whatever helps you keep His hope and grace not on some forgotten bookshelf, but on the forefront of your mind.

This morning, recount His faithfulness and revel in His history of goodness toward you and those you love. Give thanks and celebrate His powerful presence through all the days of your life.

In the future, when your children
ask what these stones mean to you,
you will tell them....These stones will always
remind the people of Israel of what happened here.
JOSHUA 4:6–7 GNT

ALWAYS HOME

Do you not know that your body is a temple of
the Holy Spirit within you, which you have from God,
and that you are not your own?
I CORINTHIANS 6:19 NRSV

Home. It's the one, comfortable place in the whole wide world where you can be the real you. Kick off your shoes and snuggle on the sofa with a really good read. Or rummage through the fridge or pantry to find the food that pleases you most. And while chores might not be the most relaxing or appealing part of home ownership, you don't mind so much because you reap the reward of a well-kept home. You decorate it, maintain it, and appreciate it because it not only tells your story in a unique way, but it's also a place to welcome those you love.

Homes must be special to God, too, because He left heaven to look for one. In the Old Testament, we see that God first walked alongside His people in a beautiful garden. Longing to be even closer, He instructed His people to build a beautiful tent so He could live right in the middle of them. Wherever they traveled, they took the tent—and God's presence—with them. Later, David and his son Solomon built a glorious temple. But it, too, wasn't quite home enough for God.

When Jesus paid for our sins on the cross, the veil of separation between us and God was torn. And for all who invite Him in, God has come to make His holy home inside our hearts. Whether we're awake or asleep, rejoicing or weeping, questioning or believing, God is at work inside our lives, making Himself a home that reflects His presence.

This morning, thank God that you are a walking, talking miracle of grace as God's presence goes with you in all that you do. Before you, behind you, beside you, and now in you, God has you completely covered by His love.

In him the whole structure is joined together and grows into a holy temple in the Lord.
EPHESIANS 2:21 NRSV

IRON IT OUT

You have been grieved by various trials,
that the genuineness of your faith…
may be found to praise, honor, and glory
at the revelation of Jesus Christ.
I PETER 1:6–7 NKJV

It's amazing what happens when you launder linen. It looks so different than it did when it was hanging so crisp and neat on the store rack. After one washing, that tablecloth has an entirely new texture, and not a desirable one. Millions of mountain ridges have risen over its landscape, and you consider scrapping the entire fabric for something easier to manage. But remembering your budget, you decide to pull out the iron and let it do its magic.

The steam builds. When the temperature is right, you test it to make sure it will have the desired effect. Then you press in, letting the heat and pressure flatten the peaks into a smooth, wide plane, pulling and straightening across the ironing board. Eventually, you realize the restoration process is complete. You have a crisp, clean cover now fit for a king's table.

In a similar way, God has declared us fit for royal dwellings. We have been chosen, forgiven, and loved fully by God. But our lives aren't wrinkle-free yet. Even though we have been laundered by Christ and declared clean in God's sight, we still contend with the wrinkles of a sin nature—that propensity to resist God's ways. But He doesn't toss us out. Instead, He allows the heat and pressure of day-to-day trials to iron out the kinks that keep us from our God-ordained destiny. We are meant for royalty, and He is at work in our lives ironing out the rough edges so we might reflect His glory.

This morning, you may feel the pull and pain of life lived in this world. Don't lose hope. Instead, give thanks that God is at work, turning your life into a beautiful covering for His grace.

Your steadfastness and faith during all your persecutions and the afflictions…is intended to make you worthy of the kingdom of God.
II THESSALONIANS 1:4–5 NRSV

PITCHER PERFECT

God has poured out His love to fill our hearts.
ROMANS 5:5 NCV

It was a curious ceramic cylinder sitting in a bucket of water. It seemed to have no purpose at all, no discernible holes or spouts springing from its side. It just boasted one, tall handle that begged lifting. Wondering why anyone would make such an unconventional contraption, you oblige your query by lifting it up and out of the water. And then it starts to pour. Secret holes on the underside allowed the bucket to fill with water until it was full. Now that you are carrying it about, it's emptying itself through those same portholes, watering whatever and wherever you walk with it. Once the water is gone, you simply return it to the bucket, where it fills up once again.

You, child of God, are like that curious watering jar. What you may have felt are weaknesses in your past—painful struggles you'd rather not remember—are the holes in your soul through which God's healing love seeps in. When we sit in His presence, we can't help but soak in His life-giving grace. We were actually designed to hold it inside. But God ordains those portholes for other purposes, too. Not only do life's difficulties draw us closer to Him, but He also intends to use them to bring comfort and nourishment to others in the world.

When God lifts you out of your comfort zone, don't panic or try to plug up the cracks. You were made for this! Instead, let the truth of God's love and grace pour through you into the wilting world around you, knowing that you are being carried in the greatest of hands.

Their buckets will brim with water,
their seed will spread life everywhere.
NUMBERS 24:7 THE MESSAGE

GONE FISHING

Jesus called out to them, "Come, follow Me!
And I will make you fishermen for the souls of men!"
MARK 1:17 TLB

You've always wanted to try it, and now that you're on vacation with your little ones and the weather is right, you decide to give it a go. So you head to the tackle shop with your kids in tow and try to act like you know exactly what you're doing. Unfortunately, you discover an umpteen number of fishing-rod options, along with an entire wall of lures and jigs that all promise success. Of course, there's always the live bait—which seems to be of particular interest to your crew. So you purchase the day's entertainment, praying that at least one person will catch something.

As you stand on the lake's shore, you recognize some potential pitfalls—weeds to the left and low-hanging branches to the right. But everyone is chomping at the bit to get their big worms on small hooks. So you get started. Though lines tangle and minnows steal the bait, eventually each kid catches a fish about the size of his or her small hands. You feel grateful for the success and the memories.

Jesus compared faith sharing with fishing. Of course, He was talking to some real-life fishermen who could easily understand the connection, but the analogy isn't lost on us either. Sharing our faith can be daunting, but God tells us not to worry. Witnessing isn't setting a hook. It's sharing your story. The lure to hearers is actually God's Spirit, who brings in the catch when He's ready. We simply make the effort to drop a line by talking to others about what God has done. Today, ask God to help you fish for people. Ask Him to place on your heart those who need to hear His encouraging words and bait your conversation with the beauty of God's love.

> *Jesus said to them, "Come with Me....*
> *I'll show you how to catch men and women*
> *instead of perch and bass."*
> MATTHEW 4:19 THE MESSAGE

SANDCASTLES

Everyone who hears these words of Mine
and acts on them will be like a sensible man
who built his house on the rock.
MATTHEW 7:24 HCSB

You're aware of the sun moving toward its peak overhead. There will be no sunburn on your watch. So you pick up the funny castle-shaped bucket and flimsy green plastic spade and get to work helping your kids finish their sandcastle. Before long, though, you feel the sweat coming on—along with your more perfectionistic urges. "We need a deeper moat and higher walls," you hear yourself say. "Keep the turrets nice and trim by adding wetter sand. And how about we find some shells and seaweed for decoration?" It's as if some alien force has put you under its power. *Why on earth am I putting so much effort into something the surf will wash away in minutes?* you wonder.

And then you think again. It's not so different from real life, really. We often spend all our mental and physical energy trying to build a successful life: the right education with the best grades, the most lucrative career, the best-decorated house, the right car, the most lavish vacations. Yet somewhere in the middle of the madness, we know those investments won't yield the lasting pleasure our hearts long for. And Jesus confirms our suspicions. He likens those pursuits to building castles in the sand. Instead, He instructs us to build our lives on the rock—God Himself. He invites us to put down our plastic shovels and move to the only solid ground that brings true joy and won't be washed away by the rising tide of adversity.

Today, will you settle for building sandcastles, or will you seek firmer ground? Commit your decisions, your dreams, and your heart to the Lord, and let Him show you the best way to build your life in Him.

Store up your treasures in heaven, where moths and rust cannot destroy them, and thieves cannot break in and steal them.
MATTHEW 6:20 CEV

In *a* Nutshell

I pray that Christ Jesus and the church will forever bring praise to God. His power at work in us can do far more than we dare ask or imagine.

EPHESIANS 3:20–21 CEV

To everyone else, it was just a legume, a soil-dweller not destined for anything fancy. Peanuts, after all, had been enjoyed for hundreds of years for what they were. But young George Washington Carver saw something more. It started with just a handful of peanut recipes and uses he discovered when applying his past experience with and knowledge of plants. But soon more ideas sprouted, and the list of applications grew. From one little peanut, Dr. Carver produced more than three hundred highly useful, versatile, and affordable products that helped sustain a strained and struggling farming economy in the South.

Dr. Carver taught a life lesson far greater than even his botanist contributions—recognizing that potential depends on our perspective. Had he acquiesced to culture and even history, he would have never pushed to see just how far that little peanut could go. You, child of God, might feel like life is just too crazy complicated, too overwhelming, or even too boring to bring any change into this world. In a nutshell, you have something in common with those peanuts. But your perspective on this day is the eternal game changer. Are you going to see yourself as only one of six billion people in this world without any real power to contribute something greater? Or will you look at your core component—the God of this universe—who declares you to be of infinite worth? If you dare to believe, you open yourself to all the potential God has packed into the person you are.

Today, let God broaden your perspective of His power working through your unique gifts and abilities. Dare to dream big, and ask Him to multiply His gifts as He pours out His grace through you today.

"If I can?" Jesus asked.
"Anything is possible if you have faith."
MARK 9:23 TLB

CURTAIN CALL

*O send out Your light and Your truth,
let them lead me.*
PSALM 43:3 NASB

The room is shrouded in darkness. Furniture silhouettes in varying shades of gray peek out from the shadows beyond your bed, but you are ready to get up and get the day started. You know from your clock the sun must be up, but your blackout drapes are doing their job, and not a peek of light slips past them. So you shuffle over to the wall of curtains on the far side of the room, being careful not to trip on anything along the way, and begin pushing apart the panels of fabric. Instantly, light floods the room, shadows vanish, color springs to life, and the beauty that had been in darkness now gleams with fresh vitality.

Our problem is, we often have blackout drapes of a different kind blocking the portals of our souls. When we indulge insecurity, shame, or regret, we find ourselves fumbling around in the shadows. But God who gives us the sun also gives us His Son—the One who radiates light and hope into every corner of our minds and lives. When we risk authentic vulnerability in His presence and allow His Spirit to push back the drapes we have used to hide our unseemly side, His beautiful light rushes in and brings life and color to our souls.

What area of your life needs God's glorious truth and light today? You are always safe in your Father's presence. Present yourself to Him in all honesty this morning and experience the rush of joy and freedom that can only come when you open yourself up fully to God's love.

In Him was life,
and the life was the Light of men.
JOHN 1:4 NASB

The Sovereign LORD has given me
His words of wisdom, so that I
know how to comfort the weary.
Morning by morning He wakens me
and opens my understanding to His will.

ISAIAH 50:4 NLT

If I ride the wings of the morning,

if I dwell by the farthest oceans,

even there Your hand will guide me,

and Your strength will support me.

PSALM 139:9–10 NLT

Swiftly dodging between scattering gamblers, he came upon the two guards quicker than they were able to react. With a crunch and a snap, the two guards dropped to the floor and began to slowly crawl away, nursing their wounds.

Cole took a slow, deliberate step toward the target and unholstered his pistol. The Modosian recoiled reflexively, pressing his back deep into the soft leather chair.

Cole offered a half smile. "You can thank me later."

Confusion flashed on the Modosian's face.

With a short draw back and a thunderous strike, Cole pistol-whipped the Modosian square on the side of the head, and he slumped down, unconscious, into his chair.

"It's done," Cole said, the message circulating through the squad's earpieces. "Prep for extraction."

Cole holstered his pistol, produced a pair of cuffs from his belt, and slapped them on the Modosian's wrists.

"Hey, golden boy," a man's voice said, clear amid the chaos.

Cole froze. As he turned slowly to face the voice, the lights flickered back on.

Cole was right to feel uneasy about the mission.

The man stood up from the table. "It's been a while."

The commotion outside had started simply enough. When the lights went out, the patrons scrambled. Some panicked and ran, some hid under the tables, and others tried to make off with whatever chips they could grab. It got a lot less simple once casino security got wind of what was happening.

At least a dozen security personnel currently clogged the doorway to the main floor. Half were ushering people out, and the other half were firing at Ram. Ram hated that other half.

He was ducked down behind a table and could only pop his head out every now and then to get a few shots off in an effort to hold them back. Gregor was doing what he could to help, but that amounted to little more than some suppressive fire. With so many civilians rushing about, he couldn't risk taking any direct shots.

Cole hadn't yet reappeared from the private room, and too much time had passed since he'd said the job was done. From Ram's current position, he couldn't even see the room without losing his head.

"Hey, kid," he shouted to Gregor. "Can you see Cole?"

Gregor looked to the doorway and the lit room beyond. "I can't see him."

"Cole," Ram yelled into the comm. "We could actually kinda use a hand out here. It would seem security has taken exception to our presence."

Nothing.

"Sol," Ram said. "Have you got eyes on?"

"Nah, mate," Sol said, clearly out of breath as he was running. "I'm a little busy with some friends of me own. I'm coming to you."

"Terrific." There was only one thing to do. Ram grabbed two grenades off his belt, primed them, and lobbed them toward the bases of a pair of statues near the entrance. They landed just right, as always. The two closely timed explosions caused the statues to come crashing down across the entryway, blocking the advancement of the security team. It may have also crushed a few of them, but that wasn't something Ram could be concerned with right now.

Cole started toward the man standing at the end of the table. He wasn't even all the way through the first step when the two guards at the man's side, having seen what happened to the other pair of bodyguards, promptly ran for it.

The man looked after them and laughed. "I guess you really do get what you pay for."

Cole slowed his advance, still silent, getting a closer look at the man in the dim light to confirm his worst fears.

"After all these years, you have nothing to say to me?"

Cole stopped and steadied himself. "Tobias, you're supposed to be d—"

"Dead?" Tobias said, cutting him off. "Funny how that works out sometimes."

Tobias stepped away from the table and started walking toward Cole.

"You know, you don't look any different," he said and then motioned to the limp body of the Modosian. "Though you do seem to be doing things a bit differently these days."

Tobias stopped in front of Cole, who remained frozen in place. He reached down and snatched Cole's pistol out of his holster. He then turned it about and presented it to Cole, handle first.

"Go on then. Why not have another *stab* at it?" Tobias said, goading Cole into action.

No action came. Cole just stared into Tobias's eyes, the same eyes that had haunted him for the last fifteen years. He couldn't process what was happening.

Tobias sighed. "No? Really?"

In an instant, Tobias spun the pistol around, pressed it firmly into the side of the Modosian's head, and pulled the trigger. Blood sprayed across the table.

Tobias turned the gun back around and presented it to Cole. "How about now?"

Cole's ears were ringing from the shot. He looked back and forth between the crumpled body of the Modosian and Tobias. His legs felt like lead.

The thud from the explosions outside echoed into the room.

Tobias let the gun fall to the floor.

"No? Well, all right, I guess we'll have to do the other thing then, won't we?" He pulled his hands back, then thrust them forward toward Cole. The force of the invisible blast knocked him clear across the room into a wall. Without wasting another second, Tobias ran for it.

"What the bloody hell is going on?" Sol shouted. He'd burst through a maintenance door just as Ram had brought the statues down. "Where's Cole?"

"Still in there," Ram said over the din, pointing to the private rooms. He was out of cover now. The statues had done their job of slowing up security.

"Uh, guys?" Gregor said from above.

"What?" they both replied.

"Who's that?" he asked, pointing to the lone figure running from the private room.

Ram's and Sol's gazes followed Gregor's outstretched arm to see a man running down the long hallway.

"Beats me," Ram said, puzzled. "Probably just a civilian."

"What's that about then?" Sol questioned as he saw Cole burst out of the room in pursuit.

"I dunno. I thought he said he got the guy," Ram said.

"Should we follow?" Gregor asked, already moving in that direction.

"I'm sure he's got it," said Sol, unholstering his pistol.

"Yeah," Ram said, heading toward the hallway. "I'm sure he's fine."

"Are you guys freaking kidding me?" Cole shouted into the comm as he ran full tilt down the hallway. That was all the prompting they needed.

Gregor had the worst of it trying to catch up. The whole upper floor was in the middle of extensive renovations, and the walkway to the outside was cluttered with boxes and equipment. He tripped at least three times, but when he eventually made it, the scene was one he hadn't expected.

With the last sunlight disappearing over the vast cityscape behind him, Tobias stood with his back to the open air and his hands held out to his sides in surrender. The balcony plaza had cleared in seconds after they had arrived. It was now just the five of them. Cole looked around and saw Gregor up on the balcony, his rifle trained on the confrontation.

"Do you have a shot?" Cole asked.

"I-I do," Gregor replied, flustered. "I have a shot, but I don't—"

"Take it," Cole said.

"What? I can't. He's not"

"Found your balls at last, have you, Cole?" Tobias called out. "It's only taken twenty years."

Tobias's words hung in the air, faint screams from elsewhere in the casino drifted on the wind.

"Take it, Gregor," Cole said sternly.

Gregor didn't know what to do. "Sir, he's an unauthorized—"

"Take the damn shot," Cole yelled, glaring up at Gregor from below.

The shot rang out and echoed across the plaza.

The moments after it was fired seemed to drag on for an age as the shot missed and flew harmlessly wide right. Tobias, from his perch on the edge of the balcony, laughed, shrugged, and then stepped backward into the ether.

"Damn it," Cole shouted as he ran to the edge. What greeted him made his blood boil.

Twenty meters or so below the lip of the balcony hovered a ship. It was medium-sized, probably a civilian model, and crouched on its roof was Tobias. He stood slowly and stared down Cole as the wind ripped furiously at his clothes. The ship began to slowly glide away into the night and before long was gone from sight entirely.

All that could be heard now was the faint rustling of leaves from the many trees that lined the plaza and the distant screams of casino-goers who didn't realize the crisis was over. Cole sighed and backed away from the edge. "Sol, bring the ship around," he said quietly.

"Already on its way."

Cole turned and pointed up at Gregor. "You," he said, far too calm for the situation. "Down here. Now."

Gregor was gone before Cole had even finished speaking.

The *Havok* came to rest hovering just near the edge of the plaza, the ramp appearing from its shimmering mass. Without a word, Ram and Sol made their way up.

"Sol, get me a fix on that ship. I want to know where it's headed," Cole said as Sol passed him.

Cole lingered on the ramp. Gregor was nowhere to be seen.

The loud repeated cracking of gunfire drew Cole's attention, and he looked up to see Gregor running full tilt down the corridor toward the ship with at least twenty security personnel in tow.

"Hey, look at him go," said Ram over the comm, doing his best to stifle a chuckle.

"A little help would be nice," Gregor shouted, firing a pistol blindly over his shoulder as he ran.

In no time at all shots rang out from the belly of the *Havok*, thinning the pursuing herd a little.

Not much, but enough.

Gregor leaped for the ramp and only just made it. Cole caught his arm and hauled him aboard in one swift motion.

"Thank you, sir," Gregor said, deeply out of breath.

"Don't thank me yet," Cole said.

Gregor scrambled to his feet and ran into the belly of the ship.

Cole turned to face the guards as the *Havok* began to drift away from the balcony and gave them a short, sharp salute before hitting the button to close up the ramp and heading inside.

As he came into the cockpit, Cole saw Sol and Ram both pouring over the displays. "Tell me you've got him."

Sol pushed back from the screen and let out a sigh of defeat. "He's gone. We lost visual, and the scanners aren't getting anything."

A yell escaped Cole's throat as he slammed his fist into a nearby panel. The lights in the cockpit flickered.

"Hey, steady," said Sol, concerned for the welfare of his ship.

"Cole," Ram said, concern evident in his voice. "Who was that?"

Unconsciously Cole ran his fingers down the large scar that ran the length of his forearm, their tips caught on a glinting piece of metal embedded in his flesh.

"A ghost."

TWO

THE MOOD ON the trip home was tense. Cole had mostly kept to himself. In truth, he'd barely spoken to anyone. When Gregor walked into the main hold, there he was, still sitting there, glass in hand. Tentatively, Gregor approached him. "Sir?"

Cole took a sip.

"I-I'm sorry," Gregor said. "I should . . ."

Another sip.

Gregor may have been young, but he knew there were times when someone didn't want to be spoken to. This was one of those times. Conceding, he joined Ram and Sol who sat around a table in the far corner of the hold.

"Might want to give that some time, kid," Ram said, looking over his shoulder at Cole.

Gregor leaned forward on the table. "So, who was that back there?"

"Just leave it, kid," Ram said.

"I'm serious, who was he?"

"No idea. Never seen 'im before," Sol said, shrugging.

"Me either," Ram said. "Look, I'm sure Cole will tell us when he's ready."

Sol laughed. "Shit, I don't know if I've got *that* long."

They sat in silence for a few moments, but Gregor was still fidgeting. He had a suspicion about the man. "Was he a Conduit?"

Ram rolled his eyes. "Here we go."

"A Condy?" Sol said with a laugh. "I dunno. Could have been. We haven't seen one for a while."

"I only ask because how else could he have survived that fall?"

"The kid has a point," Ram said, becoming a bit more interested in the conversation. "That *was* quite a jump."

Sol nodded in agreement.

Feeling a bit more confident in his assertion, Gregor pressed on. "Also, code says that the only condition under which a squad leader can go off mission to apprehend or eliminate a non-mission-critical target is if said target is a Conduit, and only if they're threatening the safety of the general populace."

Ram and Sol just stared at each other before the former broke out laughing. "Oh no," said Sol, shaking his head. "He's a reader."

Not wanting to let it go, Gregor continued. "But he wasn't."

"I'm lost. Who wasn't *what*?" Ram said, having finally pulled himself together.

"The man, he wasn't threatening anyone," Gregor said. "He was just a man, and Cole was the one chasing him. We knew nothing about him."

"He would have had a reason," Sol said.

"Code also says that any and all mission changes are to be confirmed with command and then presented to the squad before any action is taken," Gregor said, his voice rising in volume. He was all in on this now.

"Kid, you don't—" Ram said, trying to quiet him down.

"All I'm saying is that, as far as I knew, he was ordering me to kill an unarmed civilian who presented no apparent threat. I couldn't act on that information. I just cou—"

Smash.

The trio turned to follow the noise and saw Cole was no longer at the bar. The glass from which he had been sipping was no longer in his hand. It was now mostly on the floor, though some had bounced onto a nearby shelf.

"Are you saying you missed on purpose?"

They were the first words Cole had spoken in hours.

Gregor got up from the table and stood his ground. "Respectfully, sir"—he regretted the choice almost immediately—"I am. Perhaps if you had followed protocol, I—"

"Protocol?" Cole said as he advanced on Gregor.

"Oh boy," Ram said positioning himself between the two. "Easy, Cole, it's not worth it."

Ram had to fight to keep Cole in front of him.

"This is *not* the academy, kid," Cole shouted, pointing at Gregor over Ram's shoulder. "You are on this ship to follow *my* orders, not your damn books."

Ram had had enough. He shoved Cole hard enough to finally separate them. "Leave it—" and before Gregor could do anything, Ram turned to him"—and you sit the *hell* down."

As Cole backed off and turned to walk out of the hold, Ram in tow, Sol got up to follow.

Ram waved him off. "I've got this one," he said. "It's my turn anyway."

Cole fumbled at the door controls to his quarters; he was sure he'd hit the right button at least three times. With a loud and deliberate sigh, Ram reached over his shoulder and hit the right one, which was on an entirely different panel, and guided Cole inside.

"OK," Ram said. "What the hell was that?"

"What was what?"

Ram motioned to the main hold. "*That.*"

"A long story," Cole said, sitting down on the edge of his bed.

"I've got time."

Ram's offer was met with silence.

He could tell he wasn't going to get this story now, so he let it slide. "All right, well you—"

"I was too hard on him, wasn't I?" Cole said, his face falling into his hands.

"He got some of his own in there, but yeah, you were a bit of an asshole," Ram said.

Cole started to get back up but was promptly pushed back down by Ram. "Look, I'll handle him. You should call Liv, let her know you're OK."

"I don't want her to see me like this," Cole said. "She's seen it enough."

"Then where's your stuff?" Ram asked.

"My what?" Cole asked before realizing what he meant. "Oh, uh, top drawer?"

Ram walked over, retrieved a small packet from the drawer, and tore it open to reveal a small capsule. He pressed it into Cole's arm and then threw it in the bin.

"Give it some time to kick in," Ram said, "and then call her."

It was some time before Cole slumped into the chair in front of the vidcom and pressed the call button. Got it first go, even. He felt a smile creep onto his face as the image of his wife flickered in through the static.

"Did I wake you?" Cole said.

"No, no, perfect timing," Olivia said.

One thing Cole knew about his wife was that even if it had been the worst possible time to call, she'd never let it show. Cole, on the other hand, wasn't so adept at hiding things.

"What's wrong?" Olivia asked, picking up on it immediately.

"You know I can't say, Liv."

"I know."

The silence was backed by the soft whisper of the static from the long-distance vid call. The smile had faded from Olivia's face, and Cole could see a change in subject was in order.

"Zara home?" Cole said, asking after his daughter.

"You just missed her."

"Damn," said Cole. "Wait, it wasn't a boy, was it?"

"It was."

"Do I need to kick his ass when I get back?" Cole said, playing the role of overprotective father to a tee.

"He seems harmless," Olivia said, her smile returning.

"You used to think I was harmless."

"Fair point."

They laughed.

"You know, it's been good for her having you home more lately," Olivia said. "She's actually talking to people now."

Cole sat back in his chair and sighed, and he saw Olivia's expression drop yet again. Clearly, his had changed too, and she knew something was up. He wouldn't be able to keep this from her, and they both knew it.

"Something's—" he shifted uneasily in his chair "—something's come up."

Olivia had heard those three words more times than she could count, though this time they seemed especially loaded. "Cole, no."

"It won't take long," Cole said. He was on the back foot quicker than usual; something really *was* wrong. "Couple of weeks—"

"Cole, the last 'couple of weeks' ended up—"

"Three weeks. Three weeks max, I promise."

She knew that Cole knew what these impromptu missions did to her and Zara, and that he hated doing it to them. But she also knew that he could never leave a job unfinished, even if it was a job that had just "come up."

She sighed, knowing she couldn't change his mind. It was something she admired him for.

Cole smiled, trying his best to reassure her. "Liv, I'll be fine. You know I will."

"I know."

"And why will I be fine?" Cole asked, still smiling.

She knew this routine by heart.

"Because my husband is a badass," she said, truly believing it. Its repetition never dulled her sincerity.

"Look, I'll be home day after tomorrow. We can talk more about it then," Cole said.

"All right," Olivia said.

"I'll see you soon."

"OK," Olivia said. She sat and watched her husband reach for the button to end the call and his image fade from the screen.

"He'll be fine," she said to the static.

Cole stood staring out the viewport that occupied the back wall of his quarters, but the endless black of deep space wasn't really much to look at. So much had changed in the last day that he was having trouble processing it all, and the drinking hadn't helped matters. It never did. As Cole turned to head back to bed, the lights flickered and he looked back out the viewport and saw his reflection in the glass.

The pale reflection showed a body covered in row upon row upon row of jagged scars. They were crisscrossed by longer, more controlled scars, the occasional glint of metal creeping out from beneath the surface. Reminded, Cole picked up a small knife from a nearby table.

Each scar held a story, a memory, a soul.

He made a short nick on the back of his left hand.

This was for the Modosian.

Cole ran his fingers up and down the scars on his arm, catching them occasionally on the structure beneath. It too had a story.

"I'll be fine," he said to himself.

The sun glinted off the hull of the *Havok* as it shot through the upper atmosphere of Cotari IV and descended toward the surface. It was midafternoon, and a storm front was rolling across the ocean toward the capital.

The capital, Cotar, was a bustling seaside metropolis and the central command hub for the militaries of the Federation. It was established forty years ago, during the war, and since then had grown exponentially. It was also home to corporations, banks, and around thirty million citizens.

"You still here?" Ram said, poking his head into the command room. Cole sat a desk, his head buried in papers and data pads.

"Yeah, I just have to finish up this report."

"It can wait," Ram said, coming into the room. "Go home already."

Cole let out a loud sigh and pushed back from the desk.

"I screwed up, Ram," he said, shaking his head.

Ram thought now might be the time to get something out of Cole about the mystery man. "Who was he, Cole?"

"He was supposed to be dead," Cole said.

"He have a name?"

"Tobias Navarr." Cole got up and walked to the window. "I saw him die fifteen years ago."

"What happened to him?"

"Nothing good," Cole said.

"He deserve it?"

Cole nodded.

"Good enough for me." Ram walked up and stood beside Cole. "Where'd you know him from?"

"From before."

"Ah, the mystical 'before,'" Ram said. "A time of mystery and intrigue."

Details of Cole's life before he joined Penumbra were scarce, and Ram had learned over the years that if you got even a small glimpse behind the curtain, you should consider yourself lucky. They'd always nagged Cole about it, and he usually played along, but Ram could tell by the silence that followed his jab that now wasn't the time for it. Ram could feel Cole's willingness to share slipping away.

"So, what now?" Ram said, breaking the silence. "We going after him?"

"We have to," Cole said.

"All right then," Ram said. "You tell Liv?"

"I did."

"How'd that go?"

"She was . . . displeased."

"What'd you tell her?"

"Not everything."

"Man, I know *that* feeling. I'm with her. Consider me displeased too."

Cole laughed. "Screw you," he said, elbowing Ram in the side.

The tension that had been building in the room broke.

Ram sighed. "Look: go home, talk to her, get some sleep." He motioned to the paperwork all over the desk. "Forget about all this. We'll work it out tomorrow."

Cole listened as Ram left and the door slid shut behind him. He was right, the report could wait until tomorrow, but still he stayed, staring blankly out the window, watching the clouds roll in, slowly swallowing the sunset.

The wind and rain buffeted against the windows of the cab as it bumped along. The ride was rough, as usual, which Cole always found surprising for a vehicle that never actually touches the ground. It was dark out by now and the storm wasn't helping matters, but Cole could still see the gradual change in the density of the buildings as he traveled out of the city. Cole lived in a part of town that was less built up, where there was grass and everything wasn't gray. Everything was gray now, though.

The driver was trying to make conversation over the noise of the storm, but Cole wasn't interested, even if he could hear him. His mind was elsewhere, in the past.

His attention was finally grabbed when the cab swerved and came to a stop.

Cole looked out the window and saw what appeared to be a large group of people gathered on the side of the road outside his building—so large that they spilled over into the street. He couldn't work out why they'd be out there in this weather.

Cole got out of the cab, and through the crowd, his eyes saw quick successive flashes of red and blue lights.

Cole's stomach dropped.

THREE

WITH THE RAIN stinging his face, Cole pushed his way through the crowd, many of whom were residents of his building. He scanned the crowd for Olivia, but it was too dark to see clearly.

"Olivia!" Cole shouted over the noise. "Zara!"

"Cole?" a voice called back.

Cole searched for the source and found a familiar face. "Shalar?" he asked.

Shalar had been their neighbor for many years. She was very elderly and on this night looked every year of it.

"What's going on?" Cole asked, pushing his way to her.

"I don't know," she said, trembling from the cold. "Alarm, the alarm. Then we go." Her basic wasn't very good, but Cole got the gist of what she was saying.

"Have you seen the girls?" he asked, urgency in his voice.

Shalar just shook her head and started to weep. Cole placed a comforting hand on her shoulder. "It'll be OK."

He left Shalar and forced his way to the front of the group. The scene before him did nothing to calm his nerves. A boundary line spanned the front of the building, manned by police at regular intervals. Security vehicles were parked on the grass, their lights a never-ending strobe. Cole couldn't delay any longer. He had to get inside.

Cole ran for the police line, but before he could even get to it, he was cut off by three armed officers.

"Sir, please return to the group," one of the officers said calmly.

"You don't understand, I have to get in there," Cole shouted as he tried pushing through them. He was met with a rifle butt to the stomach.

"Sir, please return to the group. It's for your own safety," the officer repeated.

Cole got to his feet and, looking past the officers in his way, saw a group of eight heavily armed troops enter the building through the main doors—though the troops weren't what got his attention. The doors to his building had been blown in, bent almost entirely off their hinges.

Tobias.

"Sir, I don't want to have to tell you again."

Cole backed away, his eyes scanning the scene for any other possible point of entry. There wasn't one; they had the building completely surrounded.

Think, damn it, he said to himself, trying to force a plan into existence. Cole's hand unconsciously fell onto his pistol. Then it came to him: he knew what to do.

Forcing his way through the throng of people, Cole ducked down behind one of the vehicles parked in the street. He took out his pistol, switched off the safety, and emptied the clip into the rainy night sky.

It didn't take long for his plan to come into effect. Despite the sound of the storm, enough people heard the gunshots to start a panic. Within seconds, the crowd was running every which way. The police weren't prepared for it, and before they knew it, the containment lines had disappeared and they were being overwhelmed. Using the panicked crowd for cover, Cole sprinted for the entryway.

Inside, it was eerily quiet. The storm outside was reduced to background noise, and the screams of the crowd faded away entirely. Cole's footsteps echoed across the tiled floor. Before him, the usually pristine lobby was anything but. Light fixtures hung from the ceiling, sparks flying out in all directions. Water covered most of the floor, having flowed from a shattered tank in the wall. Bodies were scattered about, some slumped in chairs, others looking like they had been struck down trying to flee. Cole walked cautiously out into the center of the lobby, which used to be a large atrium; now it was just shattered glass and shredded plants. There was a muffled shout from above. Cole looked up.

Thud. Crack.

The body barely missed him. Its impact was a sound he didn't think he'd ever be comfortable hearing. The body was that of one of the troops he had seen rushing into the building minutes earlier. Cole crouched down to check the man's pulse. He needn't have bothered.

There was no more time to waste. Cole had to get to his family. He ran to the elevator, which was thankfully still functioning, and rode it to the top floor. Upon exiting the elevator, Cole almost slipped in a pool of blood.

He had found the remaining troops.

Cole liberated one of the fallen men of his rifle; the lights were out, and it had a flashlight. Stepping around the remaining bodies, he made his way down the long, dark corridor to his apartment, rifle up, ready to fire at a moment's notice.

He was almost there when he heard a noise behind one of the many doors that lined the corridor. With his weapon trained, he slowly slid the door open.

A pair of shrill screams shattered the silence. Illuminated only by the flashlight were the faces of two terrified children, a boy and a girl. He didn't know their names, but he had seen them around the building before.

"It's OK, it's OK," Cole said, lowering the rifle and reaching out his hand. "I'm not going to hurt you."

Without the light shining in her eyes, the little girl seemed to recognize Cole and reached out to take his hand. Her brother followed closely behind.

"Is there anyone else inside?" Cole asked them. They shook their heads.

Cole pointed to a door on the other side of the corridor. "You see that door? That's the stairs. I want you to take them all the way to the bottom. Do you understand?"

The children nodded.

"When you get there, I want you to run outside. Don't stop, no matter how scary it might seem. Don't look at anything. Just run," Cole said, looking them in the eyes. "Do you think you can do that for me?"

The children continued to nod.

"OK, go! Go now," Cole said, ushering them to the door.

As they disappeared through the doorway and headed down, Cole turned and looked back down the corridor. A faint flicker emanated from around the corner at its end. Quickly and quietly, Cole rushed to the corner and pressed up against it. He readied himself and swung around the corner, weapon raised, scanning from right to left and back. There was no one there.

The door to his apartment had been blown in—in much the same way as the main doors down below. The flicker of damaged lights flooded out into the corridor through the mangled opening.

Cole's shadow danced across the walls as he picked his way through the entryway and into the living room. Beyond the wreck of the entryway, the rest of the apartment was in almost pristine condition, not a single cushion or piece of furniture out of place.

Maybe they weren't home?

"Olivia?" Cole called out, hope entering into his voice, buoyed slightly by the state of the room. "Zara?"

They got out. He didn't find them.

Cole's focus shifted to the other rooms in the apartment. Moving down the hallway, still calling their names, Cole noticed the door to his bedroom was open ever so slightly. As he approached, he prayed he would find nothing on the other side.

He slid the door open quietly, heart pounding.

"No."

The word fell again and again from Cole's lips as he stumbled into the room. His feet dragged, and his head throbbed. It wasn't long before no sound could escape his mouth at all.

Slumped by the side of their bed was Olivia Traske. She had been placed there, the smears of blood on the ground indicating she had fallen forward. She was placed just so, so that Cole would find her as she was. The sheets had been pulled from the bed. They had wrapped around her leg as she tried to flee. They were slowly soaking up the blood that now pooled around her lifeless body.

Cole knelt down beside her. He brushed the hair away from her face. Every movement seemed to take all the strength he could muster. Fighting back the tears, Cole lifted her into his arms. She seemed lighter. He lowered her onto the bed, making sure to rest her head gently on a clean pillow.

Cole sat for a moment and looked into his wife's eyes. The glimmer had gone out of them. He passed his hand over her face, closing her eyes for the last time. He kissed her, for the last time.

"I'm sorry."

After taking a moment to compose himself, Cole acted quickly. Zara was still missing, and there was no time to waste. He hurried to the far wall of the bedroom and flicked a switch, and a panel retracted and slid into the wall. Inside was another panel. It was supposed to be closed; it had been the entire time they'd lived there. But it was open—forced, by the look of it. Its contents were gone.

Crash.

He was moving before he knew it. Upon reentering the living room, Cole saw the source of the sound: a lamp had been knocked over, and its cover had shattered on impact. Then he noticed it: a trail of blood, a fresh one. It hadn't been there when he came in, and it was leading out the door. *He was in here the whole damn time.* Running out into the corridor, Cole saw her. *Zara!*

Tobias had Zara by the arm and was dragging her toward the elevator. Blood was running down her other arm, which hung limply at her side.

"Zara!" Cole yelled, running after her.

Zara's head swung around, and she fought Tobias's grip, desperate to pull away. "Dad!" she screamed as Tobias threw her into the elevator. The impact cracked the glass on its back wall.

I won't make it, Cole thought as he sprinted toward his daughter.

He arrived a moment too late as the thick glass doors closed in front of him. Cole went to press the button to open the door, but it was no good. Tobias had trashed the exterior panel. Zara scrambled to the door and banged her bloodied palm against it. "Help me," she pleaded again and again.

Cole placed his hand over hers on the glass. There was no physical contact, but it seemed to calm Zara. "It's going to be OK, baby girl," Cole said, not knowing if he even believed his own words. "It's going to be OK. I'm going to—"

Tobias yanked Zara back, throwing her into the back wall of the elevator yet again. She went limp in a pile on the ground. She had been knocked unconscious.

"You son of a bitch," Cole shouted, rising to come face-to-face with Tobias. "I'm going to f—"

That was when he noticed it: resting in Tobias's hand was a hilt. From it extended a thin, razor-sharp blade, its surface crackled with electricity. Blood glistened along its length in the flickering light. It was Cole's sword, the same one that should have been locked away in his apartment. Tobias's sick plan came into startling focus. This was nothing more than revenge. Tobias wanted to make him suffer.

This is all my fault.

Cole looked up from the sword to see Tobias grinning back at him. The glint in Tobias's eyes was no different than it had been fifteen years ago: no shame, no remorse, only rage and pure bloodlust.

Tobias calmly pressed a button in the elevator, and it ascended into the darkness. Cole could only watch as his daughter slipped away. He punched the glass door, cracks radiating out from the impact. The pale, distorted reflection that stared back at Cole echoed the look in Tobias's eyes.

One way or another, this would end tonight.

Cole ran back down the corridor to the stairs and took them two at a time. It was only a short climb. The roof was the only place Tobias could be going.

Cole hoped that he wouldn't be too late.

The wind nearly knocked Cole backward as he came out onto the roof. The storm was at its peak, and rain lashed the concrete in waves. It was terribly dark, the spotlights from the police effort downstairs did little to illuminate the rooftop. As Cole stumbled forward into the darkness, lightning began to arc across the sky. Each successive flash gave Cole a glimpse of what awaited him like a strobing horror show.

At the edge of the roof stood Tobias. One arm held a groggy Zara, who was just coming to; the other hung at his side, the blade still resting comfortably in his hand. Cole shouted to Zara, but no reply came. The wind was just too loud. He would have to get closer. Cole moved slowly. He didn't want to spook Tobias. His first priority was getting Zara out of harm's way.

Finally within earshot, Cole made his plea. "Let her go," he shouted, straining his voice above the wind. "She has nothing to do with this."

"That's not true, though, is it, Cole?" Tobias replied. Another flash of lightning revealed the same sick grin was still on his face. His eyes continued to burn with rage.

Cole edged closer. "Let her go, Tobias."

But he had gotten too close. Saying nothing, Tobias forced Zara to her knees and held the blade to her throat.

Cole stopped dead, dropping to his knees. "Stop! Please!"

"Dad!" Zara screamed. "I'm scared!"

She had been sleeping when a loud noise woke her. She had looked out to see the front doors of her home twisted open. She had watched as a man crossed the floor and disappeared into the darkness.

She had tried to scream as the man's cracked and wrinkled hand held tightly over her mouth. She had felt the familiar hot stink of alcohol on his breath.

He had broken her arm the first time she tried to escape.

Now her knees buckled as she was forced to the ground. She could feel the cold steel of the blade dig into her throat a little more with each gust of wind, and with each drop of rain, the shocks got stronger. She could feel the man's crooked finger running down her cheek.

She could see her father, on his knees, pleading with the man for her life. She could barely hear him. She cried freely.

"I know, baby girl. It's OK, I'm here," her father said, tears rolling down his cheeks. "Just keep looking at me. Keep looking at me." He met her gaze and nodded. "Be my brave girl."

She saw the nod. She was her father's daughter.

She swung back with her good arm as hard as she could manage. She caught the man in the leg and then bit hard into his arm. The blade fell away, and the man lost his grip on her.

She ran.

For a few brief seconds, she was free, but then the man's hand came down hard on her shoulder. She saw a flash of lightning as the man spun her to face him. She felt a sharp pain as the man's blade pierced her heart. Then she felt nothing. Saw nothing.

Cole's mouth twisted in a silent scream. Time slowed. Raindrops slowly drifted to the ground, and the lightning cast a horrific glow on the scene before him.

Tobias flung Zara's lifeless body to the side. It crashed against a ventilation duct and crumpled to the ground. He retracted the blade and threw the hilt across the concrete. The smile had not left his face. He stepped back toward the edge.

Cole ran to his daughter. He cradled her head in his hands, begging for her to come back to him. He watched as the life faded from her eyes. As the rage inside him built, he looked toward the building's edge, ready to go after Tobias, but he was gone.

The fight went right out of him then, and he slumped forward and cradled his daughter. The rain began to abate, and between deep, wracking sobs, he could hear the crowd below again and the sirens. He heard the footsteps approaching, at least a dozen.

He didn't care.

This is my fault.

Cole looked up to see whom the footsteps belonged to.

Crunch.

Blinding light, then darkness.

"The girl?" a voice said in the fog.

"Dead, sir," came the reply.

"Sir, look," said a third voice, "the weapon."

"Take him."

FOUR

LIGHT LEAKED INTO the side of Cole's vision. His head throbbed like it was about to explode. He blinked a few times to try and clear his vision, but it was still slightly out of focus. His hands were bound, a short leash fixing them to the cold metal table. A single light shone on him from behind him somewhere. It sounded like there were maybe two guards back there as well. This wasn't good. The memories of the stormy night flooded back into his mind. He couldn't tell how long it had been. Hours? Days?

Olivia. Zara.

A man paced up and down the far wall of the room. He looked in Cole's direction.

"Ah, finally awake, are we?" he said, turning to face the large mirror on the left wall. "Took you long enough."

"Where am I?" Cole asked. He was still groggy, but he had a fair idea of what the reply was going to be.

"Interrogation room eighty-seven, Cotar Central Command."

"What?" Cole said. "Interrogation? What kind of bullshit is this?"

Cole struggled against the cuffs, trying to slip them. A quick jab from the guard's electro-pike put an end to that.

"Easy. No use fighting," the interrogator said, still facing the mirror.

"Fighting? What am I even doing here? I haven't done anything. My family was just—"

"Your family was just *what*?" the interrogator said, cutting him off.

"They were murdered, you ignorant little shit," Cole shot back. One of the guards stepped forward, pike at the ready. He was waved away by the interrogator, who sat down on the edge of the table. Cole could see he was young, far too young to be doing this. Cole now knew how to handle this situation.

"On whose orders am I being held here?" Cole asked calmly.

The interrogator shot a nervous look toward the mirror before refocusing on Cole. "Command."

Cole could see the small crack appear in the kid's facade. "Command?" He shook his head. "You expect me to believe that Federation Command is detaining *me*."

"Believe what you want, it won't—"

"What's your name, kid?" Cole said.

The crack widened slightly. "What?"

"Your name, we've all got one, kid," Cole said. He'd noticed that his face twitched every time he called him "kid."

"Daniels," he offered. His back straightened; the crack widened.

"Daniels," Cole said, "do you know who I am?"

"Sergeant Major Cole Traske, thirty-eight years old, newly appointed leader of Penumbra of the Forty-Second Unification Division, of which you've been a member for ten years. Fourteen-year veteran of the Federation Armed Forces and owner of the highest target acquisition rate since the end of the Fifty-Year War," Daniels said, barely drawing a breath. The crack narrowed slightly.

"So why in the hell—"

"Former Hunter, smuggler, and gun for hire. *Synth*. Known associate of war criminals. You are the target of thirty-seven outstanding arrest warrants across the border systems,"— Daniels stood up straighter now—"and sole owner of *this*." From behind his back, Daniels produced the hilt of Cole's sword and slammed it down on the table; the crack slammed shut right along with it.

Cole had misread the situation.

"And as such, you are the *sole* suspect in the murder of eight UniDiv specialists and seventeen civilians, seemingly now including your own wife and daughter."

Cole said nothing. He could see Daniels's mind ticking over, mulling his next move. The kid was deadly serious.

"So, what was it that tipped the scales? Huh?" Daniels sat back down on the table. "Life in the military getting too stress-ful? Too boring, maybe?" He leaned in closer. "Maybe those implants of yours finally shorted." Daniels smirked. "Or per-haps all that time away for all those years gave Mrs. Traske time and reason to step out on—"

Cole lurched forward, his forehead smashing into Daniels's mouth. Kicking his chair into one of the now rushing guards, Cole did his best to lock his arm around Daniels's throat and squeezed, hard. The chair only slowed one guard, though, and the other jammed his pike into Cole's ribs and held it there until Cole's body went weak and he fell, crashing into the table.

Daniels scampered away from the table, clutching at his throat.

"You'll pay dearly for this," Daniels said, catching his breath.

Cole was picked up by the guards and placed roughly back in his chair.

"You stupid son of a bitch! It wasn't me! It—"

Daniels picked up the hilt and slammed it down again for effect. "You were the only living being found anywhere in that building. The weapon is yours, and your fingerprints are the only ones on it."

Cole's eyes bore a hole in Daniels's chest.

Without warning the door opened behind Cole, and all he could see in the mirror was a large silhouette, contrasted against the brightness of the room outside. Daniels stiffened; the crack had returned.

"Enough." The voice was deep and commanded immediate attention.

Daniels wavered. "But, sir, I, uh—"

"This man is now in my custody." The perfectly pointed delivery was indicative of someone raised in the Old Core worlds. "You're dismissed, corporal."

Daniels shuffled quickly out the door, nursing his sore chin.

"Leave us," the silhouette said. The guards didn't need to be told twice and followed closely behind Daniels.

"A corporal? Really?" Cole said, bewildered. "Is this what you jackasses call a sound interrogation practice? He was barely out of diapers, for crying out loud."

"Cole, is that any way to speak to an old friend?"

The man entered the room, and his face became clear in the reflection.

"Oren?" Cole said, barely believing his eyes.

Lieutenant Commander Oren Rhey'll had been the commanding officer of UniDiv for two years now. He had inherited a division that had slowly corrupted itself in the years since the war ended. Its original mission, set twenty-five years ago during the war, was to roam the galaxy, find dissent, do what was needed to quash it, and move on. After the war, however, its name took on a more sinister connotation. UniDiv were no longer just peacekeepers, they were glorified bounty hunters. The Federation determined that the best way to create unity and peace in the galaxy was to eliminate the "problem" altogether. In that case, they deemed the problem to be Conduits. As such, UniDiv were tasked with hunting down and capturing, not killing, every last Conduit across the galaxy—men, women, and children, whether they were a threat or not. No one ever knew what happened to them once they were brought in, but more often and not, they were never seen again.

As Conduit numbers dwindled, they started going after other targets: political extremists, radicals, and basically any undesirables that Federation leadership saw fit to deal with. There weren't any restrictions on lethality with those other targets, and in the long run, it made a bad deal even worse. In more recent years, UniDiv was viewed as less of a necessity to galactic safety and more and more as a black mark on the face of the Federation. UniDiv was a wartime unit that tried to adapt to peacetime and failed.

In the short two years that Oren had been in charge, recruitment numbers were up, corruption was down, and he had recently secured funding that would keep UniDiv in action for at least the next ten years. It wasn't all good news, though: in recent months, leaks within the division had endangered and even taken many of its operatives' lives. Recruitment may have been up, but they were losing people faster than they could replace them. To Oren, the rebuilding of UniDiv was to be a lifelong battle, and he wore every struggle in the creases of a face that belied his age.

Oren Rhey'll was Cole's oldest friend, and the fact that he was even there, in that room, away from his crusade, spoke volumes.

"Aren't you supposed to be halfway across the galaxy?" Cole said, watching as Oren signaled for the cameras to be switched off.

"I swear," Oren said, seemingly not hearing the question, "I must have a word to Modell about the people they let in here."

"Oren, what are you doing here?"

"I just got back," Oren said, unlocking Cole's handcuffs. "Word filtered through about what happened." Oren sat down opposite Cole. "I'm so terribly sorry, Cole, and I can't help but feel partially responsible."

"Responsible?" Cole said. "Last night had nothing to do with you."

"Last night?" Oren said. "Cole, it's been four days."

"Four *days*?"

"They must still have the hibernation protocol in place," Oren offered. "I petitioned them two months ago to have it abolished. Lot of good that did, it seems."

Oren produced a data pad and placed it in front of Cole.

"This is the man we believe is responsible for the death of your family," Oren said. "Tobias—"

"Navarr," Cole finished.

Oren's eyebrows raised. "You know him?"

"Watched him die fifteen years ago, Oren."

"Cole, Navarr escaped from Kylgor two months ago. He'd been in there for thirteen years . . ." Oren trailed off as a thought began to form.

"Prison?" Cole said.

Oren didn't hear him. "This is starting to make much more sense now," he said. "For two months, we've been chasing him as he made a tear across the galaxy, killing seemingly at random. We'd never been able to find a motive"—Oren shifted uneasily in his chair—"until now."

"He was coming for me the whole time," Cole said, the pieces falling together in his mind.

"Unfortunately, it does seem that way," Oren said.

A somber silence fell on the room.

Cole flicked through the pages of information on the data pad.

"He was on Tragg," Cole said, suddenly remembering.

"What? When?" Oren asked.

"It'd be a week ago now, I guess," Cole said. "We were there on a job. I secured the target, turned around, and there he was, just sitting there."

"What happened?"

"He got the drop on me. I-I froze. If I hadn't . . ."

"We'd been tracking him," Oren said. "But we lost him ten days ago when he passed through Nelmar."

"A lot of people disappear there," Cole said. "And he has more of a knack for it than anyone I've ever known."

"If we hadn't lost him," Oren said, "perhaps we would have been able to intercept him and stop this whole tragedy from occurring."

Cole pushed the data pad away. He'd seen enough. "Oren, I made this bed a long time ago, and now I have to lie in it. I'm the only one to blame here. My family is dead because of me." Cole stood up from the table. "The only thing I can control is what happens now."

"You want to go after him," Oren said.

Cole looked down at the picture of Tobias on the data pad. "I want to tear his heart out."

"What can I do?"

"Well, for starters, if you could get me out of here, that'd be great."

"Already taken care of," Oren said.

"Thanks," Cole said, making for the door.

"I presume you have a plan?" Oren said, following him out.
"I do."

Oren picked up on the tone in Cole's voice, one he hadn't heard in quite a while. "I'm not going to like it, am I?"

"No. No, you're not."

FIVE

THE DAY AFTER they got back from Tragg, Ram had gone into Command, expecting Cole to be there finishing his report. However, Cole was nowhere to be found. Ram had tried calling him, but the call rang out. Sol hadn't seen him either, and they were happy enough to just assume that Cole had slept in and didn't hear the call.

Then Gregor came running into the break room like his ass was on fire.

"You haven't heard?" Gregor said.

"Heard what?" Sol said.

"It's Cole." Gregor caught his breath. "He's been arrested."

Ram laughed. "Kid, if you're trying to be funny, you're missing the mark, big time."

"I'm serious! They're saying he killed his family."

"They're saying what?" Ram couldn't believe what he was hearing.

"What the hell is going on? You can't seriously think Cole did this, can you?" Ram said, standing in the office of the Cotar police chief, Harn Modell.

"The evidence is there, Ramses. We can't ignore it," came Modell's cold reply. "No matter how much you might want us to."

"Screw your evidence!" Ram was shouting now. "There is no way that Cole could do these things. It's ridiculous! He would never touch so much as a hair on Liv's head or Zara's."

"He was the only one at the scene, Ramses," Modell continued. "His fingerprints are on the murder weapon."

Ram had heard enough. "I want to see him."

"I'm afraid that won't be possible," Modell said.

"Why the hell not?"

"Mister Traske is still currently in hibernation until our investigation is completed," Modell explained. "It could be several days."

"This is bullshit," Ram shouted, smashing his fist down onto Modell's desk.

"Ramses Barden," Modell said sternly. "The only reason I even entertained this meeting was because of my debt to your father. If he—"

"This was a waste of time," Ram said, making for the door. "If I have to go over your head, I will, and you know that I can."

"Good luck with that," Modell said.

"Drak off, old man," Ram said under his breath as he stormed out of the room.

Despite his repeated and insistent efforts, nothing Ram tried over the next four days granted him access to Cole. Early in the morning of the fifth day, however, he got news that Cole had been released the night before, only Cole hadn't made contact and no one knew where he'd gone—no one except for Ram.

As the door to the bar slid open, the familiar stench of stale sweat and alcohol wafted out into the street. The bartender saw Ram come in and hurried over to meet him.

"Hey, Rek," Ram said, "he here?"

"Been here all night," Rek said, the fatigue evident in his voice. "I couldn't bring myself to throw him out, poor bastard."

Rek pointed to the far end of the bar, where several booths lined the wall. Something resembling Cole sat slumped over in one on the far right.

"Thanks," Ram said.

Cole was fast asleep, facedown on the table, a small puddle of drool slowly expanding from the corner of his mouth. Ram gave him a few solid shakes to wake him, but he didn't stir. He was out cold.

"Rek?" Ram called out.

"Yeah?" Rek said, his head buried somewhere behind the bar.

"You got any QWake back there?"

Rek's reply came in the form of several small packets landing at Ram's feet.

"He might need a couple," Rek said, his head popping up from behind the bar. "This is the worst I've seen him since Nate."

Ram unwrapped the capsules and activated them, a small needle popping out the top of each. One by one he pressed the capsules into Cole's arm, making sure to wait the requisite thirty seconds between doses. One QWake capsule was usually enough to snap a grown man into sobriety in short order. Ram was up to the third.

"How much did he have?" Ram said.

"I cut him off about six hours ago, but before that he'd been hitting it pretty hard. We tried to get him to slow down, but I guess he just wanted to forget everything. Understandable, really."

Ram looked over to Rek. "We?"

"Yeah, there was another guy here with him," Rek said. "Officer type, real important-looking. Stick up his ass. Sounded like he was from the Old Core."

"Ah," Ram said, knowing exactly who it was.

"You know him?" Rek said.

"Knew him," Ram said. *Oren. Great.*

Thirty seconds had passed. Ram waited an extra ten for good measure and administered the fourth capsule.

"Anyway," Rek continued, "he couldn't keep up with Cole. Wigged out about two hours in and left. Asked me to keep an eye on him. He tipped well, at least."

Fifteen seconds into the fourth dose, Cole started to stir. Five seconds later, he lurched backward and came roaring into consciousness.

"Zara!" Cole yelled, lashing out at whatever was closest. In this case, it was Ram, who quickly reigned in Cole's thrashing and did his best to calm him down.

"Cole," Ram said, clear and direct, locked onto his friend's eyes. "Cole, it's Ram. Look at me. Hey, look at me. Do you know where you are?"

Cole calmed, but his hands were shaking uncontrollably. "Ram?" he said.

"Hey, welcome back," Ram said, patting Cole on the back.

The drugs had kicked in now. Unfortunately for Cole, the clarity they provided brought back every painful recollection of that stormy night. Cole's head sank to his chest.

"They're gone, Ram," he muttered, tears welling in the corners of his eyes.

"I know, buddy," Ram said, putting his arm around Cole's shoulders. "I know."

They sat in silence for a long time.

"So that's the plan?" Ram said.

"That's the plan, more or less," Cole said.

It had been some time since Ram had woken him, and any signs of intoxication were long gone. The excessive amount of QWake in his system had seen to that. Cole had been able to process what had happened as best he could and was now working on accepting it and planning for the long road ahead.

"And Oren's actually OK with this?" Ram asked.

"Some of it was actually his idea."

"Well, shit, if it's got *Lord* Rhey'll's seal of approval—"

"Ram . . ."

"Cole, you know I'm in. I'm with you on this."

"Never doubted it for a second."

Ram shifted in his seat and stretched. "Sol's not going to like it, though."

"But he'll do it," Cole said.

"Yeah, he will," Ram said. "Anyone's guess as to whether or not the kid will go for it."

"Yeah," Cole said, "I wouldn't blame him if he told me to go jump."

"He'll probably produce some deeply buried, long forgotten FedCo regulation that will absolutely prevent him from doing it," Ram said. They laughed.

It was the first time either of them had laughed in many days. Soon the laughter gave way to the quiet murmur of a bar in midmorning.

"You know," Cole said, breaking the silence, "if Nate was here, he'd probably have a much better plan."

"Maybe," Ram said. "All the same, I think he'd still prefer yours."

Cole shuffled to the side and eased himself out of the booth that had been his home for the last eighteen hours.

"Look, can you call the others?" Cole said. "Have them meet us back at base this afternoon."

"Where are you going?" Ram asked.

"I have to sort something out first."

Oren's secretary had let him through without protest. Cole assumed that meant that just about everyone knew what had happened by now.

"Yes, Captain, that's correct," Oren said, in the middle of a phone conversation. "All right. Yes. Just make sure that you do." Oren ended the call. "Blithering idiot."

"You got a minute?" Cole asked from the doorway.

"Yes, of course," Oren replied and waved Cole in. "I was actually just finalizing some of the arrangements for your mission. Everyone on board?"

"Ram's in. We're meeting with the others this afternoon to present it to them."

"And how is Ramses?" Oren said. "Still charming?"

"As ever," Cole said. "He was thrilled about your involvement."

"He's never going to let that one go, is he?"

"Can you blame him?"

"Not at all."

Cole paced the floor. His face showed a mind deep in thought.

"What do you need, Cole?" Oren asked.

"My implants, I-I need them reactivated."

"Cole . . ."

"Tobias is just as strong as he was fifteen years ago, maybe stronger." Cole stopped pacing. "I need them back up and running if I have any chance of surviving this."

"Cole, your implants were deactivated over a decade ago," Oren said. "Even if they're still in working order, we just don't have the capabilities for that here anymore. You know how things have been since the laws came in."

"I know that," Cole said. "I was hoping that maybe you, y'know, knew someone."

Oren frowned. He got up from the table and moved to a large display screen. A few simple hand gestures brought up a wealth of information.

"This is Kag Darka, the weapons dealer I was telling you about." Oren brought up a picture of Darka, a squat Virn with a face that perhaps even his own mother didn't love. "Now, he'll be providing you with your gear and ammunition, but if there were anyone who might have information on reactivating your implants, it would be him."

"Do you trust him?" Cole asked.

"Kag?" Oren said, laughing. "Not as far as I could kick him, but he knows better than to cause trouble."

Cole turned away from the display.

"Cole," Oren said, his face turning serious, "are you absolutely sure this is the way you want to do this?"

"This is my fault," Cole said. "Who knows how many people have died because of my failings. I should have put Tobias down years ago. This is how it has to be. I have to make this right."

"Very well," Oren said. "As discussed, I will do what I can to help."

"Thank you, Oren," Cole said, "for everything you're doing and have done already. This plan would be dead in the water without you."

"Cole, I owe you my life," Oren said. "There's nothing I wouldn't do."

"Think you could come by the meeting this afternoon?" Cole asked.

"Of course."

Cole got up to leave. "I'll keep Ram in line."

"Cole?" Oren said. "I was speaking to the coroner earlier, and he informed me that your family was given a proper burial. You should—"

"Thank you, I will," Cole said as he left.

The command room was empty by the time he arrived; Oren had seen to that. Cole walked over to a desk and began checking over papers related to the plan. Ram sat off to the side, reclining in an officer's chair, spinning around slowly. Oren stood nearby, looking out the large window that made up the entirety of the back wall of the room.

Noise from the doorway alerted Cole to the arrival of Sol, who was followed closely by Gregor. He had come after all, but he also hadn't heard the plan yet.

Cole was met by Sol with a strong embrace. "I'm sorry, mate," he said. "If there's anything I can do to help."

"Thanks, Sol," Cole said. "That's why you're here."

Gregor stood a few meters away, staring at his feet.

"Gregor?" Cole said.

"Sir?" Gregor looked up

"You OK?" Cole asked.

"I," Gregor's voice caught in his throat, "I'm so sorry, sir. I feel that this is all my fault. If only I had—"

"None of this is your fault, Gregor." Cole walked over to him and placed a reassuring hand on his shoulder. "It was my fault long before now."

"Y-yes, sir."

The trio walked back to the central part of the room and gathered around the large holo table. Oren and Ram were unmoved.

"What's he doing here?" Sol said, noticing Oren.

"He's here to help," Cole said.

"And have they . . ." Sol motioned to Oren and Ram.

"Spoken?" Cole said, finishing Sol's thought. "Not a word."

Sol laughed. "Babies, the pair of 'em," he said, taking a seat.

Gregor came up beside Cole. "Sir, why aren't they talking to each other?" he asked.

"Gregor, that there is a story that would take longer than we've got to do it justice," Cole said, guiding him toward a chair.

Oren turned to face the group. "Shall we begin?"

"Tobias Navarr." Cole ran his fingers over the controls and brought up a hologram of Tobias, his face looming large over the group.

"Sixty-one years old, mass murderer, suspected terrorist, one of the strongest Conduits I have ever come across"—Cole cycled some information across the displays—"and our target."

"Piece of cake," Ram said, breaking his silence.

"Fifteen years ago, at the height of the war, there was an . . . incident, and following that incident, I believed Tobias to be dead and buried, but I was wrong."

Gregor leaned forward in his chair. "This was before you joined the Federation, sir?" he asked.

"Yes, a couple of years before." Cole paced behind the holo-gram. "In actuality, Tobias survived and was tracked down and arrested by the Federation for his crimes after the end of the war. He spent the next thirteen years locked away in Kylgor Prison on Hitaari Prime until his escape two months ago."

Cole stopped and brought up a list of names. "This is a list of the people Tobias has killed since he escaped, that we know of," Cole said. "And this,"—he cycled another, much longer list onto the displays—"this is a list of all known victims of Tobias Navarr over the last forty years."

"By Andana's Grace," Sol said.

"Five nights ago, Tobias Navarr took my family from this world, from me." Cole paused, his voice catching in his throat. "Today, I'm asking for your help in hunting him down and putting an end to this."

"You don't even need to ask, mate. We're in," Sol said, pointing to himself and Gregor.

"Gregor, I would understand if you didn't want to commit to this," Cole said.

"No matter what you say, I can't help but feel responsible, sir. You have my full support, such as it is."

"Our plan to take Navarr down is unconventional and risky," Cole said. "I want you to hear all of it before you fully commit." Cole cleared his throat and continued. "We're dis-banding the squad. From today, we will no longer be soldiers of the Forty-Second Unification Division," Cole said, watching the faces of his friends closely. "The *Havok* will also be decom-missioned and removed from active service and returned to Sol as a civilian vessel."

"I'm sorry, what?" Sol blurted out.

"But why? I don't understand," Gregor asked, doubt creep-ing into his voice.

Oren stepped forward. "Plan A was to get the Council to grant Penumbra immunity and to authorize a kill mission to get Navarr," Oren said. "They wouldn't have it. Conduits are far too valuable to them, and they wouldn't agree to a revenge mission. So this is Plan B—"

"It's actually Plan C," Cole said. "The Council won't allow us to go after Tobias, so we're going to have to do it without them. Oren will be handling our separation from UniDiv, and he's seen to it that if we are successful, we should be able to be reinstated without too much trouble."

"That's also where things get a little tricky," Oren said. "You'll be acting outside the law on this. If you get caught doing anything . . . untoward,"—Oren looked straight at Ram—"I won't be able to protect you."

"We've done a pretty good job of not getting caught so far," Ram said, returning the look.

"He's serious, Ram," Cole said. "We'll be on our own, and if we get caught taking out Tobias it's—"

"Death," Gregor said grimly.

"Exactly," Cole said. "It won't be easy, but this is our best play. Our only play."

"What about weapons?" Sol asked. "I'm guessing we can't take Fed gear with us?"

"Oren has provided us with a contact who will get us the gear we need," Cole said. "Completely untraceable."

"I will also be keeping track of Navarr's movements," Oren said, "and will update you on his location as soon as we have him."

Ram scoffed. "You mean the mighty Lord Rhey'll doesn't know where he is?" he said.

"Not currently, no," Oren said. "Scanners picked him up leaving Cotari space the morning after the incident, but we lost him from there. We have found him before, and I have no doubt that we will find him again."

Gregor nervously rose to his feet and addressed Oren directly. "Commander Rhey'll, sir," he said, "you've been tracking Navarr for two months, yes?"

"That's correct," Oren replied.

"Then, if you don't mind me asking, why weren't you able to warn Cole about—"

"Gregor, until yesterday, they didn't know Tobias and I were even connected," Cole said. "I'd been on leave for six months. There was no reason to tell me."

Gregor sat back down sheepishly.

"So that's the plan," Cole said. "Anyone changed their minds?"

"Not a chance," Sol said. "Sounds like my kind of fun."

"Gregor?" Cole said.

"I will do this, sir. I believe it is the right thing to do," Gregor said.

"All right," Cole said, switching off the displays. "We leave in the morning. Get your things in order, and I'll see you then."

Cole looked across the holo table at the four men in front of him, his friends.

"I don't need to tell you all what this means to me. Just know that we're even now. Any debts, any favors owed, they're paid in full. And Gregor?"

"Yes, sir?"

"I owe you one now."

Gregor went pale. "No, sir, I couldn't possibly—"

"Take it while you can, kid," Ram said. "He doesn't hand them out that often."

They laughed.

SIX

THE AUTOMATIC GLASS doors had retracted on approach and now stayed open as Cole lingered in the doorway, unable to move. He had wanted to come here after the meeting the day before but couldn't bring himself to do it. Now, standing at the door to the Federation Memorial Gardens, Cole still wasn't sure if he could do it, but he had to. They were set to leave in a few hours for a mission from which there was every chance he would never return. This may be his only chance to say a proper good-bye. He forced himself to put one foot in front of the other.

The Memorial Gardens were set on a hill overlooking the city and harbor below and consisted of a series of interconnected glass structures that had expanded over the years to cover nearly the entire hill. The gardens were inside to protect them year-round from the extremes to which the weather in Cotar could slip to. Winters were bitterly cold, and the summers were some of the hottest on the planet. The precisely controlled climate inside protected the gardens, and the heavy security outside protected those interred there. In the years after the war, grave robbery was commonplace, which led to the construction of the gardens around the original cemetery in order to protect the dead.

"Olivia and Zara Traske," Cole said to the receptionist sitting behind a thick glass panel just inside the door.

"And your name?" she said, not even looking up.

"Cole Traske."

There was a short wait before a slip of paper appeared from a slot below the window. "We're sorry for your loss," the receptionist said, her voice a flat monotone.

Cole had passed through three separate security checkpoints before he arrived. The garden wasn't as thick with foliage as many of the others. There were ferns and some large trees scattered throughout, but a lot of the ground was covered with rock formations and sand, raked in decorative patterns. It was nice. Cole walked along the paths until he found them. Nestled between the roots of a Xerenium tree were two small stone plaques:

OLIVIA ARAIN TRASKE - 35
ZARA TALRA TRASKE - 13

It seemed wrong to Cole that only their names and ages were listed, but it was the same for everyone, always had been. It was as though it didn't matter to anyone else where and when they died or how or whom they left behind—only it did matter. It mattered more than he could put into words.

Cole knelt down and brushed away some petals that had fallen from the branches above. Then he sat. He wracked his brain for the right words to say, and even if he found them, he wasn't sure if he'd be able to speak. How could he tell them that this was his fault, that he was the one who had put them in danger? He sat for a long time in silence, as the air circulating in from the outside rustled the leaves in the trees above.

Finally, he found the courage to speak.

"You deserved better than this," Cole said, fighting back the tears. "I should have protected you from this, from him. I failed you. You trusted me to take care of you, and I failed."

The dam broke, tears flowed, and after a long while, they subsided.

"I have to go now," Cole said. "I'm going to make this right. I will make him pay for this, and I won't fail you again."

Cole leaned forward and touched Olivia's grave. "Good-bye, my love. I will see you again."

Then Zara's. "Bye, little bird. Daddy will always love you. Never forget that."

He got to his feet and turned to leave, not wanting to take his eyes off of them in case he never returned.

But he couldn't stay.

Cole entered the cockpit. Sol had been in there for a while making sure everything was ready to go. Ram and Gregor were just finishing loading the last of their supplies.

"How's she look?" Cole asked.

"Not bad," Sol said. "Surprisingly, aside from the lack of guns, it seems Oren's boys barely even touched her in the decommissioning."

"I made sure he wouldn't," Cole said.

"Thanks, mate," Sol said.

"Plus," Cole continued, "he knows what this ship means to you."

"Saved his bacon more than once," Sol said with a chuckle.

"Yes, it did, and we'd probably all be dead many times over if it wasn't for her."

Sol turned his chair to face Cole. "So, where we headed?"

"Shipyards near Nikara," Cole said.

"Looks like the old girl's getting a bit of a homecoming," Sol said, a smile crossing his face.

"I thought you'd be pleased," Cole said. "Look, we're just about loaded up. I'd say we're good to go in about thirty."

"Roger that," Sol said.

It was a four-day trip to Nikara, and Cole was thankful that it had been largely uneventful. So much had happened in such a small space of time, and he was glad for the reprieve, short though it was. They were just now entering Nikaran space, and the shipyards loomed large before them. The shipyards were essentially a space station that travelled in Nikara's orbit, but the station itself was a lot more than just a construction yard for the Federation's fleet of ships. It was also home to a couple hundred thousand people, many of whom were workers at the yards, but many more were refugees, private citizens, or criminals trying to hide right under the Federation's nose.

They were after a salesman.

Sol brought the ship down in one of the many commercial hangars that lined the port side of the station. The hangars were immense, stretching for several kilometers across the station's surface. Hundreds of ships were scattered along its length, and it seemed like tens of thousands of people were milling about on the ground.

"So, what's this guy's name again?" Ram asked.

"Kag Darka," Cole said. "Oren said he runs a salvage reclamation place in the market district. Sol, can you find him?"

"Already on it," Sol said, accessing the station's directory. "Got him: he's on the twenty-third level of the market district." Sol started laughing.

"What?" Cole asked.

Sol managed to compose himself. "His shop . . . It's called 'The Darka Side of Salvage.'"

"Wonder how long it took him to come up with that?" Ram said.

"Probably far longer than it should have," Cole said.

"I think it's quite clever," said Gregor, popping his head into the conversation.

The other three just shook their heads and laughed.

"We better get going," Cole said. "Don't want to be here any longer than we have to be."

"I hear that," Ram said. "Let's just hope that what he has for us isn't actually garbage."

The shipyards weren't the tidiest place in the galaxy, but the market district took it to a whole other level—or levels, as it were. What started as a five-level shopping complex for employees expanded over the years to become a ramshackle, cobbled-together mess of buildings that spanned just over forty levels. Somewhere along the line, it had merged with the residential district and was now said to be home to roughly a quarter of the station's population. The higher it went, the less secure everything felt. Vehicles weren't allowed past level twenty, as the roads weren't able to support the weight. Past level thirty, the buildings had to be made out of natural materials, like timber and cloth, that had to be shipped in. Using anything else further threatened the stability of the levels below. Five years ago, the Federation had intervened and put a stop to any further development past level forty-one, deeming any expansion a danger to the lives of those living beneath it.

The Darka Side of Salvage was on level twenty-three, which was sort of in the middle ground between the more organized society below and the poverty of levels thirty and beyond. It was home to the central telecommunications hub for the district, and as such, any light that might have filtered down from above was promptly blocked by thousands upon thousands of cables running to and from every dwelling across the forty-one levels. The streets were concrete, cracked even just from foot traffic, and they were lined with market stalls and shops that sold everything from a piece of bread to someone's cousin.

Squelch.

There were also animals in the market district. Ram had the unfortunate distinction of finding this out firsthand—or foot, as it were.

"Son of a bitch," Ram said, scraping his boot on the curb.

"It should be down here," Sol said, pointing down a side alley that couldn't have been more than two meters wide.

"Lead the way, Sol," Cole said.

There, hidden away in the corner, was a doorway and, next to it, a small window, caked in dust. The sign above the door did in fact read *The Darka Side of Salvage*, but the whole shop front did little to instill confidence.

"*This* is our arms dealer?" Ram said.

"I guess we'll find out," Cole said, forcing open the door that was almost rusted shut.

Inside wasn't a whole lot better. It was bigger on the inside—not huge, but bigger than they'd expected. Shelves lined the walls, and large bins covered the floor. All were filled with scrap. Nearly all of it was useless. It was dark and dusty. The few lights hanging from the ceiling were expected to illuminate the whole shop. They didn't.

"Don't touch anything," Ram said to Gregor, as he pulled him back after he got too close to a perilously unbalanced-looking pile of scrap.

Picking their way through the mess, they made it to what appeared to be a counter; it was, after all, buried under boxes and piles of junk. Behind it was a door and some shutters, both closed. On the one clear space on the counter, there was a bell.

"Hello?" Cole called out, after ringing the bell amounted to nothing.

There was a muffled grumbling from behind the door before it swung open to reveal a squat little creature, maybe half Cole's height. He wore glasses that rested on a long snout and had the look of someone who had just been woken up and might kill whoever had woken him.

"Kag Darka?" Cole asked wearily.

"Yes," Kag said with a huff. "Who are you?"

Cole motioned over his shoulder to the rest of them. "Penumbra."

Kag just looked at them. "Should that mean something to me?"

"It should . . ."

"What was the name again?"

"Penumbra," Ram said.

Kag looked over the top of his glasses, squinted, and then scrunched up his nose. His face then flickered with recognition. "Oh," he said, "Penumbra . . . like the shadow thing. Very mysterious, yes. You"—Kag pointed at Cole—"you need to speak more clearly. Also, you're late."

"Do you have our gear?" Cole asked, doing his best to ignore the chuckling of his friends behind him.

"Wait here," Kag said as he shuffled out through the back door.

"Charming little fellow, ain't he?" Sol said.

Thirty seconds had passed before the grumbling started again from beyond the door. It got louder, and soon Kag was standing in the doorway, hands on his hips. "You coming, or what?" he shouted.

They looked at each other in stunned silence before laughing and heading into the back room. It was like entering another world. You could walk around, for one, and several large crates were hovering over the much cleaner floor. There wasn't much in the way of shelving, and windows on the far wall let in the artificial light from the street outside.

"You know," Cole said, "you really should use this as your shop instead of—"

"This is my shop," Kag snapped. "You broke into my storage room, you idiots."

"Why didn't you tell us that in the first place?" Cole asked.

"Don't you think this was more fun?" Kag said, a smile appearing on his dour face. "I do."

"The gear?" Cole said, his patience wearing thin.

"Ah, yes," Kag said, heading toward the crates in the middle of the room. "Over here."

They helped Kag remove the tops of the crates. There was a crate for each of them and two others containing ammo and other supplies. Kag pulled out a short rifle from one of the crates.

"The Xanthar P23," Kag said, handing the rifle to Cole. "A .30 caliber, polycarbonate frame, laser-sighted with a folding stock. Light as a feather. Kicks like a Gurk."

Cole weighed the weapon in his hands and checked the sight.

"You'll each get a sidearm," Kag said, holding one in the air. "Peronas CR-90, silenced, low recoil. They won't know they're dead till they drop."

Kag looked around. "Where's our sniper?" he asked.

"Uh, here," Gregor said, raising his hand. "I'm the sniper."

Kag looked at Cole and raised an eyebrow. "Let me guess, he's new?"

He handed Gregor the rifle. "Tolivar Deathstrike," Kag said. "It's a hell of a thing. Three-kilometer range, computer-assisted targeting, silenced as well. You could drop ten targets, and no one would ever find you."

Kag turned to Ram and pointed to the crate floating beside him. "In there you'll find something to your liking."

Reaching into the crate Ram pulled out a small, compact weapon. "What? This little thing?"

"That 'little thing,' my large-headed friend," Kag said, testing Ram's boundaries, "is the Huris CPL60. Compact Projectile Launcher, can be configured for rockets or grenades, both of which you will have plenty. Half the size, half the weight, four times the stopping power."

"Not bad," Ram said, admiring the weapon.

"For the engineer," Kag said, walking over to Sol, "we have this, the Worth G4. Combat-spec automatic shotgun, modified for greater spread and impact. Someone surprises you, this will stop them right quick."

"Oh, and you"—Kag pointed at Ram—"you get one of these too. Believe it or not, there are times when blowing shit up isn't the best idea."

Cole punched Ram in the arm. "There's a lesson you should probably listen to."

"You love it when I blow shit up," Ram said, returning the favor.

"Now," Kag said, "all your weapons are taking the same type of rounds, shotguns and CPL excluded. These took a lot to get a hold of, so don't waste them." He pulled a box out of one of the crates and threw a bullet to each of them.

"What are these?" Cole said. "I've never seen anything like them."

"Ceramic rounds," Kag said. "White Death. Sensors inside the bullet set off a small charge just after impact. The ceramic shatters, tears shit to pieces, then vaporizes. Untraceable."

"I thought these we're only in the experimental stages of development?" Gregor asked, looking closely at the round.

"Why do you think they were so hard to get?" Kag said. "Look, I've seen these things do some scary shit to people—cut people in half kind of scary, so be careful with them."

Gregor tentatively placed the round down on a nearby bench top.

"You will also each be getting one of these," Kag said, producing a knife. "Standard-issue Federation combat knife, with a little added extra."

"Added extra?" Cole asked.

Kag pushed a button on the handle of the knife, and a small hum could be heard, when he touched it to the metal crate, sparks shot out. "The blade is electrified. It's sorta like a shock pike, but a bit more personal," Kag said. "Know where I got the idea?"

"Yeah, I do," Cole said.

"You *do*?" Kag asked, looking at Cole with astonishment.

Cole unhooked the hilt from his belt, with a flick of his wrist the metal blade extended and quickly crackled to life. He hit it on the crate. Sparks. Kag's eyes went wide.

"T-that's," Kag stammered, "that's a Conduit blade. Is it genuine?"

"It is."

"How much do you want for it?"

"It's not for sale."

"Oh," Kag said. "Wait a minute, are you—"

"I'm not a Conduit," Cole said.

"Oh good, I don't need that kind of hassle on my hands," Kag said with a sigh of relief. "Wait . . . did you kill one?"

"Might have," Cole said, raising his eyebrows.

"So you won't be needing the knife then?" Kag asked.

"Might as well throw it in," Cole replied.

Kag unceremoniously chucked the knife into the crate.

"So, are we right to go?" Cole asked.

"There is one small issue," Kag said.

Ram sighed loudly. "Let me guess, you—"

"Our mutual friend is covering your costs," Kag continued. "But he forced me down to quite a low rate, and I just can't possibly let the gear go at that price."

"And there it is," Ram said, walking toward Kag. Ram grabbed him by the front of his shirt and lifted him to eye level, clear off the ground. "Listen here, we're really grateful for what you've done for us, really, but this was a done deal. You can't renege on it just to try and get a better payday."

"Ram," Cole said sternly, "put him down."

With a shrug, Ram released him.

"OK, OK," Kag said, clearly flustered. "No money, but I do need a favor."

"Of course you do," Sol said.

"What's the favor?" Cole asked, crouching down to talk face-to-face with Kag.

"Two days ago, a small lockbox was stolen from my office," Kag said. "I know who has it. If you get it back for me, you can take the gear as agreed."

"I say we just take it anyway," Ram said, arms folded.

Cole looked up at Ram. "We're not taking it." Cole looked back to Kag. "Who has the lockbox?"

"Beren Zarr," Kag said. "He runs a competing salvage shop on the other side of level twenty-three."

"Of course he does," Ram said.

"What's the name of his shop?" Cole asked.

"Salvage Ba-Zarr," Kag said.

"That's actually not bad," Sol said, stifling a laugh.

"We'll get your lockbox back," Cole said, "and then we're leaving with our gear."

"Of course," Kag said, nodding. "Of course."

"Sol," Cole said, "I want you to stay here and keep an eye on him. Ram, Gregor, you're with me."

Ram reached into the crates, picked out three sidearms, and distributed them.

"You can't take those," Kag said.

"Think of it as a gesture of goodwill on your behalf," Ram said. "Besides, if we run into any trouble on this treasure hunt of yours, I don't want to be left without protection."

Kag went silent.

Soon after the trio had left, Sol turned to Kag.

"So," Sol said, "you named the business yourself?"

They stepped out into the bright artificial light of the street, and Ram looked up to see a rather large sign for Kag's shop above the door. "You know," he said, "for a pilot, his navigation skills leave a lot to be desired."

"Well, Ram, here's your opportunity to do one better," Cole said. "I want to find this lockbox quick and get out of here."

Ram puffed out his chest and led the way.

As they headed off down the main street, a figure peeled away from the shadows, followed closely by three others.

There were a lot of alleys and side roads in the market district, and unfortunately for Ram, many of them weren't marked or were marked incorrectly. On their fifth trip down this particular unnamed main road, having looped onto it several times, Gregor sidled up to Cole.

"Sir, can I ask you something?" Gregor asked.

"Only if you stop calling me 'sir,'" Cole said.

"Oh, of course," Gregor said, "I keep forgetting."

"What's on your mind, Gregor?" Cole asked after Gregor had gone quiet, seemingly forgetting that he had wanted to ask a question.

"Tobias," Gregor said, "how did he die? I mean, well, he's not dead but—"

"Like I said, there was an incident."

"But what *happened*?"

"I'd rather not . . ." Cole looked at Gregor and could see the eagerness in his face. "He was badly injured. The building we were in had become unstable, and it began to collapse. I barely got out, and he never did."

"Oh."

"I had no reason to think he was alive," Cole said.

"And this was during the war?" Gregor asked.

"Right near the end, yeah."

"So, if you weren't with the Federation back then, who were you with?" Gregor asked, probing for more information. "Like, what side?"

"Yeah," Ram said, pulling himself away from his desperate search for Salvage Ba-Zarr, "I've often wondered that myself."

They walked in silence for a moment as Cole thought of the best way to answer. "No side," he said. "Both sides. The lines got real blurry toward the end."

"Oh." It was all Gregor could think to say. He hadn't actually thought of a follow-up question.

They stopped at a food stand that they had passed at least three times before to get their bearings.

"Consider yourself lucky, kid," Ram said. "That's almost as much as I've gotten out of him in over ten years."

Ram turned to Gregor, but he was gone. A quick check of the area found him standing about twenty meters behind them, staring at something.

"Hey, kid," Ram shouted to him. "What are you doing?"

"It was Salvage Ba-Zarr, right?" Gregor called back, pointing in front of him.

"Yeah?" Ram said. "So?"

"Found it," Gregor said, a smile spreading across his face.

Cole and Ram walked over to him, and sure enough, there was Salvage Ba-Zarr, sign and all. They'd walked right past it.

"I knew that was there," Ram said, on the defensive immediately. "I just wanted to grab something to eat before we headed in. Was just about to mention it."

"Sure you were. Good work, kid," Cole said, patting Gregor on the back. Gregor's smile grew wider.

"Let's get this over with," Cole said, opening the door to go in.

They heard the sound of footsteps and rattling gear behind them.

"Cole Traske? I knew it was you."

Hearing the voice, Cole spun and was less than impressed with what he found.

"Charles," Cole said.

Before them stood Charles Weaver, and his squad, Eclipse, also from the Forty-Second. Cole's dealings with Charles had never been pleasant. The two of them, along with Oren, had been part of the same recruitment class. After five years of training, Oren moved into the officer ranks, while Cole and Charles went into the field. Cole was assigned to Shadow Point, which Charles always resented and had antagonized Cole about for years.

Weaver had long tried to muscle his way into Penumbra, which was seen by everyone in the division as the top squad, and he hadn't exactly been subtle about it either. Three days after the death of Nathan Revik, he petitioned to become Penumbra's new leader and to replace Cole, Ram, and Sol with his own men. This hadn't gone over well—not with Oren, whom Weaver had proposed the idea to, or with Cole, Ram, and Sol. Ram spent four days in lockup after an incident with Weaver's second-in-command, Jarak Rol. Jarak spent five days in the hospital. The other two, Darm Ju'rell and Levi Rhakti, were the textbook definition of brainless hired guns. All you had to do was point them in the direction of something and say "go," and they'd go till the job was done. Weaver and Rol ran the show, and the other two just went along with it, no questions asked. Sol had a pet name for them: "the Goons."

Gregor knew none of this, but judging from the looks on everyone's faces, he figured that they weren't a welcome addition to their travels.

"What are you doing here, Weaver?" Ram said, deep-seated anger clear in his voice.

Ignoring the question, Weaver stepped toward Cole and picked at his civilian clothes. "Huh, so the rumors were true," Weaver said.

"Rumors?" Cole said as he pushed Weaver back as politely as he could muster.

"You guys are out." A smug smile flashed across Weaver's face. "Cut and run. Couldn't run with the big boys anymore."

"If you say so," Cole said, wanting nothing more than to carry on with the task at hand.

"I mean, it's fine with me," Weaver said with a shrug. "Means we won't have to clean up after you anymore."

"What the hell are you doing here?" Ram asked again and stepped toward Weaver—though, before he got close, Jarak cut him off. Their eyes burned holes into each other.

Gregor could see that this situation was about three words from escalation.

"Just carrying out a bit of business," Weaver said. "Nothing to do with you,"—Weaver licked his lips and surveyed the situation—"which is why we're going to leave you to your . . . whatever it is you're doing."

"That'd be great," Cole said.

Weaver and his cronies backed out into the middle of the street. Cole turned to head into the store.

"Sorry about your wife," Weaver called out. "I'll really miss her."

It turned out to be eight words, but the situation did indeed escalate rather quickly.

Within seconds, Cole was on Weaver and had smashed his fist squarely into Weaver's slightly crooked nose. He felt the bone shatter underneath, and when he pulled back for another strike, Weaver's nose was more of a weirdly deflated blob. In a few swift movements, Cole had struck him in the throat, knocked him from his feet, and drawn his blade.

Ram, reacting just as quickly, whipped out his sidearm and held it to Jarak's head. Jarak returned the favor. The Goons grabbed their rifles and pointed them at Cole.

Gregor didn't even know where to look, let alone who to shoot. He'd pulled out his sidearm and was sort of loosely pointing it in the direction of the standoff.

Cole breathed heavily as he held the blade to Weaver's throat, pressing it in ever so slightly.

"One. More. Word." Cole watched Weaver's face frantically twitch from the electric shocks. "One more word and you won't like how this ends."

Gregor watched as Cole leaned in closer to the younger man's face.

Weaver forced a laugh. "Oh, won't I? We both know you won't do shit. Everyone knows the stories. You're just a—"

"We're going to go now," Cole said. "And you're going to go." Cole released the pressure on Weaver's throat and stood up, backing away off the street.

"If we see you again," Cole said, collapsing the blade and returning it to his belt, "we're going to have to finish this discussion."

Ram and Jarak still held their pistols to each other's heads. Neither wanted to be the first to withdraw.

"Ram," Cole said, "it's not worth it. We have to go."

"Lower your weapons," Weaver said, his voice a raspy whisper. "Damn it, lower them!"

All parties lowered their weapons and returned to their respective sides. The tension was still thick in the air, but by now a crowd had gathered and were taking in every action. They all knew that the authorities wouldn't be far behind. Weaver backed away, wiping the blood from his face, before turning and disappearing into the crowd, and his squad followed closely after him.

Gregor was still vaguely pointing his gun at the place where Cole had been holding Weaver down. He quickly lowered it, hoping that no one had noticed. The street was quiet now, save for a few vendors shouting at passing potential customers. With the excitement now over, the crowd had quickly lost interest and dispersed.

"I'm sensing a history," Gregor said. He then realized he'd said it out loud.

Cole and Ram both ignored him as they brushed past and entered the shop.

"Right," Gregor said to himself and hurried after them.

Inside Salvage Ba-Zarr they found something a bit unusual: there, in the middle of an aisle filled with what appeared to be salvaged food processors, was a man. The man was on his knees, staring at the floor and shaking from head to toe. Cole and Ram looked at each other and realized that he must have seen what had just transpired in front of his store.

"Beren Zarr?" Cole asked quietly, not wanting to scare the poor guy.

"Whatever you want, you take!" Beren shouted, the fear palpable in every word. "No trouble!"

"We're not here to hurt you, Mister Zarr," Gregor said, trying to reassure him.

Beren looked up at the three of them, his face was pale and sweaty.

"You took something from our friend Kag Darka recently, a lockbox." Cole said. "He would like it back."

"Out back!" Beren said, still shouting, but more in earnest to get rid of his burly visitors. "I show you."

As Beren scurried out into the back room, Ram laughed. "Maybe we should ask nicely more often?"

They followed him in only to find him staring at his desk, the top of which was completely bare. He started looking around frantically.

"So, where is it?" Cole asked.

"Was here," Beren said, clearly flustered. "Now it is gone."

"Are you sure you put it there?" Ram asked.

"Well, no," Beren said, stammering, "but it is gone."

"Well, shit," Ram said.

As Cole, Ram, and Beren proceeded to tear the room apart looking for the lockbox, Gregor decided to take a look for it in some of the boxes near the back door. He was halfway through a box filled with broken data pads when he heard a metallic banging. It wasn't coming from inside the room. Easing the back door open, he peeked out and then looked back toward the search on the other side of the room.

"What is it we're looking for again?"

"Small lockbox," Cole said amid a whirl of papers.

"Oh, right. Well, in that case, you might want to come out here," Gregor said as he disappeared through the back door.

The flurry of papers and boxes came to a halt as they watched Gregor leave. Confused, Cole, Ram, and Beren followed him out the door. The four of them stood together outside Beren's shop in the narrow alley, and together they stared.

"Is that it?" Gregor asked, pointing.

A short way down the alley was a young girl, looking to be no more than sixteen, her clothes ragged, her bare feet covered in dirt. She was bashing the lockbox against a ventilation duct, again and again, in the hope that it would break open. Hearing voices, she turned and saw four men staring at her and at the lockbox. The youngest of them locked eyes with her and, without saying a word, somewhat awkwardly raised his hand and waved. She found herself just as awkwardly returning the gesture.

She recognized Beren as she had been a frequenter of his store in recent weeks.

It seemed that Beren recognized her as well.

"Thief!" Beren shouted, angrily waving his hands in the air.

The girl grabbed the lockbox and ran.

SEVEN

"GREAT," COLE SAID.

Cole and Ram took off after the girl.

"You stay with him!" Cole shouted back over his shoulder to Gregor.

By the time they made it to the main street, the girl was gone. A quick scan of the crowd turned up empty, but then Ram caught sight of her ducking into an alley across the way. "Got her!"

They cut across the flow of the foot traffic after her, knocking over several people and a food cart in the process. The alley was dark and cluttered, and the lights above could do little to get through the cracks in the cables that ran every which way above them.

Ram caught another glimmer of movement around a distant corner, but as they gave chase and rounded it, they found themselves at the intersection of several long, cluttered alleyways.

They also found that the girl had disappeared completely.

"Wait," Cole whispered.

Unluckily for the girl, it wasn't the first time they had chased someone down. Alleys and paths crossed each other for kilometers off of the main roads. She was only just in front of them a few seconds prior and hadn't had enough time to get very far away. The girl had to be hiding somewhere nearby, hoping they would just run right by her. Cole knew how to handle this: sound would be their best help in this chase.

Cole raised his finger to his lips, signaling to Ram to stay quiet. A few short hand signals later and Ram understood the whole plan: split up, comb the area, check in and under everything, and flush her out. Ram took a pathway off to the left, and Cole continued forward.

They had moved so far into the rat's nest of alleyways that even the light from the main streets was starting to peter out. Luckily for them, the residents of this part of town were aware of this and had hung lanterns from the cabling that ran overhead. They provided enough light to aid a search, but also enough shadows for someone to hide.

Cole rounded the corner to find a row of bins lining the wall. They must have been out the back of some kind of restaurant because Cole could smell the food wafting out the back door.

Cole looked at the bins and, judging by the size and shape of them, figured them as good a candidate as any for holding a small teenage girl. He had just opened the second one when he heard a noise up the alley. He looked up to see what it was.

It was Ram. He'd come around the corner and run straight into a tower of boxes that, from the sounds of it, contained a lot of glassware. Cole shook his head before pointing to the bins.

The girl heard the crash and knew that they must be close. She also knew that the bin had been a poor choice from the instant she'd jumped in. She knew better than to trap herself.

The girl listened as the sounds of the bin lids opening and crashing down closed in from both sides. She had to move.

Crash. A bin toward the center of the group lurched forward, scattering a small amount of garbage across the ground, but that wasn't all. There, lying in the middle of the trash like a stunned Harb, was the girl, still clutching the lockbox. It seemed to take a few seconds for her to process the situation before she sprung up and burst through the back door of the restaurant.

"Ram, go!" Cole shouted, rushing after her through the door. Ram took off down the side alley to try and find the front of the place to cut her off.

It was hot and stuffy in the kitchen, and what little staff were in there quickly scattered as soon as the chase tore through. The girl managed to pull down a large stack of plates across Cole's path, but it just annoyed him more than it actually managed to slow him down.

The girl slid over the service counter and, with a quick roll, was on her feet in the main dining area of the restaurant. Dodging around tables, she ran to the door but was stopped dead in her tracks.

"Hey there," Ram said. He was breathing heavily. The girl backed up and away from Ram and turned to see Cole coming in from the kitchen, equally out of breath. She was cornered.

"Look, kid," Ram said, holding his place at the door. "It's not worth it. Hand it over."

"And why should I?" the girl said, her voice projecting an age that was not her own.

"It's not yours," Ram said. "You stole—"

"I found it," she said. "So it's mine, butthead." Ram found himself smiling at the insult.

Cole had been slowly closing the gap between them while Ram had kept her talking, but the ruse only lasted a short while. The girl spun on Cole.

"Don't even try it," she said.

Cole stepped back to show he meant no harm. "What's your name?" he asked.

"What's it to you?" she shot back.

"What's your name?" he asked again.

The girl looked between the two of them, and realizing it was probably futile to fight the situation, she sighed.

"Kira," she said, calmly and clearly so they could both hear.

Cole looked at her standing between them. She was a slight, little thing—probably didn't eat very well, but there seemed to be a strength to her. Her hair was short and tied back like she knew how to keep it from being a distraction or a liability. Her legs were set in such a way that she could make a break for it at any second. But she wouldn't. Cole could see that this was a girl who'd had to take care of herself for a long time, maybe her whole life, and that she was also smart enough to know when she was beaten.

There was something about her that reminded him so much of Zara.

Cole shook his head to chase away the memories that he couldn't deal with here and now, and took a careful step toward Kira.

"Kira," Cole said, his tone softening. "My name's Cole, and that's Ram. We're not here to hurt you." Cole pointed to the box that Kira still had clutched tightly to her chest. "That box was stolen from a friend of ours, and we're trying to get it back to—"

"OK, one: I found it, and two: you're friends with that guy?" Kira asked, incredulous. "He's a total dick."

"Little charmer, this one," Ram said, still blocking the doorway.

Cole laughed. "No. He, uh, actually stole it from our friend, and then you stole it fr—"

"Found it," Kira said.

"Right," Cole said, "then you found it."

Kira looked down at the box in her hands. "If I give this back to you, what's in it for me?"

"Not sure you're in a position to bargain, sweetheart," Ram said.

"I'm not sure *you're* in a position to bargain, butthead." Kira was more than capable of returning fire.

Cole laughed at the look that had appeared on Ram's face and then rummaged around in his pockets until he found what he was looking for. He pulled out the small chip and held it out for Kira to see. Her eyes went wide.

"See this?" Cole said. "This has five thousand credits on it. Give us the box, and it's all yours and you'll be free to go."

"Five thousand credits?" she asked, staring at the chip.

"Five *thousand*?" Ram asked, equally stunned.

"Five thousand, all yours," Cole said.

Kira shrugged. "OK, you win. But you throw me the chip first," she said, "and then I'll throw the box."

Cole threw the chip to her, and she plucked it out of the air with one hand, the other still holding the lockbox.

"Now you," Cole said, motioning for her to throw the box.

Kira turned, walked over to Ram at the door, and handed him the box.

"Here you go, butthead," she said with a self-impressed smile. "Pleasure doing business."

"Yeah, well, don't spend it all at once," Ram said, stepping out of the doorway and into the room.

With a bounce in her step, Kira disappeared out the door and into the darkness of the alleys beyond.

For the first time since they burst into the dining room, Cole looked around. There were three diners, all at separate tables. All were sitting, cutlery in hand, mouths agape. He cleared his throat and made for the door.

"Sorry about the mess," Cole said as he and Ram walked out into the alley.

"Sol?" Cole said, switching on his comms. "We have it; start loading the gear." A muffled response came through. "I don't care what he says, we have the box, so load the gear. We'll be back soon."

Kira sat on a nearby ledge and watched as the two of them disappeared out onto the main streets. She flipped the credit chip back and forth between her fingers before dropping down to the ground and following.

Cole and Ram retraced their steps as best they could and eventually made it back to Salvage Ba-Zarr, where they collected Gregor and then started the trip back to Darka. As they turned onto Darka's street, some footsteps came up behind the trio and someone tapped Gregor on the shoulder.

"So, what's your name?" Kira said.

Cole and Ram looked around to see Kira following them.

"Just terrific," Ram said.

Gregor wasn't sure where the voice had come from, but turned around to see the face of the girl from the alley. "Uh, Gregor, Gregor Mishkol," Gregor said, his voice rising in pitch toward the end.

"You sure?" Kira said, laughing. "Because that sounded like a question."

Gregor didn't know how to respond to that.

"Are you guys like mercenaries, or what?" Kira asked.

"Uh, no," Gregor said, finding his voice again. "No, nothing like that."

"We kind of are, though," Cole said without turning around, "if you think about it."

"Well, you're not Fed guys," Kira said confidently. "I'd spot that a klick off."

Ram just raised an eyebrow to Cole, who shook his head and smiled. They were now out the front of The Darka Side of Salvage—the proper entrance this time.

"So are you like private security or—"

Ram stopped and turned to Kira, who then also stopped.

"Look, Kira, was it?" Ram said. "We're kind of in a rush, so if you don't mind." Ram took Kira by the shoulders and steered her away out onto the street. "Thanks, run along now."

Gregor shrugged sheepishly as he passed.

Kira just stood there blank-faced and watched them as they headed into the shop.

"How rude."

Inside, they found Sol and Kag deep in conversation.

"So, what you're saying is that this wasn't your original choice?" Sol asked.

"No," Kag said. "As I've already mentioned many times, my second cousin up on level thirty-two stole my original idea."

Cole, Ram, and Gregor approached them, weary about interrupting their discussion.

Sol saw them out the corner of his eye. "Fellas!" Sol said. "You wouldn't read about it: Kag started this place up last year after his cousin, uh . . ."

"Tek Darka," Kag prompted.

"That's right, Tek Darka," Sol said. "He stole—"

"Kag's original idea," Ram said. "We heard."

"It was going to be a hair salon. Can you believe it?" Sol said with far too big a smile on his face.

"I really can't," Cole said, trying his best not to laugh. Ram wasn't as reserved.

"Hey," Sol said, slapping Kag on the shoulder, "tell 'em the name, tell 'em the name, go on."

"'Would You Like It Darka?'" Kag said flatly.

"Isn't that brilliant?" Sol's eyes went wide. "And Tek, the old snake, stole it right out—"

"Right out from under him, we got it, Sol," Cole said.

"Exactly!" Sol said, pointing excitedly at seemingly nothing.

Cole looked at the counter and saw two empty glasses and a half-empty bottle. Kag sat quietly next to Sol at the counter and looked at Cole with a face that could only say "help me."

"Sol," Cole said, "why have you been drinking?"

"Well, you guys took so bloody long, we had to do something to pass the time," Sol said.

Kag got up from the counter. "So you got the lockbox?" he asked.

"As promised," Cole said. "Ram?"

Ram handed the box to Kag, whose eyes widened at the state it was in. Kag ran his hands all over it, inspecting every dent and chip in the paintwork. He glared at Ram.

"This your doing?" Kag asked.

"There were some complications," Cole said. He looked over his shoulder to the outside to see if Kira was still there, but she'd gone. "I'm sure everything inside is fine."

"What's in there that's so damn important?" Ram asked, finally bringing his laughter under control.

"Um, it's some . . ." Kag seemed to be trying to avoid saying the answer. "It's some, uh, love letters. They're very—"

"Love letters?" Ram blurted out. "We did all that for some damn love letters?"

"Well, you see, there's this Rotarian—"

"Why would Zarr steal your love letters?" Cole asked.

"I, uh," Kag said, staring straight at the floor, "I might have told him there was money in there."

"Why would you do that?" Ram asked.

"He was in here the other day bragging about all his sales," Kag said as he sat back down at the counter and poured himself a drink, "so I told him I'd sold a whole heap of scrap and, well—"

Kag was interrupted by Sol, who was tapping him on the shoulder, trying to get him to pour him another glass.

"I think he's had enough," Cole said as he took Sol's glass away and turned to Ram. "You think you can get him back to the ship?"

"Not a problem," Ram said as he peeled Sol away from the counter.

"I'm assuming you've got the gear loaded, Sol?" Cole asked.

Sol shook his head. "Uh, it's on a speeder out front," he said, his words melding together. He leaned forward, nearly fell off his stool, and whispered loudly to the whole room. "Covered it up all secret-like, I did."

Cole sighed.

"Well, I guess that'll make getting him back easier," Cole said. He then realized Gregor was nowhere to be found. "Has anyone seen Gregor?"

"I'm here!" Gregor popped his head out from in the back room. "I was just looking through some of the scrap back here."

"I want you to go back with Ram and Sol, and get the ship loaded up and ready to go," Cole said.

"What about you?" Ram asked, struggling to hold Sol upright.

"I'll catch up," Cole said. "I just have to follow up on a few things here."

"All right," Ram said, half dragging Sol to the door. "See you back at the ship."

Gregor still hadn't come out of the back room.

"Get moving, kid," Ram shouted across the room. "Time's a-wasting."

As quickly as he appeared from the back room, Gregor disappeared out the door behind Ram and Sol.

"What were you two drinking?" Cole asked Kag, who looked exhausted.

"Sulvar Ale," Kag said. "It affects everyone a bit differently. Your friend, it would seem, doesn't have much of a tolerance."

"No, he never has," Cole said.

Kag got up from his chair and put the bottle away behind the counter. "I'm assuming that's not what you wanted to ask me about?" he said.

"No."

"Why do I get the feeling I'm not going to like this?" Kag asked, seeing the grimness that had come over Cole's face.

"Our mutual friend told me that you might know something about reactivating synthetic Conduit implants," Cole said.

Kag tensed up immediately. "And that's where this conversation ends. Good day to you, sir." Kag quickly made for the back room, but Cole was quicker to cut him off.

"You don't know anything?" Cole asked.

"I knew something was off about you," Kag said, looking Cole up and down. "I thought you might have been a Conduit, but a Synth? Do you have any idea what would happen to me if I was caught helping you?"

"So you *can* help?" Cole asked, his hand still firmly placed on Kag's chest.

"No," came Kag's determined reply.

"But you know anyone who can?" Cole asked.

"No, and even if I did, I wouldn't tell you," Kag said, trying to force his way past Cole. "They could still get me as an accessory. Now get out of my way!"

Cole relinquished his position and stepped back from the doorway. Kag hurried past.

"Look, if you could just tell me a name, I wouldn't even have to—"

The wooden door to the back room slammed shut and was followed by the loud rustling of the shutters being closed.

"Terrific," Cole said to the closed door.

When Cole got back to the ship, Ram was just coming down the entryway, having loaded up the last of the crates. They met at the bottom of the ramp.

"Trouble?" Ram asked.

"Just wanted to see if he had anything on Tobias," Cole said.

Ram looked at him with a raised eyebrow. "And?"

"He didn't."

Cole could tell Ram didn't believe him. He knew the time would soon come when he'd have to lay everything out about his implants, but that would mean opening up a can of worms he wasn't sure he was ready to open. Cole did actually know a place where he could get his implants reactivated, but he was fast running out of ways to avoid going there.

"Any sign of Weaver?" Cole asked, wanting desperately to change the subject.

"Nothing," Ram said, going along with it. "Maybe he actually listened this time?"

They stood in silence at the bottom of the ramp until their comms crackled to life. "Oh, back, are we?" Sol's voice cut through the static. "We right to leave this shit hole? I'm getting real . . ."

"He doesn't think he's flying us out of here, does he?" Cole asked.

"I'll jab him with some QWake," Ram said. "He'll be fine. "

"Oi!" Sol was back on. "Hurry up already!"

From across the hangar, Charles Weaver stood and watched as the ramp of the *Havok* closed and the ship slowly lifted off. Weaver wiped away the blood that was still slowly seeping from his nose.

"Is it done?" Weaver asked.

"Yes, sir," Jarak Rol said, coming up beside him. "Do we follow?"

Weaver watched as the *Havok* glided out of the hangar and into the vacuum of space.

He nodded.

"How's the head, Sol?" Ram asked as Sol emerged from the cockpit. It had taken two packets of QWake to bring him back to the real world. Cole's record was still intact.

"Getting there," Sol said. "I propose that on all future missions, we carry those bloody needles with us. Cover any *misadventures* we might have."

"How much did you have?" Cole asked.

"Enough," Sol said. "The little bugger had more than I did, and he didn't even bat an eye." Sol sat down at the table in the main hold. "And speaking of misadventure, what took you lot so bloody long?"

After having the whole afternoon laid out for him, Sol couldn't help but laugh. "You took all that time because you were outsmarted by a little girl?" he said.

"I still think we should have just taken the stuff," Ram said, "instead of turning into his errand boys."

"Well, it's done now," Cole said. "And besides, we had some fun, made a few friends." Cole managed to keep a straight face.

"Oh yeah," Ram said, rolling his eyes, "friends for life. Well, actually, Gregor might have. That girl was about his age. Hey, kid?"

Gregor looked up from his data pad. "What? No, she was just, I mean, she was too, uh, and I wouldn't, I don't even know—"

"It's OK, kid," Ram said. "I'm just messing with you."

Bang. Crash.

They all heard the sound.

Gregor spoke first. "What was—"

He was cut off by Ram, who signaled for him to shush. The sound had come from a storage room off the main hold. Slowly and quietly, Ram walked over to the door and pressed his ear up against it. Nothing. He pressed the button to open the door, and it slid open, slowly revealing the cause of the noise huddled in the corner.

Ram let out a loud sigh. "Son of a bitch."

EIGHT

KIRA STOOD IN the middle of the main hold of the *Havok*. To her right, Gregor sat at a table, eating and avoiding all eye contact. The other three were currently huddled in the far corner of the hold, arguing about what to do with her. It was a situation she had found herself in far too often in her short life.

They thought that they were being discreet about it, but she could hear every word.

"She can't stay here," Ram said.

"So what, do you want me to turn all the way back around so we can take her back?" Sol asked, gesturing wildly off into the distance.

"It's a better idea than—"

"She must have had a reason for sneaking aboard," Cole said, cutting Ram off. He'd seen the look in her eyes when she was cornered back in the restaurant. She knew when to run, and she wouldn't have just done this on a whim.

"I don't care what her reason is," Ram shouted. "She can't be here."

"We could drop her off somewhere safer maybe?" Cole said, trying to find a solution.

"We can't just go jaunting off across the galaxy to drop off some lost child," Ram said. "Or have you forgotten why we're out here in the first place?" Ram's face dropped. He knew he'd stepped over the line. "Cole, I . . ." The guilt was evident in his voice.

"It's OK, Ram," Cole said, waving the apology away.

"All I'm trying to say is," Ram said, gathering himself, "is that I wasn't sure if having her around would be the best thing for the mission or for you."

She couldn't see their faces and she didn't know what the mission was that they were yelling about, but Kira knew one thing: that their conversation had gone on too long without her getting a say.

"Excuse me?" Kira asked, her voice getting lost among the noise of the argument. She stomped over to where Gregor was sitting and took the bun that he was currently in the middle of eating.

"What are you doing?" Gregor asked.

"Getting their attention," Kira replied. She returned to the center of the room and hurled the bun at the trio. It smacked into the back of Ram's head with quite a bit of force.

"What the—" Ram said. Then, upon realizing what had happened and where it had come from, he turned to Kira. "What?"

"I would like to stay," Kira said, squaring her shoulders.

"Well, it's not up to you," Ram said.

Gregor moved to stand next to Kira. "I think it would be best if she stayed, at least—"

"It's not up to you either," Ram snapped at Gregor.

A silence fell on the room. Kira looked at Gregor and smiled. He smiled back.

Kira took a step forward toward the others. "I can't go back there," she said.

Ram took a step forward also. "Well tough sh—" He was cut off by Cole's hand on his shoulder.

"Why can't you go back, Kira?" Cole asked.

"It's . . . well . . . th-there's just nothing for me to go back to, OK?" A tear formed in the corner of her eye. "I-I'm on my own. I don't have anywhere else to go."

Cole could see she was hiding something. Ram could too.

"And that's the only reason?" Ram asked.

Kira shuffled her feet on the ground. Her strong footing from their earlier confrontation was nowhere to be seen. "There was some trouble."

"You don't say," Ram said as he walked away from the conversation.

"What happened, love?" Sol asked.

"It's OK," Cole said after a few moments of silence. "You can tell us."

Kira cleared her throat. "I, uh . . . my parents, they died when I was very young. I'd been living in a shelter in the housing district. I was one of the older kids, been there the longest." Kira walked over and sat down on the table. "For the last couple of years, every other month, a man would come, take one of the kids, and leave, like clockwork." She looked up at Cole, a tear now rolling down her cheek. "Two weeks ago, he came and he chose me."

Cole looked at her, and he couldn't quite place the look in her eyes.

"What happened, Kira?" Cole asked as he moved closer.

"I-I didn't go with him," she said. "I got away."

"Got away?" Sol asked.

Kira brushed away the tear from her cheek, and her face hardened. "He can't hurt anyone anymore."

Cole saw it now. He was sorry he hadn't seen it sooner; he might have been able to avoid putting her through reliving it. The strength he had seen in her eyes earlier had now been replaced with guilt. He'd seen it in the mirror many times before. The guilt of taking a life was something someone as young as Kira should never have to experience.

"She stays," Cole said.

Kira blinked away the tears and looked at Cole. His smile was sympathetic and sincere. She was surprised to find the same look on the other faces in the room as well, even Ram's. She smiled a small smile. "Thank you," she said, her voice quiet. Maybe this time she could truly be safe.

"Gregor?" Cole said.

"Yes?" came the reply as Gregor stepped to his side.

"Why don't you find Kira a place to sleep," Cole said.

"There's a room down by main storage that's got a spare cot in it," Sol said, pointing down the corridor.

"So, they don't let you in on the decision-making?" Kira asked, plopping down on the cot. The room was small and dark. It seemed like its main purpose was extra storage space, if the boxes stacked along the end wall were any indication.

"Oh, no," Gregor said. "No, I'm only new."

Kira scrunched up her nose. "So? I thought you guys were like a team?"

"Well, we are."

"And it doesn't bug you that you don't get any input?"

"It's not my place to give input. I haven't earned the right," Gregor said.

"Well, thanks for sticking up for me anyway," Kira said with a smile.

"Oh, uh, no problem," Gregor said, his eyes glued to the floor. "I'll, uh, let you get settled in. I have to get back. Important mission stuff to do," he said, finding any excuse to remove his awkward self from the situation.

"Important mission stuff?"

Gregor nodded. "Yes, very important."

"OK then, you better get going. Don't want you to miss the . . . stuff."

With another quick nod, Gregor hurriedly turned and made for the door.

"Gregor?" Kira said.

Gregor stopped short. "Yeah?"

"You should try sticking up for yourself sometime," she said. "You might be surprised what can happen."

"She all right?" Cole asked Gregor as he came back into the room.

"I think so," Gregor said.

"This isn't a permanent situation," Cole said to everyone this time. "I just want you all to know that. My hope is that we'll be able to find somewhere safe to drop her off along the way."

"We can only hope," grumbled Ram.

"We couldn't just blast her out the airlock, Ram," Cole said.

"I know, I know."

"Right, so now we have to talk about the next stop," Cole said.

"Where we headed?" Sol asked.

"We need to make a detour," Cole said as he leaned against the sidewall of the hold.

"What kind of detour?" Ram asked.

Cole knew they weren't going to like this. "I need to have my implants reactivated."

"Implants?" Gregor asked. Cole rolled up the sleeve of his shirt to show Gregor the scars, and the metal that poked through them.

"You're a Synth?" Gregor's mouth fell open. "But that's . . . You can't be. The Federation—"

"There was a grace period following the end of the war," Cole said. "Synths could join the Federation forces if they agreed to have their implants deactivated as a condition of—"

"But even still, it's forbidden for anyone to be a Synth now," Gregor said. "This is crazy. No one in their right mind would . . ." Gregor looked around at Ram and Sol for backup, but they just sat there. "Did you know about this?"

"We did, mate," Sol said.

"It was a bit hard to miss the scars," Ram said.

"Look, I know the risks," Cole said, "but if I don't do this, I won't be able to take out Tobias. He was just as strong as he had always been, and I've been out of that game for a long time."

"So how exactly do you plan on getting this done?" Ram asked. "The restrictions on this stuff have surely wiped out nearly everyone who did it back in the day."

"Yeah, I've kinda been finding that out," Cole said. "But there is one option left."

"What is it?" Gregor asked.

"I know someone," Cole said, his voice slow and deliberate. He wanted to make sure this was all worded just right. "Or rather, I knew someone."

"Well, where are they?" Sol asked.

Cole took a deep breath.

"Ryger." He couldn't keep this hidden any longer. He couldn't risk Tobias getting away just to keep his past bottled away.

"Ryger," Ram repeated. "*You* know someone on Ryger?"

"I was born there."

"You were *what*?" Ram said in disbelief.

"Look, it's something I've never talked about. I told the academy I was born on Volaria—"

"Mate, you told *us* you were born on Volaria," Sol said.

"Olivia didn't even know," Cole said.

Gregor leaned forward. "Why hide that all these years?"

"It was a period of my life that I'm not proud of, Gregor. I was doing whatever I could to forget it entirely. I *had* forgotten it."

"Cole, we're not angry," Ram said. "Just a little . . . surprised."

"I'm actually not surprised at all," Sol said with a laugh. "Suddenly an awful lot of things about you make a whole lot more sense than they did five minutes ago."

"Trust me when I say I've done everything I can to not have to go back there," Cole said, "but this is the only way."

"Well, if that's where we need to go," Sol said, heading for the cockpit, "then that's where we're gonna go. I'll set the course."

Ram got up to leave, but Cole remained unmoved from his position against the wall. "There's more to this than you're saying, isn't there?" Ram asked.

"There is," Cole said.

"No need to go into it now. We've got a long trip ahead of us," Ram said. "Go get some sleep."

After Ram had gone, only Cole and Gregor were left in the hold.

"Sir, uh, Cole, can I ask you something?" Gregor said.

"Shoot," Cole said.

"I didn't want to ask before, but what's on Ryger?"

"The Shek'Tarii," Cole said.

"Oh." Gregor had heard things as a child about the Shek'Tarii, but he'd always thought that they were stories created to scare children. Bands of men and monsters that would kill, pillage, or destroy anything for a payday, they were said to have mystical powers and that each of them were stronger than ten men. Gregor didn't know if he was more scared as a child or as an adult who now knew they were real. Then it all clicked into place.

"You're a . . ."

"I *was*, a long time ago," Cole said, "a lifetime."

"I don't know very much about them, only things from stories," Gregor said.

"You'd be surprised how much of that old stuff is true," Cole said.

Gregor swallowed the lump that had formed in his throat and continued. "Like I said, I don't know much about them, but I always heard that they have issues with outsiders."

Cole laughed. "That would be putting it mildly."

"Will *we* be an issue?" Gregor asked.

Cole pushed himself away from the wall and walked over to Gregor. "It should be fine. I can vouch for you."

"Oh, good."

"That's providing that they don't blow my head off first, of course."

"Oh."

"I'm kidding," Cole said, giving Gregor a light shove.

"Oh, good."

"No, really, they might actually kill me."

Gregor went white. "Oh."

Cole sat alone in his quarters. They were five days into the trip to Ryger and were due to arrive the next day. He had spent a lot of the time by himself, running through in his mind everything that had happened and everything that was about to happen. They were now hurtling through space toward a past that he had long since said good-bye to. There was no other option: he had to face the people who made him who he was, *what* he was.

He had to face all that he had done. If he didn't, there was no way he'd be able to get justice for Olivia and Zara.

Cole had avoided making the marks for them ever since that fateful night. Time and again, he had prepared himself and backed out, too afraid to make the cut. Part of him felt like if he did it, then it would be final and they would be truly gone. The other part, though, realized that they were, in fact, truly gone and that he couldn't help them any longer. He had to honor them the same way he honored all the others who had passed from this world at his hands.

No, not the same way. This has to be done properly. They deserve that.

He hadn't done it the proper way since leaving Ryger all those years ago. It was their ritual, their tradition, and he'd carried on his own bastardized version of it for years. But for his family, he would do it properly.

They were worthy.

Cole removed his shirt and picked up the hilt of his blade. He knelt in the middle of the floor, facing the deep black of space, and placed the hilt on the floor in front of him.

"Shakla es te Rel. Fir haar ne es Varidum," Cole said to the darkness.

Taken from this Realm. Find peace in the Void.

Cole reached down and gently picked up the blade with both hands. He extended it a short way, it's thin metal blade unfurling, the pieces sliding over each other before locking into place and forming a short dagger.

"Vitari e ne mortena."

Live on in death.

As Cole said the words, he took the blade and pressed it to his chest.

Cole's body was covered in the marks, the scars representing the lives he had taken, the lives lost that he was responsible for. On that night, he had failed to protect his family, and they paid the ultimate price. The only place free from marks was an area over his heart. He had known that one day he would lose those closest to him, by means natural or otherwise. He had long saved this spot for them, hoping never to use it.

"Vitari e ne mortena, Olivia."

Cole repeated the words as he made the first cut for Olivia.

His body shook from the charge, but it only helped to tighten his grip and his resolve. He cut deeper than normal, for this was a deeper hurt than normal. The blood trickled slowly down his chest.

"Vitari e ne mortena, Zara."

He took his time with the second cut for Zara.

The shock ran up his neck and made the whole side of his face twitch uncontrollably, but he pushed through. He had to. He had failed the most when it came to Zara. He had missed so much of her life, always off on a mission or just too busy. Then, on that night, the one time she needed him more than any other in her life, he failed her. He had failed his daughter again and for the last time. This cut was the deepest.

The blood flowed.

"Galtara es cerana. Yaashni ve memorta."

Gone from creation. Forever in our memory.

Cole placed the blade on the floor in front of him. He dipped his fingers in the blood dripping from the cuts and stroked it across his forehead, then a short stroke on each closed eyelid.

"Yaashni ve memorta."

He sat, eyes closed, as the blood ran down his chest. After a short while, the flow stopped.

Cole opened his eyes.

"Vitari yaashni ne eterna."

Live forever in eternity.

It was done.

After a long silence, Cole stood, the dried blood cracking from the movement, and his head swirled. He had gone deeper than he had in a long time, and he was woozy from the blood loss. Cole lay down on his bed and saw that his door was slightly ajar. His mind was wandering, and he couldn't remember if he'd left it open. Before he could even bring himself to think about closing it, the ever-closing dark swept over his mind and he fell asleep.

Cole woke to the sound of the vidcom beeping and slowly rolled out of bed. The door was closed now. He looked down at his chest, where the blood had congealed and dried in the cuts. Before he answered the call, he wiped the dried blood from his face and put on a shirt to cover the wounds.

"All right, all right," Cole said to the machine, whose beeping had only gotten louder.

Sitting down groggily in front of the display, he accepted the call. Through the static, Oren's face appeared.

"You look like hell," Oren said.

"Hello to you too," Cole said, rubbing his eyes to force himself awake.

"I was just noticing you were in the Feldar sector. Given how far that is from Nikara, I assume you've picked up your gear already," Oren said. "Did you have any trouble?"

"Not much," Cole said, shifting in his chair. "Nothing we couldn't handle." Cole thought it best not to mention the run-in with Weaver or the fact that they'd picked up a passenger.

"Did you get any help with the reactivation?" Oren asked.

"No," Cole said, "that's why we're out here. I know someone on Ryger who might be able to help, but it's a long shot."

"On Ryger?" Oren asked, eyebrows raised.

Cole also didn't feel the need to spread his past around any further than he already had.

"Just an old friend. Then hopefully it'll be a matter of finding Tobias and ending this."

Oren looked offscreen to some displays at his side. "Well, it just so happens you're in luck," he said.

"Oh?"

"We found him, Cole. Cameras picked him up in a bar on Ferris two days ago, and there are no indications he's left the planet, or the bar, since."

Cole furrowed his brow in thought and frowned. "Even if my contact can help, I'm looking at a minimum of a couple of recovery days," Cole said. "I'm going to need you to keep an eye on him for me."

Cole's door slid open. It was Ram. "We need you up front, Cole," he said.

Cole looked back to the call. "Oren, I have to go. Duty calls," he said. "Keep me posted, OK?"

Oren nodded. "Will do," he said. "If he moves, you'll be the first to know."

Cole switched off the call and headed to the door. "What's up?" he asked.

"Was that Oren?" Ram asked, motioning to the vidcom.

"Yeah, he's found Tobias," Cole said as they walked down the corridor to the main hold.

"Where?"

"Been on Ferris a few days."

"That's not far from here," Ram said.

"I know," Cole said. "He'll probably be gone again by the time we're ready, though. Oren's keeping an eye on it."

"Oh, good," Ram said, his voice dripping with sarcasm.

"What did you need me for?" Cole asked. He didn't want to get into it over Ram's and Oren's little feud. He'd been hearing it for years, and right now, he wasn't in the mood.

"We're coming up on Ryger," Ram said, "and Sol was picking up a signal from some kind of way station. Seemed to be looking to identify ships in the area."

"A way station? That's new."

As they came out into the main hold, Cole saw Kira sitting off to the side with Gregor. She was looking more settled-in than last he saw her. She had washed her hair, and Gregor had given her some of his fatigues to wear. Clothing choices aboard an in-transit starship were rather limited, as it turned out.

"You OK?" Cole asked her from across the room.

Kira didn't reply. She just looked at him for a few moments, concern readily visible in her eyes, before she returned to her conversation with Gregor. Cole didn't have time to contemplate the meaning behind her stare, as a voice called out from the cockpit doorway.

"Cole," Sol said, "I really think we might need you for this one."

In the cockpit, Cole could hear the chatter coming through the comms. It sounded impatient. Ram, Sol, and Gregor filed in behind him, while Kira stood in the doorway and watched.

"Unidentified starship, I say again, halt your progress," the voice said. "State your name and purpose for entering Ryger."

"Why haven't you said anything?" Cole asked Sol.

"Thought it might be best coming from you, mate," Sol said. "They know you. Less likely to shoot."

"You'd be surprised," Cole said as he sat in the pilot's chair. He leaned into the comms.

"This is Cole Traske, aboard the civilian vessel *Havok*, visiting a friend."

"One moment," the voice said after a short pause.

The pause that followed was longer. Eventually, the voice crackled through once again.

"Any other occupants on board?"

"Four others," Cole said. "Traveling companions."

"Traveling companions?" Ram asked.

Cole switched off the microphone for a moment. "What was I supposed to say? 'My heavily armed, trained killers are here with me'?"

"I see your point," Ram said.

It seemed like minutes had passed without so much as a word out of the way station. The silence in the cockpit was deafening.

"They're not going for it," Sol said.

Cole held up a hand. "Just wait," he said. "They know me. I'm in their records."

"Which records?" Gregor asked.

The comms crackled to life, snuffing out any chance of Gregor getting an answer. "Civilian ship *Havok*, you are cleared to proceed," the voice said. "We've sent a packet to your ship's computer. Please follow the beacon to find your landing site.

A party will be there to greet you when you arrive. Welcome to Ryger."

Cole felt a flutter in the pit of his stomach. Something was off.

"I, for one, love parties," Ram said as he headed out of the cockpit.

"They do seem friendly enough," Sol said.

"Yeah," Cole said.

That's what's got me worried.

NINE

AS THE *HAVOK* burst through a large bank of clouds, the city of Ryger, named along with the planet, spread out across the landscape before them. Kira pushed her way to the front of the cockpit to get a better view out the front viewport. It was like nothing she had ever seen.

Into the distance stretched hundreds of large, wide mesas, jutting out of a flat and barren desert landscape. They were interconnected by multi-level bridges that were built atop natural rock spires and steel pylons. Some of the bridges seemed to span kilometers. The cities, or what could be seen of them, were built into the mountains, as though the centers of the mesas had been excavated, then built up from the inside. The larger mesas appeared more built up than the smaller ones, with tall steel structures jutting out of the rock like a gathering of silent steel giants.

Cole saw the look of wonder on Kira's face. "It's quite a thing to look at, isn't it?"

Kira just stared, trying to take it all in. She had spent her whole life in the shipyards. The cluttered and slowly decaying station was the only place she'd ever really known. She'd seen pictures of other places before, in books at the shelter or on screens in a shop front, but to see this with her own two eyes, spreading far off into the distance seemingly without end, it was like something from a dream.

The beacon was leading them to one of a large grouping of smaller mesas. Each had been hollowed out, leaving a thick wall of rock protecting the hangars inside. Sol banked the ship around and gently brought it down inside one of the ringed hangars on the edge of the cluster. A small group of people were waiting for them on the far side.

Cole got up and motioned for the rest of them to stay. "Look, I'll go out first and, y'know, test the waters. If it's cool, I'll give the signal."

"And if it's not cool?" Sol asked.

"Well, I'll probably be dead, and you should leave rather quickly." He laughed to try and make a joke of it, but none of them would have it. Plus, he couldn't honestly say that that wasn't about to happen. Cole had no idea how the people of Ryger had reacted to his leaving all those years ago, and he could very well be walking to his death. But there was only one way to find out.

"Oh, and it might be best to leave the weapons behind, just for the moment," Cole said. "We can come back for them later."

As he lowered the ramp, Kira came running behind him. "Can I come with you?" she asked, eager to see more of this new world.

"If it's safe, you can come with the others when I give the signal, OK? Just make sure you stay close to us and don't wander off."

"I can do that," Kira said.

"OK, well, keep a watch for my signal. Everything should be fine."

The ramp closed behind him with a soft thud, and a whirl of dust blew up off the metallic floor. A strong wind was blowing through the large openings carved into the sides of the hangar. Now out of the ship, Cole could see that there were six in the greeting party and several of them were armed. He started the long walk toward them, and with each step, his brain screamed at him to turn around, but he kept going. As he got closer, a man at the front of the group broke away and started to walk toward him to meet him halfway. It didn't take long for Cole to recognize the face, and the anxiety he'd been feeling fell away almost instantly.

"Freelan?" Cole called out to the man.

"Holy shit, it is you," Freelan shouted back. "When they told me who it was, I thought there wasn't a chance in hell you'd ever be back here."

They met in a large embrace. Freelan Mir was Cole's best friend from his time with the Shek'Tarii. They had been friends since they were children and had grown up together in Ryger.

Freelan stepped back and took a long look at his old friend.

"How've you been?" Freelan asked.

"Better," Cole replied.

"We all thought you must have been dead," Freelan said. "Thought maybe this was going to be some skarfer trying to use your name to get in here, but here you are."

"Here I am," Cole said.

"Thought you said there were four others with you?"

"They're in the ship," Cole said. "Just wanted to make sure you weren't going to kill me."

Freelan laughed. "Well, if you hadn't turned out to be *you*, then we were actually going to kill you." Freelan pointed to the guards behind him. "What do you think they're here for?"

"So we're good?" Cole asked. "It's safe for them to come out?"

"Look, Cole, if they're friends of yours, then they're friends of Ryger," Freelan said.

Cole waved to the ship to give the signal. The ramp lowered, and the four of them appeared, starting to make their way over.

Freelan looked at them, and his eyes fell on the girl, who seemed out of place. "That girl yours, Cole?"

Hearing the question, Cole's heart skipped a beat. For a second, his eyes saw Zara walking toward him through the swirling dust. A tear threatened to form, but he quickly blinked it away, and with another cloud of dust, he could see only Kira again.

"Uh, no," Cole said finally. "Stowaway, if you can believe it."

"And you didn't just blast her out of the airlock?"

Cole laughed. "No, I didn't just blast her out of the airlock. That was a long time ago, Free."

"Yes, it was."

The four others had now arrived, and Cole motioned for them to come closer.

"Freelan Mir," Cole said, pointing to each member of his group, "I'd like you to meet Ramses Barden, Solomon Dane, Gregor Mishkol, and Kira . . ."

Cole realized he had no idea what Kira's last name was, so he looked at her for an answer.

"Uh," she said quietly, "just Kira."

Freelan stepped forward. "Well, welcome to Ryger," he said. "Now, if you will follow me, I have been instructed to take you to the Hall."

"Sounds important," Ram said.

They were led to a row of open-top vehicles that were waiting outside the hangar on the bridge. After passing through several other hangars and settlements, they came to a large, single-level bridge that stretched toward a solitary mesa. It was only a short trip to the Hall, and there was no mistaking it when they arrived.

The Hall *was* the mesa; it wasn't just built into it. The bridge itself terminated at a large balcony that had been built off of the front edge of the mesa. It was just about the only man-made thing visible from the outside. Everything else was carved stone. The entryway to the Hall was a large courtyard, set back into the rock about a hundred meters and just as far to the ceiling. Its walls were a smooth arch that met at the top, where a series of large lanterns hung down into the void below. It was the middle of the day, but the shadow from the overhang meant lighting was needed deeper into the courtyard.

They passed into a comparatively small foyer that was lit along both sides by fires that ran the length of the room, the gentle orange glow softly illuminating the bare walls. At its end stood a large set of wooden doors, fifty meters tall and inlaid with gold and stone. Freelan called a halt to the group before they passed through and pulled Cole aside.

"I feel I have to warn you," Freelan said. "Not everyone is going to be happy to see you. Everyone's heard rumors about what happened on Epheria. Not many of them were favorable to you."

"It's OK, Free," Cole said. "Not everybody liked me before. It's—"

"The way you left things caused a lot of ill will, Cole," Freelan said. "A lot of people wanted to hunt you down. Some still do."

"Lucky me."

Freelan headed toward the door.

"Everything all right?" Ram asked, tapping Cole on the shoulder.

"I sure hope so," Cole said before heading after Freelan.

Freelan and several others pushed open the heavy wooden doors and led them inside.

"Holy shit," Kira said as she looked up at the expansive ceiling above.

Unfortunately, she'd said it far too loudly, and one of the guards walking with them shot her a menacing look.

Sol pulled her back to walk closer to him. "Best keep your expletives to yourself, love," Sol said. "We don't need to go giving them any reason to kill us."

Gregor had started to lag behind, so Sol pulled him to the group as well, and he fell in line next to Kira.

The Hall was immense, easily four times as long as the courtyard and twice as high. Its walls were polished stone and arched like those in the courtyard, but instead of lights at its apex, there was a large skylight that flooded the room with natural light. There were windows along the walls, but they were narrow slits, maybe forty to a wall. Hundreds of people lined the walls, citizen and soldier alike. A large dark green carpet stretched from the entryway to the far end of the Hall, and running parallel to it were two long fire pits. At the carpet's end was a single chair, large and opulent, with several partially dressed women draped on and around it. On that chair sat a man—not one Cole thought he would ever see again or want to see.

Cole leaned in to talk to Freelan as they walked. "Free, you could have told me that Garrett was the one in charge now."

"You could have asked."

Now Cole was close enough to see him clearly. Garrett Tar, aged far beyond when Cole had last seen him, sat upon the throne, resting his head on one hand while the other tapped incessantly on the armrest. The look in Garrett's eyes brought the nervous feeling back to Cole's stomach.

Cole leaned to Freelan. "I'm assuming that he's one of—"

"One of the ones that wanted to kill you?" Freelan said with a laugh. "Cole, he started the club."

"Terrific."

They finally arrived at the base of the platform on which Garrett Tar's throne sat. Garrett's eyes burned a hole in Cole for nearly a minute before he spoke.

"So, the Ghost of Epheria has returned at last," Garrett said, his voice low and indignant.

Gregor and Kira stood back from the main group and watched as Cole spoke to the man in the chair. They didn't pay much attention to the conversation and were happy enough talking among themselves.

"This place is pretty crazy," Gregor said, looking around the large room. "You ever seen anything like it?"

"I've spent my entire life in a space station," Kira said. "I'd never seen a sky before today."

Gregor looked at her, realizing how stupid his question had been. "I'm sorry. I didn't even—"

"It's OK, dude, really," Kira said. "So,"—she pointed to the lineup of guards along the right wall—"who are these guys again? Shek . . . something?"

"Shek'Tarii," Gregor said. "Specifically, Shek'Tarii Hunters."

"Hunters of what?" Kira asked.

"A payday mostly," Gregor replied. "They'll hunt down any person, monster, ship, or piece of cargo as long as the price is right."

"Well, it looks like business has been good," Kira said.

"It's weird," Gregor said. "I'd always been told they were savages."

Kira laughed. "Pretty fancy-looking savages," she said.

"You know, I never realized these Shekkers were so . . . formal about things," Ram said to Sol.

"Me neither," Sol said. "Kinda makes you wonder how much of what everyone tells you is true and how much is just ghost stories."

"I guess there are benefits to being a secret society," Ram said. "They probably just made up the stories themselves to keep people out."

They stood in silence and watched as Cole spoke with Garrett, only catching the odd word, their voices getting lost in the cavernous room.

"That one doesn't exactly seem thrilled to see Cole," Ram said, nodding toward Garrett.

"No, he doesn't," Sol said. "And the three at nine o'clock? They haven't taken their eyes off us yet."

Ram looked over, casually. "Nah, they seem all right."

"All right?" Sol said. "I haven't seen a look like that since you stole that Vakarian's speeder right from under his nose."

"Hey, that was a fair bet," Ram said. "He shouldn't have played if he didn't want to . . ."

A few words from Cole's conversation with Garrett drifted over to them.

"Wait, what did he just say?" Ram asked.

Sol had caught it too. "Well, this just took a turn."

"Tobias Navarr is alive," Cole said.

Hushed whispers flooded through the Hall. Garrett called one of the women to him and whispered something in her ear. She turned and scampered out of the room, disappearing through a side door. Garrett sat, still tapping his fingers on the armrest, and searched Cole's face for any deception. He found none, but of course he knew that he wouldn't.

"We know," Garrett said as the tapping stopped.

"What?" Cole asked.

"After your little run-in with him on Epheria, he—"

"You call *that* a little run-in?" Cole blurted out.

Garrett simply frowned at Cole and pressed on. "After Epheria, our scouts picked up his trail, but he went into hiding. You know how he is. A few years later, though, he was snapped up by the Federation and thrown in Kylgor. We had assumed that he'd been killed or had died in custody. That was until our spies heard something about his escape several months ago."

"You knew he was alive and you didn't try to correct that?"

"Why should we?" Garrett asked.

"After what he did, I would think—"

Garrett straightened in his chair and glared at Cole. "After what *he* did?" Garrett said, his voice booming across the Hall. "What about what *you* did?"

"Garrett, you weren't even there," Cole said, barely holding his anger back. "You don't know what happened."

Garrett stood and stepped down from the throne. He raised a crooked finger at Cole. "Martiss trusted you, and you—"

Cole could hold back no longer. His voice echoed through the Hall:

"*Tobias* killed Martiss, you stupid son of a bitch!"

The guards sprang into action and moved in on Cole, but were quickly waved away by Garrett.

"Leave him," Garrett bellowed as the guards slinked back to their posts. He moved down from the pedestal and came face-to-face with Cole.

"It would seem we were told a different version of events," Garrett said quietly.

"And where'd you get yours?" Cole asked. "Tobias?"

Garrett smirked, and without answering, he turned and walked back to his throne. "Cole, what is your business here?" he asked. "And what of your interest in Tobias?"

"Tobias murdered my wife and my child. My interest is in his head leaving his shoulders."

"And you expect us to help you with that?" Garrett said. "We don't know where he is."

Cole held his ground. "I already know where he is."

"Then I ask again, what is your business here?" Garrett demanded.

"I need reactivation," Cole said.

Garrett was silent. He looked at Cole like he was trying to understand the punch line to a bad joke. He shook his head and laughed a deep, rumbling laugh.

He stopped himself for a moment to speak. "You joined the Federation?" Garrett said, barely holding it together. "*You?*"

Cole stood silently as the room broke out into muffled laughter.

"Suddenly this whole thing makes sense," Garrett said. "Epheria, Tobias, these *clowns* you have with you. Hard to believe you took the deal."

"There was nothing left for me here."

Garrett sat for a long while, staring into the distance, nodding, no doubt contemplating his next insult.

"If I grant you this, you'll leave?" Garrett said, breaking his silence.

"As soon as I've recovered," Cole said, "yes, we'll be on our way."

"I can't make any promises," Garrett said. "We haven't activated anyone in years. The crackdowns made it more trouble than it was worth."

"But you can still do it?" Cole asked.

"Perhaps."

"Sooner it gets done, the sooner I'm out of your hair."

"Very well," Garrett said. "Freelan, I will leave this to you to organize. Now get out of my sight, all of you."

They began the long walk back out of the Hall, trailed by a small group of guards. Ram hurried and caught up to Cole at the front of the pack.

"So," Ram said, "I'm assuming that *that* was the something more?"

"That was it," Cole said as they passed out into the courtyard.

Sol had caught up now as well. "You, young man, have some explaining to do," Sol said.

"I know," Cole said.

TEN

THEY HAD BEEN allowed to head back to the ship and gather their gear and supplies, then they were taken to one of the residential mesas. By this time, it was late afternoon, and the Rygerian sun hung low over the distant horizon.

The mesa was huge, easily several kilometers long and one or two wide. From the outside, its entryway was carved similarly to the Hall, but inside it had been completely hollowed out with apartment complexes lining the walls. A central thoroughfare stretched the length of the cavern, with mazes of roads heading off among the buildings.

"This is where you'll be staying," Freelan said, motioning to the large glass structure before them. "I trust you'll find it to your liking."

Ram brushed passed him. "We're not going to be here long enough to form an opinion."

"Don't mind him, Free," Cole said.

"It's fine," Freelan said. "I know his type."

"He is right, though," Cole said. "We're not going to be here long."

Freelan finished directing the helpers, who were unloading the gear from the speeders. "Well, in any case," Freelan said, "I'll be by later tonight to take you to Joran's."

Relief flashed in Cole's eyes. "Glad he's still with us. This plan was shot to hell without him."

"Yeah, not sure anything'll ever kill the old man."

"He always was a tough old bastard," Cole said.

Sol and Gregor passed the pair, pushing some of the crates into the building.

"Feel free to help, mate," Sol said. "Plenty there."

Cole and Freelan said their good-byes, and Cole set about retrieving a crate or two. When he got there, he found Kira was still standing by the side of the road, staring out at all the traffic and people, as well as the sky above and the soft white clouds floating along.

"Kira?" Cole called. No response. He approached her and tapped her on the shoulder. "Kira," he repeated.

"What? Oh," Kira said, spinning around, "I was just—"

"Looking. I could tell."

"It's just all so . . . different."

"Believe it or not, it's different to when I was here last too," Cole said. "None of these buildings were here, for starters."

"How long has it been?" Kira asked.

"A long time," Cole said. "Fifteen years."

"That seems like forever," Kira said.

"Feels like forever," Cole said. He pushed one of the crates over in Kira's direction. "Hey, you want to help push that in?"

"What's in it for me?"

"If you help now, you can go have a look around later," Cole said.

Without another word, Kira rounded up two crates and disappeared through the front doors.

Cole sat the three mugs of ale down on the table with a clunk. It was starting to get dark out, and the time had come to fill his friends in on what was going on. He felt that it might go over better with something alcoholic in their system. They sat around a table in the dining room of the apartment that they had been set up in. Its walls were a mixture of wood and metal panelling with stone columns supporting the ceiling. Cole was just about to launch into the tale when Kira came into the room.

"Can I go out now?" she asked.

Cole nodded and looked to Gregor, who was sitting in a chair off to the side, reading. "Gregor," Cole said. "Go with her, just to be safe."

"I'll be fine, really," Kira said.

"He's going," Cole said. The tone of his voice caused Gregor to follow the instruction immediately, and in no time, he was standing at Kira's side.

"And don't cause any trouble," Ram said, pointing right at Kira.

"We won't," Kira said.

"Well, go on then," Cole said. "You've got an hour."

They didn't need to be told twice, disappearing out the door.

"Ah, young love," Sol said after they'd left the room.

"Oh, leave them alone," Cole said, laughing.

"Do you think we might be able to dump her here?" Ram asked, not laughing and not mincing his words.

Cole didn't reply straight away. His mind had wandered to Zara and how he had been upset about her being out with a boy. He had regretted letting Kira stay on board. He couldn't look at her without seeing his daughter's face, and every time he was reminded of his failure to save her. It might be best if Kira were to stay on Ryger. It certainly seemed a much safer place than it had been when he was last there, more civil.

"Cole?" Ram prompted.

Snapping out of his trance, Cole took a sip of his drink. "Maybe. I don't know."

"Don't think we can't see what it's doing to you, having her around," Sol said.

Cole pretended not to hear and took another sip. "So," he began, "where should we start?"

"Beginning's as good a place as any. How'd you end up with these guys?" Sol asked.

"I was born here. My mother died when I was maybe seven," Cole said. "My father died before I was born. Martiss Darenian was a family friend and also the leader of the Shek'Tarii at the time. He took me in after my mother died and was just about the closest thing I had to a father. I was here for twenty-three years, until Epheria."

"I kept hearing that thrown around back in the Hall," Ram said. "I've never heard of it. Is it a planet?"

"It is, deep in Wild Space," Cole said. "It saw a lot of piracy during the war. A lot of bad shit went on out there." Cole sat his mug down with a sigh. "I wish I'd never heard of it either."

"What happened?" Ram asked.

"All my life, Martiss had favored me," Cole said, "and as he got on in age, he started to groom me to take over his role as leader. Tobias was born and bred here on Ryger, and had been a Hunter since age six. He had worked his way up through the ranks and had been angling for the leadership for years. So when word started to get around that Martiss wanted me to succeed him—"

"He cracked it?" Sol said.

"That's putting it mildly," Cole said. He poured each of them a fresh mug from a large pitcher in the center of the table. "At the height of the war, we were taking contracts from everyone, didn't matter which side of the conflict they were on. We'd been contracted by the Federation to rescue a group of political and business leaders who had been kidnapped and taken to Epheria. Martiss put me in charge of the mission, as a test of sorts, a test I failed."

Ram looked at Cole over the rim of his mug. "I have a feeling I know where this is going."

Cole rubbed his tired eyes and leaned back in his chair. "Tobias's plan was to kill Martiss, frame me for it, then arrest me, return a hero, and secure his place as the leader of the Shek'Tarii."

"That's some plan," Sol said.

"By the end of the day," Cole said, "the twenty-odd people we were sent to rescue were dead, along with Martiss, the two other squad members, and Tobias—or so I thought."

"He killed them all?" Sol asked.

Cole went quiet.

"Where were you in all this?" Ram asked.

"I tried to stop him," Cole said. "But he was a full-blown Conduit with forty years of training. I,"—Cole's voice caught in his throat—"even with my implants, I couldn't stop him."

Sol leaned forward. "How'd you get out of there?"

"I got lucky," Cole said. "The building was coming down, and I got to our ship just in time."

"And you never saw him come out?"

"I didn't think anyone could have survived that collapse," Cole said. "But, evidently, he did."

"Cole," Sol said, "if the implants weren't any help against him before, what good are they going to be now?"

"Physical strength is a big part of it," Cole said. "At their core, the implants amplify your senses, your strength, and your speed. I'm in better shape now than I was back then, so I'm hoping that the implants will feed off of that. Tobias is older as well, and his muscle mass has decreased since Epheria—"

"Ten years in isolation will do that to a man," Ram said.

"Exactly," Cole said. "Tobias will still have his party tricks, but his overall speed and strength should be lower. I'm hoping that, when we meet, it'll be a much more even fight than before."

"So, with this reactivation," Sol said, "will you slip right back into it? Or will it take some time?"

"It's hard to say," Cole said. "After my initial activation, it took me a couple of weeks to adjust, but then again, I was only ten years old."

"They put those things into kids?" Ram asked, his face a mask of horror. "I've seen grown men brought to the breaking point after having them done. To do that to a kid is . . . it's barbaric."

"It was different back then, Ram. You know it was," Cole said. "War makes sane people do insane things."

"I'm well aware."

Cole shifted in his seat and poured each of them another drink. "What I'm trying to say is that I don't think it'll be too bad. My body is more suited to take the process now than it was back then. I can't see me being out more than a few days."

"Let's just hope Tobias stays put on Ferris then," Sol said, "until you're ready."

"If he doesn't, Oren's on it," Cole said. "He'll let us know the second Tobias moves."

"You know what?" Ram asked.

Cole leaned toward Ram. "If this is going to be another rant about Oren then—"

"Steady on," Ram said, raising his hands in surrender. "What I was going to say was that even though we're out of the system, it is nice to have someone on the inside keeping track of things for us."

"That's very civil of you, Ramses," Sol said.

"Why, thank you, Solomon," Ram said, mocking Oren's Old Core accent. "I'm just trying to keep my eye on the bigger picture."

"That's the right idea," Cole said. "There's a lot of little cogs moving around at the moment, but the main goal is taking out Tobias. Being here is a means to that end. I would never have come here otherwise."

"And if we can dump the kid, that'll be one less distraction for us," Ram said.

"Look, I can't argue that," Cole said. "I just want to be sure that it's safe for her."

"She seems to like it here," Sol offered.

"Yeah, she does," Cole said.

"Hey, look at that," Kira said, pointing into the distance.

"What?" Gregor said.

"That," she said as she took off running.

"Kira, wait, you're not supposed to—"

When he finally caught up, she was standing in front of what looked like a large clearing in between two buildings. It was a training yard, and there were rows and rows of students practicing combat skills. Some were engaged in hand-to-hand drills, while others practiced with wooden training swords. They moved in unison, their motions fast and precise, their feet kicking up the sand and dust on the floor in small clouds.

"Look at them," Kira said with wonder. "I'd love to be able to do all that stuff."

"Maybe they could teach you," Gregor said.

"I doubt it. You'd have to be one of them and live here."

"You could live here," Gregor said. "Cole said you could only stay with us temp—"

Kira punched him in the arm. "That keen to get rid of me, are you?"

"No, no, not at all," Gregor said, rubbing the pain away. "It's just you seem to like it here."

"I'm in a place that's dry, doesn't smell like shit, and isn't threatening to crush me at any second, Gregor," Kira said. "I think I'd like it pretty much anywhere."

They stood and watched the training for a little while before moving on down the main road. They soon found themselves in a market that was set back from the main road. It seemed to be mostly food being sold. Most of it Kira had never seen before, and all of it was out of her price range, as she'd left the credit chip Cole gave her back at the apartment. She'd never let that stop her before, though.

Gregor was watching a nearby street performer when Kira came up and jabbed him in the ribs. He looked down to see she was holding two large fabar fruits in her hands.

"Where did they come from?" Gregor asked, though he felt he didn't need to.

"I bought them," Kira said, trying to force one into his hand.

Gregor frowned at her. "You don't have any money, Kira," he said, pushing the fruit back her way.

"This is true," Kira said, "but I couldn't possibly live here without first trying—" Kira's eyes went wide, and she pocketed the two fruit. "We should probably run now."

"What?" Gregor said. He turned to see what had spooked Kira: a hulk of a man lumbering in their direction. Gregor spun back to Kira to try and convince her to give the fruit back, but all he saw was her feet disappearing around a corner stall.

"Hey, you!" shouted the angry salesman. "Get back here!"

Gregor's feet were carrying him around the corner stall before he knew it.

The merchant gave up the chase long before Kira and Gregor stopped running. They ran for so long that, by the time they stopped, they were so out of breath they could barely speak. The alley in which they'd stopped had a large pile of boulders sitting right at the end of it, which Kira decided was as good a place as any to rest. She scrambled up and motioned for Gregor to follow her, which he did, but nowhere near as swiftly.

Kira handed Gregor his share of the fabar fruit and broke hers open.

"I want you to tell me something," she said, mouth half full of fruit.

"What is it you want to know?" Gregor said.

"Oh, I don't know," she said. "Something about you, something you'd tell a friend."

"Are we friends?" Gregor asked.

"I would hope so," Kira said. "I stole for you, remember."

Gregor took another bite of the fabar. "Well, my mother is a doctor, and my father is a banker."

"They must be thrilled with you," Kira said. "Runaway with a little band of mercenaries."

"I'm not a—we're not mercenaries," Gregor said.

"Oh?" Kira raised an eyebrow. "Well, what are you then?"

"I was a sniper in the Forty-Second Unification Division," Gregor said.

"Never heard of it," Kira said flatly.

"It's a division of the Federation's Armed Forces, we—"

"So you *are* Federation guys?"

"Well, we were," Gregor said, a frown starting to form at the corners of his mouth. "I graduated top of my class, the highest-rated sniper out of the academy in years, and I got assigned to Cole's squad, Penumbra, the pride of the division. Everything was supposed to be great."

"What happened?"

"I disobeyed a direct order," Gregor said, throwing the peel of the fabar fruit down off the boulder. "I let someone get away and . . . people died."

"Cole's family?" Kira asked, the pieces falling together.

"His wife and daughter," Gregor said, nodding slowly.

"I heard Cole talking about that on the way here. Don't remember hearing him blaming you, though."

"He doesn't," Gregor said. "But I can't help but feel responsible."

"But hang on: Why aren't you with the Federation anymore?"

"It's part of the plan to get the guy who did it, Tobias," Gregor said. "We couldn't do it within UniDiv, or the law, for that matter, so we had to go outside it."

"And you gave up *everything* to go along for the ride?" Kira asked.

"My mother always told me that I should own up to my mistakes," Gregor said, "and do whatever I could to make it right. I just . . ."

Kira put her hand on Gregor's shoulder. "What is it?"

"They don't trust me," Gregor said. "I've only been with them for two months, and I was a replacement for their old leader, who died, and they're forever making fun of—"

"Gregor," Kira said sternly.

"What?"

"They trust you," Kira said. "They trust you enough to send you to keep me out of trouble and—"

"Just for the record," Gregor said, "I haven't done a very good job of that."

"Well, no, but the point is that they *do* trust you," Kira said. "And if I'm reading this entirely wrong and they don't? Then make them."

"But how?"

"Help them catch that asshole," Kira said. "Do whatever you can to make it happen."

"I'm trying," Gregor said, forcing a smile.

"I know."

They sat in silence for a long while.

"We should probably head back," Gregor said, checking his watch. "It's been more than an hour."

"Oh, all right, *dad*."

They jumped down off the boulder and headed down the alley.

"Try not to steal anything on the way back, OK?" Gregor teased.

Kira punched him in the arm again.

Cole looked up as Kira and Gregor came in through the front door, followed closely by Freelan.

"Found those two walking down the main road," Freelan said. "They supposed to be out?"

"Not this long, they're not," Cole said as Kira and Gregor disappeared into the next room. "They get into any trouble?"

"No, nothing like that," Freelan said. "I was just headed this way and thought I'd save them the walk."

"Thanks, Free," Cole said as he finished up one last drink. Ram and Sol had both turned in for the night after their talk. It wasn't late, but it had been a long couple of days.

"You right to go, Cole?" Freelan asked.

"Absolutely."

"Joran's still out in the Old City," Freelan said as they tore down a bridge that stretched for kilometers into the night. "He refused to move his workshop despite Garrett offering him some pretty state-of-the-art facilities."

"It'll be good to go back," Cole said as they continued down the bridge.

Ahead was a grouping of mesas, their carved surfaces pocked with pinpoints of firelight from the many windows in the cliffs. This was the Old City, Cole's home. There were no modern buildings in these mesas. Everything was carved from the stone of the mountains or built from other natural materials. Cole had always preferred it to Ryger for the same reason he lived well outside of Cotar: he liked the quiet.

Of course the Old City used to be called Ryger, until a few years after his mother died. Martiss had pushed to expand and had set about excavating and colonizing the other mesas in the immediate area. Business had flourished during the war, and the influx of funds meant that Martiss could do anything he wanted, and he did. New Ryger was established within a year; two years later, he had established fifteen satellite colonies around the Old City; and in another five, all had been connected by the bridges. In the time since then, the people of Ryger, the Shek'Tarii, seemed to have mellowed compared to what Cole remembered. Martiss had built a thriving society, a powerful one, and it would have been Cole's to lead if Epheria had gone differently. But it hadn't.

Cole felt the soft dirt of the cavern floor shift under his feet as he stepped from the speeder. There were some people about, but not many. The Old City emptied out in the years after the expansion, with those staying behind generally being elderly, sentimental, or just stubborn.

Joran Darenian was all of these things and more, and he was also Martiss's father.

They stopped outside his workshop, which to Cole's eyes looked exactly the same as it had all those years before. The inexplicable stacks of buckets lining the front wall stood as tall as ever, and the wall itself looked like it hadn't had a new coat of paint since the building was chipped out of the rock.

"Do you want me to come in?" Freelan asked.

"I'll be fine," Cole said.

"Right. Well, I'll be off then," Freelan said. "Call me when you're ready to be picked up."

Cole pushed open the old wooden door, which creaked and scraped as it traveled over the floor. Inside the main room, it was darker than he remembered, but everything was still in its place. Everything was right where it should be, except for Joran.

"Joran?" Cole called out. No reply.

Cole noticed the door to Joran's workshop was slightly ajar, a dull orange glow flowing from the opening. He approached quietly and opened the door. There was Joran, sound asleep in front of the fire, snoring so loudly it was a wonder he didn't wake himself.

Cole walked over and tapped him on the shoulder.

"Joran," Cole said. "Get up."

Nothing.

"Joran!" Cole shouted, shaking him by the shoulder.

"Wha—? What is it?" Joran shouted, thrashing about as he came to. "Who are—what do you want?"

"Joran, it's Cole," Cole said, sitting down on a chair across from him. "Cole Traske."

Joran's jaw dropped. Cole couldn't tell if that was from shock or old age.

"Cole?" the old man said, examining every part of Cole's face. "Little snot-nosed Cole? I don't believe it!"

"Joran, they were supposed to tell you I was coming."

"Who was?" Joran asked.

"Freelan Mir," Cole replied.

Joran started nodding. "Oh yes, I do remember someone saying something about someone coming to see me."

"Do you remember what it was about?" Cole asked.

"That I do not," Joran said with a weak grin.

Indeed, Joran had not changed one bit.

Cole took Joran's hand. "I need reactivation, Joran." Joran's hand shook in Cole's; that was new. "You're the only one who can help."

"Oh yes, I remember now," Joran said. "Terrible thing. Though I will do what I can to help."

"Well, good," Cole said. "Let's get to it."

Joran raised his free hand to Cole and pointed a crooked, old finger at him.

"Not so quick," Joran said. "I need to check what sort of state you're in first. It's been a long time."

Joran got up from his chair and shuffled through the door into his workshop. As Cole passed through, he quickly discovered that the shake in Joran's hands wasn't the only thing that was new.

Freelan had mentioned that Garrett offered Joran a brand-new workshop as a motive to move, but he forgot to mention that he gave it to him anyway. The room Cole stepped into was a long way from the old dark stone workshop of the master weaponsmith of Ryger. The floor was tiled and stretched out to meet cold steel walls. The room seemed at least three times as big as it had been. There were separate areas for metalworking, electronics, and leatherwork for armor. There was even a clean room with an operating table in it.

In the far corner of the room was what Cole had come for: the activation rig. It was clearly the oldest thing in the room that wasn't Joran and looked like it hadn't been touched for years.

"Take off your shirt and sit over there," Joran said pointing to the operating table.

Cole sat and watched as Joran fumbled around in drawers and cabinets, looking for his equipment. In the cold blue light of the workshop, Cole could see just how much Joran had aged. His hair was now white, not silver, and it fell past his shoulders in a loose ponytail. The wrinkles that barely touched him years ago now etched a story into his worn face. Age had shortened him as well. His back stooped, and he no longer towered over Cole. Joran used to be like a wizard to Cole; he could make anything out of nothing and could turn an ordinary man into something much more. He had studied Conduits his whole life, and his modifications to the standard Synth implant made him a very sought-after man during the war—though no one ever found him. He was Ryger's little secret. Cole was hoping that Joran's abilities hadn't been dulled with the time that had passed.

As Joran approached Cole, he saw the scars that spread across his torso.

"Oh, my boy," Joran said, his voice wavering. "What have these years done to you?"

"Nothing I couldn't handle," Cole said. It was a lie, but he could see Joran's mood slipping and he didn't want to upset him. He needed him present and focused.

"How do they look?" Cole asked, keeping Joran on task.

Joran ran his fingers over the long surgical scars and inspected the metal that protruded from them. He frowned.

"The frame shouldn't be protruding like this," Joran said. "I will need to do a scan."

Joran hurried to the corner of the clean room and rolled back a large machine. It had a wand-like attachment that must have been the scanner. He waved it over Cole's body, and after a few minutes, some images started cycling on the machine's display. Joran blocked Cole's view of the machine, but he could still see the old man's shoulders slump after just a few seconds of viewing the images.

"What's wrong?" Cole asked, bracing for the answer.

Joran didn't remove his gaze from the machine. "My boy, is it absolutely necessary that I do this?" he asked.

"Yes," Cole said.

Joran turned to face Cole, a tear forming in the corner of his eye, his face sullen.

"Then this is going to be very difficult for the both of us."

ELEVEN

THE SHORT VERSION of the story was that the implants were trashed.

The long version of the story was that the implants were really trashed.

At length, Joran had told Cole that he would require surgery to repair the framework and inner workings of the implants before any thoughts of reactivation could be entertained. Cole had gone back to the apartment for the night to give him time to prepare for the surgery and to allow Joran to track down any spare parts that he might need.

Ram looked up from the book he'd found sitting on a shelf. "So what you're saying is that—"

"What I'm saying is that we're going to be here a bit longer than we planned," Cole said, taking a long sip of his drink. "I have to go back for the repairs first thing in the morning."

"And how long's that going to take?" Sol asked.

"Joran said he won't know how bad things really are until he gets in there," Cole said, "but a casual estimate would be a good half day."

"Well, shit," Ram said, "how'd they get so banged up?"

"Seriously?" Cole said. "Ram, think about every mission we've been on in the last decade, all the stuff that's happened. Add all the jobs from my time here, and that's a hell of a lot for almost thirty-year-old cybernetic implants to put up with."

"OK, OK," Ram said, "I get it."

"It's OK," Cole said as he threw himself into a large armchair. "Didn't mean to snap. This whole situation's got me riled up something fierce. Tobias will probably be long gone by the time I'm anywhere near ready."

"And if he is, Oren will let us know," Sol said, trying to calm the tension in the room, "and then we'll go find him again."

"Three weeks," Cole said to no one in particular.

"What?" Sol said.

"When I told Liv that something had come up after Tragg," Cole said, "I told her I'd handle it in three weeks, three weeks max."

Ram looked at Cole. "Cole don't—"

"In a couple of days, it will be three weeks," Cole said. "And I'm going to be lying in bed recovering, while Tobias runs around free to do as he likes."

"That can't be helped, mate," Sol said.

"She never even knew about Tobias. I never told her. If I'd told her everything, if I'd thought about . . ."

Cole got out of his chair and started pacing the room. "I should have seen that he'd go after them. I should have—"

"Cole," Ram said, getting up to stand in the way of Cole's pacing. "You didn't even know he was alive. You couldn't have known that he knew about your family. You were blindsided. It happens to the best of us. You—"

"It's my fault, Ram, all of this."

"It's not," Ram said. "Go to bed and get some rest. You'll need it for tomorrow."

Ram took Cole by the shoulders and pushed him in the direction of the bedrooms.

"And Cole?" Ram said.

"Yeah?"

"Tomorrow we'll wake up, and we'll kick this thing in the teeth. Then once you're right, we'll push on and take it to Tobias. Got it?"

Cole gave them a halfhearted thumbs-up as he disappeared down the hallway.

"Poor bastard," Sol said.

Ram sat back down and poured himself a drink. "He'll be fine," Ram said. "He just needs to get out of his own way."

"You're back," Kira said, popping out the door of her room. "That didn't take very long."

"Haven't done it yet," Cole said, a yawn escaping his mouth.

"Why not?"

"There were some problems," Cole said. "Have to go back in the morning."

Cole went to move, but Kira lingered in the doorway.

"Can I talk to you about something?" she asked as she stepped back into her room.

"What is it?" Cole asked, taking her place in the doorway.

"I know this isn't permanent," Kira said, "following you guys around and stuff. I know I shouldn't even be here, and—"

"Kira, it's OK," Cole said.

"But it isn't," Kira said. "Look, I know what happened. I'm not stupid. I know it can't be any good for you seeing me whenever you turn around. I'm a distraction."

Kira slumped down onto her bed, and Cole didn't know what to say, mostly because she was already saying it.

"I think I might want to stay here," Kira said, looking up at Cole. "If . . . if that's OK?"

Cole sat down on the bed next to Kira. "They don't let just anyone live here, Kira. It—"

"But you know them," Kira said. "You can talk to them, ask them."

"I guess I can," Cole said, "if it's what you really want."

"I don't want to be a burden to you," Kira said. "You've got enough to deal with."

Cole sighed. "I'll see what I can do. No promises, though."

"Thanks," Kira said.

Cole turned to her as he left. "You're a good kid, Kira. Ryger would be lucky to have you."

She was a good kid, strong and smart too. She could do a lot on Ryger, make a life for herself. Everyone had been telling Cole that she was a distraction, that it wasn't good for him having her around so soon after Zara's death. They weren't wrong, but at the same time, every day she reminded him of Zara a little bit more and it was a strange sort of comfort seeing her face.

Cole felt a small pang of sadness at the thought of leaving her behind. But if it was what she wanted, who was he to argue?

Early the next morning, Cole headed back to Joran's, alone this time. He knew the way. On entering Joran's workshop, he saw the old man sitting over by a bench, wrangling with some parts.

"Joran?"

"Ah, you're here," Joran said. He turned and saw the concerned look on Cole's face. "Oh, don't worry. These aren't for you." Joran laughed as he held up some of the scrap parts he was working with. "I was actually able to find some relatively new parts in storage. Should make my job a bit easier." Joran's smile faded. "I'm assuming you still want to go through with this?"

"I have to."

"Well, when you're ready," Joran said, "get changed and hop on the table over there, so we can begin."

Cole lay down on the table and felt the coolness of the metal on his skin. The exposed metal jutting from the scars clinked and clanked as he got into a comfortable position. He could hear Joran rustling around in a drawer, looking for some long-lost tool. Soon, though, Joran was beside him and placed a hand on his shoulder.

"Do you remember when you first had these done?"

"I do," Cole said.

"Do you remember what you said to me when it was over?"

Cole forced a smile. "Never again."

"I hated watching what you went through," Joran said. "Martiss pushed it on you far too soon. I tried to—"

"It's OK, Joran," Cole said. "Really."

Joran gently squeezed Cole's shoulder and forced a smile of his own. "Are you ready?"

Cole nodded.

Joran inserted the needle into Cole's arm and administered the anesthetic. It was only a few seconds before Cole's eyes slowly closed and he was under. Joran pulled over the couple of mobile tables he had prepared all the equipment on and picked up a scalpel.

His hand shook as the blade hovered over the scar on Cole's left arm.

"Forgive me, my boy," Joran said as he made the first cut.

There were four main components to a Synth's implants. The first was the Framework, a series of interconnected reinforcing and strengthening attachments that were fused to the skeleton of the subject. Since they were nearly always put in when the subject was a teen, the Framework was expandable to compensate for bone growth and allow for some flexibility. Second were the Impulse Nodes, thin wires that fed from the Control and Power Unit through the Framework and were grafted directly to the musculature of the subject. They served to increase muscle response, overall muscle strength, and endurance. The Control and Power Units were encased in a small box under the skin on the subject's back, its only external feature being a small access port no more than a few millimeters wide. The Power Unit amplified the subject's own bio-electricity enough that it was practically a self-sustained system. The more active a subject was, the more power it generated and the less often they would need a top up. The Control Unit was the most complex part of the whole setup. It was connected directly to the subject's spinal cord, as well as having nodes inserted into the brain stem. The implants were controlled by the subject's brain so as to work in concert with their normal movements, amplifying them. The Control Unit's purpose was to make sure the information got to where it needed to go, which was why all the Impulse Nodes originated from there.

Cole's implants had been put in twenty-eight years ago. Twenty-eight years was a long time for any piece of tech to survive inside the human body, let alone something as delicate as the implants. This was never an issue during the war as those who were getting them done weren't expected to have a long life ahead of them.

Cole's Framework had begun to rust in places and in others was so brittle it had started to crack and penetrate through the skin. The joint reinforcements were all in good enough condition, so only replacements along the limbs would be required.

From what Joran could tell, the Power Unit was still in good condition and the Control Unit was largely undamaged, only requiring minor repairs.

The biggest issues were the Impulse Nodes, many of which had worn out, been torn to pieces by bullet fire or other wounds, or had simply disintegrated. Thankfully the connections to the spinal column and the neural implants were in satisfactory condition, as Joran didn't know if his hands would be up to the delicate task of reestablishing them.

Fourteen hours had passed by the time Joran closed the final incision. He was able to replace the deteriorated parts of the Framework, and he ended up having little trouble replacing and reconnecting the Impulse Nodes. The last step was to prime, charge, and activate the implants. It required specialized equipment, yet it was actually the easiest part of the whole process. Then all Joran could do was wait. The rest of the process was entirely dependent on how Cole recovered from the operation, and it would be some time before it could be declared a success.

Following the operation, Cole had been transferred back to the apartment to rest and recover. Freelan had wanted him taken to the hospital, but Ram wouldn't allow it. He still didn't trust them. It was an intense procedure, but there weren't any complications and Cole was expected to make a full recovery, so Freelan allowed it.

It was late morning, two days post-op, but inside Cole's room, it was dark. The shutters had been drawn across the large window on the back wall. Kira stood in the doorway and could only just see the silhouette of Cole as he lay in his bed sleeping.

Closing the door behind her, she stepped slowly into the room and walked over to Cole. She turned on the small lamp beside his bed and dimmed its soft blue light just enough so that she could see.

It took her no time at all to see the scars that littered Cole's upper body. It wasn't the first time she'd seen them, of course, but it was the first time this close. One night on the trip to Ryger, she had peeked into his room and heard him speaking in a language she didn't understand. He had been facing away from her and she didn't know what he was doing, but the image of the scars covering his back never left her.

The long scars from his surgery had been sealed and covered with adhesive bandages to protect them, but the ones that weren't covered came into clear focus: hundreds of small vertical marks in groupings of four with one slashed across them—tally marks.

Kira could only imagine what they were checking off, though given what she knew about Cole and the Hunters, she could probably guess. She felt awful for staring at them, but at the same time, she couldn't peel her eyes away. The calmness she could see on Cole's face did well to hide the pain his body had endured. Before she knew what she was doing, Kira found her hand reaching out, her fingers lightly touching one of the scars on Cole's shoulder. She quickly jerked her hand back as Cole started to stir. She sat frozen in place.

The rain poured down thick and fast. Cole's head swam as he pushed through the sheets of water, desperately trying to reach his daughter. She had just broken free of Tobias's hold and was running toward him.

A flash of lightning.

Cole launched himself through the air, his outstretched hands reaching for Tobias's throat.

Flash.

Cole's sword skittered along the ground as it flew from Tobias's grip. They landed with a splash and a dull thud as Cole took Tobias to the ground. Cole brought his fist down hard on Tobias's face. Again. Again. Again. He relished each strike as he felt the bone shatter and give way under his fist.

Flash.

Tobias staggered toward him, blood pouring from the wounds in his face faster than the rain could wash it away. The rain was so heavy that Cole could barely stand. He looked down to see that his sword was in his hand now. It felt heavy, too heavy.

Flash.

Cole had his hand firmly clamped on Tobias's throat and forced him to his knees. With great relief, Cole thrust the sword clean through Tobias's chest. The blood-soaked blade was washed clean the instant it emerged from Tobias's back.

Flash.

The rain stopped. All was quiet. All Cole could hear was the sound of his own breathing. He looked down, preparing to look upon the face of his tormentor one last time.

"Daddy?"

Flash.

"Zara!" Cole yelled as he shot back into consciousness. He could see the shape of a young girl sitting beside his bed. "Zara?"

Kira brightened the bedside lamp. "Cole, it's me, Kira. You're back in the apartment. Freelan said the operation went well."

She watched as Cole's eyes frantically scanned the room, and then a calmness came over them as he slowly began to understand where he was.

"I-I should go," Kira said, getting out of her chair. "You need to rest."

"Don't," Cole said. His voice was weak.

Kira sat back down.

"I could use the company," Cole said, forcing a smile.

Kira pulled her chair closer. "Can I ask you something?"

"Well, now's your chance, kid," Cole said. "I'm a captive audience." He laughed but pulled up short from the pain.

"Your scars," Kira said, hesitant to bring them up, "what do they mean?"

Cole turned his head to look at her. He could see the concern in her eyes.

"You sure you want to know?"

Kira nodded.

"I've done a lot of things in my life, Kira," he said, "a lot of bad things."

"Oh," Kira said.

"Each mark is someone whom I've killed or who's died due to my actions," Cole said.

Kira pointed to the two scars over Cole's heart. "So, are those two—"

"Those are for my family," Cole said, "Olivia and Zara."

"Zara's your daughter?" Kira asked.

"Yes," Cole said with a smile. "I think you would have liked her."

"Then who's Alaria?"

Cole nearly jumped at hearing the name. "Where did you hear that name?"

"Earlier. You were saying it in your sleep earlier," Kira said. "Is she your mother?"

"No. No, she's not important," Cole said tersely. "Forget you heard it."

"OK. I'm sorry if I—"

"It's OK, Kira. It's just something I'd rather stay forgotten."

They sat quietly for a few minutes, neither of them feeling a need to speak.

"Y'know, I don't remember my parents at all," Kira said finally. "I only ever remember being in the shelter."

"I remember very little of my mother," Cole said. "They never told me what happened to her, only that she was gone."

Kira shifted uneasily in her chair. "Cole," she said, "am I going to be a bad person?"

"Why would you think that?"

"Because of the man at the yards," Kira said. "He died, and I—"

"No, absolutely not," Cole said, looking her right in the eyes. "Look, we both had rough upbringings. A lot of shit happened, but you have a far stronger mind than I did at your age, a stronger heart too. You're a good kid, Kira. You can't let your past dictate your future. You can be more than what you were. I haven't killed a single person since I left here fifteen years ago, not one."

"But your job—"

"Being a soldier has its challenges, but I made a choice. I wasn't going to live like that anymore. I had a family to take care of . . ." Cole trailed off. He could see Kira processing it all, and then she got up and walked over to a table by the window.

Kira had seen Ram lay out all Cole's gear earlier when they brought him back. There was stuff everywhere, and she had to dig through a pile before she found what she was looking for: the knife.

She sat back down next to Cole's bed and held the knife tightly. Without hesitation, she made a cut on the back of her hand.

"What the hell are you doing?" Cole asked. He could barely move and could only watch as Kira made the cut.

"That was for the man," Kira said quietly. "I-I don't even know his name."

Cole watched as Kira stared at her hand as the blood slowly trickled down and dripped to the floor.

"Promise me you won't ever do that again."

"I won't," Kira said. "I-I just had to. I couldn't—"

"It's OK, Kira," Cole said. "I understand, trust me. Now go clean that up. Don't want it to get infected."

Kira headed toward the bathroom that was across the hall to clean the cut but stopped short when the door opened in front of her to reveal Freelan standing there.

"Oh," Freelan said. "I didn't realize there was anyone else in here. I was just checking to see—"

"I was just leaving," Kira said.

Freelan caught sight of the blood on her hand as she pushed past him.

"I was just checking to see if you were awake," Freelan said, "which clearly you are."

Freelan sat down beside Cole's bed and noticed the blood on the floor.

"Everything OK there?" Freelan asked.

"Yeah, just a little accident," Cole said. "Nothing major."

Freelan sighed. "So Joran tells me it could be a week or two before you're ready to go."

"Really? Shit."

"Yeah," Freelan said, "and I don't need to tell you that Garrett is less than pleased you'll be hanging around."

"Screw him."

"That's exactly what I told him," Freelan said. "He wanted to whack you in a crate and ship you off, but I—"

Freelan shot to his feet as a deep rumble shook the entire room and was followed in quick succession by several more.

Kira appeared in the doorway, still only part way through bandaging her hand. "What the shit was that?"

TWELVE

KIRA RAN TO the window and threw open the shutters. "Cole?"

Her voice was wavering.

Cole was unable to see out the window from his bed. "Kira, what is it?"

Kira just continued to stare out the window. Cole's stomach sank.

"Kira?" Cole shouted. Nothing.

He looked to Freelan. "Can you help me up?"

"Are you sure that's a good—"

"Now, Free."

Freelan hurried over and hooked his arm under Cole's shoulder, easing him up from the bed. Cole's feet nearly gave way as he took the first few steps, but he soon regained his footing. With each step, the pain shot right up his back and a burst of light exploded in his field of view, but he needed to see what was going on.

Eventually, they reached the window, and Freelan propped Cole against the window frame while continuing to support him. There was no mistaking what Cole saw: there, in the distance, was a ship, and it was firing rockets toward several of the mesas of Ryger.

Cole had seen the ship before, three weeks prior, on Tragg. *Tobias.*

"Son of a bitch," Cole shouted, wincing in pain. He pushed Freelan away angrily. "You know anything about this?" he said, pointing out the window.

"Know anything about what?"

Cole just glared and continued to point out the window.

"What is it, Cole? Who is it?"

"It's Tobias, Free," Cole said. "And why do you think he's here?"

"For you."

"Exactly, and I'll give you one guess as to who tipped him off."

"Garrett," Freelan said with a frown.

Cole turned and walked uneasily under his own steam to the table where all his gear was laid out. Kira rushed over and tried to guide him back to bed. "What are you doing?"

"What I have to," Cole said as he slipped on his jacket and grimaced as it rubbed against his wounds.

"Cole, you're in no shape to be going out there. Just sit down," Freelan pleaded.

"I'll be fine."

"You'll be dead," Freelan insisted as Cole pushed past him.

Cole gathered his sword and his pistol, and limped toward the door. The sounds of fast-closing footsteps slowed his advance.

"Hey, where do you think you're going?" Ram said as he appeared in the doorway and put his hand to Cole's chest to stop him.

"It's Tobias, Ram."

"And what?" Ram stood his ground. "You have a burning desire to run off and die all of a sudden?"

"No one else is going to die because of me," Cole said. "He has to be stopped."

"And you're going to do it? In your state?" Sol said. "Mate, you can barely walk."

"I'm fine. It's getting easier," Cole said, "like riding a bike."

"Oh yeah, just like it," Sol said.

"If you want to help, you're more than welcome."

"We're not going to change your mind, are we?" Ram asked.

Cole's face remained unmoved.

Ram sighed. "Well, I guess we're helping then," he said with a huff as he got a hold of Cole's arm and helped him into the main living area.

Kira stepped into the middle of the group. Cole took one look at her and, seeing the knife in her hand, quickly snatched it away.

"Hey, what the hell?" Kira said.

"Gregor," Cole said, "I want you to stay here and take care of—"

"No," Gregor said. "I'm coming with you."

"I need you to stay here with Kira," Cole said. "Keep her safe."

"I can take care of myself," Kira said, her voice falling on deaf ears.

"And I'm coming with you," Gregor shouted as he gathered his rifle. "I am a part of this team, and I'm sick of being drakking sidelined. It's bullshit."

They all stared at Gregor.

"Well, shit," Ram said. "Hard to argue with that."

"I just want to help," Gregor said.

Cole smiled. "OK, Gregor," he said, "you're with us."

Freelan stepped forward. "I can keep an eye on Kira."

"Thanks, Free," Cole said as the four of them grabbed the rest of their gear and headed out the door.

Kira threw her hands up in the air and sat down in one of the armchairs.

"I can take care of myself," she said to Freelan.

"I'm just trying to help, kid."

Kira laid back and closed her eyes. "Yeah, that seems to be going around."

Garrett walked among the large group of Hunters that he had scrambled to meet the invading threat. They gathered in the hangar and stood, weapons raised and ready, as the attacking ship glided in and lowered to the ground with a dull thud. The dust cloud it kicked up drifted and washed over them.

"Do not open fire until I give the order," Garrett said, coming to the front of the pack.

With a hiss of steam, the boarding ramp lowered and locked into place, and light flooded out from inside. A hooded figure descended the ramp, flanked by a squad of a dozen troops heavily armed. The troops fanned out and took up defensive positions while the figure stayed at the bottom of the ramp, silhouetted against the light from within the ship.

"Leave now," Garrett shouted, waving the attackers away.

A dry and rattling laugh emanated from within the hood. The figure walked toward Garrett and removed his hood.

A murmur went through the Hunters as many of the older members recognized the man before them and disseminated the information among the rest.

Garrett walked to meet the man, chest puffed out, head held high.

"Tobias Navarr, you are no longer welcome on Ryger and are hereby ordered to return to your ship," Garrett commanded. "Comply, and we will allow you and your men to leave with your lives."

As their speeder pulled into the hangar, the ship was already down and they could see a large group of Hunters blocking the entryway. Ram, Sol, and Gregor cleared a path for Cole as they pushed through the crowd.

Tobias continued to laugh.

"One last chance, Navarr," Garrett bellowed. "If you don't—"

"Oh shut *up*, Garrett," Tobias said. "You always did love the sound of your own voice far too much for my liking. Now, where is he?"

Garrett did his best to look flabbergasted. "What? Where is who?" he stammered. "Who are you talking about?"

"I grow tired of these games, Garrett."

"I don't know what you're—"

Tobias's hand shot out and grabbed Garrett by the throat, then lifted him clear off the ground. Garrett's legs kicked in the air, trying in vain to find solid ground.

Cole and the squad now stood several rows back from the clearing where Tobias was holding Garrett.

"Ram, Sol, I need you to be ready to help take out Tobias's men if shit breaks down, OK?" Cole said.

"Got it," Ram said as he and Sol headed off amongst the crowd.

"Gregor?" Cole said.

"Yes?"

"I want you on Tobias," Cole said. "If this goes really south, I want you to take the shot, understand?"

"Yes," Gregor said. "I will do my best."

"I know you will," Cole said. "Now get in position."

As Gregor disappeared into the crowd, Cole couldn't help but wonder if this was it. Was this the last time he would see his friends? He didn't know if he'd be able to beat Tobias. The pain was still intense and his head was swimming, but his muscles were tensing and he could feel the strength starting to flow through his body. He had to try.

"Where is Cole Traske?" Tobias asked, tightening his grip on Garrett's throat. "You very kindly told me he was here and that he was weak. So please, where might I find him?"

The murmuring of the crowd intensified as they realized that Garrett had betrayed their world by letting Tobias in. Some of the group even began to leave, which thinned the Hunters' resistance.

"Put him down, Tobias," Cole said as he stepped from the crowd, his sword drawn and crackling to life at his side.

"What? Even after he sold you out?" Tobias said.

"Stupidity isn't reason enough to kill him," Cole said. "Let him go. This has nothing to do with him."

"Very well, my arm was getting tired anyway." With a short flourish, Tobias launched Garrett clear across the hangar and into the hull of a cargo vessel. Garrett fell to the ground in a crumpled pile and didn't move.

No one went to check on him.

"I will admit," Tobias said, "this wasn't the plan, but I've never really been one to let an opportunity go by *unexploited.*"

Cole limped toward Tobias, and with each step, the pain got a little easier to bear—but only a little.

"Oh, Cole," Tobias said with a sigh. "Gold star for at least trying to make this a challenge for me. But even with your little gizmos up and running, surely you realize you don't stand a chance. They didn't do you any good on Epheria, and they'll do you no good now."

Cole broke into a slow run and raised his sword at Tobias.

"Oh, all right then." Tobias drew his own sword and launched himself toward Cole.

Their blades met with a crash and a shower of sparks. Tobias attempted to force Cole to the ground, but with his implants starting to kick in, Cole was able to fend him off. A few parries later and Tobias sprung back for a reprieve.

"You always were skilled with a blade, Cole," Tobias said. "I always admired that about you. Shame this fight won't go on long enough for me to enjoy it."

Tobias thrust his hands forward and blasted Cole, knocking him off his feet and sending him rolling through the dust. His sword skittered away across the ground after him. Able to right himself mid-roll and dig his heels in, Cole looked up to Tobias, ready to defend, but he was nowhere to be seen. He sensed movement to his side, but as he turned to look, Tobias's elbow smashed into the side of Cole's face and sent him careening into a nearby crate.

Cole's vision had tripled and all of it was blurry, but he could see the vague shape of Tobias stalking toward him, sword at his side.

"Gregor!" Cole managed to shout, but the pain that shot through his head sent his vision spinning yet again.

Tobias smiled and turned to face the crowd. He raised the sword and pointed it to a high balcony that overlooked the hangar.

"I see you there, boy," Tobias called out, his voice booming across the hangar. "Back for another shot?"

Through the scope, Gregor saw the sunlight glint off the blade that was pointed directly at him and slowly raised his head to get a better look. Then he froze.

"Look, I can make it fair. I'll give you one free shot," Tobias called out from below. "And when you miss, I'm going to kill him, OK?"

"What a dick," Gregor said to no one in particular.

Tobias's arrogance had snapped Gregor out of his trance, and he returned his eye to the scope. The computer-aided sight had adjusted for the wind that had begun whipping through the hangar, and he settled the crosshair just to the right of the smirk on Tobias's face.

Gregor calmly emptied his lungs and pulled the trigger.

The shot rang out clear amongst the silence that had fallen on the hangar after Tobias's dare. A split second later, Tobias's feet shifted and he brought his blade around in a swift arc that intercepted the bullet mid-flight. Unfortunately for Tobias, he wasn't aware that the bullet was of the White Death variety. The slug exploded, sending high-velocity ceramic fragments in every direction. Several of them sliced across Tobias's face leaving a deep gash in his cheek surrounded by several smaller ones. Unfortunately for Cole, this did little to deter Tobias, who was now stalking back toward him, blade at the ready, blood dripping from his cheek.

As Cole's vision began to clear, he could see the crowd of Hunters and Tobias's troops all staring at the spectacle. The hangar was deathly quiet as Tobias's boots scraped over the ground.

"It's a shame, really," Tobias said as he lifted his sword and brought it down toward Cole's chest.

A piercing scream tore through the hangar.

The blade never found its mark.

With great force, Tobias was flung backward and collided heavily with the hull of his ship, along with several of his troops unlucky enough to be caught in the blast.

Cole was thrown back also, but since he'd been on the ground, he only rolled a short distance in a swirl of dust. His vision still blurry, Cole looked around for the source. His eyes settled on the group of Hunters—or, rather, the area between the group of Hunters, who had split in two.

There stood a figure, staring blankly into space, arms limp at her side, her legs shaking, her whole body shaking.

Cole blinked several more times to clear his vision.

"Kira?"

THIRTEEN

KIRA STARED.

Her eyes watered.

Her mind raced.

Her muscles ached and burned.

She couldn't feel her feet.

Unbeknownst to her, the tremors had started there and quickly worked their way upward.

They quickly took over her whole body.

The convulsions started.

Her vision shook, then blurred.

Shadows flew through the air in slow motion.

"Not again," she whispered.

And the world went dark.

Ram and Sol passed through the crowd, keeping their eyes squarely on the fight between Cole and Tobias.

"I don't like this, mate," Sol said. "We have to do something."

"No, we wait," Ram said. "Cole knows what he's doing."

They watched as Tobias caught Cole with an elbow that sent him flying.

Ram grimaced. "Hopefully."

Before they could act, the sound of rapidly approaching boots and heavy breathing drew their attention, and they turned to see Freelan run right up to them.

"What the hell are you doing here?" Ram asked.

"That girl of yours is quick."

"Put one over on you, did she?" Sol asked.

"So where is she?" Ram asked.

Crack.

Gregor's shot rang out, and the exploding round scattered several of the Hunters who were within its range.

The explosion was soon followed by a scream and a loud rush of air. In its wake, Tobias and several of his men were thrown across the hangar.

Sol pointed toward the quickly widening gap in the crowd of Hunters. "There she is."

"What the hell?" Ram said.

Freelan looked around and saw Kira standing among the Hunters. Her body was trembling. "Wait, where's Garrett?"

"Over there," Ram said, pointing over his shoulder, never taking his eyes off Kira.

Freelan looked and saw the crumpled pile that appeared to be Garrett slumped against a ship.

Both sides of the conflict had just been staring at Kira for what felt like an age. Action needed to be taken.

Kira's shaking became more violent until she suddenly collapsed to the ground.

This was the moment.

"Fire!" Freelan shouted. "Drive them out!"

Freelan's voice carried over the group and simultaneously brought their focus back to the conflict. Within seconds, gunfire erupted and filled the air.

Tobias shook his head, trying his best to clear the fog from his vision. He'd taken a pretty hard bump into his ship and was still slightly woozy when he finally found his feet.

He looked in the direction from which the blast had come.

It can't be.

He took a few slow and uneasy steps forward.

That girl did this?

Tobias looked down at Cole, who was a few meters away and was staring directly at the girl, shock clear in his eyes.

Why? Why would she—

Tobias's train of thought was cut off as the girl collapsed, shouts rang out, and the air became thick with gunfire. He stood there for several moments staring at the girl, transfixed.

Several rounds ricocheted off the hull near Tobias's head and brought him back to the moment. He looked around and saw that almost all of his men had been killed in the hail of bullets. Quickly, he retreated back up the ramp of his ship and slammed his fist on the button to close it.

The engines of Tobias's ship roared to life overhead, and Cole looked up to see it tear out of the hangar, smoke trailing from its hull. He heard a voice shouting among the gunfire.

"Cease fire!"

It sounded like Freelan, but he couldn't be sure. As the bullets stopped flying, Cole struggled to his feet. His left leg gave way almost immediately, but he regained his balance and hobbled toward where he had last seen Kira.

He pushed his way through the crowd that had now gathered over Kira's motionless body. Sol was at her side.

"Sol, is she—"

Sol looked up at Cole. "She's fine, mate, just out," he said. "You, on the other hand, that's a different story."

Cole looked down and could see the blood pouring from his right arm, where the surgical wounds had reopened. Blood was also seeping through his jacket. He'd taken quite a licking.

"I'll be fine. Where's Ram?"

"Gone to get the speeder."

"Good," Cole said. "We need to get her out of here, now. Where's Gregor?"

"Here," Gregor said, running up to the group. He'd only just gotten down from the balcony and was seeing Kira for the first time. "Kira? What happened? Is she—"

"She's OK, Gregor," Cole said. "Well, hopefully she is."

"I don't know what happened," Gregor said, speaking faster than his mouth could keep up with. "The shot was on target, and then it-it just exp—"

"You did good, Gregor," Cole said as Ram pulled up in the speeder. "Now help Sol with Kira."

Sol and Gregor gently lifted Kira off the ground and settled her into the middle seat of the speeder. She hadn't so much as stirred. Cole climbed gingerly in next to Ram and winced.

"You OK?" Ram asked.

"I will admit I've felt better."

Freelan ran up to the side of the speeder. "Where are you going?"

"Joran's," Cole said. "He might be able to help her."

"Right, I'll catch up," Freelan said.

Cole hit his hand on the speeder's dashboard. "Ram, we need to go, now."

Ram pushed the speeder through the crowd and then gunned it down the bridge toward the Old City.

Joran's door crashed open as Ram burst through carrying Kira in his arms. Joran shot out of his chair. "Who are you?" he shouted. "And who the hell is that?"

"They're with me, Joran," Cole said as Sol and Gregor assisted him into the room. "She needs your help."

Joran's attention wasn't on the girl now; it was on the blood pouring from Cole's arm. "My boy, what happened?" he asked. "Let me take a look at you."

"I'll be fine," Cole said as he waved him away, convincing no one.

"Just let him take a look at you, mate," Sol said. "Close up that wound."

"No," Cole said. "Not until we know Kira's OK."

"Kira?" Joran asked.

"The girl, Joran," Cole said. "Help her."

"What happened?"

Cole shrugged. "Can't really be sure. But it's possible she's a Conduit."

"Oh, right." Joran pointed at Ram. "You, the big one, lay the child down on the lounge there, and you two,"—Joran pointed Sol and Gregor to his workshop—"take him in there and put him on the table."

"I-I'd like to stay with her," Gregor said.

"Not a problem," Sol said. "I can get the stubborn arse in there myself."

Gregor sat down in the chair next to Kira as Joran began to check her over. "Is she all right?"

Joran checked her pulse. "Pulse is good," he said. "She's got a bit of a fever, but on the whole, I think she'll be OK. She's just unconscious."

"Oh, good," Gregor said. He looked at Kira and smiled.

"Keep an eye on her and come get me if anything changes," Joran said as he got up and headed into the workshop.

Gregor brushed a strand of hair away from Kira's face and noticed that her eyes were frantically flicking back and forth behind her eyelids.

"She OK?" Cole asked as Joran entered.

"The girl will be fine," Joran said. "You, on the other hand, you are going to need to sit very still."

Joran set about resealing the wounds that had broken open during the fight.

"What happened? Who did this?" Joran asked.

"It was Tobias," Cole said. "He attacked the hangars."

"What? When?" Joran said.

"Just now," Ram said. "You didn't hear the explosions?"

"No?"

"Really?" Sol asked incredulously.

"He got the better of me," Cole said.

"You were foolish to even try and face him in your condition," Joran said to Cole, closing up the wound on his arm.

"That's what we tried to tell him," Ram said.

Joran dumped some bloody bandages in a nearby bin. "He always was a stubborn one as a child."

"Why am I not surprised to hear that?" Sol said.

"Forever throwing tantrums until he was allowed to do exactly what he wanted."

"That does sound about right," Ram said.

"Guys, I'm right here," Cole said, grimacing. He laughed, and the pain rippled up his spine.

There was a knock at the door.

"How's everyone doing?" Freelan said as he entered the workshop.

Crunch.

Ram caught Freelan in the side of the face with a well-placed right, then pushed him back against the wall, his forearm pressed firmly into his throat.

"You son of a bitch," Ram said through gritted teeth. "You set us up, sold Cole out. You nearly got him killed!"

"Ram!" Cole shouted. "Let him go. It wasn't him. It was Garrett."

Ram released Freelan and turned to Cole. "I know it was Garrett, but this piece of shit,"—Ram shoved Freelan hard into the wall—"is his second-in-command. Do you honestly believe he knew nothing about it?"

Cole looked Freelan in the eyes and didn't like what he saw.

"Free," Cole said, "did you know?"

"I didn't know, I swear," Freelan said, his voice hoarse.

"What is the meaning of this?" Joran shouted, throwing his tools on the table. "What are you all talking about?"

"They tipped off Tobias that Cole was here, that he was weak, ripe for the picking," Ram shouted.

"Freelan?" Joran said. "Is this true?"

"It would seem so," Freelan said. "But as I said, I had nothing to do with it, and the identities of those involved died with Garrett."

"Garrett's dead?" Cole asked.

"Yes," Freelan answered. "His neck was broken."

"So what, you're in charge then?" Ram asked.

"For the time being, yes."

"I feel safer already," Ram said, his voice dripping with sarcasm.

"What's more," Sol said, "we've got people on the outside tracking Tobias. They would have warned us. Why didn't we—"

Ram scoffed. "Given everything else, they probably blocked the transmissions."

"May I speak?" Freelan asked.

"Make it worth our time," Ram said.

"Go on, Free," Cole said.

"I will admit," Freelan said, "that the communications were blocked, but—"

Crunch.

"Ram!" Cole shouted.

"Sorry," Ram said, not even close to meaning it.

"They were blocked," Freelan said, "but it's standard procedure now to block all unauthorized incoming communications."

Cole stood up from the table and leaned against it. "Free," he said, "it might have been nice if you'd told us that."

Freelan wiped the blood away from his nose. "Well, it might have been nice if you'd told us your little *stowaway* was a damn Conduit!"

Sol got right up in Freelan's face. "Mate, bear with me here, but do these look like the faces of people who knew she was a bloody Condy?"

Cole pushed the two of them apart. "Free, I don't even think *she* knew or, at least, understood."

Freelan backed up toward the door. "Clearly this is the wrong time to try and discuss this," he said. "I'll come back tomorrow, and we—"

"We're leaving," Cole said.

"What?" Freelan asked.

Cole pressed on. "In the morning. As soon as we can get organized, we're gone."

"But Cole," Freelan said.

"But nothing, Free," Cole said. "It's not safe here, and it's clear now that nothing has changed. No matter how many shiny buildings you put up, it's still the same rotten place it always has been. We're leaving."

Freelan straightened. "The girl as well?" he asked. "She'd expressed a desire to stay, and it would—"

"If you think for one second I'm leaving her here," Cole said, "then you're sadly mistaken."

"I tried to help you back there," Freelan said. "This plan was all Garrett's. I had—"

"I don't care whose plan it was," Cole said. "You've screwed our whole mission, set us back who knows how long. We knew where Tobias was. We had him. Now he's in the wind, and who knows how long it'll take us to find him again?"

"Cole, we can help with that," Freelan said. "We can open up the communications and track—"

"Freelan, I think you've done enough already. I think it's time you left," Cole said. "Guys, can you see that he does?"

"With pleasure," Ram said.

Ram grabbed Freelan by the arm, twisted it behind his back and pushed him through the door. Sol followed.

"Well, this is quite a mess, isn't it?" Joran said.

"You can say that again," Cole said with a deep sigh.

Joran finished sealing the last of Cole's wounds. "There you are, all done. Thankfully there didn't seem to be any significant damage to the nodes." Joran looked out the door to where Kira was still lying with Gregor by her side. "What happened out there, Cole?" Joran asked. "With the girl, I mean. You think she's a Conduit?"

"I don't really know," Cole said. "I was fighting Tobias, he knocked me down, and then there was a scream—"

"The girl?"

"I wasn't sure at the time," Cole continued. "There was a rush of wind, and a bunch of us went flying. When I looked up, there she was, just standing there, shaking all over."

"And then she collapsed?"

"Yeah," Cole said. "It was a hell of a thing. She saved me. Tobias had me dead to rights."

"You're lucky she was there."

"She wasn't meant to be," Cole said, putting his jacket back on. "I tried to keep her away from it."

"I don't believe it," Joran said flatly.

"What?"

"You found someone else as stubborn as you," Joran said with a laugh.

"Do you think it's possible she's a Conduit and doesn't know?" Cole asked.

"It's possible," Joran said. "If this was the first manifestation of her—"

"I don't think it was the first time," Cole said. "There was another incident recently. She hasn't said a lot about it, but it could be related."

"If you were to stay a bit longer, I could run some tests and—"

"We can't stay, Joran," Cole said, "not after today. It's not safe."

"I understand."

"Before we go, though, there is something I need from you," Cole said.

"Anything, my boy," Joran said.

"I need that," Cole said as he pointed to the back wall of the workshop.

"I-I don't . . . That was—"

"I know I have no right to ask you for it," Cole said, "but it's for her. She's going to need to be able to protect herself. I can teach her, but a quality blade is hard to come by these days and Martiss always had the best."

"Truth be told, my boy, you have more claim to that blade than I," Joran said. "You always were his favorite."

Joran reached up and plucked the hilt of the aged blade from its mount on the wall and turned it over in his hands.

"Time has not been kind to this one," Joran continued. "It's going to need some work."

"Think you can have it working by tomorrow morning?" Cole asked.

Joran laughed, a wry grin wrinkling the corners of his eyes. "It always was hard saying no to you."

Cole stood underneath the hull of the *Havok*, shielding himself from the harsh midmorning sun, as a speeder came into the hangar, kicking up dust as it glided toward him.

"That's the last of it," Sol called down from the top of the ramp. "We should be right to leave whenever you're ready."

"All right. Thanks, Sol," Cole said as he watched Joran exit the speeder.

Cole walked to meet him. "You made it."

Joran produced the hilt of Martiss's sword and handed it to Cole. "The blade was rather stuck and the electronics were almost rusted out, but she's as good as new now."

"Thank you for this, Joran," Cole said. "I know it can't be easy to—"

"Say no more of it," Joran said, holding up his hands in protest. "You just make sure she knows how important that blade is."

"I will," Cole said.

"You know, I never did thank you for getting that back to me," Joran said.

Cole smiled gently at the old man. "It was the least I could do after everything that happened."

A somber silence hung in the air between the two of them. Cole looked down and noticed that Joran was carrying something else: a book. "What's that you've got there?"

Joran handed him the book. It was thick and felt heavy in Cole's hands. "Something of mine for the girl. Everything I've gathered about Conduits over the years," Joran said. "I thought it might help her understand her situation a bit better."

"Well, one thing's for sure," Cole said, "you'd do a better job of explaining it than I would."

"How is she this morning?"

"No change."

"I really wish you would both stay. You need rest, and I can help her."

"You know we can't, Joran," Cole said. "It's not safe for her here."

"Is it any safer for her out there?"

"Probably not," Cole said, "but I can't stay here, and I won't leave her on her own, not now. As for the rest, our ship's med pods should have me right in a few days."

Another speeder raced into the hangar and was closing on them. Cole could see Freelan sitting in the passenger seat. Cole didn't have the time or patience to deal with him.

"We have to go now, Joran."

"Farewell, my boy," Joran said, embracing him tightly. "Travel safe, and don't do anything else reckless."

Cole pulled back. "Reckless? Me?" he said with a chuckle. "I hope we can see each other again under better circumstances."

"I do too."

"Good-bye, Joran," Cole said as he turned and walked up the ramp. He stopped and looked to see Freelan getting out of his speeder and rushing toward him. Cole just stared him down, said nothing, then went into the depths of the *Havok*. The ramp closed behind him.

"Can I shoot him?" Ram asked Cole as he entered the cockpit. Ram's finger was already resting on the trigger of the

Havok's main cannons. The sights were squared firmly on Freelan's chest. "Please?"

"Not sure that'd be the best idea, Ram," Cole said, "as much as I'd probably like you to."

"Hey, look, it's the fun police."

"We right to go?" Sol asked.

"Take us up, Sol," Cole said. "I've had just about enough of this place."

Beep. Beep. Beep. Beep. Beep.

A while after they were well clear of Rygerian space, the communications console in the cockpit lit up in a frantic flurry of light and sound.

"What is it, Sol?" Cole asked.

"Whole bunch of stuff just started flowing in," Sol said. "I guess they really did have the comms blocked."

"Anything from Oren?"

Sol looked over the logs. "They're nearly all from Oren, actually."

"Can you bring one of them up?" Cole asked. "The earliest?"

"Sure thing."

A few quick taps of the controls, and Oren's face appeared on the screen.

"This one's from about a week ago," Sol said, "just after we got to Ryger."

"Cole," Oren said in the message. "Navarr has been seen meeting with a group of Shek'Tarii Hunters in a bar on Ferris. He's still there, but given your current location, I just want you to be aware that you may have been compromised."

"Yeah, no shit," Ram said.

"Play the next one, Sol," Cole said.

"Next one's the same," Sol said.

"Find the next unique one then."

"Got it," Sol said as he flicked through the logs. "Here we go. This one's from five days ago."

Oren flickered onscreen once again. "Cole," Oren said. "Navarr was just flagged leaving a spaceport on Ferris. His vector had him headed straight for Ryger. If he maintains his current course and speed, he should get there sometime tomorrow. I hope you can be prepared in time. I don't know why you aren't responding, perhaps communications have been disrupted by the Shek'Tarii. I will keep attempting to make contact."

"He wasn't kidding," Sol said. "He sent that fifteen times."

Cole sat down in one of the chairs in the cockpit and let out a loud sigh.

"Sol," Cole said, "can you get him on the comms?"

"Sure can," Sol said. "Gimme a sec."

They waited a few minutes before a live image of Oren flickered onto the screen.

"Cole?" Oren said.

"Yeah, it's me," Cole said.

"Where the bloody hell have you been?" Oren asked. "I've been trying to contact you for a week."

"We just got the messages now," Cole said. "As you thought, they'd blocked incoming comms. Wasn't the only thing you were right about either."

"Tobias was there?"

"Sure was," Cole said. "They tipped him off. I was only a couple of days clear of the surgery when he attacked."

"Are you all right?"

"Nothing a few days in a med pod can't fix," Cole said.

"Charles and his crew were nearby on some business, and I tried to send them to Ryger to help, but they wouldn't let them in," Oren said.

"The last thing that situation needed was Charles Weaver," Cole said sternly.

"No, you're probably right," Oren said. "So where is Tobias now?"

"No idea," Cole said. "He escaped. We were kind of hoping that you had some idea where he was."

"Escaped?" Oren said.

Cole had to be careful with his words. "Yeah, some of the Hunters weren't up with the plan and apparently didn't care for Tobias's intrusion. They killed his men and chased him off."

"His men?"

Ram popped his head in front of the camera. "Oh yeah, that's the fun part," he said. "The jackass rolled in with about a dozen armed troops."

"That is troubling," Oren said. "Perhaps he recruited them on Ferris?"

"Who knows," Cole said. "They're dead now anyway."

"Unless he has more," Ram said, "which he probably does."

"So, do you have anything on Tobias?" Cole asked.

"No," Oren said. "Our scanners haven't picked him up for a while. We only knew he was on the way to Ryger because of the local authorities on Ferris. He could be anywhere."

"Not necessarily," Sol said. "His ship was pretty beat up when he tore out of there. I don't think he could have gotten very far."

"Hmm, it's possible then that he returned to Ferris," Oren said.

"Well, that's probably our best shot," Cole said, "for now, anyway. I'll take a few days to rest up, and then we'll head over and check it out."

"All right," Oren said. "I'll keep looking on this end in case he's gone somewhere else, and I'll have my contacts keep an eye out for him on Ferris. If I find him, I'll be in touch."

Oren's face flickered and disappeared into the static.

Cole pushed away from the comms station. "Where's Gregor?"

"Where do you think?" Ram said, pointing over his shoulder.

FOURTEEN

COLE STOOD IN the doorway to Kira's room. She was stretched out on the cot, facing away from the door, and Gregor was sitting, leaning against the wall by the door.

"How's she doing?" Cole asked.

Gregor jumped and looked up at Cole. He yawned. "Oh, um, still no—"

"I'm fine," Kira said.

Cole stepped into the room. "How long have you been—"

"A little while."

"You did a good job of hiding it," Gregor said.

Kira rolled over to face them. She looked like she hadn't slept for weeks. Heavy bags hung under her eyes, and her skin was pale. "Pretty easy to do when *you've* been snoring the whole time," she said. "I didn't want to wake you."

"Gregor, go get some rest," Cole said. "I can keep an eye on her."

"Uh, sure," Gregor said. He got up and navigated his way to the door, barely keeping his eyes open.

Cole noticed that he'd left a small package behind on the floor.

"That yours?" he asked Gregor.

"What? Oh," Gregor mumbled. "Yes. Thank you."

He hurried back, picked up the package, and disappeared out the door.

Cole sat down on a box that was beside Kira's cot. "So how are you feeling?" he asked. "For real, this time."

"Why are we back on the ship?" Kira asked. "What happened?"

"Tobias found us," Cole said. "The Hunters, they . . . It wasn't safe there anymore."

"But I was going to stay," Kira said. "I thought that—"

"They weren't good people, Kira," Cole said. "They put on a good show, but they hadn't changed as much as it looked like they had. I'm sorry, I know you were looking forward to staying."

"It's OK," Kira said with a sigh. "There'll be somewhere else."

Kira rolled onto her back and stared at the ceiling.

"I remember what happened," Kira said. "Sort of."

Cole sat forward on the box. "What do you remember?"

"I remember . . . getting away from Freelan," Kira said, "and running to the hangar, and Tobias, he was,"—Kira sat up and looked at Cole—"I-I wasn't going to let him hurt you."

"And he didn't," Cole said. "Well, not much, anyway."

"Did he get away?"

"Yeah," Cole said. "But we're looking for him."

"Tobias is a Conduit, right?"

"Yes, he is."

"Am I?"

"Yes," Cole said. "I believe so."

"Oh," Kira said as she sat back against the wall. "I'm not going to end up like him, am I?"

"No, not at all," Cole said. "Despite what most people will tell you these days, Conduits aren't bad people. In fact, that reminds me: hold on a sec, I have something for you."

Cole disappeared out the door, and when he returned, he was carrying the book that Joran had given him for Kira.

"What's that?"

"This is a book written by my friend Joran," Cole said. "Now, he's forgotten more about Conduits than most people learn in a lifetime, but thankfully he got into the habit of writing it all down. He gave me this book for you, to help you understand, and learn."

Cole placed the book down beside her. He had considered giving her the sword, but thought it might be best to leave that for when she'd gotten a grasp on the whole being-a-Conduit thing.

Cole moved and sat next to Kira on the edge of her cot. "Kira, what happened back there, it isn't the first time something like that's happened, is it?"

Kira shook her head.

"What happened with the man?"

Kira took a deep breath and exhaled just as deeply. "When he came for me, I didn't want to go," she said. "He tried to drag me out of the shelter . . ."

A tear rolled down Kira's cheek.

"It's OK," Cole said. He placed a reassuring hand on her arm.

"The next thing I remember was that everything was very loud and the man flew across the room," Kira said. "I blacked out, and when I woke up, they'd tied me up. They told me the man had died and that some people were coming to collect me. 'Handle me,' they said. I was able to escape just before they got there."

A thought started to form in Cole's mind. He didn't like the feeling it gave him.

"How long ago was this?" Cole asked.

"About two weeks before I met you," Kira replied. "I spent most of that time living on the streets and, well, stealing stuff to survive, but you already know about—"

"And that's why you can't go back to the yards, right?" Cole asked. "Because of them?"

Kira nodded. "I figured I'd be safer if I was anywhere but there."

"These people who were after you," Cole said, speaking slowly and clearly, "were there four of them?"

"Yeah," Kira said. "How did—"

"One of them was about my age, graying hair with a goatee?"

Kira nodded.

Weaver.

"One was darker skinned, with tattoos?"

Kira nodded.

Jarak.

"The other two look as dumb as a bag of rocks?"

Kira nodded.

The Goons.

"Shit," Cole said under his breath.

Concern washed over Kira's face. "Cole, what's going on?"

"I know who's after you," Cole said.

"What? Who?"

"No one good," Cole said. "But don't worry. I can sort this out."

If Weaver and his cronies were after Kira, there was only one place the order could have come from.

Oren.

Cole came into the main hold with a huff and his eyes blazing.

"Ram, Gregor," Cole said, "I need you to do a sweep and scan of the ship, right now."

Ram looked up from his drink. "What are we looking for?"

"A tracker of some kind," Cole said.

Sol laughed. "If we were being tracked, mate, I think I'd—"

"Find it, and shut it down." Cole turned to Sol. "Sol, I need you to get back on comms with Oren and patch it through to my quarters, got it?"

"What's this about?" Sol asked.

"Remember how Weaver was at the yards?" Cole replied.

"Yeah?"

"They're after Kira," Cole said, "and they've probably been tracking us for weeks."

"All right then," Sol said, "one call to the boss man coming right up."

"And Sol?"

"Yeah?"

"Do whatever you can to make this ship as invisible as possible," Cole said. "It's going to take a few days for me to heal up, and I don't want any surprises."

"Got it."

Cole stormed out of the hold toward his quarters.

"Well, shit," Ram said. "I wouldn't want to be Oren right now."

"He did seem angry," Gregor said.

"What I would give to be in that room right now," Ram said. "But we've got a scan to do. Come on, kid."

"Cole? What's going on?"

"I need another favor, Oren," Cole said.

"What do you need?"

"It's about Weaver."

"Is this about your run-in with him at the shipyards?" Oren asked. "Because I've already told him to drop—"

"It's about what they were doing at the yards in the first place," Cole said.

"I don't follow," Oren said.

"They were there to snatch up a Conduit, a young girl," Cole said. "She'd killed someone with her abilities."

"Uh, yes, that does sound right," Oren said. "How in the world do you know that?"

"Because she's on my ship," Cole said, "has been since we left the yards."

"How exactly did that happen?"

"She snuck on board while we were loading our gear," Cole said. "We didn't find her till we were well out of Nikaran space."

"I see. So, what's the favor?"

"I need you to call off the dogs," Cole said. "Weaver must have gotten a tracker on the *Havok*. That's why he was already so close at Ryger. He'd been following us the whole time."

"Charles did mention to me that they were following a ship that he thought the girl was on," Oren said. "Clearly he neglected to mention that it was your ship or that you had anything to do with the girl. Calling this off goes against a lot of Federation regulations, Cole."

"Screw the regulations," Cole shouted. "She's just a kid, a scared one at that. She's only just found out she's a Conduit, and she saved my life, Oren. Tobias was *this* close to killing me on Ryger, and she saved me. I owe her this. She doesn't deserve to be 'disappeared.' Call them off."

Oren thought it over for a moment. "OK," he said finally. "Consider it done. It would seem the girl eluded the Federation's grasp and has disappe—"

"Mark her as dead," Cole said.

"What?"

"Mark her as dead. That way no one will come after her again."

"Very well," Oren said. "I will inform Charles and give him some other errand to run. Though I have to mention, you know what Charles is like, what he's always been like."

"Look," Cole said, "you can tell him that if he comes anywhere near her or me again, I'll shoot him on sight."

"I will gladly pass that along," Oren said with a smile.

"I've got the others searching for the tracker and securing the ship," Cole said. "I'm about to hop in the med pod for a day or two."

"Very well, I will keep Solomon up to date regarding Tobias's location," Oren said. "Hopefully by the time you're out, we'll have him."

"Hope so," Cole said. "I'm getting tired of chasing him across the galaxy."

Cole ended the call.

Everyone was back from their assignments when Cole came back into the main hold. Kira was sitting at the table leafing through her book, and Gregor was reading over her shoulder. The lights had been lowered throughout the hold, but there was still a light on over the table for them to read by.

"So, how'd we all do?"

"Cloak's up," Sol said. "All noncritical systems have been powered down. We're practically invisible. Kept one med pod running."

"Thanks," Cole said. "Ram?"

"Found it," Ram said. "Scanner picked it up on the forward hull. We put a temporary signal blocker on it, but we'll have to wait to actually pull it until we land on Ferris."

"Good job," Cole said. "So, anyone got any ideas on how to best approach the search for Tobias once we land?"

"I've got a mate there," Sol said. "Owns a club. His name's Whil T'Qar. Good bloke. Knows a lot about things he shouldn't. If Tobias is there, I'd be pretty shocked if he didn't have some idea as to his location."

"Are you able to contact him before we arrive?" Cole asked. "Might give us a bit of an advantage."

"We'll have to wait until we're closer to Ferris," Sol said. "Comms from this far out might get picked up by Weaver and give us away."

"Ah, right," Cole said. "Good thinking."

"Speaking of the trip to Ferris," Sol said, "you wanted to sit just out of Ferris space, yeah?"

"Yeah?" Cole said.

"Well, given our current circumstance," Sol said, "I thought I'd plot us a nice, slow scenic route. How many days do you need?"

"Oh, two, maybe three," Cole said. "Make it three."

"Done. We will arrive at Ferris in three days, and we'll never stop moving."

"All right, now that that's all under control," Cole said, "I think I might head into the pod. I feel like ten pounds of shit in a five-pound bag."

The med bay on the *Havok* was pretty small compared to those in most vessels of the Federation fleet, but Sol had still managed to fit four full-sized pods in there. However, that meant that there wasn't a lot of room for much else, which meant that for almost every injury, they relied on the pods to heal them. The newer models were especially good at handling most things. They could do everything from heal small cuts and bruises to repair organ damage and set broken bones. The only issue with them was the time it took for everything to work. Sure, it was faster than natural healing, but Cole always felt they could be quicker. The new units had been installed about four months ago, in the wake of Nate Revik's death. For years, Nate had insisted on keeping the old legacy models in the *Havok*. He didn't like change, and it ended up costing him his life.

Cole slid back the cover on the pod and hopped in. He entered in the treatment time on the internal controls and made himself comfortable. After a short countdown, the cover closed with a hiss and the pod pressurized. Cole felt as though he hadn't slept for weeks. He'd been rocketing from one disaster to the next and never had an opportunity to properly rest. As the pod slowly began to fill with the aerosolized anesthetic, Cole smiled. He could finally rest.

Cole's vision blurred, and soon everything was in triplicate. There was shouting coming from somewhere in the distance, but he couldn't discern its origin.

Crackle.

He heard the sound of a blade activating, and his vision snapped into clear focus. It was behind him.

There stood Tobias, at the base of the ramp to his ship, surrounded by his troops. They were back on Ryger.

"I'm sorry, Cole," Tobias said.

"Sorry?" Cole asked. "For what?"

Crunch.

Tobias's elbow caught Cole in the cheek just as it had before, only Cole was able to react quicker this time and spun in the air, landing squarely back on his feet. He launched himself at Tobias, and his fist made contact with Tobias's midsection. Cole drove his fist up into the underside of Tobias's chin, feeling the bone crack and chip under the force of the hit.

Cole's blade was in his hand now. It crackled to life. With a swift spin, he drove it cleanly into Tobias's chest. He was face-to-face with him now, staring into his eyes—eyes that were filled with untold rage, madness, and fear?

Cole blinked several times, trying to focus on his tormentor's face.

"Cole?"

The voice was not Tobias's. The eyes were no longer Tobias's.

"Olivia?" Cole said.

Ryger vanished around them in a flurry of wind. Blackness now stretched to eternity. A light came from somewhere above, just where, Cole had no idea. His hand still grasped the hilt of his sword tightly, but its blade was now buried deep in his wife's chest.

She showed no emotion, spoke as if she felt no pain at all.

"Is this it?"

Blood flowed freely from her chest and trickled slowly from the corners of her mouth.

"What?" Cole said, unable to release his grip on the sword.

"This," she said, pointing to the sword. "Is this what you want?"

Her face morphed back to Tobias's briefly before changing back.

"I want him to pay for what he did to you," Cole said, "for what he did to Zara."

"Did he do it, though?"

"W-what do you mean?"

"Tobias may have struck the killing blows," Olivia said. "But who set this wheel of terror in motion? Who truly held the blade?"

"It was him," Cole said, tears flowing freely. "I saw him."

"Whose blade was it, Cole?"

Cole felt a sharp pain in his stomach and then an intense heat. He looked down to see his own blade buried deep in his midsection, blood rushing from the wound. Olivia's hand was clenched tight around the hilt and was twisting it in the wound, forcing it deeper.

Cole didn't scream, couldn't scream.

As his vision began to blur once again, he looked back into his wife's eyes—only his wife was no longer there. Cole's own face stared back at him, bloodied and twisted. His own blood-shot eyes had sunk deep in their sockets—eyes that were filled with untold rage, madness, and fear.

Cole woke in a cold sweat to the beeping of the med pod cycling down. His heart felt like it would explode, and his head didn't feel much better. He lay for a while, calming himself, before finally getting out of the pod. Hallucinations and nightmares were a common side effect of being a Synth, with the cause being attributed to the amount of neural inter-actions involved with the implants. Cole could still remember the terrors that had gripped him as a child as he went through the adjustment period after his initial activation. It took many years for him to get used to them, but he was thankful that they stopped when he was deactivated and that there was no lasting damage.

But the visions that had been disturbing his sleep since the reactivation were different. They felt more real, more lucid than anything he remembered experiencing before.

"Pull it together," Cole said to himself as he slapped his face several times to help wake himself up. The sleep had been refreshing, nightmare notwithstanding, but now it was time to get to work. Three days had passed, his wounds had healed, and he could feel the strength in his body, could feel his senses heightened. He was ready.

"Oh good, you're up," Sol said as Cole entered back into the main hold. "Save us, please."

Cole looked at him, puzzled, then he looked around the hold. There were papers scattered about, and several lights were broken. Kira was still sitting at the table reading her book, and Sol and Ram were sitting at the bar.

"What exactly happened here?" Cole asked.

"That one thought she would practice," Ram said, pointing at Kira.

"Practice?"

"You know, Condy stuff," Sol said.

"Really?" Cole said. He walked over to Kira. "This was you?"

Kira nodded hesitantly.

"How exactly did you—"

"There was stuff in the book," Kira said, "about, y'know, training and stuff."

"And stuff?" Cole laughed. "Well, I think for now it might be a good idea to hold off on the practical side of things," he said. "We kind of need the ship in one piece."

"Very funny," Kira said.

"Look, for now, just focus on reading and learning as much as you can," Cole said. "There'll be plenty of time for training 'and stuff' later."

"Oh, she's been doing plenty of learning while you've been out," Sol said.

"Yeah," Ram said. "Did you know that Conduits have longer lifespans than normal beings of their species? And they can heal faster too."

"And did you know," Sol said, "that Conduit abilities can sometimes present much later in life?"

"And that no one knows the full extent of what a Conduit is capable of? Or that if a Conduit is—"

"Oh quiet, butthead," Kira said, laughing. "You love my trivia."

"In small doses, kid," Ram said, "very small."

Cole couldn't help but smile. As the last remnants of his hallucination faded away, he noticed that they were one short. "Where's Gregor?"

Ram and Sol started laughing. Kira soon joined in.

"What happened?"

"Like I said, she was practicing," Sol said.

"He's in his room," Ram said.

"Right, OK. Sol, you have any luck with your friend?" Cole asked as he headed toward Gregor's quarters.

"Whil? Spoke to him 'bout a half hour ago. Says a ship matching the description of Tobias's landed in a spaceport on Ferris a couple of days ago."

"I presume he told you which one?" Cole asked.

"He did," Sol said. "Course is already programmed in and ready to go."

"Well, let's get going then," Cole said. "Don't want to keep him waiting."

FIFTEEN

THE HAVOK GLIDED silently above the expansive cityscape that sparkled below. Ferris was a dwarf planet that over centuries had been enveloped by one large megalopolis covering almost three-quarters of its surface. The only regions that hadn't been colonized were a large ocean that reached nearly the entire way around its equator and the mountainous regions at the poles, which were too cold and treacherous for habitation.

Their destination was one of the massive spaceports toward the center of the city, a large, flat expanse of concrete and steel dotted with thousands of hangars, landing pads, markets, and other amenities.

"So, where's his ship?" Cole asked.

"It was spotted getting repairs somewhere over on Platform 451," Sol said.

"Which one's that? Ram asked.

Sol pointed to the rows of concrete pylons out west. "See the maglev lines over there?"

"Yeah, I see them."

"And see that over there?" Sol pointed to the large building far off in the east that housed thousands of markets and retail outlets.

"Yeah?"

Sol then held his hands out to the span of ground between them. "Platform 451."

"Oh," Ram said, laughing. "Well, shit, this should be a piece of cake."

Sol brought the ship down onto a large open concrete landing pad nearer to the markets with a gentle thud. There were only a few other ships in the immediate vicinity, and they were near a transport station, so they would have easy access to the rest of the city—and to escape, if needed.

A city as large as Ferris would be crippled if it weren't for its intricate transport system. For a planet so small, it boasted the largest isolated maglev train system in the quadrant. Millions upon millions of kilometers of tracks crisscrossed over the surface of the city and often under it as well. Road-based vehicles, along with the roads they used, had long been abandoned in favor of speeders and other light aircraft, which travelled above and between the buildings of the city.

They sat in the cockpit and watched as the Ferris inspection team hurried over to their ship, scanned it, and did all the checks they would normally do for any vessel that entered Ferris. After about ten minutes, they scurried away into their speeder and were gone.

"Guess we passed the test," Sol said.

"I wonder if they'll ever realize that they should probably look *inside* the ships as well?" Ram said.

"Probably not," Cole said, resting his rifle against the back of Sol's seat. "Sol, can you get out there and yank that tracker?"

"Sure thing." A silence followed in Sol's wake.

Ram turned to Cole. "You think we'll find him here?"

"He was hurt, his ship was damaged, and this was the closest civilized planet for a long way," Cole said. "If he hasn't skipped out on another ship, he'll be here."

"One tracker," Sol said as he came back up the ramp, "as requested. Where do you want it?"

"It's deactivated?" Cole asked.

"Sure is," Sol replied. "Gave it a bit of whack for good measure."

"Ah, just chuck it over there then," Cole said. "Might make a good paperweight."

Sol did as he was told and threw the tracker down on the table in the main hold, where Kira was sitting reading her book yet again. She looked at it briefly before returning her eyes to the pages.

"Where's Gregor now?" Cole asked. It had been two hours since he told him to get ready, and he had yet to appear.

"I'll get him." Ram walked a few steps to the opening of the corridor that led to the crew quarters. "Hey, kid! Get out here. We're leaving."

"Don't exert yourself too much there, Ramses," Sol said.

Cole heard Gregor's door open and his quiet footsteps as he came down the corridor. When Gregor rounded the corner into the hold, Cole had to try to keep a straight face.

"So how exactly did *that* happen?" Cole asked, stifling a laugh.

Gregor hung his head. "I-it was an . . . um . . ."

Cole couldn't help but stare at Gregor's right eye, which was the blackest one he'd seen in a long while, and wondered what Kira had done.

"It was an accident," Kira said as she jumped up and stood by Gregor's side.

"Yeah, but what hit him?" Cole asked. "You?"

"Uhh . . ."

"It was a rogue boot," Sol chimed in.

Cole looked at Kira. "You kicked him in the face?"

"Well," Kira said, "not exactly."

Ram piped up. "It was mine—"

"*You* kicked him in the face?"

Ram laughed. "It was over by the wall. She was trying to levitate it or . . . something."

Cole laughed. "Or something . . . Right, well, like I said, best if you hold off on training for now."

"OK," Kira said.

"And especially no levitating," Cole said.

"All right already," Kira said, folding her arms across her chest. "No levitating."

"Gregor, you right to go? You don't need to lie down or anything?" Cole asked.

Gregor nodded.

"Um, actually, can I just borrow him for a sec first?" Kira asked.

"Sure," Cole said.

"Looking to finish the job?" Ram asked, laughing.

"Shut up, butthead," Kira shot back.

Kira pulled Gregor to the side. "I really am sorry," she whispered.

"It's OK," Gregor said with a smile.

"But this is what I was talking about," Kira said. "They're making fun of you again. You have to stand up for yourself."

"It's not always that easy."

"But it can be," Kira said. "Show them you belong, that you can handle all this, give them some of their own back."

"I don't know if I—"

"Promise me," Kira said, "promise me that you'll try."

Gregor nodded.

Kira hugged him and pushed him back toward the group.

"Hey, looks like he made it out unscathed," Ram said.

Gregor waited just a moment too long to make his come-back: "Shut up, butthead."

An awkward silence hung in the air.

Ram laughed. "Well, points for effort, but that's *her* line."

Gregor looked back at Kira, whose face was a sort of half smile, half grimace.

Cole cleared his throat. "Can we go?"

"Absolutely," Sol said.

They all headed down the ramp, with Cole at the rear. As they reached the bottom of the ramp, Cole could hear footsteps behind him, and he turned to find Kira following close behind them.

"And where do you think you're off to?" Cole asked.

"I, uh, thought I'd, uh, come with . . . you?" she said.

"No."

"Look at the markets?"

"No."

"Clean the ship?"

"No," Cole said. "But you can stay *in* the ship until we get back."

"But—"

"But nothing," Cole said. "Inside, now. It's not safe for you to be out here. Stay in the ship."

"Fine," Kira said as she stomped back up the ramp.

Cole watched her go and then turned back to the group. "Close her up, Sol," he said. "No one in or out."

After a few taps of his wrist communicator, the ramp of the *Havok* raised into the hull of the ship and locked itself.

They exited the carriage of the maglev train onto a busy platform. All the platforms on Ferris were busy, but the ones in the entertainment district were especially crowded. Luckily for them, Ferris attracted a wide range of visitors, so no one batted an eyelash at four armed men stepping off a train.

"So how do you know this Whil guy?" Cole asked. "I've never heard you mention him before."

"Met him in training about twenty-five, maybe twenty-six years ago," Sol said. "I ended up being assigned to Nate, and he went into Fed Security."

"The FSF?" Gregor asked. "I thought you said he owned a club?"

"He does," Sol said. "He's way undercover, like deep. He'd probably kill me for saying that out loud."

"What's this place called anyway?" Cole asked.

"Keltar's."

"Will you be able to find us the *front* door this time, Sol?" Ram asked.

"Thought I might find us a food stand instead," Sol replied, grinning from ear to ear.

Ram punched Cole in the arm. "You told him about that?"

"Actually, I told him," Gregor said.

Ram punched Gregor in the arm and nearly knocked him off his feet.

Sol laughed. "It's not far now."

Kira sat at the table in the main hold of the *Havok*, staring blankly at the pages of her Conduit book. She couldn't focus on the words at all, so she pushed it aside and started aimlessly spinning the mangled tracker on the tabletop. That soon grew tiresome as well. Her mind and legs were restless from being cooped up in the ship for days. She needed to get out of there.

Kira had spent so much of her formative years breaking into places, whether to sleep or to find food or something shiny, that she was surprised how hard it was to get the ramp down. After many, many attempts, she finally touched the right wire to the right connector and the ramp unlocked with a clunk, slowly lowering to the ground.

The temperature outside was cool, much cooler than in the ship, and a light breeze blew Kira's hair into her face. She had decided to let her hair out for once. It was short, but being freed from its ties felt strangely liberating. Looking around, she could see a bunch of ships, many smaller than the *Havok*, but a lot that were larger as well. In the distance, she could see a large freighter like the ones she used to see all the time back at the yards. Feeling slightly nostalgic, she decided to go over and take a look around.

In most areas of Ferris, the buildings reached over two hundred stories with the ground below often never seeing sunlight. In the entertainment district, it wasn't uncommon for buildings to reach far beyond that. Keltar's was on the 342nd level and was connected to its neighboring buildings by a series of interconnected walkways and plazas that were teeming with people.

Keltar's was right in the heart of the district, among all the other bars, casinos, and theaters, but it clearly stood out from the rest. An endless surge of people flowed in and out of its front doors, and the entire facade of the building stretched over a hundred meters into the air. Its neon surface flashed and pulsed without ever stopping, illuminating the plaza in front of the club in a wash of color.

Inside, it was hard to move through the other people, but they eventually forced their way to the bar. Sol tapped the bartender on the shoulder. "We're here to see Mister Keltar."

"So's everyone else, buddy," he replied. The bartender grunted and turned back to his work.

"He's expecting us, mate," Sol said, louder this time.

The bartender sighed and turned to face them. He leaned on the bench, his less-than-fresh breath wafting over them. "Name?"

"Solomon Dane."

The bartender eyed Cole and the others. "They with you?" Sol nodded.

"Hang on," the bartender said and disappeared through a door.

When he returned, he looked sourer than when he had left.

"Over there, red door," the bartender said, pointing over his shoulder. "Take the stairs to the top. It's the first door on your left."

Kira rounded a corner and stopped dead. There before her was something she hadn't planned on seeing on her little sojourn: Tobias's ship. She was sure of it. It had set in her mind so clearly when she saw it out the window on Ryger that there could be no doubt that it was the same one.

It looked like it was pretty beat up, and Kira wondered if any of the damage had been her doing. She still didn't remember a whole lot about that day, just the broad strokes.

There didn't appear to be anyone about, but she didn't want to take any chances, so she approached the ship slowly and carefully, making sure to stay out of plain sight.

It was locked up tight. Almost instantly, Kira's mind flashed and she knew what she had to do.

The tracker.

They followed the bartender's instructions and found themselves in a lavish office, decked out from floor to ceiling in glass, gold, and red velvet. A window occupied the entirety of the far wall, and it looked out over the club floor below.

"Fancy," Ram said, taking it all in.

A man stood at the window and, on hearing them enter, turned to greet them.

"Solomon," Whil said. "You made it."

Whil T'Qar was not what Cole had expected. By any description, he was just a man: average height, average build, neatly trimmed beard, nice suit. He certainly didn't look like a master spy, but then again, that was probably the idea.

Solomon introduced each of them, and Whil shook their hands in turn—a firm handshake.

"Sol tells me you might be able to help us out," Cole said.

"Ah yes," Whil said. "Follow me."

Whil walked over to his desk and pressed a button on his computer. A screen appeared from a panel on the right-hand wall of the office. A picture of Tobias's ship flickered onto it. "That your man's ship?"

"It is," Cole said.

"This is a live shot from Platform 451," Whil said. "From the looks of it, repairs are not yet complete. It's been parked there for three days, but as far as we've seen, he hasn't been anywhere near it."

"Who's that there?" Sol asked, pointing to a small figure jogging away from the ship.

"No idea," Whil said. "Could be part of the maintenance crew. They've been back and forth for days."

"Is it possible he's left on another ship?" Cole asked.

Whil raised a finger in the air, and a new image appeared on the screen. "This was taken around four hours ago at the Telravia Casino. My contact there has been watching him. He hasn't seen him leave."

On the screen was Tobias, sitting at a table, playing cards like he didn't have a care in the world. The cuts on his face looked like they'd only just started to heal.

"Looks like he loves to gamble as much as you love to drink, Cole," Gregor said.

Ram and Sol chuckled to themselves. "There you go, kid," Ram said. "That's more like it. A little on the nose, sure, but not bad."

Cole ignored them. "And you're sure he's there?"

"As sure as I can be," Whil said.

"Anything else you can tell us?"

"What do you want to know?"

"Is there anyone else with him?"

"Like who?"

"Private security," Ram said.

"As far as we've been able to tell, he's alone," Whil said.

"And what's security like in general at the Telravia?" Cole asked. "Will we have any trouble getting to him?"

"Security's pretty tight," Whil said. "However, they're surprisingly lenient on patrons carrying weapons, so you won't have any issues there."

"But we will have issues?" Cole said.

"Look, you're not going to be able to go in there and start a big shit-fight with the guy. I heard about Tragg," Whil said. "Getting him out of there is your biggest issue."

"We'll think of something," Cole said.

"So where is this joint?" Ram asked.

"Not far from here," Whil said. "Solomon knows where it is. Don't you, Sol?"

"You're not going to let me live that down, are you?"

"Not on your life."

Ram looked at Sol. "Should I ask?"

"I'd really rather you didn't."

"Oh, I'm saving that one for a rainy day," Ram said with a gleeful smile.

"Well, OK then," Cole said. "I guess we should go say hi."

They left Keltar's and forced their way through the mass of life into the plaza. Gregor couldn't help but look up and around at all the lights and advertising screens that seemed to cover every square meter of every building as far as his eyes could see. It was like a canyon of light, a big shiny metal canyon of light.

"It's just down here a ways," Sol said, pointing down the avenue.

Gregor pulled his eyes away finally and turned to Cole. "So, do you have any idea how we're going to get Tobias out of there?"

"Not a one," Cole replied. "Like I said, we'll think of something."

They headed off in the direction of the Telravia, making sure to go with the flow of foot traffic. They hadn't gotten far when the crowd slowly began to come to a halt. Then it began to reverse its flow, and before long, it was surging the opposite direction. Screams traveled down to them on the wind.

"What's going on?" Ram shouted over the noise.

"No idea!" Sol shouted back.

Several police speeders tore through the air above their heads in the direction of the Telravia, the lights from their sirens getting absorbed into the glow of the lights surrounding them.

"He can't have made it that easy for us?" Ram shouted.

"It could be nothing," Sol offered.

Cole tried to maintain his footing against the rush of the crowd. "Can't hurt to take a look."

The four of them proceeded to force their way through the crowd and headed off slowly toward the source of the disturbance.

Kira had a problem. She'd retrieved the tracker from the *Havok* easily enough, but it was trashed. Sol wasn't kidding when he said he whacked it. She figured her best bet was to head to the market to try and find a replacement, but she'd already been through several stores, and they'd all chased her out or told her to beat it. She couldn't hang around in the market much longer. She'd had to leave the ramp of the *Havok* down; otherwise, she wouldn't have been able to get back in.

Kira spied an electronics store across a small plaza. It was her last hope. She ran into the store but was pulled up by the owner, a large, overweight Valdar.

"What do you want?" he asked.

"I need your help," Kira said.

"Do you now?"

"I need a new one of these," Kira said as she held out the mangled tracker before her.

The owner took it and turned it over a few times in his hands. "I'll say you do. What was it—in its former life, that is?"

"A tracker. I need another one."

"What sort do you need?" the owner asked.

"Um, a good one?"

"You have no idea, do you?"

"Not really, no."

"What are you tracking? A ship? A person? Cargo?"

"A ship. My friends are following someone."

"Your friends?" the owner asked, raising an eyebrow.

"Yep," Kira said. "My friends."

"You're not planning on breaking any laws with this, are you?"

Kira smiled. "Nope, just following someone very legally."

The owner eyed her suspiciously for a moment and then shrugged. "In that case, I think the Portana XC-93 is what you're after. Deep space tracking, resistant to tampering and signal blocking—it's waterproof too. Magnetic locking mechanism won't come off unless you turn it off. Perfect for what you're looking to do."

Kira's face beamed. "Do you have one?"

"No," the owner said.

"What?"

"Well, I have *one*," he said, "but it's on hold for another customer and I—"

"How much is it?"

"What?"

"How much?"

"Fifteen hundred credits," he said. "Which is probably out of range of your allowance anyway, kid."

Kira rummaged around in her pockets and produced the credit chip Cole had given her.

"This has five thousand credits on it," Kira said. "Give me the tracker, and it's yours."

"You really want it that much?"

Kira nodded.

"Well, shit, who am I to argue?" The owner laughed and disappeared out the back. He soon returned with a small box in his hands and put it on the countertop.

Kira confidently strode to the counter, threw the credit chip to the man, picked up the tracker, and made for the door.

"Hey, kid," the owner said.

Kira stopped. "What?"

"You have any idea how to use that thing?"

"Does it have instructions?" Kira asked.

"Well, yeah, but—"

"Well, there you go," Kira said as she walked out of the store, package in hand. "Butthead."

The exterior of the Telravia Casino was even more extravagant and gaudy than Keltar's. You'd hurt your eyes if you looked at it for too long. But as night fell on Ferris, nobody was looking at the casino. All eyes that had not yet fled had fallen on the plaza in front.

As Cole pushed through to the edge of the ever-widening circle of humanity, he saw what they were all looking at.

"Shit."

In the center of the circle was Tobias, sword drawn, eyes wild. He had a man by the throat, and several security personnel littered the ground between him and the entrance to the casino. Several other security members were lingering along the clearing's edge, hesitant to enter the fray.

"Maybe he was counting cards?" Ram offered.

Cole surveyed the scene, and a plan formed quickly in his mind.

"Ram, Sol, go through the crowd, get on either side of him," Cole said. "Don't let him run. Gregor, I want you to—"

"Cole Traske!"

Tobias's voice boomed across the plaza, and every mouth in the area fell silent.

"I see you there, boy," Tobias yelled as he singled Cole out in the crowd with his sword. "Why don't you and your little friends come out to play?"

Cole removed the hilt from his belt and stepped from the crowd. Ram, Sol, and Gregor followed slowly behind him. Clear from the crowd, Cole extended his blade and activated it. The crackle could be heard across the plaza.

"This *your* man?" Tobias asked, raising his captive a little higher off the ground. "Caught him spying on me. Not nearly as sneaky as he thought he was."

"He's not with me, Tobias," Cole said. *He must be Whil's man.*

Tobias looked at the man squirming in his grip and frowned. "He's not much use to me then, is he?" He then forced the man to his knees and held his sword to his throat.

Tobias sighed. "We really have to stop meeting like this, Cole," he said. He drew back his arm.

Cole reached out a hand. "Tobias, don't—"

Tobias's blade shot through the man's chest, a fountain of blood spraying across the white-tiled plaza. He threw the man with such force that he skidded to a stop at Cole's feet, and then Tobias ran straight back into the casino.

"Damn it," Cole shouted as the four of them ran off in pursuit, leaving the entire congregation staring dumbfounded at what had just happened before their eyes.

Kira was very pleased with herself. Not only had she had the idea of putting the tracker on Tobias's ship, but she'd also been able to procure a brand-new tracker and was able to get it on the ship using only half the instructions. When she got back in visual range of the *Havok*, she was doubly pleased that it was still there. She knew she'd be in trouble for leaving it open and unattended for so long, but Kira was hoping that getting the tracker onto Tobias's ship would make up for it.

Kira began the walk back to the *Havok*, but she was so wrapped up in her success that she didn't hear the footsteps behind her, didn't see the shadows spreading out either side of her.

Someone pushed her to the ground, and she hit hard.

The next thing she knew, she was being pulled to her feet by her hair.

I've made a mistake.

The man lifted Kira by her hair until she was at eye level. Her vision was blurry after hitting the ground, but she thought she could make out three others.

"I've been looking for you," he said menacingly.

Kira recognised his voice, his face.

Weaver.

"Where is he?" Cole shouted as his eyes scanned the casino floor for any sign of Tobias. If he was in there, the patrons weren't aware of it. Everyone was calmly going about gambling away their life savings without a care in the world.

"Spread out," Cole said. "If anyone sees him, shout."

They'd gotten about three steps when Gregor suddenly bolted across the floor, patrons jumping out of the way in shock as he ran past.

"Kid, where are you going?" Ram shouted after him.

Gregor was already out of vocal range, but his reply came clear over the comms. "Glass elevator, far wall."

It was all he said and all he needed to say.

Cole, Ram, and Sol looked, and sure enough, there was Tobias, calmly riding the elevator up until it disappeared into the ceiling of the casino.

The interior of the casino was at least ten stories high and Cole had no idea what was at the top, but there was no time to think about it. They all took off after Gregor through the corridor of people that had formed in his wake. They skidded to a stop outside the elevators and all rushed inside when one arrived—all except for Ram, who lingered just outside the door.

Cole furrowed his brow. "Now is *not* the time, Ram," he said as he grabbed Ram by the arm and pulled him into the elevator.

They all managed to squeeze into the elevator that would have been fine for normal people but was much too small for four fully armed, fully grown men.

"Where to?" Gregor asked.

"As high as it goes," Cole said. "Sol, do you have any idea what's up there? I need something to work with."

"There's . . . there's,"—Sol pounded the palm of his hand on his forehead as if trying to force an answer from his mind—"some gardens, big rooftop gardens, couple of restaurants, and it all backs onto the parking for the casino."

"Parking?" Cole said.

"Yeah, big, multi-level thing."

"He's trying to run again," Ram said.

"Not if I have anything to say about it," Cole said.

The casino floor passed out of view, and the elevator ascended into darkness.

"Are you sure about this, Weaver?" Jarak Rol asked. "Rhey'll told us pretty explicitly to let her go."

Weaver had Kira sitting on the ground now, his hand firmly on her shoulder. "But we're not getting these Condies for Rhey'll, are we?" Weaver said. "They're for the Federation. We have a reputation to uphold and a job to do, so I'm doing it."

"But—"

"We're taking the girl," Weaver said as he dug his fingers into Kira's shoulder. "End of story."

"So why are we hanging around? Let's just go," Jarak said.

Weaver ignored Jarak and knelt down to talk to Kira. "So tell me, you little shit," he said, "where's Cole?"

Kira looked out the corner of her eye and saw that the *Havok* was a straight shot, a couple of hundred meters away. She could make it.

Kira spat in his face.

Weaver smiled and shook her shoulder hard. "Where is he?" he said calmly.

Kira closed her eyes and focused. She hadn't practiced much, but if there was one thing she had gotten the hang of doing, it was making people fly.

She bit down hard on Weaver's hand, and when he released his grip, she was able to make it to her feet. She focused her mind on what she wanted to do, and she screamed. She honestly had no idea if the screaming actually helped, but it wasn't the time to move away from tradition. When she opened her eyes again, Weaver and his men were scattered across the platform a few meters away. She turned to the *Havok* and ran.

Kira's feet seemed to carry her faster than she'd ever remembered them doing before. Her head was swimming, and she didn't feel like she was going to be able to maintain her balance for much longer, but she finally made it to the lowered ramp of the *Havok*. She scampered inside and fumbled with the wires before she made the right connection, and the ramp closed without any of them getting inside.

As she stumbled into the cockpit, she could see Weaver and his men approaching the *Havok*. They started shouting at her, and two of them, the dumb-looking ones, started firing on the ship at Weaver's command.

She was trapped.

The elevator came to a stop, and they burst out onto the rooftop plaza, guns at the ready. It didn't take very long for them to find Tobias. All they had to do was follow the screams and the bodies.

"There!" Ram shouted as he spotted Tobias running into the parking structure.

As they turned a corner into the structure, Cole could see Tobias running down the long corridor in front of them. They were running full speed after him when Sol began to hear a beeping sound.

It took him a while, but eventually Sol realized it was the comms. "It's from the ship!"

Cole slowed slightly but stayed in pursuit of Tobias. "Kira?"

"Has to be."

"Patch her through to all of us," Cole said.

"Got it."

The comms crackled to life. There was only silence on the other end.

"Kira, we're kind of in the middle of something," Cole shouted as he ran.

"Cole?" Kira said.

The fear in her voice stopped Cole short.

"Kira, what is it?"

"I think I'm in trouble."

She sounded completely out of it.

Cole turned and saw that Tobias too had stopped running and was just staring blankly at them, blood dripping off the end of his sword.

"Kira, take a deep breath and tell me what's going on," Cole said. "Can you do that?"

"It's Weaver," Kira said. "He's here."

SIXTEEN

COLE PROCESSED THE situation and exhaled. "Kira, I need you to listen to me and do exactly what I say, OK?"

Kira's voice came back a whimper: "OK."

"I need you to stay out of sight," Cole kept his voice as reassuring as he could muster. "The ship is secure. They shouldn't be able to get in. Just stay hidden, and you should be safe until we get there, OK?"

"OK."

"We'll be there soon," Cole said. "Hold tight."

"Hurry," Kira whispered just as the call cut out.

Remembering the pursuit, Cole turned, fully expecting Tobias to be long gone, but he wasn't. There he was, standing no more than a hundred meters or so away, barely moving, eyes fixed on them.

Without taking his eyes off of Tobias, Cole set the plan in motion: "Ram, Sol, I need you to get back there now."

"What do you want us to do about Weaver?" Ram asked.

"Handle it."

"Say no more," Ram said as he and Sol turned and ran back toward the casino at a full sprint.

Gregor started after them but stopped when Cole grabbed him by the shoulder.

"Don't."

"But I have to help her," Gregor said. "I can help."

Cole locked eyes with Gregor. "I need your help here, OK?"

Gregor nodded in agreement.

"All right," Cole said. "Just follow my lead and be ready for anything."

Tobias remained unmoved, but even from this distance, Cole could see the nervous tension coursing through him. He could see it in the way he was continuously shifting his weight. It was like he was getting ready to make a run for it at any second, but something was holding him firmly in place. The tension flowed outward from him and spread thick through the air, slowly muffling the screams and sirens of the chaos left in the wake of their chase.

After what seemed like an eternity, Cole couldn't maintain the standoff any longer and began to slowly advance on Tobias's position with Gregor in tow. Tobias too broke his trance and started backing away.

Ding.

Cole stopped as an elevator door opened along the side-wall, and several rather drunk patrons stumbled out, completely oblivious to what was going on around them. They were laughing hysterically about something that none of them would remember the next day. Some of them would never remember anything again.

Tobias moved quickly. Cole couldn't get there in time.

The blade flashed and crackled in the still night air, and in moments, two of the men were lying crumpled at Tobias's feet, blood slowly pooling. The rest screamed and ran, able to escape only because Tobias had found something of more interest to him. He casually knelt down and picked up something that had fallen from one of the men's hands: keys.

Cole began sprinting, but could only watch as Tobias found the speeder that the keys belonged to, hopped in, and promptly sped off into the ever-deepening night.

"Damn it!" Cole shouted as he skidded to a halt. There was no time to waste as he ran to the nearest speeder he could find and jumped in. After ripping the cover off the dash, he started messing with wires, trying to jump start the engine. It was no good. He was going into it blind and didn't know how to get it started. Every second wasted meant Tobias was getting farther away.

Cole's hot-wiring effort was interrupted by the soft rumble of an engine somewhere close by. He looked up to see Gregor's beaming face.

"Coming?"

Cole leapt out and ran to the waiting speeder. He only had to stand at the driver's side for a few seconds before Gregor got the hint and moved over. In a burst of exhaust fumes and scraping metal, the speeder tore out of the parking garage in pursuit of Tobias.

As traffic rushed by the sides of their speeder, Cole and Gregor did their best to scan ahead and spot any sign of Tobias. The speeder that he had taken was red, blood red, but even taking that into consideration, finding it in the middle of the Ferris rush hour was going to be a task. It didn't help that half the district had been thrown into chaos by Tobias's little escapade and there was quite a lot of air traffic that wasn't exactly sticking to their lanes.

"How did you do that?" Cole shouted above the rush of wind in the cockpit.

"Do what?" Gregor shouted back.

Cole made a sweeping gesture with his free arm, indicating the speeder.

"Oh," Gregor said, a confident smile breaking out on his face. "Well, you see, I was friends with this guy at the academy and he, well, he was kind of involved with some shady characters—well, not shady. They were kind of loners, I guess, and anyway, there was this girl and—"

Cole held up a hand. "Is this a long story?"

Gregor nodded, the smile fading slightly.

"Is there a short version?"

He nodded again, slower this time.

"Well?"

"I know things," Gregor said quickly.

"You know 'things?'"

"Yes," Gregor said, as he returned his gaze to the search.

"Well, I guess you're just full of surprises," Cole said, weaving through the traffic with ease. They rounded a corner at a great rate of speed and nearly clipped a cargo freighter, dipping at the last second to avoid a premature end to the pursuit. Up ahead, the traffic was at a near standstill.

"Cole, there!" Gregor shouted, pointing into the distance.

Sure enough, there was Tobias's blood-red speeder, frantically weaving in and out of the stagnant traffic, with two police speeders close behind.

"Hold on, kid," Cole said. "This might get bumpy."

Cole put the speeder into a dive, and Gregor's stomach leapt into his throat. It wasn't a long descent, though, as Cole soon leveled out and gunned it. Gregor's stomach dropped and was then pushed back into his seat. Now below the traffic, they were able to make ground and close the gap on Tobias.

An explosion drew Cole's gaze upward just in time to see one of the police speeders career into several stalled civilian vehicles and break apart. The wreckage of all three vehicles promptly began the long descent into the depths of Ferris, followed closely by Tobias, who was attempting to evade the other police speeder. Luckily for Tobias, it seemed to have worked as no one followed him. Unluckily for him, though, Cole had him in his sights.

The engines of Cole's speeder whined as they sped toward the fleeing speeder. It was unlikely they'd ever been put under this kind of strain before or that they were even designed to be. They managed to pull up beside Tobias in no time at all, and for a short time, it seemed as though Tobias didn't even realize they were there.

Cole banked sharply and gave Tobias's speeder a solid nudge, just to help things along. It worked. Tobias's head snapped to the side, and he glared at them long and hard before he swerved and rammed them. Again and again, he slammed his speeder into them, the screech of grinding metal ringing out over the roar of the engines.

After a sustained attack, Tobias abruptly peeled off and disappeared between a pair of tall glass buildings. Cole quickly adjusted his flight path and headed after him.

It was several minutes before they were able to catch up to Tobias again, and by the time they had, they had emerged onto the large industrial flatlands near the landing platforms. It was a sea of shipyards, cargo bays, construction yards, and hangars that stretched as far as the eye could see.

Tobias's speeder was outpacing them, the gap between them widening with each passing moment.

"Shoot out his engine," Cole shouted to Gregor.

"Right." Gregor grabbed his rifle and stood up in the cockpit. The wind rushing past nearly knocked him off his feet, but he was able to steady himself by resting his knee on the dashboard. He tried to line up the shot, but the reticle was going haywire.

"It's no good! Our speed is messing up the tracking. I can't get the shot!"

Cole turned to look at Gregor but kept one eye on Tobias. "You're kidding me."

"What?"

"You were top of your class, right?"

"Yeah, well, actually I was only—"

"Best sniper in the academy?"

"But Cole, I—"

"Can you make the shot or not?"

Gregor looked ahead at Tobias's speeder. It was a good couple of hundred meters away, with the wind and the speed they were traveling, it'd be tough. Gregor steeled himself and nodded.

"Well, take the shot then," Cole shouted.

Resting the barrel of his rifle on the windshield, Gregor settled in and took a look through the scope. He felt the wind rushing past his face. Adjusted the shot. He did his best to slow his breathing. Adjusted the shot. Followed Tobias's speeder as it bobbed along in front of them. Adjusted the shot. Finally, he placed his finger on the trigger. A final adjustment.

With a silent prayer, Gregor exhaled and slowly depressed the trigger, and the recoil nearly kicked him from the speeder. He watched intently, waiting for the round to find its mark.

He didn't have to wait long.

The starboard engine of Tobias's speeder erupted in a ball of sparks and flames, the ceramic round making short work of the internals. Hot metal flew outward before being caught by the wind and trailing off into the ether.

"Nice work, kid," Cole said as he pulled a stunned Gregor back into the cockpit.

Cole gunned it and closed the gap on the ailing speeder in no time at all. It still had one engine, so it was still mobile, but it had been severely crippled. Cole brought their speeder alongside and, at full speed, smashed it into the side of the badly smoking speeder.

As his hands were wrenched from the controls, Tobias could feel a subtle warmth radiating from somewhere in his midsection, and the dull ache slowly grew into a sharp pain. He knew he'd been hit with some sort of shrapnel from the explosion, but there wasn't a lot he could do about it in his current situation.

Regaining control of his flagging speeder, he turned his gaze to his assailant and found himself locking eyes yet again with Cole. He could see the determination flickering behind the rage, and in that instant, he knew there was only one way this was going to end.

Ahead, he could see the crisscross of maglev lines with a constant flow of cargo trains shooting across them.

"No point waiting around," Tobias said under his breath, to no one in particular.

Utilizing what little power his speeder had in reserve, he slammed his speeder yet again into the side of Cole's—only this time there was no turning back. Metal shrieked and sparked, and flames sprung anew from his mangled engine. Their two craft had become one, fused and tangled together.

He could see Cole wrenching at the controls, trying to separate them, but it was no use. The boy was even firing at his remaining engine trying to destroy it completely, but it only entwined them tighter.

A short stab indicated that another piece of shrapnel had made its way into the cockpit. This one seemed to pass through him somewhere below the previous wound, not that it mattered now.

They were closing on the maglev lines fast, and it looked like their arrival would coincide with an approaching cargo train. Tobias strained at the controls and steered the speeders into a collision course.

It wasn't supposed to be this way.

"What are you doing?" Cole shouted over the din.

Gregor popped his head briefly from under the dashboard. "We need more power."

"Can you do it?"

"Give me a sec," Gregor shouted, returning to his work.

Through the smoke and flames, Cole could see the rapidly approaching train lines. They had to do something fast. He was just about to ask after Gregor again when the mangled speeders shot forward. He could feel that they were back in majority control of the wreck, and not a moment too soon.

"Stay down!" Cole shouted.

He pushed hard on the controls, and despite screeching in defiance, the speeders dipped just enough to miss the train line.

The brief reprieve was short-lived.

They cleared the underside of the maglev line, but in a violent collision, the port side of Cole's speeder clipped the steel and concrete pylon. Cole was thrown forward into the controls and, with a bright flash, into darkness.

The force of the impact broke the two speeders apart, and they each spiraled off in a different direction. Trailing smoke and embers, they each fell from the sky like stones.

The impacts were heard by no one.

In fact, the only real signs that something had gone wrong were the two slowly rising pillars of smoke among an endless field of cargo containers.

SEVENTEEN

A DAMPNESS HUNG in the air as Ram and Sol slid into a position a safe distance from the *Havok*. Their footsteps were silent against the concrete, the only sound being the light rustling of their gear, imperceptible against the voices of Weaver and his crew.

They hadn't been seen.

Night had fully fallen on Ferris, and a low fog spread across Platform 451. Large floodlights bathed the entire area in a sterile glow, creating an obscure shadow play among the spacecraft scattered across its surface. Cracks of sound cut through the air, and their accompanying flashes of light indicated that Weaver was still trying to get into the *Havok*.

Ram exhaled sharply. Sol shot him a concerned look.

"What's the plan?" Sol asked.

Seemingly not hearing the question, Ram unhooked the launcher from his back and started loading rockets into the mag.

"No. No way," Sol said sternly.

"What? Why not?" Ram said.

"We don't need Laatschi all over again."

Ram scoffed. "Really? You don't think I learned from that?"

"You can be a little *reluctant* at times, Ramses."

"Look, I've got this," Ram said. "In fact, I was thinking it'd be more along the lines of Raavi."

Sol laughed. "Oh, well, that should be all right then. That'll work nicely, actually."

"Thank you," Ram said as he finished loading the magazine.

Ram hoisted the launcher up onto his shoulder and began to dial in the aim.

Sol cleared his throat. "Just remember that there is a rather expensive ship over there that's *mine*."

"I know."

"And a girl, inside said ship, that we're trying to save."

"I *know*."

Ram shifted his weight and made the final adjustments to the shot.

Sol tapped Ram on the shoulder. "Ramses?"

"Yes, Solomon?"

"Just a little to the right," Sol said. "If you don't mind."

Ram let out a loud, disgruntled sigh and shifted his aim a fraction to the right.

Kira's heart was racing, and she swore it skipped a beat every time a round skipped off the hull of the *Havok*. She'd been hunkered down under the main control console of the cockpit ever since Cole told her to stay out of sight. She could hear muffled voices shouting at her in between the cracks of gunfire, but not clear enough to make out any words. She didn't need to; she knew what they wanted, why they were there: her.

The sound dropped away for a moment, as it had several times before, but this was different. The hairs on the back of her neck stood on end, and she felt a flutter in the pit of her stomach. *Something's wrong.*

Still dazed and weak from her escape, Kira managed to force herself to stand and peer over the top of the control console and out the front viewport. Through the fog, she could just make out the shadowy shapes of Weaver and his men, standing in a close group, taunting her. Taking a few steps back, she rested gently into the pilot's chair. Her head was throbbing now, but she couldn't take her eyes off the men outside. Something inside her compelled her to look.

Then she saw it: in the distance, there was a flash followed by a dull thud. The spiraling rocket cut through the fog like a knife as it tore across the platform toward the ship. Everything inside her was telling her to run for cover, but still, she couldn't take her eyes away.

The rocket left a trail of smoke that slowly dissolved into the fog. As it neared Weaver and his men, Kira could tell the rocket was not headed for them. It dipped and contacted the ground a good distance to the right of them. The fireball was brief but bright, and the *Havok* shuddered from the blast.

It had only taken a few seconds, but to Kira, it felt like an eternity.

The explosion had cleared the immediate area of the fog, and for a moment, Kira was able to take in the aftermath: there was a crater, though it was much smaller than she would have expected, and several crates and pieces of equipment had been scattered, laying smoking or sparking or both. She could see that Weaver and his men had also been thrown by the blast, and they lay scattered near a pile of crates. They were moving slowly, but it seemed they had survived. As the fog began to encroach, Kira saw two figures emerge from behind a large cargo container. She breathed a sigh of relief when she saw it was Ram and Sol.

By the time they reached Weaver and his men, the fog had swallowed the scene entirely. However, she could make out their silhouettes enough to work out what was going on: two of them, the bigger ones—"The Goons," as Cole had called them—were trying to crawl away as Ram and Sol arrived. Two bright flashes and dull thuds later, they stopped crawling.

The other two, Weaver and Jarak, slowly struggled to their feet as Ram and Sol trained their weapons on them.

Something in the back of Kira's mind told her that now was the time to look away.

Everything was a wash of blurred color when Cole came to. His head was ringing, and the smell of fried electronics and smoke filled his nostrils. It took a few moments, but when his vision cleared, he was able to get a better sense of the situation. He was still in the speeder—or what was left of it. His foot was pinned in the wreckage, and he couldn't see Gregor anywhere.

"Hey, kid," Cole shouted. "You all right?"

Nothing.

From what he could tell, it looked like their speeder had taken a nose dive into the side of a stack of shipping containers. The stack was about three containers high, and given the groans coming from the steel at the bottom container, Cole got the sense that the stability of the stack had been compromised. He didn't particularly feel like hanging around to find out if he was right.

Part of the footwell had collapsed during the crash and trapped his foot. It didn't feel like it was broken, just stuck. With a bit of careful positioning, there was enough room to be able to reach down the side of his leg to try and free it, but it was no good.

Clank.

The sound had come from outside the wreckage.

"That you, kid?" Cole called.

There was a moment of silence before Gregor's face popped into view. "I feel like that could have gone better."

"You're telling me. You all right?"

"Yeah," Gregor said as he looked up and noticed the containers. "Bump on the head and my rifle's gone, but otherwise I'm OK. You?"

"Foot's stuck."

Gregor looked into the cockpit to get a better view. "How stuck?"

"Pretty stuck."

"Right. You wait there, I'll—"

The look on Cole's face pulled Gregor up short. "Oh, sorry. Look, I'll just go and find something to try and get you out of there."

"Wait," Cole said. "There isn't time. I'm going to be a pancake any second now. We'll just have to brute force it."

"What?"

"Help pull me out, Gregor," Cole said flatly.

"Oh, right."

They locked arms, and Gregor found traction against the side of the wreckage and started to lift Cole free of the speeder. A sudden scream stopped progress.

"What is it?" Gregor asked.

"Leg snagged on something," Cole said, the pain evident in his voice.

"So, what now?"

The bottom container buckled slightly, and the stack tilted ever more perilously toward them.

"All right, screw the leg," Cole shouted.

"But Cole—"

The container buckled further.

"Now, kid!"

Gregor latched back on and with all his strength was able to lift Cole clear of the wreckage. As they hit the ground, the stack of containers gave in and came crashing down on the wreckage.

As the dust cleared and Gregor caught his breath, he turned to see Cole getting to his feet, limping badly. A glance at his leg was all that was needed to see why: blood was running freely from a gash on his calf.

"Cole, I need to take a look at that," Gregor said, getting to his feet.

"You got a weapon?" Cole asked.

"I, uh, no, I don't," Gregor stammered. "Cole, your leg—"

"My leg's fine," Cole said sternly. He reached to his holster, produced his pistol, and threw it to Gregor. "Use that. We need to get going. Who knows how much of a head start Tobias has."

Before Gregor could protest, Cole was already heading off into the maze of containers, sword hilt in hand.

"Watch my back, kid," Cole called over his shoulder.

Gregor took a deep breath and headed into the maze, pistol at the ready.

It didn't take them long to find Tobias's ship. It had come down a few hundred meters away. The pillar of smoke was visible above the container stacks, providing an easy guide. When they got there, the wreckage was empty and there was no sign Tobias had hung around.

"Cole, look," Gregor said pointing off to the side.

There was a blood trail, and from the looks of it, Tobias was badly hurt.

"OK, stick close," Cole said. Cole activated his sword and headed off, following the trail, Gregor close behind.

The trail led deep into the container field, and the farther in they went, the higher the containers were stacked, the darker the corridors between them got. The floodlights above barely reached the ground, and it got harder and harder to follow the trail.

"How'd he even get this far in?" Gregor asked.

"No idea," Cole said, his breath leaving a fog in the cold air. "He's lost a lot of blood, though."

"Speaking of, how's the leg?"

"Bleeding's stopped," Cole said. "Head's still a bit fuzzy."

"You really should have let me look at—"

"Damn it!" Cole shouted.

"Sorry, I'm just trying to—"

"No, not that . . . Look."

They had arrived at a T-intersection, and as Gregor's gaze moved to the ground, he saw the problem. The blood trail broke off in both directions.

"He's trying to throw us off," Cole said.

"We should split up," Gregor offered.

"No, that's what he wants."

"But it'll be quicker if we—"

"No, we need to—"

Gregor slammed the butt of the pistol against the side of one of the containers, the clang echoed along the corridor.

"Damn it, Cole," he shouted. "Just let me do this. Trust me to do this."

Cole could see the determination in Gregor's face. He could see that he'd made up his mind and that it'd be hard to change it. Gregor had proven himself several times already, and despite a few hiccups, he really hadn't given Cole any reason not to trust him.

Cole let out a sigh.

"OK," Cole said, his voice calm.

"All right, I'll take the right—"

Cole raised a hand to stop him. "Just cool it for a second."

"You said it yourself, Cole, we don't know what kind of head start Tobias has. We need to move."

"I know," Cole said. "Is your radio working?"

"I think so," Gregor replied.

"OK, so you follow that trail, and I'll follow this one," Cole said. "If you find him, call me the instant that you do and—"

"Can do," Gregor said.

"Do *not* engage him, Gregor," Cole said, his tone leaving no room for argument.

"I won't," Gregor said confidently. "You have my word."

"All right," Cole said, backing toward his trail. "Get going. We can't waste any more time. I'll let you know if I find him."

Cole lingered a moment and watched as Gregor headed down the corridor of containers and disappeared around the corner.

"Good luck, kid."

"'Allo Charles."

Sol followed his greeting with a swift strike to Weaver's face with the butt of his shotgun. Ram had just finished giving the same greeting to Jarak, although with slightly more force than was probably necessary.

"That's for shooting up my ship," Sol said.

Trying to catch his breath, Weaver was able to eke out a sentence: "We just want . . . the girl."

Sol shook his head. "Mate, does anything that's happened here even remotely look like that's something we're willing to let happen?"

"I guess not," Weaver said, getting to his feet once again.

Crack.

Ram hit Jarak once more.

"Come on, Ramses," Sol said with a laugh. "Ease up on the poor bastard. He can't even defend himself."

"I know, isn't it great?" Ram said as he kicked Jarak in the side.

Sol turned his attention back to Weaver. "Now, Charles," he said, "I think we should talk this out like men and resolve things peacefully."

"Peacefully? You just killed two of my men," Weaver said flatly.

Ram laughed. "Come on, you never liked them anyway, Chuckles."

"Look, here's the deal," Sol said. "You and Mister Rol here pick yourselves up, dust yourselves off, and politely piss off, never to come near Kira or us again."

"I'm assuming there's another option?" Weaver asked.

"Yeah, but I'm not really sure you'd like it."

"Try me."

"You know what the other option is, Charles," Sol said. "So what'll it be then?"

"I guess we'll be on our way," Weaver said.

Weaver walked over to Jarak and helped him to his feet. As he was doing so, Sol saw his hand grab something off of Jarak's belt.

"Don't even try it," Sol shouted.

It was too late. Weaver had grabbed a small stun grenade, and on impact, a blinding light seared the back of Ram's and

Sol's eyeballs. In the next instant, they found themselves being tackled to the ground, punches raining down on them.

It was a furious scrap, and luckily for all involved, Ram's and Sol's weapons had been knocked aside and out of reach. With the element of surprise worn off and their eyesight returning, Ram and Sol were able to regain the upper hand on their injured opponents.

Though they weren't yet aware of it, the Ferris Police Force had begun scrambling units in response to reports of violence across the city, including an explosion and gunfight on Platform 451.

As Cole followed the blood trail through the labyrinth of containers, the only sounds he could hear were his own breathing and the low hum and crackle of his blade. All other sounds failed to filter into the container field, which added a strange sense of serenity to the task at hand. In the faint light, Cole noticed a bloody handprint on the corner of one of the containers. He was getting close.

Pressing on, he found more light beginning to filter through, and the stacks of containers started to get lower and lower until he found himself in a clearing that backed onto some kind of loading dock.

The floodlights were so bright in the clearing that it took a few moments for his eyes to adjust to the glare. When they did, his gaze fell immediately on a small crumpled form in the distance. It was still a good couple of hundred meters away, but it was clearly a body, slumped against the platform of the loading dock. Blade at the ready, Cole began the long walk to the platform, and as he got closer, a feeling of dread welled up in the pit of his stomach.

It's not him.

Cole crouched beside the body and lifted its face, just to make sure. It was a man, but not the man he was looking for. He looked like he must have been a worker who had been unlucky enough to cross paths with Tobias. His throat had been cut, which more than accounted for the amount of blood that made up the trail.

"You poor bastard," Cole said out loud.

Cole surveyed the scene, half expecting Tobias to leap out of the shadows and attack. But no attack came; instead, Cole noticed that leading back toward the containers from the body was a separate blood trail. It was thinner, but distinct.

He doubled back.

The rest of Tobias's plan fell into place, and the consequences became apparent.

Gregor.

Cole grabbed his radio. "Kid, you there?"

No answer.

"Gregor?" Cole shouted.

Gregor's reply came as a harsh whisper. "What? Did you find him?"

"No," Cole said, relieved that he was OK. "Listen to me, the trail I followed was a decoy. You're headed right for him. I want you to stay put and wait till I get there."

"OK," Gregor said, "staying put."

"I'll be there soon."

Cole ended the transmission and took off as fast as his leg would allow him back into the dark depths of the container field.

"I'll be there soon."

Cole's words hung in the air as Gregor placed his radio back on his belt. He had followed the trail to what looked like a large warehouse, but after Cole's call, he found himself resting somewhat comfortably against one of the containers just outside. The steel felt cool against his back, but it did little to relieve the nervous tension and anxiety that was wracking him at the moment.

Do not engage him.

Cole's voice echoed through his mind once again. It was like his subconscious telling him what he should do, even though his waking mind could only focus on one thing. No matter what he tried, he couldn't stop his eyes from glancing at the door. The rusted door through which the crimson path disappeared had been left slightly ajar, a bloody handprint smeared across its surface. He knew that Tobias had come this way, that he was in all likelihood inside the warehouse, and that he was hurt badly. It seemed like it was laid out perfectly.

Show them you belong.

It was Kira's voice that drifted into his mind now, and as he pictured her face, he could feel the pain from his injuries fading away and a confidence growing inside him.

"I could just take a look," Gregor said to himself. "One quick look, see what's going on in there and come right back."

I can do that.

Exhaling sharply, Gregor pushed himself away from the container and, pistol raised, set off toward the warehouse. The door creaked quietly as he slowly pulled it open, and just as quietly, he slipped inside.

The entryway was a dimly lit corridor lined with office spaces and a checking station. The blood trail passed all of them to disappear through a large opening at the end of the corridor. Passing through, Gregor found himself in darkness, but a quick fumble around on a nearby wall located a light switch. A few steps in and Gregor's foot slipped on the ground beneath him. It was a pool of blood. There, just inside the doorway, was the body of a man, clearly not Tobias, with a large flesh wound to his midsection. A quick check of his pulse confirmed the obvious, but the body was still warm. Tobias was close. There was a small blood trail leading away from the corpse that went deeper into the warehouse, so without wasting any more time, he headed after it.

Gregor rounded a stack of crates and found himself in a clearing. The lighting was patchy; it seemed not all of the lights had come on earlier. Pistol at the ready, his hands shook as he scanned the room, and his breath caught in his throat when he noticed him.

Kneeling in the middle of the clearing, at the end of the trail, was Tobias. There could be no mistaking it. Gregor knew he should turn back and wait for Cole, but still he kept moving forward, pistol raised. As he got closer, he could see that Tobias's sword hilt was laid on the ground in front of him. Tobias's arms hung limply at his sides and his head hung low.

"Hey!" Gregor shouted.

No response.

Gregor approached with caution and kicked the sword hilt away, sending it skittering across the concrete floor. He nudged Tobias with the toe of his boot. Nothing.

He slowly removed the handcuffs from the back of his belt and knelt behind Tobias. As he clasped the cuffs onto Tobias's wrists, he noticed the large blood stain on the side of his torso.

Gregor decided to give him another nudge.

Tobias let out a pained groan as Gregor pushed the toe of his boot into his wound.

"What?" Tobias said, his voice extremely groggy. "Who—who's there? Cole?"

"Not quite," Gregor said as he pistol whipped Tobias in the back of the head, sending him to the ground in a heap.

Beep.

The pain in Cole's ankle was blinding as he tore along the corridors of containers, but even still he only slowed to a jog to answer the call.

"What is it, kid?" Cole said.

There was a long enough silence on the other end that it brought Cole to a stop.

"Gregor, what is it?"

"It's Tobias," Gregor said finally.

Cole could hear the confidence in Gregor's voice, and he knew what was coming next. He didn't know how it had happened, but he could tell it was coming.

"I've got him."

"What?"

"In cuffs, on the ground in front of me."

"OK, just don't let him move," Cole shouted as he broke into a full sprint. "If he tries anything, shoot him in the leg."

"Got it," Gregor said as he ended the transmission and static took over.

As Cole ran, he could feel the sharp, stabbing pain in his leg. He could feel the blood starting to run anew from the wound, but none of it mattered now.

Gregor was in danger, and he had no idea.

EIGHTEEN

"ALL RIGHT THEN," Sol said, wiping away some blood from the corner of his mouth. "I think that's enough of that."

The scuffle had been short, but Ram and Sol had won it easily. Now they stood over Weaver and Jarak, weapons back in their possession.

"Ramses?" Sol said.

"Yes, Solomon?"

"Now that they've gotten that out of their system, do you think we should make the offer again?"

"Which one's that again?"

"The one where they either piss off or we . . . "

Sol trailed off as something caught his attention. The sound of sirens drifted on the wind, and in the distance, he could see dozens of flashing lights against the night sky. Red-and-blue flashing lights. They were closing on them quickly.

Weaver noticed them too. "If it's all right with you two knuckleheads," he said, "we might take option one."

"Shut up," Ram said.

Weaver laughed. "Look, it's fine by me if we all hang around and finish this, but I highly doubt you two are in a position where you want to be caught with four dead bodies on your hands."

The sirens got closer. It was clear to all of them that the police had sent quite the response team.

"Am I wrong?" Weaver shouted.

Sol and Ram exchanged concerned looks and started backing toward the *Havok*. Spotlights flooded the area as police vehicles flew in and hovered overhead, the wind from the engine exhausts clearing the immediate area of fog.

"We see you again, you're dead," Ram shouted over the increasing noise of the sirens.

The gunfire started suddenly, and Ram and Sol were forced to make a run for it back to the ship. A few quick commands into his wrist controller and Sol had the ramp down just in time for their arrival and started closing as soon as they reached it.

"Get a lock on Cole's position," Ram said, just about out of breath. "We need to—"

"We need to go," Sol shouted. "Yeah, I kind of got that."

As Sol ran into the cockpit, Ram noticed that Kira had been standing in the hold along with them the whole time. She hadn't said a word and was just staring blankly into space. Ram approached her and put his hand on her shoulder.

"You OK?" Ram asked.

Kira threw herself at Ram, embraced him tightly, and didn't let go. She didn't say a word, just wept quietly into his shoulder.

Ram didn't feel the need to fight it.

"It's OK, kiddo," he said, gently brushing her hair. "We're here now."

The rattle of gunfire against the hull of the *Havok* faded slightly as Sol took off and broke away from the police. It'd be a task, but if there was any way they were getting out of this alive, he'd have to lose them, quick.

卌

When Cole burst into the main area of the warehouse, a wave of relief washed over him. Gregor was OK, and everything was exactly as he'd said it was: Tobias was indeed on the ground, slumped at his feet in handcuffs.

"How in the hell did you manage that?" Cole asked.

"Trade secret," Gregor said with a pained smile. He was starting to feel the effects of the battering he took in the crash.

"Is that so?" Cole said. He looked down at Tobias, who seemed barely conscious. "So you didn't have to shoot him?"

"I think I kinda already did," Gregor said. "He's got some shrapnel in his side. Looks like it might have come from his engine. I took his weapons as well."

"Good work, Gregor," Cole said. "Get him up."

Gregor reached down and lifted Tobias to his feet.

"Hey," Cole said, snapping his fingers in front of Tobias's face. "You with us, old man?"

Tobias shook his head slightly and peered at Cole, his eyes glazed over.

"Oh, you made it," Tobias said. "I was wondering how much lon—"

With a stiff right hook, Cole dropped Tobias to his knees. A slow laugh crawled its way out of Tobias's mouth, and he spat out a gob of blood and teeth.

"You know, Cole," Tobias said, his words slightly garbled and raspy after the punch, "I'm pretty impressed with your little lackey here. Snapped me up without an ounce of trouble. Though I am kind of surprised you didn't bring that girl for backup again."

Gregor grabbed Tobias and forced the muzzle of his pistol into the back of his skull. "Watch your mouth before I—"

"Gregor, back off," Cole said.

Gregor released him, and Tobias laughed yet again as he rested back on his knees. "Like I said, I'm impressed."

"Enough talking," Cole said as he drove his knee into Tobias's chest.

In one swift motion, he drew his sword, activated it, and pinned Tobias to the ground with his knee. He pressed the crackling blade into the flesh of Tobias's neck and watched as the right side of his face began to twitch.

"Is this it?" Tobias said, laughing through the pain.

Cole's grip loosened, and his knees went weak. His mind swirled, and suddenly he was thrown back to the nightmare from his time in the med pod. For a brief moment, his wife's bloodied face replaced Tobias's once again.

"Is this what you want?" she asked, echoing the dream.

Cole shook his head, and the vision of his wife faded back to the bloodied face of her killer. He released the pressure on Tobias's chest and withdrew his sword. "What did you say?"

Tobias wasn't quite sure what was going on, but something had rattled Cole. Regardless, he pressed on. "*This* is how you want to get your *revenge?*" he scoffed, the twitching in his face subsiding. "Striking down a defenseless man?"

"My family was defenseless," Cole said. "You? Not so much."

"They weren't defenseless, Cole. They had you. Oh, wait . . ." Tobias made a halfhearted attempt to stifle a chuckle. "Oh no, you forget I know you, boy." Tobias spat another gob of blood onto the concrete. "Long as I've known you, since you were yay high, nothing worse to you than a job that was too easy."

"Easy?" Cole shouted. "None of this has been *easy.*"

"Now, I didn't say it was easy. I said it was *too* easy."

Tobias watched as the doubt crept into Cole's face, the same way it always had. He was as predictable as ever.

"This *is* too easy," Tobias said, a sinister smile spreading across his face. "Isn't it?"

Gregor couldn't believe what he was seeing. Cole deactivated his sword, stood up, and walked away, leaving Tobias on his back on the ground.

"What the hell are you doing?" Gregor shouted.

"I-I don't know," Cole said quietly. "Just give me a sec."

"You don't know? What the hell does that mean?"

Cole remained silent, deep in thought.

"He's right here, Cole! End this!"

Cole let out a sigh and looked at Gregor. "Get him up. The others will be here soon."

Gregor stormed over to where Tobias was lying, lifted him to his knees, and pressed his pistol against the back of his skull.

"No," Gregor said. "You get over here and finish this, or *I* will."

Cole started to walk back over, hand outstretched to try and calm Gregor down. "Stand down, Gregor," Cole said. "That's an order."

Despite the gun pressed against the back of his head, Tobias couldn't help but laugh. They were so distracted that they never even heard the click.

"The girl's made you soft, Cole," Tobias said, interrupting their argument. "What was her name again? Kira?"

He could feel the muzzle of the pistol press farther into the base of his skull. "Don't you *dare* say her name."

It was subtle, but it was there. The intention in the boy's voice clearly indicated an emotional attachment, an attachment that Tobias was more than happy to exploit.

"What's it going to take, Cole?" Tobias asked. "What's it going to take for you to finally follow through on this?"

"You've done more than enough already," Cole said gruffly.

"Then what's the damn holdup, golden boy?" Tobias said. "Are you that much of a coward? Or am I going to have to gut the little bitch as w—"

There was a flash of light and a sharp pain as the pistol cracked into the back of Tobias's head. Through the fog that followed, Tobias could feel Cole pull Gregor away from him and he vaguely heard shouting between the two of them. By the time he was fully aware of his surroundings again, Cole was standing over him.

"I've had enough of this," Cole said. "This ends now."

Not yet, it doesn't.

"Oh, just one last thing," Tobias said.

What now?

Even before Cole could get the question out, he felt the air become charged. Tobias kneeled at his feet, hands still bound behind him, and from somewhere deep down, a powerful yell rose up. The air shifted once again and became a fast-moving wall, which headed directly for Cole. Something was different, though.

As Cole was being thrown back, Tobias's yell turned swiftly into a pained scream and suddenly the attack ceased. Cole dropped to the ground only a few feet away from where he had been standing and skidded a couple more. Gregor was unaffected by the blast and had retrained his pistol on Tobias. It would seem the attack had been a last-ditch effort, but Tobias was too injured to follow through. He was now doubled over, panting heavily, blood dripping from his mouth. He was spent.

Cole regained his footing and once again found himself standing over his family's killer. He activated his sword and held it to Tobias's chest.

"You're pathetic," Cole said. "Get up."

"Very well," Tobias said coldly.

Tobias wasn't sure he'd ever get tired of seeing confusion spread across Cole's face. It'd happened so many times recently and historically, and every time it pleased him just that little bit more. As Tobias stood bolt upright with ease, the handcuffs fell to the ground with a clatter.

"I really don't understand what Martiss ever saw in you," Tobias said.

Cole had his sword held just under Tobias's chin now.

"You're no leader," he continued. "Weak-willed and weak-minded."

The blade trembled, occasionally contacting Tobias's flesh. He never even blinked.

"Oh, don't look so surprised, Cole. I'm honestly shocked you fell for that for as long as you did."

Tobias could see the flood of thoughts and emotions racing behind Cole's eyes.

"In the end, I guess I just got bored," Tobias said.

In an instant, Tobias's hand shot out and sent a blast thudding into Cole's chest, propelling him across the warehouse into the side of an unloaded cargo container. The sound of the impact echoed across the warehouse.

Tobias casually turned to face Gregor.

Gregor stumbled back, shocked by what he'd just seen. Cole was now on the other side of the warehouse unconscious—or worse. Tobias seemed entirely unaffected by everything that had happened.

Does he not even feel it?

Gregor trembled as he found himself face-to-face with the older man. He could feel the warmth of his breath and smell the iron in the blood that still trickled from the corner of his mouth. His face was calm, but his eyes were wide and wild.

"I liked you, boy," Tobias hissed, spattering blood across Gregor's face. "I really did."

Before he could react, Gregor felt the hand clasp onto his throat, felt the grip tighten, the cartilage begin to buckle. His vision began to blur, and soon dark patches floated in and out of his view. He felt his feet lift clear off the ground. They began to swing freely.

Tobias's grip tightened again, and Gregor could have sworn he could see Cole running toward him.

Help me.

Gregor's arms went limp, and Tobias's sword hilt and the pistol Cole had given him fell to the floor.

The grip tightened.

Somewhere in the distance, he could have sworn he heard the roar of an engine.

I hope she's OK.

The last thing he remembered seeing was Tobias's cold gray eyes staring back at him. He still hadn't blinked.

Kira.

Cole stared in horror as Tobias nonchalantly dropped Gregor's lifeless body to the ground and stepped over it to retrieve his weapon. Tobias then turned and ran, disappearing into the darkness.

Everything seemed to move in slow motion as Cole made his way across the warehouse floor. He barely noticed the spotlights from the *Havok* flash across the large windows along the far wall, and the engine was but a distant murmur to him. The last few steps toward Gregor's body were even slower, and Cole's feet dragged to a stop by his side. He fell to his knees, and tears started to well up in the corners of his eyes.

"I'm so sorry, kid," Cole said, placing his hand on Gregor's chest.

The *Havok* ramp lowered with a hiss of steam, and Sol emerged, shotgun at the ready, but it wasn't needed. The first thing he noticed was the blood trail leading into the warehouse, and soon after following it, he found the body of the slain worker slumped against a wall. As he rounded the corner into the warehouse, his blood ran cold.

"Bloody hell," Sol said as he broke into a run.

Cole was still at Gregor's side and was in the midst of a furious attempt to revive him. He didn't even notice that Sol was there.

"Ram?" Sol shouted into his radio. "Prep a pod. Yeah, it's the kid."

Sol reached down and shook Cole by the shoulder.

"Cole?" Sol said, no reply. "Cole, what happened?"

"Tobias, he—I mean, I-I was too . . ."

He trailed off, and Sol could tell now wasn't the time for questions.

"It's OK, mate," Sol said. "Let's get him up and onto the ship, OK?"

"I-I, yeah, t-that," Cole stammered as he got to his feet. "Is Kira all right?"

"She's fine, mate," Sol said. "We got there in time."

"Weaver?"

"Don't worry about that, it's handled."

Sol scooped up Gregor and carried him back to the ship. His breathing was rough and faint, and the bruising on his neck was some of the darkest he'd ever seen. "Hold on, kid."

Kira stood frozen as Sol ran through the main hold with Gregor lying motionless in his arms. She went to follow but stopped when she saw Cole coming up the ramp. He looked beaten up and shaken. His eyes were red and staring off nowhere in particular.

"What happened?" Kira asked, her voice wavering.

"Tobias, he . . ." Cole slid down a nearby wall and sat on the floor. "I-it's my fault."

Kira sat down next to him and held his hand. "He's going to be OK," she said, doing her best to sound encouraging. "He has to be."

"It's my fault," Cole said, not hearing the question. "All of this."

The lights flickered and the floor shook beneath them as the *Havok* lifted off. Muffled against the sound of the engines, sirens could be heard closing in.

"We're about to have company," Ram said as he rushed into the cockpit.

"I am well aware of that, Ramses," Sol replied. "How's the kid?"

"It's not good," Ram said with a sigh. "Tobias really did a number on him. The pods are barely keeping him above water."

An explosion rocked the ship, and the dull thud echoed throughout the cockpit.

"Ah, there they are," Sol said as he banked the ship around a glass-covered high-rise, the facade of which was currently shattering from the hail of gunfire coming from behind.

"Can you get us out?" Ram asked.

"The question isn't can I get us out, it's where are we going?" Sol replied.

"Anywhere but here?"

"I was hoping for something a little more"—another explosion rocked the cockpit—"exact, if I'm honest."

Ram spun his chair around and started dialing in something on the comms center.

"What are you doing?" Sol asked.

"Just get us off-planet, Sol," Ram said. "I've got a plan."

Sol put the *Havok* into a steep climb and made for outer space. Before long the police began to drop off one by one; their ships were only made for atmospheric travel and weren't able to keep pace. When they finally broke through the atmosphere and shot into the vacuum of space, the last of their pursuers peeled off and the sounds of the chase faded away.

"How's that plan coming along?" Sol asked.

"Hang on," Ram said. "I never realized the comms were so complicated in here."

"They're not," Sol said flatly.

"Not to you."

"Look, what are you trying to do?"

"Call Oren," Ram replied.

"*You're* going to call Oren—"

"Shut up."

"For *help*?"

"Look, I don't want the kid to die, and our pods just aren't going to cut it," Ram said. "And it won't be long before the cops catch up. We *need* his help. So can you just tell me what damn button to push already?"

Sol pointed to the console. "That one."

"Really? I thought I already—"

"Well, clearly you didn't."

A quick button press later and the screen switched to static as the transmission began to go through. Soon the face of Oren Rhey'll filtered through the static and his expression quickly changed to concern.

"Well, clearly something's wrong," Oren said. "What is it, Ramses?"

It didn't take long to give Oren the rundown of the day's events, and even though he didn't know the full details of Cole's encounter with Tobias, Ram felt like he got the most important points across.

Oren's brow furrowed. "All right, I'm sending you some coordinates. I can meet you there, and we'll get Gregor the care he needs. I'll also see if I can pull some strings to get the Ferris police off your back."

"You can do that?" Ram asked.

"You'd be surprised what flashing Federation rank can get you."

"I'll have to try that when I get mine back," Ram said.

"Indeed," Oren said. "OK, I'll be at the rendezvous in twelve hours."

"All right," Ram said, "we'll be there."

The transmission ended, and the image of Oren faded back into static.

"Twelve hours," Sol said. "Kid'll be lucky if he lasts that long."

Ram got up from his chair and headed for the door. "He'll make it. Just get us there."

"With pleasure," Sol said as he entered the coordinates and made the slip.

As Ram came into the main hold, he saw Cole lying down up against the wall, sound asleep. His head was resting on a folded-up jacket, and a blanket had been laid over him. A soft voice caught his attention.

"I couldn't bring myself to make him move," Kira said.

"He OK?" Ram asked.

"I think so. I patched a cut on his head and one on his leg. Most of the bleeding had stopped. But I think he's mostly just tired, and I—"

"You did good, kid," Ram said.

Kira smiled briefly, but it quickly faded. "Is Gregor going to be OK? I was going to check on him but didn't know if—"

"I was just on my way in there," Ram said. "You can come with, if you think you're up to it."

"I want to be there when he wakes up."

"Well, that settles it," Ram said, motioning for her to get up. "After you, kid."

Kira got up and slowly headed off toward the med bay. Ram lingered for a moment, his gaze hanging on Cole as he slept. He couldn't help but wonder just how much worse this was all going to get and if it would be worth it in the end.

NINETEEN

THE GLASS FELT cool and wet in Cole's hands, and the liquor burnt its way down his throat. He didn't care, he could barely taste it by this point. He set the glass down on the bench beside him and pushed it around aimlessly.

The orange glow from Gregor's med pod cast a faint light across the bay. It was the only light in the room, save for the multitude of blinking lights and meters that covered the sides of the pods. As the mechanical arms skittered over Gregor's body within the pod, they cast a macabre shadow play on the ceiling. Cole emptied the last of the liquor from his glass and found himself staring through the bottom of it.

This is my fault.

Cole's grip tightened on the glass, and before he realized it, his implants kicked in and the strength of his grip was magnified. The glass shattered into a thousand pieces falling to the floor, and those that didn't embedded themselves in his hand. He watched as blood began to drip slowly from the wounds, each drop catching a small bit of the light from Gregor's pod.

I deserve this.

A knock on the door brought him out of his daze.

"Cole?" Kira said. She lingered in the doorway. "Can I come in?"

Cole nodded.

Kira stepped in quietly and stood beside Gregor's pod, peering down into it.

"His color's better," she said. "The bruises look like they're getting better too."

"He's got a long way to go," Cole said, his voice croaky and slow from the drink.

Kira came over and sat down beside him, immediately noticing his hand. "What did you do?"

"It's nothing," Cole said gruffly.

"It's not nothing, wait there." Kira grabbed some first aid supplies from a nearby cabinet and set about cleaning Cole's hand.

Cole tried to resist the treatment but quickly realized it was futile and relented. "What are you doing in here? You shouldn't see him like this—or me, for that matter."

"I wanted to see how you were doing, both of you. Clearly, it's just as well I did."

"Thank you," Cole said as he reached for the bottle of liquor on the bench.

Kira grabbed his arm. "I think you've had enough."

"It's for the pain," Cole said with a forced smile.

"*One* sip," Kira said with all the authority of a strict parent.

Cole took one very long sip, and Kira eyed him disapprovingly. "My dad used to drink, y'know. He died when I was little. My mom always said it was some kind of work accident, but I know it must have been the drinking."

"I'm sorry," Cole said, putting the bottle down and pushing it away.

"It's OK, I never really knew him anyway," Kira said.

"Join the club."

"I guess what I'm trying to say is . . ." Kira trailed off, and a tear rolled down her cheek.

"Go on," Cole said reassuringly.

Kira wiped away the tear. "I've lost a lot lately, and I just, I just don't want to lose anything else," she said as she looked at Gregor's pod and then back at Cole.

"You won't."

Kira smiled. "Speaking of losing things, I wanted to talk to you about Tobias."

"Hey, I didn't lose him," Cole said. "He got away. There's a difference, a big one."

"All the same, I think I can find him," Kira said.

"Come again?"

"I mean, I know how *we* can find him."

"Go on."

"Promise you won't get mad?"

"Promise."

"Well, with all the stuff with Gregor and you and Tobias esca—getting away, I completely forgot to mention it, but I put a tracker on Tobias's ship."

Cole's jaw hung loose in shock. "You what?"

Kira shifted uneasily in her chair. "I put a tracker on his ship."

"Care to explain exactly how you managed to do that?"

It took a little while, but Kira ran Cole through the story about going for a walk, finding the ship, getting the tracker, Weaver, and everything else. When she finished, Cole remained silent for a good minute.

"You're mad, aren't you?" Kira said finally.

"So you left the ship," Cole said. "After I expressly told you not to?"

Kira nodded and finished working on Cole's hand.

"I see. Does it work?"

"Does what work?"

"The tracker."

"I'd bloody well hope so," Kira said. "I paid five thousand credits for it."

Cole laughed. "Oh, so you mean *I* paid five thousand credits for it."

"Hey, you gave that to me fair and square!"

Kira got up to put the supplies away in the cabinet.

"Anyone ever tell you you're kind of an amazing, kid?" Cole said with a smile.

"No, not really," Kira said. "But I could get used to it."

"Yeah, I bet you could."

The loudspeaker in the corner of the room crackled to life. It was Sol: "Cole, we're coming up on the rendezvous. Might want to sober up."

"How'd he know?" Cole asked Kira.

"You're not very discreet," Kira said as she chucked him a packet of QWake.

The *Havok*'s hull shuddered as it came out of the slip to find itself in the vast blackness of deep space.

"Where are we?" Cole asked as he came into the cockpit.

"Somewhere between Ferris and the arse end of nowhere, by the looks of it," Sol said. "It does make sense to meet somewhere remote, though."

"Oren's idea?"

"Yeah."

"I'm just surprised Ram was the one to call him," Cole said as he sat down beside Sol.

"You should have seen it," Sol said. "He was civil and everything, even thanked him."

"Well, I guess impending death or imprisonment can do strange things to people," Cole said with a chuckle.

"I can hear you, y'know," Ram shouted from somewhere out in the hold.

"So, how's the kid?" Sol asked.

"No change, but at least he made it this far," Cole said. "I just hope Oren's people can help him."

"Speaking of, where is he?"

No sooner had the words come out of his mouth when a bright point of light appeared in the distance and from it emerged the bulk of a Federation flagship. It closed on them quickly, and soon it loomed large in front of them.

"You think he's compensating for something?" Ram asked, standing in the doorway. "I mean, come on, a ship that size—"

Cole laughed. "Well, I guess it couldn't last forever."

The comms in the cockpit cracked to life. "This is the FCV *Retribution*. Power down primary systems and await tractor lock." The transmission cut off with a clunk.

"Chatty bunch," Sol said as he complied with the instructions.

Kira pushed her way to the front of the cockpit. "Holy shit," she said, her eyes wide at the sight of Oren's ship. "That thing's huge. Is that a Federation cruiser?"

"Sure is," Sol said.

The *Havok* rocked gently as the *Retribution*'s tractor beam grabbed hold and started pulling them closer.

Kira chuckled. "He is *absolutely* compensating for something . . ."

"I know, right?" Ram said, giving her a slight nudge.

"All right, you two, that's enough," Cole said, getting out of his seat. "Kira, I want you to go help Ram prep Gregor for the transfer. You need to be ready to go as soon as we're inside."

"Got it," Kira said as she and Ram left the cockpit.

"She tell you what she did?" Cole asked.

"With the tracker?" Sol said. "Yeah, hell of a thing. She's a brave kid."

"Yeah, she is."

As the *Havok* was drawn into the bowels of the *Retribution*, light began to flood into the cockpit. The docking bay they had been brought into was brightly lit from end to end as if no corner were allowed to be in the shadows. Ground crews hurried about, prepping the area for their arrival, while other crews tended to an array of fighter craft that were neatly lined on the floor of the bay or docked in large structures on the walls. A small thud indicated that they had landed.

On the far wall of the docking bay, a large blast door slid open to reveal a group of people heading toward the *Havok*. At the tip of the spear was Oren, and the rest seemed to be medical staff. Cole hurried ahead to meet them.

"How is he?" Oren asked.

"He barely made it," Cole said. "It's hard to say."

"Well, he'll get the best of care here," Oren said. He signaled for the medical staff to collect Gregor's pod. They hurried over in a group, grabbed the pod, and promptly disappeared back through the blast doors.

"And who have we here?" Oren asked, noticing Kira for the first time.

"Kira," she said meekly as she stepped forward slightly, then returned to the group.

"Ah yes, of course," Oren said. "I've heard much about you. It's nice to finally meet. I only wish it were under better circumstances."

"Thank you, again, for doing this," Cole said. "I know the situation we've put you in."

Oren laughed. "It's no problem. This has gone down as simply providing aid to a civilian vessel in distress. No one at command knows you're here."

"Good, that helps."

Oren looked Cole up and down. "You look like hell."

Cole let out a loud sigh. "It's been a rough couple of days."

"Well, I've had quarters set up for all of you on the upper deck," Oren said. "If you follow Ensign Mackenzie here, he'll get you settled in."

Mackenzie was a young, slender man, and he stood nervously waiting to Oren's side. Cole had the feeling that being Oren's assistant probably wasn't the easiest job in the galaxy, so the kid must have some toughness somewhere under his unassuming exterior.

"Hey, Rhey'll," Sol said.

"Yes, Solomon?"

"Can you get your guys to give the *Havok* a once-over? The old girl copped a bit of a beating on the way out."

"Absolutely," Oren said. "I'll get that organized."

"Well, if it's all right with everyone, I'm going to hang around here and supervise," Sol said. "I'll be up later."

"Good, everything's settled then," Oren said.

Ensign Mackenzie extended a slightly trembling arm and motioned for them to follow him. As Cole, Ram, and Kira headed off after him, Oren called out to Cole.

"Once you're settled in, come and see me," Oren said. "We need to talk about where we go from here."

"Will do." Cole gave a nod of approval and turned to catch up to the group.

‖‖‖

"Thank you for letting me know," Oren said. "I will pass it along."

Oren ended the call and exhaled deeply. *Damn.* Cole would be there any moment and he had hoped that he would have some good news for him concerning Gregor, but it seemed fate had other ideas.

The beep of the intercom interrupted his train of thought.

"I have Mister Traske here for you, sir."

"Thank you, Caroline," Oren said. "Send him through."

The door slid open, and Cole entered. His head was on a swivel, looking around at Oren's office. Oren got up from his desk and met him halfway.

"This is some ship you've got here," Cole said. "No wonder you're bloody halfway across the galaxy for months on end. I'd never want to leave."

Oren laughed. "Well, maybe I can get my guys to install some cushions in the *Havok* for you."

"Could you?" Cole asked, only half joking.

"Have a seat, Cole," Oren said, motioning toward the chairs by his desk. "Drink?"

"Nah, I'm good."

Oren raised his eyebrows at the denial.

"I've had enough already today," Cole said. "Trust me."

"Fair enough," Oren said as he sat back down. "Now, Navarr."

"We have a way to find him."

"You do?"

"If you can believe it, Kira put a tracker on his ship on Ferris."

"Really?" Oren said, genuine surprise in his voice.

Cole nodded. "She said the packaging should still be in the main hold of the *Havok*. Should be a serial number or something on there to help track it. We would have set it up, but—"

"It's OK, Cole. I'll get my people on it right away. I promised you that we'd find him, and find him, we shall."

Cole noticed the intensity in Oren's eyes. He was fully committed.

"You don't stop, do you?"

"Sorry?"

"You've always been like that. You give your word on something and that's it, you're with it till the end. I just want you to know that I appreciate that."

Oren laughed. "Well, it's just about the only useful thing I've ever gotten from my father."

"At least you got something. My mother always told me I had my father's eyes, but what good does that do me? Not a damn bit, I'll tell you."

Oren poured himself a drink and took a long slow sip. "Kira seems like a smart kid."

"Tell me about it," Cole said with a chuckle.

"From what I've seen and heard, she reminds me quite a bit of Zara."

Cole smiled to himself. "Yeah, she does, doesn't she?"

"How's that been for you?" Oren asked tentatively. He wasn't sure if he'd overstepped a boundary. "It can't have been easy."

"At first, it wasn't," Cole said, shifting in his chair. "I'll be honest, I just about threw her off the ship when we found her."

"You must be getting slow in your old age if people are sneaking onto your ship, Cole," Oren said, trying to lighten the mood.

"She's determined, that's for sure. When she told us what had happened to her, and about Weaver, and then with everything that happened on Ryger, we couldn't abandon her."

"I'm sorry about Charles, by the way. It was rather out of my hands, and I had no idea your paths would cross like that. And for them to pursue it further like they did was just—"

"It's all right, Ram and Sol took care of them," Cole said.

"Oh, did they?"

"You haven't heard from them?"

"No," Oren said, furrowing his brow. "*Should* I be hearing from them?"

"*Some* of them. Maybe."

"I see."

"We did warn them, Oren, several times," Cole said. "Besides, they've had it coming for a while."

"I can't deny that."

A long silence filled the room. The low hum of activity on the ship was all that could be heard.

"It was hard, with Kira," Cole said at last, "but now having her around is . . . it's better. "

"She's lucky to have you," Oren said, and he meant it.

"I just hope I don't get her hurt," Cole said, shifting in his chair again. "Seems to be all I do lately."

"Don't do that," Oren said sternly. "It helps no one, least of all you."

"How is Gregor? Any word?"

"I spoke to the doctor just before you arrived," Oren said, then went silent.

"And?"

"His condition hasn't improved."

"But it hasn't gotten worse?"

"No, but Cole,"—Oren caught himself trying to find the right words—"you may need to prepare for the worst."

"It won't come to that."

"I pray that it doesn't."

Cole pushed back his chair and got up. "Hey, is it all right with you if I borrow one of your cargo holds?"

Oren looked at him, puzzled. "Whatever for?"

"I need to train," Cole said. His tone was grim. "When we find Tobias, I can't let him run again. I have to be ready."

"Cole, we've got a top-of-the-line training facility on board," Oren said. "You're more than welcome to use it."

"I just need something quiet and out of the way. I'd prefer to keep these out of the public eye." Cole tapped the metal frame jutting from a scar on the back of his hand.

"You got them reactivated?"

"Yeah, lot of bloody good they've done me so far, though."

"It'll come back to you," Oren said. "Go see Mackenzie, he'll show you to the holds. They're yours as long as you need them."

"Thanks, Oren," Cole said as he headed for the door.

As the door slid shut, Oren was left once again in the quiet of his quarters. He poured himself another glass of liquor and took a long, slow sip.

"And I won't be interrupted?" Cole asked.

"No, sir. Apparently, there was some kind of bad chemical spill in here," Mackenzie said with a knowing smirk. "It was a terrible mess. Won't be cleared for days, apparently."

"That's a shame."

"Of course we will notify you in case of an emergency and—"

"If it isn't about Gregor or Tobias, I don't need to know about it."

"Y-yes, sir."

"Thank you, ensign. That'll be all."

Cole watched him go and the door shut behind him, then he returned his gaze to the hold. It was a large, square room lit by three rows of floodlights, and it was lined on two sides by stacks of crates. The floor was clear for the most part, which was ideal for his purposes.

When he went to remove his jacket, a pain shot straight up his side, but he pushed through it. He hadn't fully recovered from the injuries he sustained in the speeder crash, but since it was mostly bruising, he figured it wasn't worth the time in a pod.

Cole removed his sword from his belt and activated it, the faint crackle filling the air around him. He knew that if he was to take Tobias out once and for all that he needed to be better. He had to try and remember everything that Martiss had taught him. Too many times Tobias had gotten the better of him. No more.

Cole exhaled, slid his foot back, and lowered his center of gravity into a ready stance. He held it for what felt like minutes, and yet it was nowhere near as long as what Martiss used to have him do. As he felt the strength build in his legs, Cole sprung forward, slashed his blade in a wide arc, and then spun sharply. Moving in perfect counterbalance to his movements, he brought the slender blade around and thrust it into the empty air behind him.

The shadow fight carried on and on, and time faded into something that had no bearing. The events of the past few weeks ran through Cole's mind like a freighter. Every encounter with Tobias, every moment, played through on repeat, again and again. He repeated every strike, every dodge, and went over every misstep and every mistake.

There had been too many, far too many.

A sound caught his attention: something had fallen on the other side of the hold. He froze, blade at the ready. He was breathing hard, and sweat dripped from the tip of his nose. That was when he saw her.

"You can come out now."

Almost sheepishly, Kira slowly walked out from behind a stack of crates.

"Sorry," Kira said. "I was just—"

The tension across Cole's whole body fell away. "It's OK. Anyone know you're down here?"

"I left Ram a note," Kira said. "He was sleeping."

Cole noticed that Kira seemed rather tense. "You all right?"

"I wanted to ask you something," she said. "A favor."

"Shoot."

Kira squared her shoulders and looked Cole directly in the eyes. "I want you to teach me."

"I'm not sure how much help I can be," Cole said. "I wouldn't know where to start with your abilities."

"I can handle those on my own," Kira said.

"Oh, you can, can you?"

Kira gave a short, sharp nod in reply.

"Well, all right, so what then?"

"I want you to teach me how to fight," Kira said. "With a sword."

"I don't know, it'd be—"

"Oh, come on, you *have* to teach me."

"Do I, now?" Cole asked. "Why do I *have* to teach you?"

"It's my birthday," Kira said, a smile spreading across her face. "It'd be like a, y'know, a present."

Cole eyed Kira suspiciously. "Is it *really* your birthday?"

He could see her counting in her head. "I mean, it'd have to be pretty close," Kira said with a somewhat convincing smile. "Close enough, anyway."

"Where's your sword?" Cole asked.

"I don't know, I thought you had it?"

Cole sat on the edge of his bed holding the hilt of Martiss Darenian in his hands. Its brass casing was ornate, decorated with intricate geometric patterns and designs. It had been years since Cole had seen it and held it. It felt heavy in his hands, heavier than he remembered, but then the weight it carried was something beyond the blade itself. One day, he would have to tell Kira its true history, but that day was long off yet.

Cole had been genuinely surprised when Joran agreed to give the sword to Kira. Clearly, Joran had a belief that she was worthy of it, and now it was Cole's job to make sure she was able to live up to it. He hooked the sword on his belt next to his own and made his way out into the corridor.

There were workmen scurrying around everywhere inside the *Havok*, checking systems, repairing wiring. The old girl hadn't had this good of a checkup in years, and given what she'd been through the last few weeks, she probably deserved it.

Cole passed the door to Gregor's quarters and stopped. *I wonder.*

A quick search through his storage compartments turned up exactly what he'd been looking for. He put the small box inside his jacket and headed down the boarding ramp.

Outside, there were even more workers running around, and from the looks of things, the *Havok* was getting a bit more than a checkup. Cole noticed Sol standing nearby, having a discussion with one of the workers.

"Hey, Sol!" Cole shouted, getting his attention.

Sol came jogging over. "Oh, hey mate," he said, excitement clear in his voice. "What's up? Any word on the kid?"

"No change."

"Damn," Sol said, shaking his head. "What brings you down here?"

"Just had to grab a few things," Cole said. "So tell me, what exactly are you doing to my ship?"

"*Your* ship?"

Cole laughed; that always got Sol to bite. "*Our* ship."

"Oren agreed to restore the weapons systems," Sol said. "Given our last few encounters with Navarr, I figured it'd be best to head into the next one fully prepared. Getting a few upgrades thrown in for free too."

"Free's always good," Cole said. "They doing everything to your *exacting* standards?"

"So far," Sol said with a chuckle. "I've only had to yell at a couple of them. Poor kids are barely out of diapers."

"How long till she's ready?"

"About a day, tops."

"All right, sounds good," Cole said. "Get back to work."

He slapped Sol on the back and headed off toward the blast doors.

The door to the cargo hold slid open, and Cole shook his head at the sight before him. There, in the middle of the hold, was Kira, arms outstretched, and before her a small cargo crate. That in and of itself wasn't unusual—it was a cargo hold, after all—but the crate was floating a meter off the ground.

"What did I say about levitating things?" Cole called out as he made his way over.

"You said not to," Kira called back, not taking her concentration away from the crate. "It's OK, though, I've got it."

Cole inspected the crate as it floated in the air and gave it a shove. It wobbled a short distance away before Kira brought it drifting back to its original position. "Sure seems like it."

"Watch this," Kira said. She closed her eyes and furrowed her brow, and slowly the crate started to move away from her while slowly spinning.

"Fancy," Cole said. He didn't show it, but he was genuinely surprised at her progress. "All right, that'll do, come on."

"Just look," Kira said. With a short, sharp flick of her wrist, the crate began to move faster, then suddenly it shot across the hold and smashed into the wall, its contents spilling out onto the floor. Towels.

Cole stifled a laugh. "Mean to do that?"

"Yes, absolutely, and yet, no, no I didn't," Kira said. "No one has to know. Do they?"

"I'm sure Oren can afford the damages," Cole said. "Sit down, I have something for you."

Kira jumped up on a nearby crate, and Cole removed the hilt from his belt. Her eyes lit up when he handed it to her.

"Happy close-enough birthday."

Kira turned the hilt over and over in her hands and ran her fingers over the details. For a long while, she stared at it intently, saying nothing before she finally looked up at Cole.

"Can I turn it on?"

"Hard to fight with it off," Cole said. "Just press that switch—"

Kira had already found it. A whirring started from within the hilt, and in seconds the thin shards of metal extended and unfolded before locking into place. The blade's familiar hum filled the air. Kira waved the sword around a little, and the floodlights above caught the blade's surface and revealed that it too was as ornate as the hilt.

"OK, that's enough for the moment," Cole said. "There's something else."

Kira deactivated the sword and sat it down on the crate. "Is it a belt for hanging this thing on? I could do with one of—"

"It's from Gregor," Cole said.

"W-what do you mean?" Kira asked. "He didn't know it was my birthday. He couldn't have."

"After Ryger, I spotted him with this," Cole produced the small box from his jacket and handed it to her. "I haven't looked at it."

Slowly she turned it over in her hands and then lifted off the lid. Wordlessly, she lifted up a small necklace. A small purple jewel hung from the chain.

"Where did he get this?" Kira asked.

Cole went back in his mind, trying to think if he'd seen Gregor take anything, and then it hit him: *Kag's shop.*

"I think I know," Cole said. "Back at the yards, we'd just got our gear and were about to leave, but he was nowhere to be seen. He'd been digging about in the back of the salvage shop, and I wouldn't mind betting that's when he found it."

"But we'd only just met," Kira said, staring at the necklace.

"I guess you made an impression."

Kira jumped forward and threw her arms around Cole. "Thank you."

"Now how about I teach you a few things?"

Kira pulled away, smiled, put the necklace on, and kept staring down at it as she walked back out into the open floor of the cargo hold.

Cole took his sword in his hand, activated it, and held it to his side.

Taking her attention away from the necklace, Kira did the same.

Cole looked her square in the eyes. "You ready?"

Time faded away as Cole took her through the same basic training that Martiss had run him through as a child—or what he could remember of it, anyway. Kira caught on to most of it pretty quickly, but the thing that surprised him most of all was how quickly she got a handle on the footwork. Maybe it was a natural talent or it was influenced by her abilities, but she was almost dancing rings around him.

After a while, the training fell into a lull as they both found themselves out of breath. The hum from both their swords faintly echoed through the hold.

"How am I doing?" Kira asked.

"Not bad, a bit behind where I was at your age, but not bad. Footwork could use some work." Cole didn't want her getting overconfident.

"Really?"

"Nothing to be ashamed of," Cole said. "It took me a while to—"

"Wait, no, hold on. I had you *at least* five times," Kira said, and she held up five fingers for added emphasis.

"Really? You think so?"

"I do."

"I'm not so sure about that."

Kira punched him in the arm. Hard.

"All right, all right," Cole said. "*Four* times."

"Five."

Cole laughed. "Well, come at me then."

"What?"

"Make it five," Cole said. "If you can."

Kira wiped the sweat from her brow and settled back into a ready stance. Without giving Cole a chance to ready himself, she lunged, yet he was still able to block her downward swinging blade. She absorbed the force of the hit and slipped to the right, but Cole followed her the whole way, their blades still clashing and sparking. She jumped back and waited for him to advance. When he did, it was thankfully in the same way he had been for the last hour. He was holding back.

As was her way, Kira saw an opportunity and took it.

Cole swung hard just to the right of Kira, and she easily sidestepped the strike. Drifting to the left, she took three steps and then spun, struck out with her leg, and caught Cole in the back of the knee with the sole of her foot. Cole fell to one knee, and Kira pushed him to the ground and held her blade to his chest.

"That's *six*."

"All right, all right, you win," Cole said, sliding his way out from under Kira's blade and getting to his feet.

The sound of the door to the hold sliding open interrupted any comeback Kira may have mounted. A solitary figure ran toward them, and as they got closer, she could see that it was Ensign Mackenzie.

Something's wrong.

Mackenzie skidded to a halt in front of them, and Cole stepped forward slowly.

"What is it?" he asked.

Now that he was closer, Kira could see Mackenzie's face was ashen. She could see their mouths moving but could hear no words of their exchange.

She didn't need to.

TWENTY

THE ROOM WAS cold and dark, and something felt off even before she crossed the threshold. It was silent, no beeping machines, no voices. Sol paced silently back and forth across the entryway and avoided eye contact. Ram was slumped on the floor in the corner, his eyes red raw. Above him, a metal cabinet hung loosely from the wall, its door caved in.

I'm too late.

At the end of the room, bathed in a pale blue light, lay Gregor. Kira felt as though she was floating when she walked over to the bed. The closer she got, the more she began to shake. As she arrived at Gregor's bedside, she could see that his chest was still, his face still.

Kira was vaguely aware of Cole and Sol talking quietly in the background, but soon the ringing in her ears drowned everything out. She reached out and held Gregor's hand and squeezed it tight. It was still warm. With her other hand, she held her necklace tight.

"Thank you for my present," she said, barely hearing herself.

Kira quickly lost track of how long she had been standing there. Minutes? Hours? It could have been days for all she knew. A hand gently squeezed her shoulder, bringing her out of her daze. Kira turned her head to see that it was Cole.

"You want some time alone?" Cole asked.

"Can you stay?"

Cole smiled warmly. "Yeah. We can stay."

Cole's head fell forward and shocked him into consciousness. He looked down at Kira, who was sound asleep next to him, using his jacket as a pillow.

Ram and Sol were talking quietly in the corner, Sol having joined Ram on the floor hours ago. It'd been some time since Gregor's passing, and credit to Oren's people, they had been left uninterrupted to mourn their loss. Cole got up and headed for the door, but before he even got there, it slid open quietly to reveal Oren.

"Hey," Cole said. He rubbed his eyes to wake himself.

"I'm truly sorry about Gregor," Oren said.

"Thanks."

Hearing Oren's voice, Ram and Sol walked out of the medical bay to join them.

"Look, I don't mean to intrude at a time like this," Oren said, "but there's news."

"Tobias?" Cole asked.

"We've got him."

That woke Cole up. "You found the tracker?"

Oren nodded.

"How can you be sure it's him?" Sol asked.

"Well, if our projections are correct and he stays on his current trajectory, he's headed directly for Epheria."

"Ah, right," Sol said, understanding the implication.

"He's trying to drag me back to where this all started," Cole said.

"It would seem so," Oren said.

"How far ahead of us is he?" Cole asked.

"Well, unfortunately, we've been heading in opposite directions for almost a full day," Oren said. "We can be in Epherian space in about two and a half days' time."

"What do you want to do, Cole?" Ram asked.

"He was hurt pretty badly in the speeder crash," Cole said. "If we hurry, maybe we can get there before he's had time to recover."

"I'll make the arrangements and get us underway immediately," Oren said.

"Vitari e ne mortena, Gregor."

"Vitari yaashni ne eterna."

The blood trickled slowly from the incision on his arm, and Cole breathed deeply as it ran down and dripped from his fingertips. He was responsible for what had happened to Gregor, and as such, his memory needed to be preserved in flesh. Once the bleeding had stopped and dried, he cleaned and dressed the wound. As he passed the mirror, the light caught on the ridges of all the scars that covered his torso. It shamed him to admit it, but over the years, he had lost count of how many times the marks had been made, and no matter how much he wanted to, he couldn't bring himself to count them.

When Cole walked back into the main room of their quarters, he found Kira still lying on the lounge facing the wall. It had been two days since Gregor's passing, and she had barely said a word.

Cole sat down on the lounge beside her and squeezed her shoulder gently. She sharply pulled it away.

"I know it's tough," Cole said. "Trust me, I do, but you can't just lie here forever."

"Then what?" Kira said finally. "What am I supposed to do?"

She rolled over to face him, and Cole noticed her eyes were clear. She hadn't been crying. When he thought about it, he couldn't remember her crying once since it happened.

Cole noticed Kira's sword lying on the floor next to the lounge.

"I'm going down to the hold to do some training," Cole said. "Might do you some good to get out of here. What do you say?"

Without saying a word, Kira rolled back over to face the wall.

"OK," Cole said. "Well, you know where I am if you need anything."

Before he left, he picked up Kira's sword and placed it beside her on the lounge.

Cole had just finished stretching when he heard the foot-steps coming toward him. He looked up to see that it was Kira. "You came."

It didn't take long before Cole noticed the bandage plastered on Kira's shoulder. "What happened there?"

Kira pointed at Cole's arm. "What happened there?"

"You promised me you wouldn't do that again."

"It was for him," Kira said. "I had to."

"What happened to Gregor wasn't your fault at all."

Cole noticed Kira's grip tighten on the hilt of her sword and pain flashed across her face.

"I told him to stand up for himself," Kira said, her voice wavering. A tear began to form in the corner of her eye.

"What? Kira, it's not—"

"I told him to prove to the rest of you that he belonged," Kira shouted. Her voice broke mid-sentence.

"He did, Kira," Cole said, moving closer to her. "He proved himself, more than once."

"Really?"

"He chased Tobias through a crowded casino before any of us had even seen him. He shot out the engine of Tobias's speeder mid-flight."

The tear started to roll down Kira's cheek.

Cole continued. "Kira, Gregor was the one who got Tobias in cuffs."

The tear fell to the ground. "Then what the hell happened? What went wrong?"

"I underestimated Tobias, again," Cole said. "If anyone's to blame for this, it's me."

"No," Kira said. "If anyone's to blame, it's Tobias. He's the one who has to pay."

"And he will."

Kira activated her sword and walked a few paces away from Cole. "We doing this or what?"

"Absolutely."

The first few exchanges went calmly enough, but as the sparring session progressed, Kira became more emotional and more forceful. She was no longer pulling any of her strikes and was clearly not concentrating. Each swing became more labored than the last, as if the full weight of her grief was in her blade. Cole realized that it was a mistake to bring her into this environment now. It was too soon. Their blades were locked together, grinding and sparking, and he could see the fire burning in Kira's eyes. He had to end the session now, before one or both of them got hurt.

Cole pushed his sword against Kira's and forced her back a few steps. When she lunged for him, swinging wildly, Cole was able to sidestep her and grab her wrist. In one swift motion, he knocked her sword from her hand and threw her to the ground as gently as he could.

"What are you doing?" Kira shouted, her face red from exhaustion.

"We're done for today," Cole said sternly.

"No, I can keep going," Kira said as she struggled to her feet. "I have to."

Cole's expression softened, as did his voice. "Why? What good will it do?"

Kira's face hardened. "I have to be ready."

"For what?"

"Tobias."

Cole put his hands on Kira's shoulders. "That's not your fight. I can handle him."

"*Can* you?"

"I can," Cole said, and for the first time in a long while, he believed himself when he said it.

For a long while, Kira stared tensely, and Cole could see that she was trying to find the right words. Eventually her face softened and then began to waver. "He was *my* friend," Kira said, pushing Cole away, tears forming anew in her eyes.

"I know," Cole said.

Kira's knees buckled, and she fell to the floor. Gasping sobs wracked her body, and the tears flowed freely as the emotion poured from her.

Cole sat down beside her and held her in his arms.

"I miss him," Kira said between sobs, her face buried in Cole's shoulder.

Cole brushed her hair and fought back tears of his own.

"I know, little bird," he said. "I do too."

Oren strode through the open door to the cargo hold and saw Cole and Kira sitting in the middle of the room, facing away from him. They appeared to be deep in discussion. As he got closer, he caught the tail end of their conversation.

"So we're all on the ship, security's closing in on us, and Gregor's nowhere to be seen. I'm on the boarding ramp, and I hear gunshots. Next thing you know, here's Gregor busting out onto the plaza with half the security force on his heels."

"He told me about that," Kira said. "You caught him as he jumped onto the boarding ramp."

"He's lucky I did too." Cole caught himself, realizing what he'd just said. "Sorry."

"It's OK," Kira said, smiling for the first time in days. "If you hadn't, I might not even be here."

"Sorry to interrupt," Oren said, stepping up beside them.

Cole and Kira just about jumped out of their skins.

"You trying to give us a heart attack?" Kira asked.

"Sorry, I didn't mean to startle you."

Kira looked Oren up and down. "You're very proper, aren't you?"

Oren smiled. "It's all my parents' fault, unfortunately."

"Don't believe him, Kira," Cole said with a laugh. "Underneath that shiny exterior, he's just as wild as the rest of us. He could outdrink anyone in the academy back in the day."

"Even you?" Kira asked with surprise.

"Even me."

"Well, shit, now I've heard everything."

Oren laughed. "We all have our hidden talents."

"What's up, Oren?" Cole asked.

"I just wanted to let you know that we'll be arriving at the edge of Epherian space shortly and that our long-range scanners have brought some slightly troubling elements to light."

"What are you talking about?

"I think it might be best if you see for yourself."

The bridge was a hive of activity when they arrived, with officers and attendants skittering every which way. Through the front viewport, backed by the vast darkness of space, a small bright orb could be seen: Epheria. The one place in the universe Cole had neither the want nor the inclination to ever see again, and yet it was exactly where fate had seen fit to send him.

Cole and the others gathered around a central display screen in the middle of the expansive bridge, and after a few quiet words from Oren to an attendant, surface scans of Epheria began to cycle through before them.

Oren stepped forward to address the group. "What you are looking at here are scans of the immediate area around where the tracker was located."

The display zoomed in on a vast compound that seemed to spread for kilometers in every direction. "It appears to be an abandoned cosmo—"

"It's a cosmodrome—or was," Cole said, stepping forward. "At the end of the war, this was one of the last remaining holds for the splinter groups."

"What happened to it?" Kira asked, gazing up at the displays.

Cole hesitated in answering, and Oren spoke up, making the save: "It was the site of a large-scale battle, one of the last of the war, the result of which ended up being peace . . . eventually."

"And you were there?" Kira asked, looking at Cole.

"I was," Cole said. "I wish every day that I hadn't been, but yeah, I was there."

"And Tobias was there?" Ram asked.

It was a few moments before Cole answered. "Yeah, he was."

"So where is he?" Kira asked.

Oren cycled the display through to a new image, one that showed a three-dimensional schematic of the main hangars. They were like rows of massive obelisks jutting out of the rock. "From what we've been able to work out, Tobias's ship docked in these hangars, and shortly afterward, the signal from the tracker went dead."

"So he found it," Kira said.

"It would seem so."

"How long ago was this?" Sol asked.

Oren checked the details on the scans. "A few hours ago."

"So he could be anywhere then," Sol said.

"Not necessarily," Oren said, bringing up a new diagram. "It would appear that power has been restored to around sixty percent of the compound, with the bulk of it focused on the tower where he landed." Oren pointed the tower out on the display. "From what we've been able to find in old records, that tower held the command center for this entire region."

"So?" Ram asked.

"Within the command center is an advanced medical bay, presumably for treating officers and noncombat personnel."

The display zoomed in on the medical bay. Its walls were lined with medical pods. "If Tobias was as injured as Cole reported, I see no reason not to presume that that's where he would be."

Ram jumped forward. "If he's in a pod, he's a sitting duck," he said. "Why don't we just go in and ice the bastard?" He looked to Cole for approval but found him looking intently at some imagery on a display off to the side. "Cole?"

Seemingly not even hearing Ram, Cole spoke without taking his eyes off the displays. "Oren, you said something before about there being some troubling elements?"

"Yes, I was just getting to that," Oren said, eyeing Ram.

A new image appeared on the displays: it was an overhead view of the compound, and around half of it was crisscrossed with blobs and streaks of color.

"Ramses," Oren said, "this is why we can't just go in and ice the bastard."

Ram shot him a dirty look. He may have been thankful for the assist after Ferris, but Ram hadn't forgotten any of their history and had no plans to anytime soon.

"This is a heat map showing the movement of personnel on the ground within the compound," Oren said.

"Personnel?" Sol asked. "You're saying he's got an army down there?"

Oren shook his head. "Not an army as such," he said. "Estimates put them at maybe two to three hundred men. We had reports for years that these ruins had been occupied by militia but had never put much stock in them. If Tobias somehow has them working for him, this just got a whole lot more difficult."

"So what you're saying is we're heading into a trap," Sol said.

"Doesn't matter," Cole said, stepping back toward the center console. "He found the tracker, so he knows we're coming.

Thing is, he would have been expecting us to charge in on our own, straight into whatever he had waiting for us. He didn't count on us knowing exactly what was down there."

"It's also safe to assume he wouldn't be expecting there to be a Federation flagship in orbit in case he tries to escape," Oren said.

"Exactly," Cole said. "We take the *Havok*, cloak in, and we'll be on his doorstep before he knows what hit him."

Oren smiled. "He's the one who's trapped."

"And he has no idea."

Sol jumped out of his seat. "Well, that settles it, I'll go get the old girl ready to go, shall I?"

Cole nodded. "Ram, get the gear ready. I want to be gone within the hour."

Sol and Ram jogged out of the bridge, and Kira took off after them before Cole could stop her. He slumped into one of the chairs by the central console.

"She's going to be pissed when I tell her she's not going," Cole said.

Oren leaned against the console beside him. "She trusts you, Cole," he said. "She'll understand."

"I sure hope so. Can you have someone keep an eye on her, keep her out of trouble?"

"And make sure she doesn't sneak onto a certain ship again, perhaps?" Oren asked with a smile.

Cole laughed.

"I'll put Mackenzie on it," Oren said, "and I'll check in with her as well. She'll be fine."

"Thanks." Cole got out of his chair and started to make his way off the bridge before Oren's voice stopped him.

"Cole," Oren said, "if you get into any trouble down there, just say the word and we'll do what we can."

"What about all your fancy regulations?" Cole asked with a laugh.

"Screw my fancy regulations," Oren said. "I'm probably going to get court-martialed for all this anyway."

"Why am I getting the feeling our break from the Federation went a bit *too* smoothly?" Cole asked.

"Look, maybe I'll tell them that any rules that may or may not have been bent were bent in the pursuit of justice," Oren said with a sheepish smile. "They like justice."

"They like their rules more, though, Oren. You know that."

"True," Oren said. "Well, it doesn't matter now anyway. What matters now is that this ends, once and for all, and I want to do whatever I can to help make that happen. So you say the word, and I'm there."

"It'll be fine," Cole said. "We'll be in and out before you know it."

"Well, the offer stands."

"Thanks, Oren," Cole said. "For everything."

"How's she look?" Cole asked as he leaned against the back of Sol's pilot's chair.

"She hasn't been in this good a nick since the day I got her," Sol said, running his fingers over the controls, checking the instruments and gauges.

"Kira about?" Cole asked.

"She was helping Ram load the gear," Sol said. "Ought to be around here somewhere."

"So you're ready to go?"

"Ready and waiting."

Cole walked out into the hold to find a large crate hovering up from the boarding ramp followed closely by Kira. As soon as she noticed him, the crate clunked to the floor, and she stared at him. The look in her eyes was pure determination.

Cole took a deep breath. "Kira—"

"Don't even say it," Kira snapped. "You wanted the ship loaded fast, so I'm doing it the fastest way I know how. Is getting on me about levitating stuff the best use of your—"

"That's not what this is about—"

"Oh, so it's the other thing," Kira said, lifting the crate back up and walking it across the hold.

Cole stepped in front of Kira and the crate. "And which thing would that be?"

The crate crashed to the ground again, narrowly missing Cole's feet.

"I'm coming," Kira said.

"You're not. I'm sorry."

"Why?"

"Because it's too dangerous."

Kira leaned against the wall of the hold and folded her arms across her chest. "Why?"

"Because Tobias is dangerous, Kira," Cole said sternly.

"Kinda worked that one out myself, thanks."

"How many people has he killed in the last couple of weeks? Huh?" Cole took a step closer to Kira. "My wife. My daughter. *Gregor*—I've lost count of how many more."

Cole could see cracks begin to appear in Kira's tough exterior when he mentioned Gregor's name.

"I'm not her," Kira said.

"What did you say?"

The tone of Cole's voice caused Kira's facade to falter further. "I-I'm not Zara," she said. She immediately regretted it. Her voice trembled and betrayed the words that came out of her mouth. "I can take care of myself. I've handled him before, and I can—"

"But you *can't*, kid. You're not ready," Cole said, his tone softening. "Hell, I don't even know if I am." Cole walked over to Kira and put his hand on her shoulder. "I know you want to get justice for Gregor, but he wouldn't want you to put yourself in danger just to—"

"Don't tell me what he would have wanted," Kira said. Her voice was barely audible. A tear started to well in the corner of her eye.

Cole squeezed her shoulder gently. "Kira, I've lost too many people these last few weeks," he said. "I'm not going to add you to that list."

"But I can—"

"Don't."

Kira remained silent for a short while before clearing her throat. Cole could see her mind working overtime. "But if I stay," she said, "how am I supposed to save your stupid butt again?"

The tension in the room dissipated immediately, and both Cole's and Kira's body language relaxed.

"I'll have Ram and Sol with me, and Oren as backup in case anything goes wrong," Cole said. "I'll be fine."

Kira wiped away the tear in her eye. "You better be."

"So you'll stay?"

Kira nodded.

"Good, now I want—"

"I have three conditions," Kira said.

"Three?"

Kira undid the clasp of her necklace and forced it into Cole's hand. "First, you're taking this, for luck."

"Kira, I can't take this from you. I wouldn't feel—"

"You're taking it," Kira said. "That way you have to come back to give it to me."

Not seeing any angle to argue, Cole put the necklace securely in his jacket.

"Second, kind of tied to the first one," Kira said, wasting no time. "Don't die."

Cole laughed. "Sure."

Kira pushed away from the wall.

"And third?"

"Kill him," Kira said. "Make him pay for everything he's done."

"I will."

The quiet moment that followed was soon shattered when Ram came up the ramp pushing some crates on a lift pad and promptly smashed them into the side of the entryway.

"That the last of it?" Cole asked.

"I sure hope so," Ram said as he picked up a fallen crate and placed it back on the lift pad.

"Well, I guess we better get going then," Cole said.

Kira rushed forward and embraced Cole, squeezing tightly. Before Cole had a chance to react, she had pulled away.

Kira made for the door but turned back as she reached the boarding ramp. "Remember,"—she pointed at him with mock authority—"no dying."

Cole gave a quick salute. "Yes, ma'am."

Kira turned and disappeared down into the bright light of the hangar.

"That sounds like a really good strategy. I'd listen to her," Ram said as he closed the ramp behind her.

Kira stood on a balcony overlooking the hangar and watched as the ground crews disconnected fuel and power lines and cleared the area around the *Havok* in preparation for its departure. The sound of approaching footsteps got her attention, and soon Oren was standing beside her at the railing.

"You my babysitter?" Kira asked.

"No, Ensign Mackenzie is supposed to be handling that," Oren said.

"I can take care of myself, you know."

"I have no doubt of that, Kira," Oren said. "You seem like a very capable young woman. But I promised Cole that you would be looked after, and I intend on keeping that promise."

"It's not like I can go anywhere."

Oren let out a bemused chuckle. "All the same, he wants you kept safe, and safe is where we'll keep you."

A wry smile spread across Kira's face. "You're more than welcome to try."

Below them, the low whine of the *Havok*'s engines cycled up quickly into a roar. The locks on the landing gear disengaged with an audible crack, and the *Havok* gently lifted off the ground. It hovered for a moment and then slowly glided forward, pitched down, and disappeared through the large magnetically shielded entryway in the floor of the hangar.

Moments after the *Havok* disappeared from view, Oren turned and strode from the hangar, leaving Kira alone on the balcony. Her gaze remained fixed on the spot where the *Havok* disappeared from view, and it was a good long while before she realized she had been holding her breath.

TWENTY-ONE

AS THE HAVOK broke through a cloud bank and began to descend, the vast, barren, and rocky terrain of Epheria spread out before them. In the distance, the tops of the monolith-like hangars of the cosmodrome could be seen peeking over a ridge. To the west, low on the horizon, the large bright sun of Epheria burned a stark red, and the shadows it cast across the landscape seemed to stretch for kilometers. The ground that rushed below them was littered with the hulking wrecks of cruisers and pockmarked with impact craters—evidence of and scars from the battle that took place fifteen years prior.

"Set us down, Sol," Cole said as they approached the ridge, "and get us some scans. I want to know exactly what it is we're heading into."

The *Havok* slowed to a crawl and came to a gentle stop on the ridge overlooking the valley and the cosmodrome complex below. The hangars and command buildings were central to the complex, surrounded by residential and industrial districts that looked to spread for kilometers all around them. Large parts of these districts were in ruins, while the rest remained completely abandoned, save for a sizable residential section nearer to the cosmodrome that appeared to have power.

After a few minutes, the console beeped to indicate the scans were complete. Sol began to look them over, and his face quickly turned sour. "Oren wasn't joking. Looks like we've got heat signatures for men on the ground."

"Hazard a guess as to how many?" Cole asked.

"The estimates were a bit off," Sol said. "Looks to me like there's at least five hundred guys down there."

"Terrific," Ram said. "So it *is* a trap."

"Looks that way," Cole said.

"Well then, it's a good thing that's when we do our best work," Ram said.

Cole sighed and looked down at the scans. "Always seems to work out that way, doesn't—"

"Not to interrupt, gents," Sol said. "But we might have a bit more of a problem."

Ram laughed. "More of a problem than five hundred guys between us and Navarr?"

Sol pointed to the scans on the display. "They've got fighters," he said. "Looks like maybe fifteen of them in flight. Might be more in the hangars, though."

Cole checked the scan for himself, and sure enough, there they were. "What are they doing?"

"Just flying around," Sol said.

They all looked out the front viewport and could just make out the small shapes flying around near the base of the hangars. From this distance, they might as well have been birds.

"Must have salvaged them from the war," Ram said. "All kinds of crap must have been left behind."

As Cole and Sol took their eyes off the fighters and turned to discussions about the best plan of action, Ram found himself looking closer at the fighters, watching their movements closely. They were flying circuits around the central hangar buildings, right up until the point that they weren't.

"Uh, Sol?" Ram asked.

"Yeah, mate?"

"We're cloaked, right?"

"Yeah," Sol said.

"So it's just a coincidence that some of those fighters broke off and are headed this way?"

Sol and Cole joined Ram in looking out at the fighters that were closing on their position.

Sol shrugged. "Must be. Cloak's up and running just fine. They're probably running a patrol or something."

"A patrol?" Ram asked flatly. "To this abandoned ridge?"

Sol sighed dramatically and tapped hard on the cloak's gauge for effect. "Look, the cloak's fine, they can't—"

In response to Sol's dramatic tapping, the light indicating a functioning cloak flickered and died, and the needle of the gauge fell to the left, indicating a loss of power.

Sol's face went blank. "Ah, that's,"—he exhaled sharply—"that's not ideal. Needle must have been stuck or—"

"Did you check it before we left?" Ram asked.

"I checked a lot of things before we left, Ramses," Sol said, frantically fiddling with the controls to get power back to the cloak.

"Did you check *the cloak*?" Ram asked again, losing patience.

"I—I may have skipped it," Sol said very quickly and quietly in the hope that it would go unnoticed.

"Oh, you *may* have skipped it?"

"We were in a rush to leave, and besides, I only—"

"Can we save this for later, please, ladies?" Cole asked, having to shout to be heard above their argument. "We need to move, now."

The sound of bullets ricocheting off of the hull was all the prompting Sol needed, and before they knew it, the *Havok* shot off the edge of the ridge with a roar. The fighters, however, were quick to react to the sudden movement and broke off in all directions in an effort to surround the ship.

"What's the plan?" Sol asked as he ducked and weaved the *Havok* to avoid the fighters' attacks.

"Get us closer to the hangars," Cole said, holding onto the back of Sol's chair for stability.

"Closer?"

"Look, we've lost the element of surprise," Cole said. "So I say we just smash in his front door. Sound good?"

"Well, I don't know about good, but it is certainly a plan."

The five fighters were in hot pursuit, firing on the *Havok* any chance they had. Ahead, the remainder of the fighters they had seen earlier were now heading in their direction and closing fast.

Sol gunned the throttle and headed straight for them. When they were only a few hundred meters away, Sol put the *Havok* into a spin and opened fire. The arc of gunfire cut through the air and managed to tear apart the two lead fighters. Their explosions sent a shower of hot metal bouncing off the hull as the *Havok* flew through the space they had just occupied. The remaining fighters scrambled every which way to avoid the hail of bullets.

The *Havok* was now flying low over the residential district, closing on the cosmodrome fast. The pursuing fighters swooped down to follow and remained close behind as Sol navigated the ship over and around the ruined buildings. They heard an explosion somewhere behind them.

"That's two more gone," Cole said, watching the displays. "Must have clipped something."

"How many left?" Sol asked.

Cole counted them quickly. "Eleven."

"Right then," Sol said. "Watch this."

He pulled the *Havok* into a vertical ascent and waited until all the fighters had gone into the same maneuver. After giving it a few more seconds, he pulled a lever on the control panel, and a light started to flash in the cockpit. No sooner had he pulled the lever, then Sol engaged the reverse thrusters and pulled back hard on the controls. The *Havok* came to a shuddering halt in midair as it stalled and began to turn around to face the ground. As the ship rolled over, Cole and Ram could see what Sol was up to. In front of them, a bright new cluster of countermeasure flares was burning in the ever-darkening sky, almost completely obscuring their view. It was worse for the fighters, though: one by one, they flew through the bright mass of flares and were picked off by the *Havok*. The last few got wise to the act and diverted their course before falling into the trap.

"That's a new one," Ram said.

"Never really had a chance to try it," Sol said.

"Three left," Cole said.

"Not for long." Sol tore off in pursuit of the three remaining fighters, who were now fleeing back to the hangars. Before long, he was on them, and a few bursts of gunfire later, the fighters were reduced to a cluster of falling shrapnel, raining down on the buildings below.

"That's all of them," Cole said, exhaling for the first time in what felt like hours. "Take us—"

An explosion rocked the ship violently, almost knocking Cole from his feet. Emergency lights began flashing in the cockpit, and from somewhere else in the ship, a warning siren began to blare.

"What the bloody hell was that?" Sol shouted.

"They've got rockets," Ram said.

"What?" Sol said. "They weren't on the scans."

Ram pointed out the front viewport at a smoke trail that was closing at a rapid pace. "Look out!"

Sol was able to bank hard just in time to avoid a direct hit, but the rocket exploded somewhere near the engines, and more sirens began blaring throughout the ship.

"I'm really beginning to wish I hadn't used those flares," Sol said.

"Just get us out of here, Sol," Cole shouted over the sirens.

The *Havok* turned sharply and shot away from the hangars, heading back toward the residential district. A shrill beeping from one of the displays indicated that several more rockets were close on their tail. Sol put the *Havok* into a climb. He figured their best bet was to get out of the rockets' operating altitudes.

It was too late.

Three separate explosions rocked the ship, and for a few seconds, the *Havok* lost all power and began to drop from the sky. It soon came back, though, and Sol was able to wrestle the ship into a controlled descent, but it was still a descent.

"Gents, we're going down," Sol said, all too calm for the situation. "Get to the escape pods."

Ram rushed out of the cockpit, and Cole went to follow but stopped. Before Cole could speak, Sol preempted him: "I'm right behind you."

Smoke had begun filling the main hold, and the backup lighting was a dull red that made visibility tough. Cole had the presence of mind to grab his pistol and some ammo, which he then holstered on his belt alongside his sword. When he came into the escape pod bay, he found Ram standing there, staring at the escape pods with a blank expression. The pods on the *Havok* were four small pods that were only big enough for a single occupant and a small amount of gear. Cole grabbed Ram by the shoulder and shoved him into the open pod.

"Now is *not* the time," Cole shouted at him as he hit the switch inside the pod to close the door. A few seconds later, Ram's pale face disappeared from view as the pod was jettisoned from the ship.

Cole waited anxiously for Sol to come through the doorway but many moments passed, and he hadn't appeared. "Sol, get the hell in here!" Cole shouted toward the cockpit.

A few seconds later, Sol came rushing into the room. "Turns out when your ship is in the middle of exploding, it's kind of hard to get the autopilot to work," Sol said with a half-smile.

Cole could see it in Sol's face that his heart was breaking. "Sol, I'm sorry."

"Can't be helped," Sol said. "Now get the bloody hell in there."

Sol hurried Cole into his pod. "I'm right behind you."

"See you on the ground," Cole said as he punched the release button and the pod door closed.

After Cole's pod had disappeared from view, Sol stood alone, listening to the groaning of the metal around him and to the blaring sirens echoing throughout the *Havok*. He reached out and laid a hand gently on the wall. "Sorry, old girl," he said, a lump forming in his throat. "We had a good run."

Blinking away tears, Sol stepped into the escape pod and pressed the release.

Through the small viewport on the side of the escape pod, Cole could see that he was in a spin. Every few seconds, the image of the burning *Havok* came into view and disappeared again, and from what he could see, the ground was a long way away. The radio on the wall of the pod crackled to life.

"Cole?" Ram said.

"How we doing, Ram?"

"I ever tell you I hate these things?" Ram asked, the anxiety clear in his voice.

"You might have mentioned it," Cole said, feeling slightly bad about forcing Ram into the pod the way he had—but only slightly.

"Never could make Nate understand that we needed bigger ones," Ram said.

An explosion nearby rocked Cole's pod, knocking it into even more of a spin, and shrapnel tore a hole in the side of its casing.

"I'm sure you'll be fine," Cole said. "How you traveling, Sol?"

Static.

"Sol?" A few more seconds had passed before the radio crackled to life once more.

"Sorry, gents," Sol said, his voice calm and matter of fact. "Not sure I'll be joining you."

"What the hell are you talking about?" Ram asked.

"It's my pod," Sol said. "It's stuck."

Cole's stomach dropped. "Can you get the door open onto the ship? Try one of the others?"

After a brief pause, Sol came back on. "Nah, mate," he said. "Dropped halfway down the chute, heard a loud bang, then nothing."

Ram cut back in. "Can you fire the thrusters to try and dislodge yourself?" Ram asked. Desperation was overtaking the anxiety wholesale now. "There should be a way to do that, right? You'd be able to figure it—"

"I guess that might work," Sol said. "Hold on."

The calmness in Sol's voice unsettled Cole, and the long silence that followed made it even worse.

"How's it going, Sol?" Ram asked. "Sol?"

"All right, all right, calm down, I'm working on it," Sol said. Moments passed. "Hey Ram, you remember that time, what was it, second year at the academy?

"What?" Ram said, taken aback by the strange question.

"The girl at Forina. Y'know, the one with the . . . thing—"

"Cetra?" Ram said.

"Yeah, that's her, Cetra. Redhead. Cole, you should have seen the look on Ram's face when—"

A cacophonous silence followed a sharp burst of static as Sol's radio cut out entirely. Cole sat back, unable to speak as his pod continued to tumble. Out the viewport, he thought he caught a glimpse of the *Havok* smoking heavily from the starboard side. It looked roughly where the escape pods were, but he couldn't be sure.

As the pod tumbled once more, Cole saw the ground rushing toward him, then darkness.

"Jenkins, you're sure that's where the pods went down?"

"Yes, Captain Sharma," Jenkins said. "Right over there in the residential district. See the smoke?"

From his position on the rise, Captain Sharma looked out over the field of buildings and saw two thin plumes of smoke rising from the ruins. "Ah, yes," Sharma said. "Good work, Jenkins. What of their ship?"

Jenkins sighed and pointed off to the west. "Uh, sir, that's the *big* plume of smoke over there. See it?"

"Ah, so it is," Sharma said. "Very good. Take four men and go inspect the pods. I shall take the rest of you and go check the ship for survivors."

"Sure, whatever," Jenkins said as he rounded up four men and trudged off down the slope into the maze of crumbling buildings.

A loud beeping alerted Captain Sharma to an incoming call. "Yes, sir?" he said into the radio. "Yes, sir. Absolutely. No need to worry at all, Mister Navarr, I've just sent some men to go inspect the escape pods. Yes, yes, I've also sent some men to check the crash site for survivors." Sharma began frantically waving for the remaining soldiers to get going to the ship. "No, of course not, I'll do my best to see that you aren't disturbed. All right then. Oh, sir, if I may I—"

The call ended suddenly. "He hung up," Sharma said to himself, now standing alone on the rise. "How rude."

Several search craft flew overhead and out into the deepening night, their spotlights on full, searching the ruins.

"Well, I think that's under control," Sharma said as he turned and headed back down the rise toward the cosmodrome.

TWENTY-TWO

THE CREAKING AND scraping of metal as the door of his escape pod was pulled open brought Cole back into consciousness. His head was ringing, and he could feel some blood trickling down his forehead, where it must have hit the inside of the pod. A dull warmth radiated from his side, but he couldn't nail down a cause. His vision, blurry to start, soon began to clear, and he saw Ram's determined face staring down at him, framed against the night sky.

"You OK?" Ram asked.

"Uh, yeah," Cole said, though he couldn't really be sure. He grabbed Ram's outstretched hand and clambered out of the pod. Looking around, Cole could see that his pod had crashed through the roof of a ruined building and come to rest at the bottom of a pile of rubble. Through a large hole in the far wall, Cole could see the very tops of the hangars, but they were a long way away. Ram's pod was nowhere to be seen.

"How long was I out?" Cole asked.

"Took me about ten minutes to get to you," Ram said over his shoulder as he began charging off in the opposite direction of the hangars.

"Hey, where are you going?" Cole called after him.

"I spotted some smoke way west of here on my way to you," Ram said. "It has to be where Sol went down."

Cole let out a sigh as he watched Ram clambering up the side of the pile of rubble toward an opening. "Ram, stop."

"What?" Ram said as he turned to face Cole. "We have to get to him."

A lump began to form in Cole's throat. He'd seen the damage the *Havok* had taken. "Ram, there's no—"

"Don't even say it," Ram said as he pointed angrily down the pile at Cole. "He's fine."

The tension hung thick in the air between them until the shuddering sound of rotors could be heard getting closer and spotlights began to sweep across the ruins above their heads. It was the shouts of approaching soldiers carried on the wind that finally broke their silence.

"We can't be here," Cole said. "Look, let's just get somewhere safe, and we can work out our next move."

Ram went to say something but held his tongue and strode down the side of the rubble pile with a slight limp. As he brushed past him, Cole could see the mix of anger, sadness, and desperation festering inside Ram, but there was nothing for it. They had to move or risk being discovered.

They were able to slip out through the far wall just as a search craft roared overhead, its spotlight flooding the area, scattering shadows in all directions. Luckily for them, the wash from its rotors blew up enough dust to cover their escape.

As they rounded a corner, they found themselves in an alley—though it was more like a tunnel, as one of the buildings on the side had begun to collapse and had fallen into the other. It provided adequate cover from the spotlights of the search craft and gave Cole and Ram a chance to catch their breath.

"We need to get to the tower," Cole said, sucking in deep breaths of air. "Tobias knows we're here. We can't let him run again."

Expecting an argument Cole looked at Ram but found none. Instead, Ram was leaning against the sloping wall of the crumbling building, and he was breathing hard.

"You OK?" Cole asked.

Ram wiped the sweat from his brow and looked up at Cole. "Just a cracked rib or two," he said. His face was pale. "Nothing I can't handle."

A flash of light at the end of the alley caught Cole's attention, and he could pick out what looked like the beams of several torches approaching the intersection. Acting quickly, he kicked in the door behind him, glass shattering everywhere, and gave the interior a quick look over. "In here."

Ram pushed himself away from the wall and limped through the doorway. "They probably heard that."

Cole stuck his head out the doorway and watched as five soldiers appeared and lingered for a moment in the intersection. One of them flashed his torch down the alleyway, forcing Cole to duck back behind cover. Once the light had passed, he peered back out and saw the soldiers move on. "We're good."

"For now," Ram said.

The building they'd run into looked to be a derelict barracks, and for the most part, the first couple of floors seemed like they could be in pretty good shape. Given the building's surroundings, it was a minor miracle it was even standing.

"Just have a look around," Cole said. "See if there's anything we can use."

Without argument, Ram disappeared off through a door to the left. Cole went the opposite direction and, after following a long, dark hallway, came out into a locker room. The ceiling and the floors above were trashed, and moonlight flooded in, casting the entire room in a pale blue glow. In the center of the room, there was a pile of lockers that had been ripped from the walls. It was looking more and more like looters had been through the place a long time ago and cleared it out.

"Hey, Cole," Ram shouted. His muffled voice sounded like it was coming from somewhere on the second floor.

"What?" Cole shouted back.

After a brief pause, Ram's head popped out over the edge of the shattered ceiling. "Come check this out."

Cole jogged up the stairs and met Ram at the entryway to the room he had discovered. Faintly lit by the moonlight, Cole could see walls that were lined with racks of guns, with more scattered across the floor. They'd found the armory.

"Now this we can use," Cole said as he made his way into the room.

"What are they even doing here?" Ram asked. "Rest of the place has been picked clean, and they leave a room full of guns?"

Cole picked up a rifle off the ground and looked it over. The metal was weathered and beaten up, rust was present on the barrel and body. As the joy of the armory's discovery began to rapidly fade, Cole pulled the trigger. It didn't budge. "They're rusted to shit, that's why."

Ram was in the process of finding out the same thing and threw the shotgun he'd found against the wall. Epheria was known for its temperamental rain; it could rain for months on end, then not rain at all for years. The armory had been rendered useless long ago.

"So what now?" Ram asked. "We can't go charging in there with a pistol and a sword between us."

"We have to try," Cole said. "We can't let him run again."

"I say we go find the ship. The rest of our guns are there. Sol's probably wondering what's taking us so long anyway."

Cole sighed. "Sol's gone, Ram."

"You don't know that," Ram said, his voice trembling. Cole could tell he was struggling to hold it together. He had to tread carefully.

"His pod got stuck in the chute," Cole said, slowly and calmly. "We know that." Cole walked over to Ram and put his hand on his shoulder. "There was an explosion just as his radio cut out. I know that. I saw it."

Without a word, Ram brushed Cole's hand off his shoulder and walked a few steps away.

"Even if he survived that, I-I don't know if . . ." Cole's voice caught in his throat. "Look, I don't want to admit it either. He was my friend too. But he's gone, Ram. He's gone."

A gust of wind blew through the room, rattling the lockers.

"This is your fault," Ram said. His voice was cold.

Cole took a few steps in Ram's direction. "Ram, don't."

Ram turned to face Cole, but he didn't appear angry at all. He just looked completely drained.

"When Nate brought you in all those years ago, he told me you were *the guy*, and you were," Ram said. "You were the whole package. But Cole, as long as I've known you, you've kept secrets, secrets about your past, about where you came from, about those scars and who knows what else. But I let it slide because I knew the sort of shit that went on during that war and figured if someone wanted to forget that time of their lives, it was their right. It wasn't hurting anyone. But now people are dying, Cole, dying because of *your* secrets."

"Don't you think I know that?" Cole asked. "Don't you think I feel guilty about all of this?"

"Do you?"

Cole took a step back. "How can you even ask me that? Of course I do." Cole lifted the bottom of his shirt up to reveal the rows of jagged scarring. "What the hell do you think *these* are for?"

"How would I know? You'd never tell us. I mean sure, we all had our theories, but we had no idea. Did Olivia know?"

"To a point," Cole said.

"Did she know about Tobias?" Ram's question hung in the air, and Cole's silence provided the answer. "So there's a madman out there with a thing for you, and you don't tell your *wife*?"

"That's not fair, Ram, and you know it," Cole said, the muscles in his neck beginning to tense. "I had no idea he was out there. I thought he was dead—"

"Seems to be a thing with you."

"Ram, stop it."

"No, *you* stop it!" Ram shouted, pointing his finger angrily at Cole. "Just stop. Stop lying. Stop hiding. Stop believing your own bullshit. Maybe if you'd done that sooner, your kid would still be alive!"

Cole could see that Ram instantly regretted saying it, but that didn't lessen the sting one bit. "I would think very carefully about the next thing you say."

The air crackled with aggravated tension as Cole and Ram stared each other down, neither saying a word or backing down. Before long, though, Ram broke the stalemate as he let out a loud, frustrated sigh.

"Damn it, Cole," he said, the anger fading in his tone but still there. "I love you like a brother, but I'm finding it real hard not to punch you in the throat right now."

Cole spread his arms out to his side. "Go on then, I deserve it."

Ram shook his head and took a step back. "I'm not gonna hit you."

"Then what?" Cole said, exasperated. "What do you want me to do?"

"I want you to stop running."

"I'm not—"

"Stop running from the truth and stop running from your past, because it sure as hell seems like they've already caught up."

"I'm not running."

"You sure about that?" Ram asked. "What happened here?"

"What?"

"With Tobias. Tell me, the whole thing, start to finish."

"Ram, we really don't have time to—"

Ram stepped closer to Cole and put his hands on his shoulders. "I followed you into this because you're my brother and I trusted you. I didn't need any other reason, none of us did, because you're *the guy.*"

Cole backed away, and Ram's hands fell off his shoulders.

"If I'm gonna go any further with this, I need a reason. I need to know."

"You know why we're here," Cole said.

"I know we're here to kill Tobias," Ram said. "What I don't know is why he's so set on tearing you apart."

Cole slumped down on a bench along the sidewall. He rubbed the just-forming tears from his eyes, swallowed his pride, and looked Ram dead in the eye.

"OK."

TWENTY-THREE

EPHERIA: FIFTEEN YEARS AGO

The strained kicking and scraping of leather boots on the hard ground echoed quietly along the otherwise quiet corridor.

Cole's eyes remained fixed on the junction at its end, watching for the slightest hint of movement. Gloved hands groped frantically at his face, and yet he paid them no mind. A light flickered somewhere beyond the distant corner, and for a moment his attention was diverted, but only for a moment. A sudden, vain attempt at escape was nullified by the tightening of his arm around the man's neck.

No one was coming.

Cole loosened his grip for a second, and in that second, he was sure that the man thought he was free as he began to try and fight his way out yet again. A sigh and a sharp twist later, there was a crunch and a crack, and then the fight was gone.

And no one had come.

As he lowered the body to the ground, Cole exhaled for the first time in what felt like minutes. The sound of footsteps behind him finally brought him out of his daze, and he turned to find Martiss Darenian looking back at him expectantly.

"We good?"

It took Cole a moment to find his voice. "Yeah. Yeah, I think so. I don't think they know we're here."

"Well, let's try and keep it that way," Martiss said. "We can't afford to spook 'em."

"No, sir," Cole said, wiping the blood away from a fresh cut on his face.

Martiss laughed. It was raspy but genuine. "Cut that out," he said. "I'm answering to you on this one, remember?"

Despite his minor slip, it was hard for Cole to forget: twenty-two years old and running point on a mission with the leader of his people, whom he'd been handpicked to replace. Martiss had been like a father to him for most of his life; he had taken him in at the age of seven, after his mother had died, and raised him the best he knew how. For Cole, the weight of the responsibility that had been laid upon him on this mission threatened to break him. But he wouldn't let it—couldn't.

Martiss placed a reassuring hand on Cole's shoulder. "Let's get in there. They're waiting."

Upon entering the security room, Cole saw that Yarik Kolmer, a long-time friend, was busying himself dragging one of the room's former occupants out of the way behind a bank of consoles.

To his left, Xan Navarr was already knee-deep in the security systems, with at least a dozen different camera feeds flashing across the displays gathered around him.

"How's it look?" Cole asked.

"Want the good news or the bad?" Xan replied.

"Start with the good."

"Scans show the hostages all seem to be in one place," Xan said.

"All right, and the bad news?"

"Well, the bad news is they're all in one place," Xan said. "They've got them bunched up, right near the top of some sort of observation level."

"I'm not following," Cole said.

"Well, it looks like there's a lot of guys between us and them."

"Never been a problem for us before," Tobias Navarr—Xan's father—said, slithering his way into the conversation.

Cole shot Tobias a disapproving look. He'd argued with Martiss that Tobias shouldn't be on this job, that his behavior was too *erratic* for something this crucial. He'd lost, of course. Tobias was here because he was the best fighter they had, and Cole couldn't dispute it no matter how hard he tried. Tobias's presence was an inconvenience, but one he felt he could control.

Cole sighed. "Define 'a lot,' Xan."

"Initial scans showed at least a hundred, but it could easily be more."

Cole felt Tobias shift his weight uneasily beside him.

"Well," Tobias said, "that might be a *bit* of a problem."

Cole looked over Xan's shoulder at the display. Sure enough, there were a large number of heat signatures scattered throughout the building. However, there was a reason Cole had been chosen to lead this mission: his ability to spot weaknesses and exploit them. It took him no time at all to see that the threat of the situation could be easily minimized. "It won't be a problem at all. If we take this service elevator, we should be able to skip a good chunk of them. Might be a bit more work on the way out, but it's the quickest way in."

Tobias's face flashed a scowl, as he resented the fact he'd missed such an obvious solution. Cole saw it and had to hide his enjoyment. "From there, we just need to be careful. Try to isolate groups we come across and then take them out as quickly and quietly as possible, so no one else is alerted. If we can get to the observation level without springing the alarm, we're home free."

Cole looked to Martiss for confirmation and received the subtle nod he was hoping for. He looked to everyone else in the room and got looks that indicated they were all on board as well, even Tobias.

"Let's head out then," Cole said. "Don't want to keep them waiting."

As Xan and Yarik collected their gear and headed out into the corridor, Cole lingered by the displays, his eyes fixed on the scans of the tower.

The look of concern on Cole's face didn't escape Martiss. "What's wrong?"

"It's nothing."

Something had felt off to Cole from the moment Martiss had accepted the contract. It had all happened too fast, with no more than three days transpiring between when they were presented with it to now being neck deep in the middle of it. Despite that, things had run smoothly, almost surprisingly so, but there was a constant doubt scratching at the back of Cole's mind. Something was off.

"Hey," Martiss said, hitting Cole in the arm, "you ready for this?"

Before Cole could answer, Tobias scoffed and started to stride out of the room. "Of course he's ready," he called out over his shoulder. "Golden boy's *always* ready."

"Ignore him," Martiss said as Tobias disappeared out into the corridor. "He's had a bug up his ass about this thing from the start."

"I think there might just be one up there permanently."

Martiss laughed. "I would not be surprised."

"Someone care to remind me why we're the ones walking into this death trap?" Yarik asked as they headed down yet another nondescript corridor.

They'd managed to skirt around a couple of patrols so far, though others had been less fortunate. Xan assured them that they would be coming up on the service elevators soon and that it was pretty much a clear shot from there.

"Feds wouldn't touch it," Martiss said. "Too risky."

"That's kinda my point. Why are *we* touching it?"

Martiss looked back over his shoulder at Yarik. "The money was good."

"*Really* good," Tobias chimed in from the rear.

Yarik sighed. "Yeah, no, I figured that. That's kind of our deal. I mean, why *us*? Y'know, specifically. Given how things are, the Feds don't usually jump at the chance to work with our kind."

"Simple. No one will miss us if we die," Tobias said as he pushed past Yarik. "And we won't take the credit if we don't."

"I'm sorry?" Xan said. "We're not going to be getting recogn—"

"We're getting paid. That's enough." Martiss turned and walked backward for a bit. "If this goes south, then it just looks like these assholes killed everyone and the Feds get their reason to make a big show and end this damn war."

"And if we get them out and, y'know, don't die?"

From the point position, Cole stopped and turned to face Yarik. "Then they get their people back, they get the credit, and we get paid and go home. That's the arrangement. That's the de—"

Cole's head snapped to the side, and he held up his hand to silence the group. Up ahead, the sound of raucous laughter and shouting carried down the corridor.

"Wait here," Cole whispered.

At the end of the corridor was an antechamber, and along its far wall were the service elevators. Problem was, there was a group of pirates in the middle. They had to go.

"How many?" Martiss asked as Cole returned to the group.

"Fifteen, maybe twenty. How do you want to do this?"

"Not my decision, Cole," Martiss said. "This is all you."

"Right. Well, they seemed to be drinking, so they're distracted. I figure if we can get either side of them, with surprise on our side, we should be able to get through pretty quick. I spotted another access way in there, so if we split up and send—"

Tobias sighed loudly. "Oh, enough already."

And with that he marched around the corner, sword drawn, gun in hand.

The only thing Cole and the others had heard before the gunfire started was, "You guys got some for me?"

They rounded the corner into the room and found it a blur of motion. Tobias, having already taken down a good third of the pirates, pulled his blade from its place in one pirate's chest before slashing it in a wide arc and relieving another of his head.

His eyes were wild.

What followed was neither neat nor clean, but fast and brutal. It took what seemed only seconds for them to clear the room.

As the last whimpering of an injured pirate was silenced with a deafening shot, Cole stood and surveyed the aftermath. The cold metal floor was slick with blood and littered with limbs. He looked over at Tobias, who was wiping his blade clean on the leg of his pants, and was just about to unload on him when Martiss beat him to it.

"What the hell was that?" Martiss shouted, pointing an accusatory finger in Tobias's direction.

Tobias scoffed.

"You follow *his* orders, understand?" Martiss pointed at Cole but kept his eyes firmly locked on Tobias. "You don't get to go wild here. Not now. Not—"

A deep hacking cough cut Martiss off mid-sentence, and he stumbled back against the nearby wall.

"I'm sorry, what was that?" Tobias asked mockingly. "I didn't quite—"

Unable to contain himself, Cole struck out and caught Tobias across the jaw with a right hook. "That's enough. This is done."

"Oh, this is a long way from done, golden b—"

Cole shoved Tobias hard in the chest. "It's *done*. Now get your shit in order, and get ready to move. We have a job to do."

Cole walked away from Tobias before he had a chance to respond and headed over to where Martiss was bracing himself against the wall. As Cole approached, he saw him wipe some blood away from the corner of his mouth.

"You OK?" Cole asked, knowing the answer.

"I'm fine."

It was the reply he expected, but it was far from the truth. Martiss Darenian was a proud man, some would say to a fault. For several months now, he'd been getting progressively less well, and while he had never said the exact cause, it was becoming increasingly clear that his time with the living was shortening.

It was Martiss's pride, Cole believed, that led to them taking this job.

It was true that the Federation rarely associated with the Shek'Tarii and vice versa, but they had a reputation for getting things done and the pay was considerable. Cole didn't know the exact figure, but Martiss had told him even the portion they got in advance would provide for their people for years and that the full amount could last generations.

Martiss knew that this was his last chance to provide a future for his people, and Cole knew that he would do it or die trying.

"What about you?" Martiss asked, clearing his throat.

"What?"

"You've been off your game ever since we landed."

Cole sighed. "It's just a lot to juggle."

Martiss offered a warm smile. "Don't I know it."

Behind them, Xan had gotten the service elevator down to their level, and he, Yarik, and Tobias were already standing inside waiting.

"If you've finished dying over there, old man," Tobias called out, "I believe we have a job to do."

Cole began to guide Martiss over to the elevator. "Y'know, we could always just juggle one less ball."

Martiss winced as he laughed. "Just get through this, and we can deal with that later."

They had only been traveling upward for a short time when the elevator car suddenly shuddered, the lights flickered, and it ground to a halt.

"I guess they know we're here," Tobias said.

"We don't know that." Cole stepped forward and tried to pry the doors open but had no luck. "Xan, can you get us moving again?"

Wordlessly, Xan hurried to the elevator's control panel, ripped it open, and got to work. It wasn't long before he sat back against the wall in defeat. "They've jammed it remotely. Locked the brakes and the doors."

"Can you at least unlock the door?" Cole asked.

Xan nodded in reply, and moments later the locks could be heard disengaging.

Cole pried open the door to reveal a blank wall and the bottom half of a door to whatever floor they were on.

"Yarik, Xan, hold the door. Tobias, give me a boost."

Surprisingly enough, Tobias complied without saying a word.

Captivity and potential death tended to be a good motivator for the petulant.

It wasn't too much of a struggle for Cole to push the outer door open and squeeze through the gap into the room beyond—a room that was quiet, empty, and void of alarms or personnel, just banks and banks of consoles and displays. Perhaps they hadn't been discovered after all.

The struggle came when he had to widen the gap so that everyone else could vacate the elevator. Even with his implants bolstering his considerable natural strength, Cole had to fight to pull the elevator up. The brakes fought back initially before finally giving way with a screech and a clang. Cole got his shoulder under the opening, pushed the elevator up the rest of the way, and held it while the others stepped out.

Tobias lingered in the elevator car. "Is that heavy? It looks heavy."

Cole forced a smile despite carrying the entire weight of the elevator on his shoulder. "I'm more than happy to let go."

"Oh, well, I better get out then. Don't want you straining anything."

"How kind of you."

As Tobias brushed past him, Cole dropped the elevator off his shoulder, and it screeched its way down into the blackness below. Several seconds passed before a thunderous crash echoed up the shaft.

Cole turned to see Xan already hard at work at a nearby console. "All right, Xan, where are we?"

"Looks like we're about three-quarters of the way up the tower. Appears to be one of the communications levels."

Martiss stepped forward and looked over the display. "Are we blown?"

Xan shrugged. "I'm not seeing any signs of increased activity or alarms being tripped, so no, I think we're in the clear for now."

No sooner had the words been spoken than a loud crackle shattered the ensuing silence as speakers around the room came to life.

"Gentlemen," a voice boomed, it was deep and resonant, male, by the sound of it.

They all froze.

"Who are we speaking to?" Cole asked the air.

All around the room, displays blinked to life, all showing the same image: a slender red face stared back at them, humanoid but clearly alien. It belied the voice coming from the speakers.

"You speak to no one, human!" the pirate barked.

Cole took the hint and remained silent.

The pirate took a deep breath, settled himself, and stared right into the camera, right at Cole.

"Kolar is speaking. You are not. Do we understand?"

Cole nodded.

"You will leave this place, all of you. *Now*. If you come for our guests, none of us will leave."

Around half the displays flickered to static and then faded into a wide shot showing a large room—the observation floor at the top of the tower. Along its end wall, the "guests" were huddled. A quick head count revealed they were all accounted for.

"Your *Federation* has our demands. Unless you are here to bestow unto us our gifts, you will leave. If not, like I said, you never will."

Several displays flickered and brought up a schematic of the building. Xan quickly scrolled through the readouts at his station, and his face dropped.

"It's rigged to blow," Xan said, his face white.

Cole cleared his throat and stepped forward. "Kolar, forgive us, but we are here to meet your demands. If we could arrange a meeting, we can resolve this without bloodshed."

"Without bloodshed? You think Kolar is without eyes? You think that he is blind?"

"I—"

"*No*. Trust that Kolar has seen your . . . efforts." His brow furrowed. "You bear no gifts, only death."

Cole straightened. "Any lives we have taken today have been both in self-defense and in the service of bringing you your . . . gifts. The Federation wants its people returned. We had to be willing to go to great lengths to secure their safety. Surely you can appreciate that?"

Silence.

Cole looked around nervously. Xan and Yarik were fixed to the screens, eyes wide, and Tobias was standing in the back shaking his head. Martiss simply shrugged.

After what felt like an age, a low rumbling laughter emanated from the speakers.

"Kolar likes you, little man. Very well. We will receive your *gifts*."

"Thank y—"

"Come alone."

And with that, all of the speakers and displays in the room cut out, leaving the room in silence.

Tobias chuckled. "Well, *that* was a shit-show. *'Surely you can appreciate that?'* Give me a—"

"Cole bought us some time, Tobias," Martiss snapped. "Or would you rather they just blow the building right now?"

Tobias rolled his eyes and relented.

Ignoring Tobias, Cole turned to Xan. "How did we not know about the bombs?"

"I-I don't know," Xan said, exasperated. "The scans showed nothing."

"Maybe they're bluffing?" Yarik posited.

"We can't take that chance. Xan, did you see where they were?"

Xan closed his eyes and tried to remember what he'd seen on the monitors.

"Uhh . . . there was a big one at ground level and maybe . . . maybe a dozen or more smaller ones scattered throughout."

"It was a lot," Yarik offered unhelpfully.

"All right. Xan, take Yarik and get down to ground level. If we can at the very least disarm the big one, we stand a chance. I'll go and see Kolar."

"Where do you want us?" Martiss asked.

"I need you and Tobias to circle around and be ready to hit them from the sides."

Tobias chuckled again. "Oh, you're not going to try and talk this out with ol' Kolar?"

Cole wheeled on Tobias. "He's going to try and kill me the second I walk through those doors. So no, no I'm not. I figure we hit them all at once from three sides. Run 'em through, quick and clean."

Tobias nodded eagerly. "I can get behind that."

"Good, I'm glad you're happy. We better get moving."

With the briefing over, such as it was, Martiss took Cole aside. "You're sure about this?"

Cole nodded. "It's what you'd do."

"Yeah, it is," Martiss said with a knowing smile.

"Are you going to be OK?"

"I'll be fine," Martiss said. "I've made it this far, haven't I?"

"*Barely.*"

Martiss punched Cole in the arm. It was a solid hit and started throbbing immediately.

He was fine.

Cole looked over Martiss's shoulder and saw Tobias and Xan deep in conversation. Xan's face was draped with concern, Tobias's with reassurance. Cole could have easily passed it off as simple fatherly concern, only Tobias wasn't the fatherly type. At all.

Cole watched as Tobias gave Xan a nod filled with eagerness and determination, and something about it caused the pit of doubt in Cole's stomach to open into a chasm.

He needed to stay alert.

Something was up.

Cole stepped off the elevator into yet another wide, empty corridor. He figured Kolar must have pulled as many men back as possible since he had made it to the observation level untouched.

A crackle in his ear indicated an incoming radio message.

"Cole, you there?"

It was Xan. He sounded nervous.

"What's up?"

"It's bad down here, Cole. The main charge is wired up every which way from Soldan. I don't know if—"

"You can do it, Xan. We need you to do it."

There was a long pause before Xan crackled through once more. "Cole, we ran checks, and there are twenty-three supplemental charges, and we've got no way of telling if they're in a chain or activated individually. It's possible that if the main charge blows that—"

"Just breathe, Xan. If everything goes smoothly up here, you won't have a thing to worry about."

Cole's stomach fluttered.

"It *better* go smoothly," Yarik chimed in from the background.

Cole smiled uneasily. "Look, just keep at it. This'll all be over soon. I promise."

Without another word from Xan, the radio cut out with a beep.

Up ahead, the open maw of a blast door beckoned to him, but Cole could see no activity inside. With a quick tap of his radio, he switched frequencies.

"Martiss, you in position?"

Silence.

"Martiss?"

His heartbeat quickened, thrumming loudly in his ears, and drowned out the static. He waited what felt like an age before a voice finally crackled through.

"Come on in, golden boy." It was Tobias. "Party's already over."

Cole's mouth went dry. He didn't even reply.

Inside, Cole expected to find chaos, but instead he found calm. The bulk of the hostages were standing in a group to the side, talking among themselves. Some looked relieved, others fearful. Several just stared into thin air, almost catatonic.

A short distance away, a pair of hostages, a man and a woman, stood in quiet conversation with Tobias. Martiss was nowhere to be seen.

As he looked around the room, it was clear that he had missed the chaos almost entirely. It was impossible for him to tell just how many pirates there had been, for now they lay scattered in pieces and bloody piles all across the vast observation deck.

The floor was slick with blood, and he had to be careful to keep his footing as he headed for Tobias.

"Tobias? What happened?"

Tobias turned and Cole could barely recognize him. His clothes were drenched in blood, and a fresh wound on his forehead seeped even more blood down the side of his face. It had begun to congeal in his beard, and his long hair had matted to his neck. He looked a mess, and yet he seemed in good spirits, which was even odder.

"Quick and clean, just like you said. Well, more quick than clean I guess, but look, the important thing is everyone's safe and sound. Not a hair out of place on a single one." He laughed to himself and playfully nudged the man he was speaking to. The man, who was completely bald, looked mortified. Tobias gave a halfhearted smile. "Oh . . . sorry."

"Tobias, where's Martiss?" Cole asked, doing his best to hide his apprehension.

"Rounding up a few stragglers that made a run for it. He should be back any minute."

"I couldn't get him on comms."

"I'm sure he's fine."

"We need to go find him. He might need our help."

"Calm down, Cole. What we need to do is our job. We need to secure these folk and get them out of here. Martiss will catch up. Now, where are my manners . . ."

Tobias made a grand gesture toward the man and woman beside him. "Cole, I'd like to introduce to you Yanis Safarin, Federation senator and Treasury secretary, and his lovely wife, Alaria."

Cole gave them a curt nod of recognition, but little else.

"What about the bombs?" Cole asked, impatiently turning his attention back to Tobias.

"I-I'm sorry," Yanis stammered, "but what bombs?"

"Dead man's switch," Tobias replied, ignoring Yanis. "It's handled. Should give them plenty of time to disarm downstairs."

Tobias pointed to the wall behind Cole. There, Kolar sat slumped against the wall, his arm outstretched, his hand clutching the dead man's switch, and a blood-soaked sword pinning his hand to the wall. As Cole got closer, he could hear the hum of the sword. The electricity running through it was keeping the switch held tight. Faint wisps of steam rose from the bloody blade.

"You always liked creative solutions, Tobias," Cole said, actually finding himself admiring Tobias's handiwork to a degree.

However, when he looked back to Tobias, who had already returned to his conversation with Yanis, Cole saw his hilt firmly stored on his belt.

His heart sank.

Cole ran his fingers lightly over the hilt stuck in the wall and wiped away a thin layer of blood to reveal distinct brass engravings that were all too familiar.

It was Martiss's sword.

A chill ran up Cole's spine.

There were no stragglers.

Martiss wasn't coming back.

With grave purpose, Cole strode toward Tobias, drew his sword, and in one quick motion, pressed the tip up under his chin.

Tobias froze.

Alaria Safarin gasped.

"What is the meaning of this?" Yanis blustered.

"What did you do?" Cole said through gritted teeth, barely containing his emotion.

Tobias's eyes went wide. "Cole, I-I don't know what you mean, what are you—"

Cole pushed the blade in ever so slightly, and Tobias's face began to twitch.

"Don't even try and talk your way out of this . . ."

Tobias's facade slipped, and a smirk spread wide. He didn't say a word.

He didn't have to.

His face said it all.

In a blink, he slapped away Cole's blade and snatched Yanis by the back of the neck, holding him steady with one arm. In futile panic, Alaria rushed at Tobias only to receive a swift backhand strike that sent her staggering back toward the other hostages.

"Right. You try that again, he dies. If anyone runs, he dies." Tobias locked eyes with Cole and drew his sword. It crackled to life at his side. "And if you take just one step closer, guess what?"

It was now Cole's turn to freeze. "Tobias, what are y—"

"He *dies*. Now toss the blade."

Cole had no choice but to relent, and so he retracted his blade and tossed the hilt off to the side. There was no way Martiss would want the hostages harmed. There was too much riding on their safe return. Their people's very future relied on their safe return. No, if Martiss was truly gone, they were *his* people now. There was a way out; he just had to find it.

"Tobias, what are you doing?" He had to fight to keep his voice calm.

"I'm making things right."

"What the hell are you talking about?"

"He shouldn't have chosen you," Tobias growled, pointing his sword right at Cole's chest. "Some dirt-born son of a whore has no business leading anyone, let alone the Shek'Tarii. You have no place, no right!"

Yanis attempted to wriggle his way out of Tobias's grasp, but his feeble attempt was quickly and forcefully shut down.

"But no," Tobias continued. "The stupid old bastard just had to choose his golden boy."

"You know why he didn't choose you, Tobias?" Cole shouted, no longer bothering to hold back. "It's because of shit like this! You can't control yourself. You're insa—"

"*I* should be the one leading my people forward, not you. It's that simple."

Cole scoffed. "You want to lead *your* people forward, Tobias? You want this to be simple? Then cut this shit out. Let's finish the job, get these people home, and get paid."

"I intend to, once you give me what I want."

"I can't do that," Cole said. He began slowly stepping back. "Martiss would never want—"

"Oh, who cares what Martiss would want, Cole? He's gone. Dead. Done. It's time to grow up, boy. Be your own damn man for once in your life!"

Cole stopped his retreat when he felt the back of his foot bump into Kolar's leg. It was only when he looked down that he realized it was no longer attached to Kolar.

He'd played every eventuality out in his head. The only way to get the hostages—all the hostages—out alive was to relent.

But relenting to Tobias's demands would mean condemning their people to the rule of a madman.

That was something he could not do.

And yet capitulation was the only remaining "good" option.

Cole locked eyes with Tobias once more, and in them, he could see nothing but madness.

He couldn't give in.

The bad options were all he had left.

Cole exhaled deeply. "All right. Let's say I give it to you, the leadership . . ."

"That'd be awfully nice of you," Tobias said.

"It's only natural you're going to want an heir, right? Someone to carry on your legacy?"

Tobias couldn't contain his laughter. "Oh . . . wow. Really? You—wow. That's . . . Look, I appreciate the offer, Cole, really, but I've already got one, thanks."

Cole exhaled deeply.

Reached back.

Clasped his hand tightly around the hilt of Martiss's sword.

Made sure Tobias saw.

"Do you?"

Tobias's eyes widened ever so slightly.

Just enough to confirm he understood the implication.

"You wouldn't. You'd kill us all."

Cole shrugged. "Maybe. Maybe not." He barely recognized his own voice; it was like ice. "But your 'legacy' would sure as shit be in a bunch of pieces."

Cole's stomach turned. Xan was a good friend, Yarik too. He hoped they would understand, and yet he wasn't even sure if he understood himself. "Now let him go."

The doubt that had crept into Tobias's demeanor evaporated, and he stood tall. He raised his blade and held it just under Yanis's chin. "You're bluffing. You don't have the balls, never have."

"Are you really willing to bet your son's life on that? *Your* life?"

Tobias scoffed. "I guess we're going to find out."

Cole watched as Tobias pushed the edge of his blade toward Yanis's neck. Heard Yanis yelp. Heard Alaria scream out from across the room.

As if on autopilot, Cole pulled the blade from its mooring in Kolar's wrist.

Everything went quiet. The only sound was that of the dead man's switch clattering to the ground and then . . .

Silence. Deafening silence.

Moments passed and . . . nothing.

Tobias locked Cole with a cold stare and drew his blade across Yanis's throat in one swift motion. He held the stare as Yanis bled out, then let him fall unceremoniously to the floor.

From across the room, Alaria Safarin wailed.

The sound of her screams would echo in Cole's ears for the rest of his days.

Before Yanis's corpse even hit the ground, Cole felt a thunderous blast slam into his chest, and he was shot back, pinned to the wall behind him.

Bursts of light spread across his vision as his head bounced off the steel.

He vaguely heard Martiss's sword fall to the ground.

Tobias chuckled.

"Y'know, I'll admit it. That was a hell of a plan, Cole. *Hell* of a—"

A deep rumble from far below cut Tobias short.

Dust shook free and fell from the ceiling.

Cole's vision cleared, and he saw Tobias's bravado falter.

"You were saying?"

A succession of thuds gained pace and drew closer.

In a brilliant flash, the far wall broke open.

The fireball tore through.

Tore apart.

The last thing Cole saw as his vision whited out was the agonized face of Alaria Safarin and then . . .

Nothing.

When the smoke cleared, there was no one left—no one, save for Cole and Tobias. Tobias hadn't moved. Hadn't so much as blinked during the fury of the blast. Hadn't taken his eyes off Cole.

Now, as the building creaked and groaned around them, his face twisted into a snarl.

"I said, hell of a plan, *golden b*—"

The words, however, caught in his throat, and a sharp cough shot a spattering of blood from his mouth. Unconsciously his hand went to his stomach and felt the end of the metal rod that had pierced it.

Blood ran freely from the wound.

Tobias stumbled backward, threw Cole to the side with the last of his strength, and fell to a knee.

Cole rolled to a stop and got his bearings. His hilt lay on the ground beside him. He scooped it up and struggled to his feet.

Tobias was now on both knees, doubled over.

Slowly, he turned his head in Cole's direction.

But Cole had no way of knowing the emotion that Tobias carried on his face in that moment—be it madness, anger, or fear—for he was but a silhouette backed against the light streaming through the fissure caused by the explosion.

With a sudden and earsplitting crack, the floor fell away and Tobias slipped from view. Cole rushed to the edge of the gaping crater, but all he could see below was a pile of rubble several floors down.

Tobias was nowhere to be seen.

In shock, Cole stumbled backward a step and felt his foot bump up against something. He looked down and saw Martiss's sword laying there, still activated.

He stood transfixed as the horror of what had occurred washed over him.

It was all lost.

This was his failure. His alone.

EPHERIA: PRESENT DAY

Cole sat in silence. He'd drifted off mid-sentence and was now staring blankly at the floor.

"How'd you get out?" Ram asked, gently trying to prompt Cole.

After a long moment, Cole looked up. "I-I don't know. Almost everything after the . . . it's a blank for everything . . . *after*. I lost days."

"It's all right. I get it," Ram said. "You don't need to say anything else."

Cole let out a deep sigh.

Ram put a hand on his friend's shoulder and squeezed. "Now . . . what do you say we get out of here and—"

From somewhere below shouting drifted up to meet them.

"Wait, wait, quiet," Cole whispered. He listened closely, and his fears were soon confirmed. There were footsteps downstairs, which meant they were about to have company. They wouldn't be able to get out of the building without being spotted, and they were no doubt outnumbered. Cole rushed to the door and closed it as quickly and quietly as he could, but it wasn't quiet enough.

"Up there!" a voice shouted from below.

Cole grabbed one of the rusted rifles from the ground and jammed it through the door handles. It was as close to a lock as they were going to get. It was just in time too, as the loud footsteps of the soldiers clattered onto the floor outside and the beams of their torches flashed across the windows in the doors.

"All right, spread out and find them," the soldier said on the other side of the door. "Let's get this over with already."

Cole pressed up against the wall to the right of the door and Ram rushed to get out of sight to the other side.

Crash.

In the dark, Ram's foot clipped an empty ammo crate on the floor and sent it skittering across the floor, banging into the door.

"Damn it," Ram said under his breath.

"Hold up," the soldier shouted from outside.

Cole and Ram froze. Neither of them were game to even breathe. The torch beams flashed across the door once again.

"We know you're in there," the soldier shouted. "Might as well come on out."

TWENTY-FOUR

"COME ON NOW, we've wasted enough time on you as it is," the soldier shouted, and he banged on the door.

Ram edged closer to the door and was able to peek around the corner and through the window to see the soldiers. He counted them and held up five fingers to Cole to report his findings.

The soldier bashed on the door once more, and the rifle almost rattled free. "Come out now, or we will be forced to open fire."

From the look on Ram's face, Cole could tell that an idea was dawning on him, and things tended to go a little pear-shaped when he got that look. Before he could stop him, Ram was back at the doors.

"Damn it, kid!" Ram shouted at the top of his voice. "Do you have any damn idea what the hell you're doing?"

There was a stunned silence on the other side, and then the lead soldier spoke. "Come again?"

"That's come again, *sir*, to you," Ram shouted back.

Cole looked at Ram in shock. In an instant, Ram had become a perfect vision of his father. It was almost scary. "What the hell are *you* doing?" he said in a whisper.

"Keldara," Ram said quietly.

"What?"

Ram made his hand into a gun, pointed it at his knees, and made a shooting motion.

"Oh yeah, that'll work," Cole said. It'd been about eight years since they'd been on Keldara, but he remembered it well enough. To his left, there was a hole that had crumbled away in the wall, and getting down on his hands and knees, he was able to get a sightline on the soldiers. Their kneecaps were all in clear view. He gave Ram the signal that he was set.

The lead soldier spoke up again. "Who *exactly* am I speaking to?"

"General Teodor Barden of the Federation Defense Force," Ram shouted. "I'm sure you've heard of me, even all the way out here on this godforsaken rock."

"I served the Federation during the war," the soldier said, his voice trembling ever so slightly. "I know who you are, sir, I just don't understand what you're—"

"What's your name, son?"

"Jenkins, sir," came the reply.

"Well, damn it, Jenkins," Ram said. "You are, right now, interfering with an official Federation task force."

"Sir, I wasn't aware the Federation was operating this far—"

"Jenkins, you are already in violation of several key Federation mandates and laws," Ram shouted. He was firmly entrenched in the role now. "Hell, you and your idjit buddies there just shot down a goddamn Federation vessel."

"As I said, General Barden, sir, we weren't aware that the Federation was operating in this sector. We had no way of—"

"Son, that's why it's called a *covert* operation."

They heard Jenkins audibly clear his throat. "Forgive me for saying this, sir, but you weren't exactly being very covert."

Ram stepped back from the door and gave Cole a shrug. "He's got me there."

"Can we move this along?" Cole asked under his breath.

"Absolutely," Ram said and then turned back to the door. "Jenkins?"

"Yes, sir?"

"Stand down," Ram said, lowering his voice. "I'm coming out."

"You're alone, sir?"

"Alone and unarmed."

"All right, do it slowly."

Ram gave Cole a nod, removed the rifle from the door, and, after a deep breath, pushed the doors open.

As Ram emerged from the darkness into the light of the torch beams, it didn't take long for Jenkins and his colleagues to notice that something was off. In short order, they surmised that he wasn't old enough to be General Barden and that neither his gear nor his clothing bore any Federation markings. This wasn't to be considered a failure, though; in fact, it was exactly how the plan went.

Even before the soldiers had begun to raise their weapons and start shouting obscenities, Ram was already stepping back behind the doorway. Moments later, Cole let off several targeted rounds, each impacting a knee, a shin, a foot, or whatever was in view, really. The soldiers dropped to the ground one by one and proceeded to grab at whatever part of them was bleeding. Amid the chaos, Ram rushed out and scooped up all the soldiers' weapons that were now scattered across the floor, what with their owners' attentions being directed elsewhere. As the dust settled, Cole joined Ram in the doorway, and they looked over the five men currently curled up and sobbing quietly in front of them. Ram gave one of them a nudge that elicited a yelp.

"Hey, which one of you was I talking to?"

Ram caught Jenkins raising his free hand; the other one was clasped tightly on his knee.

"Right," Ram said. He then went and knocked the other four soldiers out with the butt of his newly acquired rifle. "Now that we're alone."

Cole crouched down in front of Jenkins and snapped his fingers in front of his face to get his attention. "Hey! Who's your commanding officer?"

"C-Captain Sharma," Jenkins said between pained gasps for air.

"And who does he report to?"

"I-I don't know, I swear."

Cole pressed lightly on Jenkins's knee with the barrel of his rifle. "Think."

"Look, man," Jenkins said, half whimpering. "I've been here for like a month. I don't even know. They don't tell us anything."

Cole stood up and gave Ram a puzzled look, and he picked up on it immediately.

"Wait, a month?" Ram asked.

Jenkins looked over to Ram. "I-I was with a group of mercenaries, and like, around a month ago we got scooped up and brought here to this shit hole."

"How many of you are there?" Cole asked.

"There were ten in my group originally," Jenkins said. "But there were a few hundred other guys already here when we arrived."

Ram and Cole stepped away from Jenkins and turned their backs on him.

"Tobias must have figured we'd be coming for him and beefed up his security," Cole said.

Ram scratched his chin in thought. "Yeah, but why even have security in the first place?"

Cole walked over to one of the unconscious soldiers, crouched down, and began digging through the bag he'd been carrying.

Jenkins's eyes were wide. "Wait, you guys already know who he is?"

"Yeah, sorry about that," Ram said with an awkward smile.

"So why the hell did you have to shoot us?" Jenkins shouted.

"Well, self-preservation mostly," Ram said. "I mean, you were just about to shoot *us*."

Cole removed a small data pad from the soldier's bag and began looking through it as he walked back over to Jenkins. "So, where is he?"

"What?" Jenkins asked. He was getting woozy from the blood loss.

"We know he's in the compound," Cole said. "But we were hoping you'd be able to give us something more solid."

"He hasn't been here the whole time," Jenkins said. "He only got here a few days ago, a-and as far as I know, he hasn't left the main tower since he got back."

Cole crouched back down to talk to Jenkins face-to-face. "We're going to need a way—"

He was cut off by a harsh static burst from Jenkins's radio, and soon a pompous-sounding voice began echoing through the ruined room.

"Jenkins, this is Captain Sharma. Do you have anything to report?"

Jenkins was about to press the answer when Cole snatched the radio off of his vest.

"Jenkins?" Sharma prompted.

"Tell him you spotted us heading deeper into the ruins and that you're pursuing on foot," Cole said, and he held out the radio to Jenkins's mouth.

Nodding nervously, Jenkins complied. "Sir, we spotted them heading deeper into the ruins. We're currently pursuing them on foot."

It was a few moments before Sharma crackled in again. "Are you all right, Jenkins? You sound winded."

"Tell him you're fine," Cole said. He held the radio out again but quickly pulled it back. "Tell him to send as much backup as he can spare."

Jenkins leaned forward to the radio. "I'm fine, sir, they've just had us running for a while now, is all. We could use all the help we can get."

"Very well, Jenkins," Sharma said. "I believe the search at the crash site turned up no sign of survivors, so I shall send those men to your location, as well as a few squads from Command."

Cole looked at Ram, but he'd turned away from them. That wasn't what he had wanted to hear, but maybe it was what he'd needed to hear.

"Thank you, sir," Jenkins said.

"Good work, Jenkins," Sharma said. "Sharma out."

"That should thin out the herd a little," Cole said.

"There still could be a lot of guys in there," Ram said.

Cole tossed the data pad to Jenkins. "We need to get in there, preferably quietly and unseen."

Jenkins exhaled deeply and began tapping away at the data pad. "All right, I think this will be your best option," he said, holding the pad up for Cole and Ram to see. "There's a grid of stormwater drains crisscrossing this district. They lead straight into the compound. There's an access point a few blocks from here."

"OK, that's a start," Cole said. "Will they get us into the tower?"

"No, they terminate inside the outer perimeter," Jenkins said. "But it's a fairly straight shot from there. You'll need a keycard to get inside. Mine's on my pack there."

Ram followed Jenkins's directions, found the card, and pocketed it. "Then what?"

"From there, look for the maintenance elevators. They should get you close to the top levels."

"Close?" Ram asked.

"They only go so far, f-for security reasons," Jenkins said. "It's to stop people using them as access points for an infiltration."

"That's cute," Ram said. "So how do we get in there?"

"I honestly don't know," Jenkins said. "I've never been up there. That's all on you guys."

"Cole, you been up there?" Ram asked.

"Only the other tower."

"How similar's the layout," Ram asked Cole.

Cole scratched his chin. "Looks similar, but it shouldn't be too hard to work out."

"Oh good," Ram said.

"Anything else we need to know?" Cole asked.

"You'll be coming out of the drains just inside the north wall," Jenkins said. "There'll be a gate there. It's usually only manned by a couple of guys."

"Good work, Jenkins," Cole said.

Ram walked over, stood beside Jenkins, and flipped his rifle around.

"Wai-wai-wait!" Jenkins shouted as he winced and covered his face with his hands.

"What is it?" Cole asked.

"This Tobias guy," Jenkins said. "You're going in there to kill him, right?"

"That is the plan."

"Good," Jenkins said and almost immediately the tension in his body visibly dissipated. Cole got the distinct impression they'd be doing the guy a favor.

Jenkins closed his eyes, awaiting the hit, and Ram reared back with the rifle, but on the downswing, Cole caught his arm. "Ram, wait."

Jenkins opened one eye to see what was going on.

Cole held up the radio again. "This call out?"

"Call out?"

"Yeah, like if we happened to have a ship in orbit that we needed to contact."

"You have a ship in orbit?"

"Focus, Jenkins," Ram said.

"It's short range only, I'm afraid," Jenkins said. "If you need to get a message into orbit, you'll need to get into the comms center."

"And where's that?" Ram asked.

"Forty-seventh floor," Jenkins said.

"How many people in there?" Cole asked.

"No idea."

"All right, that's better than nothing," Cole said. Ram motioned, asking if he should hit Jenkins, but Cole waved it off. "I think he's earned his consciousness."

"So you're just gonna leave us here?" Jenkins asked.

"We are," Cole said, "but there's bound to be some med kits in your packs. You should be able to patch you and your men up well enough to hold out until help arrives."

"You've been a great help," Ram said, almost looking sad that he didn't get to hit Jenkins. "But we are going to have to take some of your gear."

Several minutes later, Cole and Ram had outfitted themselves in some pieces of the unconscious soldiers' gear and commandeered their weapons. They'd stand a better chance of infiltrating the compound if they were able to blend into the surroundings. They left Jenkins to tend to his men and made their way down the stairs and into the alleyway. Seeing the coast was clear, they headed down the street and made the short journey to where Jenkins had shown them the entry point for the drainage system was.

When they arrived at the intersection, it was much more out in the open than they'd anticipated. In the middle of the clearing was a large crater that gave direct access to the pipeline. It was no more than 150 meters away. A search craft hovered overhead and was strafing the area with its spotlights.

"You ready for this?" Cole asked.

Ram nodded.

"OK, we move on my go."

Cole watched the timing of the spotlight as it swept across the rubble, and after waiting for a few more passes, he had the timing down. As soon as the light passed the lip of the crater, Cole broke into a dead sprint for the opening. He didn't look back to see if Ram was following; he didn't need to, he could hear him panting right behind him.

They were about twenty meters from the opening when the spotlight suddenly started to swing back toward them, breaking its pattern. Cole pushed it the last few meters, diving and sliding toward the lip of the crater. He slipped over the edge just as the light swept over his position and fell a few meters onto a pile of rubble inside the crater, proceeding to tumble down to the ground. A moment later, he looked up to see the bulky silhouette of Ram diving over the edge of the crater. He rolled to a stop in a crumpled pile next to Cole.

"You OK?" Cole asked.

Ram groaned and rolled over onto his back.
"This jacket's too damn small."

TWENTY-FIVE

THE DRAIN CAME out right where Jenkins said it would, just inside the northern wall of the compound. In front of the exit was a small hill that overlooked the base of the towers. The concrete base of an abandoned watchtower provided ample cover for Cole and Ram to survey the situation.

Before them, the main command tower stretched up high into the night sky. It was lit from below by large spotlights, whose light failed to reach the upper floors. Instead, the black walls of the tower were dotted by hundreds of smaller lights—no doubt internal light leaking out through small windows. From their current position, it almost looked like the top of the tower simply faded into the darkness.

"Try him again," Ram said.

"I've tried four times already, Ram," Cole said. "He's not there."

Ram snatched the radio away. "I'll do it then." Ram dialed in Sol's frequency. "Sol? You there? Come in." There was no reply, only static.

"Ram, it's no use—"

"He'll be fine," Ram said. "His radio probably got busted up in the crash."

"Give it here," Cole said, holding out his hand to receive the radio.

Reluctantly Ram dialed it back to the soldiers' frequency, gave it back to Cole, and then turned his attention to the clearing in front of them.

"Well, the info was good," Ram said. "Looks like there's not much of a presence at the gate."

"Let's get a closer look," Cole said.

A burst of static from the radio was followed by the digitized, hurried shouts of soldiers. In the distance behind them, several red flares shot straight up into the sky and floated like fireworks in the wind.

"Guess they found Jenkins," Ram said.

Cole got up and grabbed his rifle. "Time to go."

In front of the gate was a large expanse of land that must have once been the vehicle depot. The dusty ground was scattered with disused transport and support vehicles, many of which were beginning to rust. Between the vehicular cover and the cover of darkness, Cole and Ram were able to make the sprint to the gate without being seen. They took cover behind a large truck about a hundred meters from the gate.

Now that they were close, they could see that the gate was manned by two soldiers. A younger soldier stood in front of the boom, and an older one was sitting in the booth.

"What do you want to do?" Ram asked.

Cole took a moment to weigh his options. "Follow my lead."

Cole ran out from behind the truck and headed straight for the gate. Just as soon as he got over the shock, Ram followed suit. Cole's plan called for them to act like they were beaten to hell—easy, because they were.

They skidded to a stop in front of the gate and startled the younger soldier, who fumbled with his rifle, eventually pointing it at them.

Cole didn't blink.

"Oh, damn. Hey, hey, you have to hurry!" Cole shouted.

The younger guard stepped forward cautiously and waved his torch over their faces. "What's going on?" he asked. "Who are you?"

"Our squad was,"—Cole did his best to appear winded—"w-we were just, we were right on them, but they got the jump on us."

Out of the corner of his eye, he could see the older guard standing in the booth's doorway, taking notice of what was going on and watching it carefully.

Cole pressed on. "They sent us back to get help."

"Help?" the younger guard asked.

Ram stepped forward. "Navarr put the word out for all available units to assist in the search, but these guys, they're like madmen," he said. "They took down almost our whole squad on their own."

Cole watched as the older guard left the confines of his booth and sidled over to them, eyeing them.

"How many are there?" the older guard asked. His voice was gruff and clearly laced with suspicion.

"Had to have been four or five guys," Cole said.

The older guard kept pressing. "And where were they?"

"In the residential district. See the flares up there? That's where they were," Cole said. "We were able to escape into the pipeline and make our way back here."

"What's your name, soldier?"

"Barnes," Cole said and pointed to Ram, "and that's Moss."

The older guard began backing up toward the booth. "Well, all right then," he said. "We'll just grab our gear, and we'll head back with you."

The younger guard turned to the older guard with a puzzled look on his face. "But, sir, what about the gate?"

Cole saw the expression on the older guard's face shift ever so slightly, just enough to know that they were blown. A quick look at Ram told Cole he'd come to the same conclusion.

Cole took off after the older guard, who now had his back turned to them.

"Sorry, kid," Ram said.

The younger guard turned back to face Ram. "Huh?"

He was met with a solid right and crumpled to the ground in an unconscious heap.

Before the older guard was able to make it back to the booth, Cole was on him. He tackled him to the ground and, after a brief struggle, was able to get him into choke hold. It wasn't long before the older guard passed out.

Cole dragged the older guard into the booth and looked up to see Ram with the younger one slung over his shoulder.

"You know, I'm actually surprised that didn't work," Ram said as he dumped the younger guard on the ground next to his comrade.

Cole wiped the sweat off his brow. "I know, right?"

"I mean, that's a solid play," Ram said. "That's worked, what, at least four times before, right?"

"Five. Remember Praxis?"

"Oh yeah, I'd forgotten about that one."

"Can't say I blame you."

The run to the tower was short and uneventful. They left the guards tied up inside the booth, just in case either of them tried to raise the alarm. Now they were standing in front of a large service door. It looked to be an entry point for maintenance vehicles. Cole produced the key card from his jacket pocket and swiped it through the reader.

"I sure hope this works," Cole said.

Beep. Beep. There was a clicking sound and then. . . nothing.

Ram frowned at the development. "Was that a good beep-beep or . . . ?"

Before Cole could answer, a series of further clicks sounded from within the door and a green light started blinking above the panel.

"Good beep-beep," Ram said with a smile.

"About time something went our way," Cole said.

The door slid open to reveal a wide concrete corridor lined with lights in the floor that barely provided enough light to illuminate the pipework running overhead. The light was good enough, however, to see that the corridor was completely deserted. It stretched twenty meters or so before bending to the right. They followed it for a short time before they came out into a large open room. On one side, there were large storage sheds, and on the other, the service elevators. Ram hit the button to call the elevator, and it wasn't long before the doors slid open with a screech. They stepped into the elevator, and it sagged slightly under their weight. Ram's face went pale.

"You all right?" Cole asked.

"Shut up," Ram said as he hit the button for the forty-seventh floor far harder than was necessary.

The elevator lurched upward, screeching and shaking the whole way. It probably hadn't been used since the war.

"How many do you think we're going to run into up here?" Ram asked. He was holding on to the handrail so tight that his knuckles matched the paleness of his face.

Cole thought it over. "Standard comms centers like this would normally have ten to fifteen guys at a minimum," he said. "If they're trying to coordinate a search, could be twice as many."

"Terrific," Ram said.

The elevator came to a grinding halt at the forty-seventh floor, and no sooner had the doors begun to slide open than Ram shot through them and was out in the corridor. When Cole joined him, they both noticed it at the same time: the corridor was empty and barely lit, just like the maintenance areas below. It was also deathly quiet.

"This is weird, right?" Ram asked.

"Let's check it out," Cole said.

They rounded a few corners in silence before the sound of a solitary voice drifted down to them. Following the voice, they came out into a vast room, and at its center was a glass-walled area, flooded in bright light.

"Well, I wasn't expecting that," Ram said.

Inside the comms center, a young man was frantically rushing from console to console, checking readouts and speaking into microphones, though he was talking to himself more than he was into the microphones. Cole and Ram exchanged bemused looks and walked right in without the man even noticing. They sat down on a table just inside the door, and Cole cleared his throat, loudly.

The young man jumped with a yelp and erupted in a flurry of papers. He turned around and scanned the room for the sound before his vision settled on Cole and Ram.

"Hi," Cole said, giving him a wave.

"W-who are you?" the young man said in heavily accented basic.

"Navarr sent us," Ram said.

This only seemed to rattle the already nervous young man further, and he sat down in a chair, chewing his fingernails.

"You run all this yourself?" Cole asked.

"I try," he replied, nodding repeatedly.

"You have a name, kid?" Ram asked.

"I-I am Darvan," he said. "My name is Darvan."

"Ah, I knew a Darvan once," Ram said as he got up and leaned on the console next to where Darvan was sitting.

Darvan looked up at Ram expectantly and forced a smile.

"He was an asshole."

"Oh," Darvan said, his smile fading quickly.

Ram patted Darvan on the back. "But you seem much nicer, much more helpful."

"Y-you need my help?" Darvan asked.

"We need to get a message into orbit," Cole said.

"Oh," Darvan said. "I'm very sorry, that's not possible."

"Why not?" Cole asked.

"Mister Navarr said no outbound communications, and he was very, very clear about it," Darvan said. "He made me disable functionality. I'm very sorry. He was very clear."

Ram squeezed Darvan's shoulder gently. "We're going to need you to turn that back on, very much so."

Darvan began shaking his head furiously. "No, no, I can't," he said. "Mister Navarr would, he would—"

Ram squeezed a little harder. "Mister Navarr might be the least of your problems, Darvan."

"Y-you were not sent by Mister Navarr, were you?"

Ram shook his head slowly, and Darvan's eyes went wide as he realized his error.

"You are the ones I have been searching for, for M-Mister Navarr," Darvan said, his voice shaking.

"We've got a quick one here," Ram said with a chuckle.

"Ram, knock it off," Cole said. "You've had your fun, give the kid a break."

Ram released Darvan's shoulder and stepped away. Cole came over and sat down beside Darvan.

"Darvan," Cole said, adopting a friendlier tone than Ram. "Are you able to turn it back on?"

Darvan nodded slowly.

"OK, and how long would that take?"

"Uh, not long," Darvan said. "Not long at all, I very quick."

"Would you be able to do that for us?"

"Yes," Darvan said, his nodding increasing in speed.

Darvan jumped up from his chair, rushed over to a console on the far side of the room, and began typing away. Ram followed close behind him.

"Hey, Darvan," Ram said. "Were you tracking our ship in here?"

"Yes, yes," Darvan replied. "Mister Navarr said that was to be Darvan's top priority."

"Did you see where it went down?"

"Yes," Darvan replied, and he pointed to a large table in the center of the room. "There is printout over there with scans from crash site."

Cole stepped over to the table and soon found the scans Darvan was referring to.

"How's it look?" Ram asked.

Cole shook his head. "It's not great. I mean, she looks pretty intact, but . . ."

"What?"

"Ram, the pod bay's wrecked."

Ram put his hand on Darvan's shoulder again, and he flinched.

"Did you see anyone come out of that ship?"

"No."

"No one? You're sure?" Ram pressed.

"I saw no one," Darvan said. "But I haven't been able to monitor it whole time."

Ram's face lit up. "So you're saying there's a chance?"

"It is possible that, while Darvan not looking, someone could—"

"Ram, he was stuck in the chute, there's—"

"He's fine," Ram shouted.

Cole walked over and held the printout out to Ram. "Look at it."

Ram took the printout and stared at it for a long time. Without a word, he dropped it on the floor and walked away from Cole and Darvan.

"I'm sorry, Ram," Cole said.

No response. Ram just stood silent and unmoving, facing out into the darkness beyond the comms center.

Darvan pulled on the sleeve of Cole's jacket. "I-it is done."

"Where do I—"

Darvan pointed to a console a few meters away.

"Thanks," Cole said.

Darvan fidgeted nervously in his chair. "C-can I go now?"

"Not yet," Ram said, breaking his silence. He turned and walked back over to Darvan. "Can you get us into the upper levels?"

Darvan's eyes went even wider than they already were. "Mister Navarr's private levels?"

"Those would be the ones," Ram said.

"I don't—no, I couldn't possibly, there's—"

Ram gave him a very serious-looking scowl, and in no time at all, Darvan's fingers were rattling away at the keyboard.

"There," Darvan said. "I have unlocked Mister Navarr's private elevators. That is all I can do."

"I don't suppose you could unlock the stairs for us too?" Ram asked.

"Oh, well, I guess I can. Just a mo—"

"It's OK, Darvan," Cole said. "The elevators will do just fine."

"Oh, OK," Darvan said as his hands hovered over the keyboard.

Ram reached down and spun Darvan's chair to face the doorway.

"Go on, kid," Ram said. "Get out of here."

"I-I can go?"

"Don't make me change my mind."

Darvan jumped out of his seat and shot out the door, grabbing a bag off the table as he ran. His footsteps echoed from down the corridor and eventually faded into silence.

"That was nice of you," Cole said.

Ram laughed. "I can be nice."

Cole sat down at the comms console and put in the call to Oren. It took a while, but eventually the shaky image of Oren's face flickered in through the static.

"Cole?" Oren asked.

"Yeah."

"What happened? We lost your signal hours ago. I was just about to come down my—"

"We were shot down, Oren," Cole said. "Ram and I got out, but Sol—we don't know for sure what's happened to him, but it doesn't look good. He was still in the ship when . . ."

"I'm sorry, Cole," Oren said.

Cole sighed and shrugged his shoulders. "Like I said, we don't know where he is. If he's anywhere at all."

"Where are you now?" Oren asked.

"Inside the main tower," Cole said. "We were just on our way up to pop in on Tobias."

"So he's still there?"

"Seems that way," Cole said. "Look, if you could send some of that backup down to help with our exfil, it'd be great."

"They're prepped and ready to go," Oren said. "I'll send a search party to look for Solomon as well."

"Thanks, Oren."

"Good luck, my friend."

The image of Oren faded into the static, and Cole sat in silence at the console. He ran his hand up and down the scar on his arm, felt the cool metal brush past his fingertips, the gentle ripple of the scars.

"Ready to go?" Ram asked, but Cole remained unmoved and stared blankly at the console in front of him. "Cole?"

"I can't ask you to come with me, Ram," Cole said finally.

"Well, tough shit, I'm coming, and that's that."

Cole turned to face him. "An hour ago, you were ready to walk—"

"And now here I am about to walk into the garda's den, I know," Ram said.

"You don't have to come. I won't—"

"Get up," Ram said as he grabbed Cole under the shoulder and tried to lift him to his feet.

"What?"

"Get up."

Cole complied, and Ram sighed deeply, then placed his hands on Cole's shoulders. "We've been in this together for ten years," he said. "We've gone through every imaginable form of shit together. If you think for one second I'm going to back out on you now, you've got another thing coming."

Cole forced a smile. "You know, you can be pretty convincing when you want to be."

"Damn right, I can. Now pound it," Ram said holding out his fist expectantly.

Cole looked at him with bemusement. "That's, uh, not something we do, Ram."

"It is now. Now do it."

"We've literally never done this."

"Just do it."

Cole bumped his fist against Ram's, and together they gathered their rifles, made their way out of the comms center, and headed toward the elevators that would take them to Tobias.

"So you think he's still up there?" Ram asked as they waited for the elevator.

"He has to be," Cole said. "This has to end. Just promise me one thing?"

"What?"

"Just this once, try not to run in like a madman. Let me handle him."

"You're the boss."

A loud ding indicated the elevator's arrival, and the doors slid open, revealing a large, brightly lit interior. Cole waved Ram into the elevator. "After you."

Ram punched Cole in the arm and headed in. "Y'know, just because this one's bigger than the other, doesn't mean that I'm any less—"

Thud.

With a short, sharp strike, Cole hit Ram on the back of the neck with the butt of his rifle, and Ram dropped to the ground. Cole dragged him out and propped him up against the opposite wall.

"I'm sorry, Ram," Cole said quietly. "I just can't lose anyone else."

Cole set his rifle down beside Ram and left him some of his spare ammo. He wouldn't need any of it where he was going. There was only one way that this was going to be decided and that was with steel and blood.

As the elevator doors closed, he got one last look at Ram, sleeping peacefully against the wall, and he came to the realization that it might be the last time he saw him. But he couldn't worry about that now.

The image of Ram was soon replaced by Cole's own faint reflection staring back at him from the doors. But he didn't look at it, he couldn't. Instead, Cole closed his eyes and focused his mind.

He listened to the hum of the elevator and to his own heartbeat, which was slow and calm. It was calmer than it had been in weeks—even years, maybe. He felt the strength and tension build in his muscles; they were primed to react at a moment's notice.

Cole's scars began to itch, and all at once, he was hit with a flood of emotion. He was reminded with stark clarity of every life marked on his body and of their deaths. Pushing the feeling to the back of his mind, the itch soon turned to a burning that was only matched by his desire to avenge his family, to destroy the man that took them from him.

The time had come to put an end to this once and for all.

He was ready.

TWENTY-SIX

YOU'RE MORE THAN welcome to try.

Of all the times to be overconfident and mouthy, Kira had chosen the wrong one. Oren had been more than up to her challenge. In a plain room with a bench stretching the length of its back wall and a simple table and chairs in the middle, Kira sat on the ground, defiant.

She wasn't being held prisoner. The door to the room remained open the entire time, and she was free to come and go as she pleased. The only counter to her freedom were the two guards assigned to her. "Personal escorts," Oren had called them. They insisted on shadowing her if she ventured out, and it seemed that her reputation preceded her, since any time she even turned in the direction of the hangar, they began to corral her back toward her room. She contemplated trying to incapacitate them in some way, but she couldn't think of a scenario that ended with her not being detained for real.

So now, while they stood vigil outside, Kira sat and practiced levitating a small jug of water that had been left on the table for her. Back and forth, she glided it across the room, about a meter off the ground, paying special attention to keeping it upright and its contents inside.

Tiring of the exercise, she began to guide the jug back to the table, but as she did, someone ran past the door in the direction of the hangar. Thinking nothing of it, Kira returned her focus to the jug, but before long, several others ran past and a klaxon began to ring out in the distance. This was enough to break her concentration, and the jug dropped just enough to clip the edge of the table, clatter to the floor, and void its contents.

However, Kira didn't even notice. She was already halfway to the door before it hit the ground. As she ran out into the corridor, it became quickly apparent that the flow of people was, in fact, heading in the general direction of the main hangar.

Something had to have gone wrong on the surface.

Behind her, Kira could feel her "shadows" approaching.

"If you want to follow me, you better like running," she said and took off down the corridor.

She soon found herself overlooking the hangar from the same walkway she had watched Cole and the others depart from hours earlier. Below her, ground crews rushed back and forth between fighters and troop transports quickly filled and began filing out of the hangar.

She turned to head down to the lower levels but ran straight into one of her guards, out of breath. The other must have given up somewhere along the way. Behind him, Kira noticed someone else appear from an entrance farther along the walkway.

"Look, kid," the guard started, forcing his words out between deep breaths. "Can you please just stay where we tell you to? We're gonna catch all sorts of—"

Without a word, Kira walked straight past him and made a beeline for the entourage spilling out into the hangar. At its head was Oren, and trailing behind him was Ensign Mackenzie. Before she could get within twenty meters of the group, Mackenzie spotted her and was already moving to head her off.

Without breaking stride, he took Kira gently by the arm and began leading her away from the hangar. "What are you doing out here?"

Kira pulled her arm from his grip and stood her ground. "Something's gone wrong, hasn't it?"

"What?"

"Down there. Cole's in trouble, isn't he?" Kira began to pace back and forth. "Damn it, I should be—"

"Look, all I know is that Mister Traske contacted the commander from the surface and requested assistance."

Kira stopped pacing. "Assistance? What sort of assistance?"

"Covering their escape, I believe."

"This seems like an awful lot for an escape," Kira said, motioning to the activity in the hangar.

Mackenzie shifted his weight uneasily. "They ran into some resistance on the ground."

"Are they OK?"

"As far as I have been told, yes."

"I need to be down there."

"No. No, absolutely not. That won't be necessary. Not at all. Look, the commander is overseeing the operation personally. It'll be fine. There's no need for you to put yourself in harm's way."

Kira went silent for a moment as she looked over the craft present in the hangar below. She was no pilot, so stealing a fighter was off the table. But if Oren was going down there, then surely . . .

There it was.

She hadn't noticed it earlier, as it had been hidden behind a troop transport that had since vacated the hangar. It could only be Oren's personal shuttle. There was a neatness and precision to its smooth black curves and close sweeping wings that could only belong to someone as *proper* as Oren. It appeared to be in the midst of refueling, which would buy her some time.

It was just then that she realized that she probably had that look on her face that she gets when she comes up with a spectacularly bad idea. She looked to her left and was shocked to see that Oren was looking right at her. Had he seen her looking at his ship? If he had, it wouldn't be much of a leap to guess her plans.

However, even though it had felt like a protracted judgement, in reality, Oren had only glanced at her for a moment, given a small smile of acknowledgement, and then carried on with his entourage down into the hangar.

If she was going to get on that ship, she had to move, *now*.

Her progress, however, was quickly halted as she turned to be faced with Mackenzie and both of her shadows, the other having finally caught up.

She sighed. "Oh, I'd forgotten about you."

"I would really suggest you head back to your quarters," Mackenzie said. "It's where you'll be safest."

Running wasn't an option, nor was fighting, not in the middle of the hangar, at least.

"*Fine*," Kira said.

There was always a third option.

The main corridor was virtually deserted as they headed back, with almost all required personnel where they needed to be. Her two guards walled off her retreat while Mackenzie walked beside her.

"This is for the best, really," he began, but before he could continue, he found himself interrupted.

Without warning, Kira gasped loudly and fell to her knees, one hand clutching her stomach.

Mackenzie rushed to her side. "What's wrong?"

Between somewhat convincing pained groans, Kira "managed" to get some words out. "I don't-I don't know."

She let out a final yell, fell completely to the floor, and remained motionless.

From the sound of Mackenzie's boots on the floor by her head, Kira could tell he was panicking. He soon stopped pacing and shouted at the guards to go get help.

Kira heard, much to her relief, the sound of two sets of boots run off down the corridor. She popped her eyes open and saw the guards disappear around a corner.

She got to her feet and was just finishing dusting herself off when Mackenzie finally turned around.

His eyes went wide. "A-are you OK?"

Kira nodded. "I'm fine. But for what it's worth, I do feel really bad about this . . ."

"About wh—"

Kira had never knocked anyone out cold before. Sure, she'd tried, but she'd never actually succeeded.

For a moment, she looked down at her hand, which was gently throbbing. She'd been in fights before—her life at the shipyards had been an ever-ongoing fight—but this felt different.

Perhaps it was guilt.

She looked down at Mackenzie lying on the floor at her feet. Despite the slowly reddening bruise on his cheek, he seemed to be sleeping peacefully.

Kira looked around and spotted a gathering of supply crates against the opposite wall. She quickly dragged Mackenzie behind them and arranged them in a way so as to hide him from anyone going past.

Wanting to waste no more time, Kira took off toward the hangar.

Thanks largely in part to the heightened activity on board, Kira was able to make it all the way down to the hangar floor without raising so much as an eyebrow. Ahead, she could see Oren's shuttle, which looked to be in the final stages of its preparation for departure.

She still had time.

Leaning against a pylon, Kira watched as Oren and his entourage lingered at the front of the shuttle. She could make a run for it and hope no one would see her—except someone would definitely see her.

As she scanned the hangar for another opportunity, her eyes soon settled on a cargo crane sitting unattended a short distance away.

"Well," Kira said quietly to herself, "here goes nothing."

She closed her eyes and visualized the crane: saw it moving, spinning slowly on its axis; saw it pushing over a stack of crates to create her window of opportunity.

When she opened her eyes, Kira felt a mix of surprise, guilt, and amusement as she found the beam of the crane was actually spinning wildly and scattering crates left, right, and center. It came to a sudden stop when it teetered just enough and clipped the portside wing of a nearby fighter.

That should do it.

Sure enough, she watched as a large portion of the hangar crews hurried to see what was going on, and Oren and his entourage also turned their attention to the ruckus she'd caused.

There was no point in lingering.

Kira stepped away from the pylon and broke into a dead sprint to Oren's shuttle.

Amid the chaos, no one saw a thing.

Cole stood in silence as the elevator rose to the upper levels. When the doors finally slid open, a burst of cool air rushed in to greet him. Stepping out into the space beyond, Cole found that it was indeed cooler up there than on the lower floors. His breath misted into the air in front of him as he scanned the room. A solitary corridor ran perpendicular to the elevator's exit, and there were no indicative markers providing a direction to the command center. Deciding that left was as good an option as any, Cole headed down the brightly lit corridor.

Soon the smooth steel walls gave way to glass as the corridor opened up onto a viewing platform that overlooked one of the hangars below—presumably the one that would have served command personnel during the war. Cole peered through the crystal-clear panes to see a small amount of activity beneath him. Several fighters were scattered about with a minimal crew tending to each. Some were being refueled from the row of tanks lining the wall beside them. On the opposite side of the hangar was Tobias's ship, unattended and still bearing many of the scars from their encounter on Ryger.

Looking past Tobias's ship, out of the mouth of the hangar, Cole could see the toppled ruins of the other tower, lit from below by dozens of spotlights. Part of him wondered if Tobias had the ruins lit up to mock him with the memory of that day. That tower was where the horrible chain of events that Cole found himself in had started. It seemed fitting then that only a short distance away would be the place where it would all end, one way or the other.

Cole held on to the memory for a moment, then pushed it from his mind and continued on along the corridor. He followed it to its end, where it terminated in a small alcove with a wide staircase leading up and around to his left. A red light emanated from each step of the staircase and cast the area in a faint glow. Thick power cables ran out of a wall and led up into the room above. As Cole slowly ascended the flight, the command center came into view—or what used to be the command center.

It was still as starkly lit as it would have been during the war, with the red glow of the stairwell giving way to a bright white light, but the command center looked anything but war-ready. Computer consoles were gutted, with tangles of wires and circuitry covering large sections of the floor. Half the room was covered with tarpaulins, making it look more like Kag's storage room back at the yards than a command hub. Many of the glass divider panels remained intact, but those that weren't as fortunate were shattered into thousands of pieces that glittered in the stark light. On the far right wall, Cole could see a hint of the bank of med pods, but his view was obscured by a bank of displays. Cole exhaled slowly and headed inside with his hand hovering over the hilt of his sword.

Cole saw him before he'd even made it to the med bay.

Tobias was in the center med pod, and it seemed to be the only one that was functional. With scattered papers and shattered glass crunching beneath the soles of his boots, Cole crossed the last few meters and came to a stop just in front of Tobias's pod.

A green glow flooded the interior of the pod and made Tobias's shirtless body look almost alien. It appeared as though the injuries he sustained on Ferris had mostly healed. The scars were still a pale pink, indicating they were fresh. Despite being unconscious, it was as though every muscle in his body was tensed to the point of breaking. This was a function of the med pod to ensure that a patient didn't lose any muscle mass while being treated for extended periods of time. Tobias's torso was covered with scars, but they were nothing like the one's Cole had given himself over the years. Many of them came from a long life of war, but many were ones that Cole had never seen before. They were precise, surgical even. Dozens of small, deliberately placed incision scars littered Tobias's skin. Almost hidden among them were what looked like hundreds of needle marks. Cole wondered just what had happened to him since that fateful day fifteen years ago. For most of that time, he'd been in Federation custody.

Cole stepped closer to the pod. "What happened to you?"

Tobias's face was still and emotionless, and his long, thinning hair was matted across his forehead. His eyes moved back and forth rapidly beneath their lids. In all the time Cole had known Tobias, he had never seen him this vulnerable. It would be so easy to just shoot him as he lay in state inside the pod, but bullets would never pierce the hardened glass of the door. There was only one way this could go.

Cole reached for the pod's control panel, and the lights in the room flickered slightly and then steadied. Cole glanced at Tobias, and there was no movement, save for the slight rise and fall of his chest. His shallow breaths continued to lightly fog the glass door of the pod.

He keyed in the command to shut down Tobias's treatment and open the pod. A series of valves released bursts of air with a hiss, and a low beeping began slowly and sped up before stopping altogether. The lighting inside the pod switched from green to red, and the lights in the command center flickered once more.

The countdown started, and a cold mechanical voice echoed throughout the empty room. Cole unhooked his hilt from his belt and kept his gaze fixed on Tobias, watching for any sign of movement.

"Five."

The lights flickered outward from the pod in a ripple, and Cole shifted his weight uneasily.

"Four."

Cole activated his sword, its slender metal blade unfolding and clicking into place. His grip tightened on the hilt.

"Three."

Sparks shot from several places along the ceiling as all the lights cut out with a crack. Cole stepped back into a ready stance, bathed in the red light from the pod.

"Two."

Tobias's eyes snapped open, and their cold gray stare caught Cole off guard. An instant later, the glass door of the pod shattered and broke from its hinges. The blast wave showered Cole with broken glass before snatching him off his feet and sending him hurtling across the room through several of the remaining glass panels and into a bank of consoles.

The computerized voice, now distorted, crackled in.

"O-o-one . . ."

Tobias stepped slowly from the pod, his bare feet crunching the broken glass beneath them. As he walked farther from the pod, the leads and tubes that had once been attached to him began to pop off one by one and were left in a tangled mess on the floor.

He took a few deep breaths, and with every one, he felt his heart rate slow and his senses heighten. His muscles tensed, and his skin was soaked with sweat.

A groan drew his attention back to Cole, who was just starting to stir.

A low, sinister chuckle escaped Tobias's mouth.

"Glad you could make it, Cole."

TWENTY-SEVEN

"WHAT A PITY that you've arrived on your own," Tobias said as he stepped closer to Cole. "I would have so enjoyed ticking a few more of your friends off my list, but I guess this will have to do."

Tobias lunged forward and planted a boot squarely in Cole's stomach. The force of the kick drove Cole back into the console he had hit moments earlier. Tobias crouched down and grabbed Cole by the throat. For a long moment, he simply stared into Cole's glazed-over eyes, and then, with a slight chuckle, he hoisted him to his feet.

"We've been dancing around this for a lot of years, boy," Tobias said, as he tightened his grip and Cole struggled to break free. "But there's no running from it now. It's time to find out if you can really be the man Martiss kept insisting you were—or if you're the man I've known you were all along."

Cole lashed out with a strike and caught Tobias in the chest, causing him to relinquish the hold on his throat. "What are you talking about?" Cole said, catching his breath.

"Born leader or born killer," Tobias said with a smirk. "I mean, history clearly shows you've got a preference, but Martiss was *always* banging on about how you could be more than that. I've always known who you are. *What* you are."

Cole's jaw tensed. "You did all this to prove a point?"

"No!" Tobias shouted. "You killed my son, Cole. Damn near killed me. Not to mention those poor bastards we were sent in there to save. All because you wouldn't get out of the way of your own ego."

"I was never going to let you rule."

Tobias laughed. "See? That's the shit I'm talking about. It wasn't up to you, Cole. It wasn't up to Martiss. No one back home wanted you to lead. *No one.* I was just doing what I had to in order to—"

Cole stood his ground. "And I did what I had to."

"You killed my son," Tobias snarled.

"Xan would have unders—"

Tobias shoved Cole hard back into the console. "Don't say his name."

Cole spotted his sword laying on the ground beside him out the corner of his eye and took a slight step toward it. "Come off it, Tobias. You were as much as father to that boy as—"

"He was my *son!*" Tobias snapped, and he threw a punch clean through the metal casing of a nearby console. In the moments after, his face went from utter rage to complete serenity. A single tear rolled down his cheek. "When I found out you were alive and that you had a *family?* Hell, that wasn't an opportunity I could pass up. No, sir . . . No, I could not let that stand."

Cole could see that Tobias was barely holding it together. He had to play this just right to regain the upper hand. There had always been a fine tipping point with Tobias between being so angry he was dangerous and so angry he was careless. Cole was standing right next to his sword now, and in a swift movement, he ducked down, grabbed it, and lunged for Tobias.

But Tobias was ready. He sidestepped the strike, grabbed Cole's wrist, and twisted it, the sword falling back to the ground. Tobias head-butted Cole hard and forced him back against one of the computer consoles.

"That was a nice try," Tobias said. "But if you think I'm going to let this end *that* easily, then you just haven't been paying attention."

Cole spat a gob of blood into Tobias's face. "Then why don't we just do this?"

Blood trickled down Tobias's forehead and dripped off the end of his nose. His eyes were wide and wild.

"I thought you'd never ask."

Tobias punched Cole in the stomach, grabbed him by the throat, and threw him toward the window. Mid-flight he hit Cole with a blast that propelled him across the room, through the plate glass, and down to the hangar below. As Cole dropped out of view, Tobias looked down and scooped up Cole's sword from the floor.

"You'll be needing this!" Tobias shouted as he hurled the hilt out the window after Cole.

Tobias began walking toward the shattered window as large sections of it continued to break away and fall down into the hangar below. On a small table to his right was his own sword, and he picked it up as he passed.

He paused at the edge of the new opening in the window and turned the hilt over and over in his hands as he watched Cole struggling to his feet far below.

"I'm going to enjoy this," Tobias said as he stepped off the edge.

Going through the window wasn't part of the plan, but that was how it turned out. Cole had been able to get his bearings enough during the fall to orient himself in a way that the impact wasn't so bad. He still hit hard, though, and as he skidded to a stop, he heard a clattering of metal. Cole got to his feet and found his sword laying just a few meters away on the hangar floor. Moments after he picked it up, Cole heard a thud and pounding footsteps approaching fast from behind. He spun at the last second to catch Tobias's blade before it met his neck.

Their blades clashed, and sparks spat from their edges as they tried to force each other backward. The small crews that had been tending to the fighters in the hangar scrambled at the sight of the ensuing fight and fled into the darkness. The deadlock broke as Tobias kicked Cole in the shin and pushed him back. He continued on the offensive and walked Cole backward into the center of the hangar. Tobias grinned as Cole seemed to be barely deflecting the onslaught of strikes, but unbeknownst to him, despite the barrage, Cole was in complete control.

Cole gave up only as much ground as he was willing to. He had to let Tobias think he had the upper hand once again and wait for the time to strike. Cole set his feet and held his position, dodging and weaving Tobias's attacks with ease. As Tobias's shimmering blade buzzed and crackled past Cole's ear, he saw that the force of the wild swing had begun to throw Tobias off balance. Striking quickly, Cole hit out with his fist and landed a solid blow to Tobias's midsection, right where his wounds had recently healed. The impact staggered him. Cole spun and struck Tobias in the side of the head with his elbow and followed it up by dropping to the ground and sweeping the older man's legs out from under him.

Tobias groaned, rolled over onto all fours, and spat out a glob of blood. "I knew you were just playing, boy."

Cole drove his boot into Tobias side. "Yeah, well, playtime's over."

The force of the kick, enhanced by Cole's implants, sent Tobias skidding across the hangar floor before he rolled through and regained his footing. Giving him no reprieve, Cole rushed after him and swung hard for his neck. However, Tobias was able to turn to meet him just in time to block the strike, and as their blades clashed together, another shower of sparks shot out.

This time Cole pushed the attack and forced Tobias back toward his own ship. With each strike, he could feel him getting weaker. Tobias hadn't been in the pod long enough to properly recover from his injuries, and Cole knew that was how he was going to beat him.

Cole ducked under an errant swing from Tobias and drove his free fist right into his gut yet again. Blood sprayed from Tobias's mouth as he doubled over and fell to his knees, hands clutched tightly to his midsection. Cole deactivated his sword and hung it on his belt. He walked over to Tobias, and without blinking, he delivered a hard right hook to the side of Tobias's head that dropped him to the ground.

The sound of rapid footsteps smacking against the hangar floor caught Cole's attention, and he looked up to see Ram running toward them.

"Ram, stay back," Cole shouted. Ram complied, but Cole could see by the look on his face that he was, understandably, less than pleased.

It had only been a moment, but Cole's attention was drawn away just long enough for Tobias to retaliate. He sent a blast square into Cole's chest, throwing him hard into the hull of Tobias's ship. He dropped to the ground in a heap.

Ram snapped into action, raised his rifle to Tobias, and pulled the trigger, but the rounds never found their mark. Tobias simply stood, hand outstretched, with the rounds hanging in midair in front of him. A swift hand gesture sent the rounds flying back toward Ram, but they again stopped just short.

Ram froze at the sight of the rounds hovering in front of him. He wasn't game to move.

"Stay out of this," Tobias said in a tone that could not be argued with.

Tobias lowered his hand, and the rounds simply fell to the floor at Ram's feet with a rattle. Ram sharply let out the breath he'd been holding and watched as Tobias collected his sword and limped over to Cole's prone body.

Cole could hear the crackle of Tobias's blade as he approached and figured he only had a short time to come up with a plan. His head was ringing, but he found his way to his feet and unhooked his sword from his belt. As his vision cleared, he saw Tobias favoring one leg, his free hand clutching at his side.

"You look tired," Cole said with a chuckle.

"You look scared," Tobias said, his eyes unblinking.

"Of you?" Cole mocked. "I doubt it."

Tobias lunged, but Cole quickly sidestepped the strike and pushed him, almost sending him to the ground. Tobias came back again with a flurry, but each strike was parried and pushed aside with ease. Cole pressed the attack and dodged Tobias's labored counters. Every chance Cole got, he struck at Tobias's midsection and the vulnerable scars that spread across it. It wasn't long before the skin began to part and blood slowly seeped from the wounds.

With every desperate swipe of his sword, Tobias got weaker, and with every strike from Cole, he faltered a little more. His torso was now covered with deep bruising, and the blood continued to pour.

Cole stepped back to avoid another strike, but he needn't have bothered, as Tobias's sword flailed harmlessly to the right.

Cole looked at Tobias as he wavered.

This has gone on long enough.

He thrust his hand hard into Tobias's throat and staggered him.

He spun, and the hangar lights glinted off his blade.

With all his strength, he drove his blade back and it bit deep into Tobias's side.

The rush of air escaping Tobias's lungs was the only sound he made.

Without looking back, Cole pulled the blade out, and the blood glistened in the light. He heard Tobias crumple to the floor behind him, but that wasn't the only sound in the hangar.

A low rumble rose from somewhere outside, and Cole turned to see a sleek shuttle glide into view. It slid into the hangar, touching down among the fighters and refueling tanks with a soft thud.

Cole stared as the boarding ramp lowered and two dozen armed Federation troops hurried out, taking up defensive positions around the shuttle. Following closely behind them was Oren.

"Nice of you to join us," Cole called out.

"Thought you might need some help," Oren shouted back.

"I think I've got it," Cole replied calmly as he held up a hand to wave off Oren and his men. A short nod from Oren was all the response he needed, and he watched as Oren's men all stood down and lowered their weapons.

Cole turned his attention back to Tobias to find that he had struggled to his knees. He deactivated his sword and crouched down to get face-to-face with the man who had taken everything from him. Blood was trickling from the corner of his mouth, and his right eye had begun to swell shut. His head rocked back and forth like he was trying to keep conscious. Cole could see now that he had beaten him. Broken him.

"Do you know why I did it?" Cole asked.

Tobias spat at Cole, but it fell short of the mark.

"Because even then I could see it," Cole said. "I could see that you were just a sad old man trying to do whatever he could to hold on to something that wasn't his. You couldn't stand that Martiss chose me over you, so you tried to destroy everything that we built."

Tobias groaned, and he kept his eyes on the floor.

Cole shook his head. "You're unstable. Angry. The rule of a madman wasn't something I was willing to submit our people to."

Tobias laughed weakly.

"There's one thing I still don't understand," Cole said as he crouched down in front of Tobias. "Was this your plan all along? To die on some forsaken rock? Hasn't really worked out great for you, has it?"

Tobias struggled to lift his head and look Cole in the eye. "How's it worked out for you?"

Cole punched Tobias hard in the stomach, and he let out a gasp of pain.

Tobias looked up at Cole and then around at Ram, Oren, and the Federation troops. He realized that he was surrounded and beaten.

A chuckle escaped his lips, and soon it turned to a deep, guttural laugh. Cole reached out and grabbed Tobias by the throat, silencing the laughter. "Get up."

Cole stood up and activated his sword, and after a long hesitation, Tobias struggled to his feet.

The blood loss had left him woozy, and he suddenly fell forward into Cole and latched on, his bony hands scrambling for a hold. He coughed and sprayed blood onto Cole's chest.

"Finish it, golden boy," Tobias said, his voice barely a whisper.

Cole stared into Tobias's cold gray eyes, and he could see that he actually wanted to die. He wanted Cole to kill him.

Cole pushed Tobias away and stepped back.

Tobias fell to the ground and rolled onto his back. Blood spattered from his mouth as he continued to laugh and groan.

Cole stared down at Tobias and let out a deep sigh. Tobias had reminded him on Ferris that he hated when a job was too easy, and he was right. He had already killed him, but to speed up that process in any way would be too easy—

For Tobias.

"No. You have to suffer."

Cole dropped the hilt of his sword to the floor.

He turned his back on Tobias and walked away.

It was done.

"You all right?" Ram asked as he jogged over to meet Cole.

Cole just nodded in reply and finally allowed himself to breathe.

"You know I'm going to kick your ass for what you did, right?" Ram said. The words were serious, but his expression was anything but.

Cole laughed. It hurt. "Can you at least give me a couple of days?"

"For you? Absolutely." Ram placed a hand on Cole's shoulder. "You did good."

"Yeah, well, I don't know about good, but at least—"

"Well, shit," Ram said, a slight smirk beginning to spread across his face.

Something had caught Ram's eye across the hangar, and as Cole followed his gaze, he saw it too: Kira.

She had been standing behind the group of Federation soldiers, who seemed completely oblivious to the fact she was even there. When she realized she'd been spotted, she broke into a run toward Cole and met him in an embrace that staggered him a little.

"Easy, kid," Cole said, wincing in pain.

Kira pulled back. "Oh, sorry."

"What are you doing here?" Cole asked. He looked over to Oren for the answer, but he just laughed.

"Well, I guess now she's put one over on both of us," Oren called out.

Cole returned his attention to Kira. "You all right?"

"Yeah, you?"

Cole offered a half smile. "I'm fine."

"Sure you are," Kira said, looking him up and down.

She continued to look around the hangar, and that was when she noticed that something was missing or, rather, someone. "Where's Sol?"

Cole hesitated. She could see in his face that he'd give anything to not say the words. She'd seen that look before, so she knew what was coming.

Ram stepped past Cole and put his hand on Kira's shoulder. "Kira, he's—"

Before he could finish, Kira wrapped her arms around him. "You don't have to say it."

After what felt like an age, Kira let go and wiped away a tear that threatened to fall from her cheek.

She turned to look at Cole and instead found her eyes coming to rest on Tobias's crumpled body a short distance away. "Is he dead?" she asked, glancing back to Cole.

He shook his head. "Not yet. It'll be slow."

The damage had been done. Even though Conduits were resilient and the bleeding would slow in time, this was a death that Tobias would not be coming back from.

"Good." Her voice was cold.

Kira could feel her fingernails digging into the palms of her hands as she stared once again at Tobias's motionless body. She was glad that he would die, but she wished more than anything that she could have been the one to do it, that she could have avenged Gregor, that she could have just—

She felt a hand in the small of her back, and it snapped her out of her reverie. She had unconsciously been walking toward Tobias and was now being guided back to Ram.

"Watch her," she heard Cole say before he turned and headed to meet Oren.

"You all right?" Oren asked.

Cole sighed. "Everyone keeps asking me that."

They had met close to where Tobias lay, and for a moment, they said nothing, just looking at the broken man before them. His breathing was shallow, his skin pale, and even the slightest of movements caused a pained expression to flash across his face.

"It is truly what he deserves," Oren said, breaking the silence. He reached out and placed his hand on Cole's shoulder. "A quick death would be a mercy."

Cole took his gaze away from Tobias and looked at Oren. There was an intensity in his eyes he had not seen for a long time.

"After everything that has been done," Oren continued. "This is the only way this can end."

Cole felt Oren's hand tighten on his shoulder.

"Thank you, Cole."

The faint clicking of metal locking into place was quickly drowned out by the thrumming of his pulse rushing through his ears. Cole didn't hear the crackle of the blade nor did he feel it as it pierced his side.

Time slowed.

The blade twisted.

The electricity coursing through his body held him firmly in place.

Kept his eyes from closing. Forced him to look upon Oren's face—a face that remained unmoved, emotionless.

But his eyes . . .

In Oren's eyes, Cole saw a rage that burned with the fire of a thousand suns.

A rage held for far too long.

A rage set free.

TWENTY-EIGHT

TIME AND THE world hung frozen around Cole.

Soon, motion returned to his vision, but it was slowed. It seemed stretched somehow.

Everything in his being told him to react, to do something, *anything*—but all he could do was look.

He found himself staring down at the blade buried hilt-deep in his midsection—

Oren's blade.

Blood began to slowly seep from the wound and drip silently onto the floor.

He felt a dull ache as the blade was withdrawn. It glistened in the light. Cole staggered back a step and lifted his head to look once more at Oren. He saw Oren's eyes dart to the side.

Somewhere behind him, he heard muffled shouting, and through watering eyes, he saw Ram and Kira rush past him toward Oren. And yet he could only watch as Oren raised a single hand to Ram and sent him flying out of view. Kira had her blade drawn, and to Cole's surprise, as well as Oren's, she closed the gap quickly. Oren was only able to block her strike at the very last second. Any later and she would have taken his head. As it was, he was left with a fresh cut on his cheek.

With a look of mild bemusement on his face, Oren quickly took advantage of Kira's forward momentum, struck her hard on the back of the neck, and dropped her to the ground unconscious.

Oren raised a hand and motioned to the troops gathered across the hanger. They hurried over, and after a short exchange of words, they picked up Kira, along with her sword, and carried her away into the belly of the awaiting shuttle. As they got farther away, the roaring in Cole's ears subsided, and he could hear the distant sounds of their boots on the hangar floor.

Time settled into its normal rhythm, and yet Oren remained unmoved. Throughout the entire skirmish, he hadn't taken a single step, and even now, he stared at Cole, exceedingly calm.

Cole reached down to his abdomen and felt the wound Oren had left him with. It was deep, but already the bleeding had seemed to slow, so perhaps it wasn't as bad as he first thought.

"You needn't worry about that," Oren said, breaking his long silence. "I didn't hit anything vital."

The suddenness of his voice caught Cole off guard, and he could offer nothing but a blank stare in reply.

Oren sighed and deactivated his sword. He hung it on his belt before the blade even finished collapsing in on itself.

"You're no doubt a little confused, yes?" he asked in a disturbingly even tone.

Before Cole could respond, Oren grabbed him by the back of the neck and turned his head to look out the gaping mouth of the hangar bay. There in front of him was the broken and crumbling second spire, lit up like a beacon in the ever-deepening night. The shadows cast by the lights from below highlighted the pockmarked and deeply scarred surface of the structure.

Cole tried to look away from it, but Oren tightened his grip, and suddenly he was beside him, right in his ear.

"*Yanis Safarin*," Oren hissed.

Cole's heart skipped a beat.

"*Alaria Saf—*" Oren's voice caught in his throat as he said her name.

Oren released his grip, and Cole's legs went from under him as he fell to the floor.

Cole couldn't find the air to breathe.

No.

Two scars on Cole's back began to burn, and as he stared at the ground beneath him, he feared the fire would consume him.

Oren crouched before Cole and grabbed him by the jaw, forcing him to look him in the eye. Cole could see tears threatening to break in Oren's eyes, yet his face remained unmoved.

Cole coughed. "Y-you're Aam—"

"Aamon Safarin, yes."

"But Aamon disappeared. It's not—"

Oren tightened his grip on Cole's jaw, silencing him. "You were supposed to rescue them. *Protect* them."

Cole could feel Oren's hand shaking.

"I-I'm sor—"

Oren's eyes flashed with wordless anger, and he pushed Cole's face away in disgust. As quickly as it had appeared, the emotion slipped from Oren's face once again.

"You honestly think I want an apology? From you?" Oren asked, his tone indignant, his face twitching ever so slightly. He rose to his feet and turned away from Cole to face the opening of the hangar, to face the spire.

"There was nothing I could do. I had no—"

Oren could contain his anger no longer. He whirled to face Cole, eyes ablaze.

"Nothing you could do?! *Nothing?*" Oren bellowed. He pointed emphatically at Tobias's near-motionless body. "You stood there and *watched* as that madman slit my father's throat."

"Oren, I—"

"You *willingly* set off those explosives. You watched them *tear* her apart. You—" Oren's voice caught once again.

Cole sighed deeply and straightened. "You're right. I did. But Oren, it's not that simple—"

"It is *exactly* that bloody simple!"

"I'm not denying what happened," Cole said, his voice even and measured. "All I'm saying is you can't possibly have the full story. Because if you've only gotten Tobias's side of things, there's a lot you don't—"

The look of complete pity on Oren's face stopped Cole short.

"Oh, Cole, give me a little bit of credit. This ball was rolling *long* before he entered the picture." Oren began to pace slowly around Cole. "I read the reports, Cole, the ones from the Federation recovery teams."

"Reports aren't always reliable. You of all people should know that."

"Are you really trying to talk your way out of this? The reports were more than thorough. Combined with the tapes, it all started to become clear."

"Tapes?"

"They were beyond my clearance level at first, but I knew I had to see them. So for years I worked and I clawed my way to them, so that I could finally . . . finally put a face to the phantom that haunted me all these years."

Oren stopped in front of Cole but did not look at him.

"Imagine my surprise when I finally watched the tapes and the face that I saw . . . was yours." Oren turned and offered a sad smile. "My *best* friend."

Oren let out a sigh that sounded as though it was borne more from frustration than anger.

"No, I know what happened that day, Cole—all of it. Do you honestly think I would have done *all* this?" Oren held his arms out to his sides as if trying to encompass his achievement. "That I would have gone to *all* this trouble without proof?"

Cole sat back on his feet, slumping slightly, still clutching the wound in his side.

All this? Cole thought.

"You know me better than that, Cole," Oren said. "You know that I . . ."

But Oren's words fell on deaf ears. Cole's attentions had been driven internally, as his mind worked overtime trying to work out just how deeply Oren's retribution had run.

There it is.

Granted, it had taken a while longer for it to register than he had expected, but the look in Cole's eyes was exactly the one Oren had waited all these years to see: confusion and despair.

"Everything's falling into place, is it?" Oren said calmly as he took a step back to take it all in.

The anger had dissipated quicker than he'd anticipated. After building up in containment for so long, he was afraid that it would consume him when unleashed. However, he now found that he was able to take that anger, that hatred, and turn it into a focused resolve to make good on the promise he made by his parents' graveside all those years ago.

Oren felt a thin smile begin to creep into the corners of his mouth. To Cole, it probably came across as smug, but Oren couldn't care less.

He'd earned this. He deserved it.

It was owed.

After what felt like an age, Cole finally spoke: "Why not just kill me and be done with it?"

Oren stood before Cole and looked down on him.

I would have loved to, believe me. However . . .

"Like I said: a quick death would be a mercy. You had to suffer for what was done. For what *you* did. You had to feel every *bit* of the pain that they felt. That *I* felt. Every *second* of it. No, this could not end until I had taken *everything* from you."

Oren took a deliberate step closer to Cole.

"Your men. Your career."

It really is quite remarkable how quickly you threw it all away.

As Oren watched Cole's mind go into overdrive, he let the smile grow a little wider. Just a little.

All you needed was a little . . . push . . .

"Your family."

Cole's eyes flashed with a fire equal to Oren's own, but it was of little consequence to him. Seemingly fueled by the mounting rage inside him, Cole began to struggle to his feet.

It's a shame, really. I would have given anything to be the one to have taken them from you, but it was too risky. Oh well, you can't always be the one holding the blade.

Cole took a step toward Oren and now stood over him.

"*Nate.*"

The anger in Cole's face dropped away and gave way to a mix of shock and confusion that pleased Oren to no end.

Oren's smile widened just a little more. "Oh, the look on your face."

Honestly, if you had any idea how hard it was to pull that off, I almost think you'd be impressed.

Behind him, Oren heard the boarding ramp to his shuttle close with a hiss, and as the engines cycled up and it left the hangar floor, he saw that Cole had noticed it as well.

"And now, the girl."

Cole's eyes went wide as he heard the implication in Oren's voice. "If you so much as touch a hair on her head, I'll—"

"Oh, she won't come to harm. I gave you my word on that, remember?" Oren leaned in toward Cole. "And like you said, Cole, above all, I am a man of my word."

And I said I would take everything.

"Ah, of course," Oren said as he abruptly took a step to the side and motioned grandly to where Tobias remained. "How could I forget? The man who, without him, none of this would have been possible: Tobias Navarr."

Somehow the smirk spread across Oren's face seemed to widen.

Oh, the things that you will find . . .

Before he could suppress it, a rattling laugh sprung from Cole's throat. It belied the anger building inside him.

"You're kidding yourself if you think I give a shit what happens to him," he said, his voice shaking. "He's nothing to me."

For a moment Cole studied Oren's face, searching for any sign that this was just some play, some *diversion*, but he found nothing. Oren's face remained fixed in a self-impressed smirk.

Cole placed his hand on the hilt of his sword. "You smug son of a bitch, this is between you and me now. He doesn't—"

"Oh, Cole," Oren said, cutting him off. "You don't even see it . . . do you?"

In the blink of an eye, Oren struck out and buried a fist squarely in Cole's stomach. And as the air rushed out of his lungs, Oren grabbed him by the back of the neck, dragged him to where Tobias lay, and forced him to his knees.

"Look at him," Oren hissed in his ear.

"What?"

Oren's grip tightened, and he shoved Cole's face close to Tobias's.

"Look at him!" Oren screamed, and he relinquished his grip.

Released, Cole nearly fell forward onto Tobias, but he was able to catch himself. Tobias's breathing was shallow and labored, and it was punctuated every now and then by a haggard cough that sent blood and spittle spattering across his face and the ground beneath him.

Tobias's gaze was vacant, and his barely blinking eyes looked right through Cole as though he were staring at something several light-years away. In all the years Cole had known him, there had been a fire burning behind those eyes, a spark, but now it lay dormant.

No anger. No fear. No malice.

Stripped of all emotion, Tobias's eyes seemed brighter, clearer somehow. He blinked slowly and then, seeming to finally notice Cole, turned his gaze to him. The light caught his eyes as he turned his head, highlighting their pale gray and . . . flecks of green?

"Your mother was right, Cole," Oren said calmly. "You do have his eyes."

No.

Words failed him. For a moment, it felt as though his heart might fail him too. It wasn't possible. It couldn't be. He wanted to deny it, to cast the thought from his mind, cast the very notion from reality.

But he couldn't.

From somewhere deep within himself, it rang true.

All their lives they had drifted in and out of each other's orbits, like a pair of planets being drawn slowly into the white flame of a star.

As those flames now licked at their heels, Cole couldn't help but stare at Tobias's face: his father's face. He looked for some kind of recognition, some hint of awareness of what was happening, what had been said.

But there was none.

Had he known all along?

Despite his instability, Cole knew what family meant to Tobias, and he couldn't believe that he would willingly murder his own granddaughter.

He was a pawn. A pawn in Oren's sick game, just as Cole's family had been.

Shuffled into place at the whim of a vengeful son.

Cole leaned back on his feet and sighed deeply.

He had killed his father.

He had killed his brother.

His wife and child were gone.

The crackle of electricity cut the ensuing silence as Oren drew his sword and activated it. "Now you know my pain."

Oren was the last of his family. Just as Cole was now the last of his.

"Cole," Oren said. "You are my best friend, *truly.*"

Cole caught sight of his hilt in the corner of his eye, laying just a few feet away.

He was the sole survivor.

The only one left who could avenge them all.

"I wish this could have gone differently."

Cole was momentarily caught off guard by the seemingly genuine sadness in Oren's voice—but only for a moment. He rocked back on his heels and attempted to draw as much strength from his implants as he could muster. The bleeding had slowed almost entirely now, and the adrenaline flooding his system pushed the pain to the back of his mind.

In an instant, he pushed off with one foot and launched into a roll that finished with a long slide, leaving him positioned right where he had earlier seen his blade. He could hear

Oren's boots as they slapped against the hangar floor, rapidly increasing in pace as he closed the gap.

Cole scooped up his hilt from the cold floor, and before he even activated it, he spun on the ball of his foot and launched himself at Oren.

Moments later, there was a clash and grinding of metal and a bright shower of sparks.

TWENTY-NINE

THE INITIAL FLURRY of strikes launched by Cole were just that: a flurry. All his mustered strength seemed to evaporate in the face of Oren's defense. Each strike was deflected with an efficiency that Cole had never seen before. Nothing he could do could break the wall Oren had set in place.

Before long, Cole's arms began to feel heavy, as though his blade were made from lead, and each strike took more out of him than the counterstrikes Oren was dealing in return.

"Always rushing into things headlong, Cole," Oren said as he spun his blade with an arrogant flourish. "That's always been your problem. The amount of times you've—"

Cole had taken a few steps back to try and get a reprieve, and as expected, Oren had taken the time to gloat. Catching him mid-sentence, Cole lunged and struck out. The blade bit deep into Oren's bicep causing him to curse and turn away, out of Cole's range.

"That's always been *your* problem, Oren," Cole smiled. "Always too in love with the sound of your own voice."

Not wanting to give up any ground, Cole pressed the attack. Oren's defense had been weakened, but even fighting with one arm, he was still able to shed the majority of the force being directed his way with ease.

On one wayward cross-body slash, Cole misjudged his footwork and stumbled. It was all the opening Oren needed to take control. Efficient, brutal strikes peppered Cole, and it was all he could do to get out of the way of Oren's blade as it sang through the air. There wasn't a single wasted motion in Oren's attack.

Without warning, Oren lashed out and head-butted Cole so hard his vision blurred and momentarily went dark. It snapped back into clear focus as Oren buried a fist deep into Cole's midsection with a force that didn't seem possible.

The shock of the blow sent air rushing from Cole's lungs and blood along with it. His blade slipped from his grasp, and his knees buckled, sending him to the floor once again.

"You know, Cole," Oren said, "even after all this, I would have expected you to put up more of a fight."

As he gasped for air, Cole saw movement in his periphery. Ram had begun to stir and was now determinedly making his way into the fray.

"Ram!" Cole shouted, finding his voice. "Stay back! I-I've got this."

Oren laughed freely then. "Oh, you've 'got this,' do you?" He laughed again and turned to face Ram. "Ramses, does it look like he's 'got this' to y—"

Arrogance had once again foiled Oren's game plan. The moment he turned his attention away, Cole gathered his feet under him and launched himself upward. Returning the favor, his shoulder caught Oren square in the midsection, spearing him. For a brief moment, they both flew through the air before crashing down hard onto the metal floor.

Taking advantage of the impact, Cole was able to knock Oren's blade away from him, sending it tumbling to the ground.

They wrestled, each of them gaining an advantage then losing it, as elbows caught faces and fists left their marks. But after a quick strike to Oren's throat, Cole got control and began to rain down strikes on his face and body. It wasn't long before Oren's retaliations began to falter, and seeing his window, Cole wrapped his bloodied hands around his neck.

Cole watched as Oren's eyes grew panicked; he tightened his grip in response. He was so focused on watching the life slowly drain from Oren's face that he didn't see him reaching for his blade. He did, however, see the light glint off it as it sliced through the air, and unable to react in time, he felt it slice into his side and emerge from his back.

He felt Oren place a hand on his chest and send a blast thudding into it.

As he arced through the air, the wind rushing in his ears, he could see Ram charging toward Oren, only to be met with a similar fate. Then, as he tumbled, a support beam rushed into his field of view. Then, darkness.

Ram came skidding to a stop, aided only by a stack of crates that he was now digging himself out of. By the time he got the last crate free and rose to his feet, he saw Oren closing in on Cole once more. His blade was drawn, and there was a purpose in his step that could only mean he was ready to end things.

He knew he wouldn't be able to get there in time, but Ram wasn't one to let inevitability get in the way, and without a second thought, he took off at a dead sprint toward Oren.

He noticed the sound first: a low, distant grumble slowly rising in clarity. Something about it told him to slow his approach, and it was clear that Oren had heard it too, as he'd stopped altogether.

With a roar, and a plume of smoke trailing it, the *Havok* hefted itself into view and began to scrape, somewhat askew, into the hangar.

However, before Ram was given a chance to register this, the hangar erupted with flashes of light as the *Havok* opened fire. Rounds hammered the ground between Oren and Cole, causing Oren to dive out of the way. The hull of the *Havok* clipped a support beam, which turned it abruptly, throwing a volley of rounds off course.

In a blinding flash, it became quickly apparent that the errant shots had hit several of the fuel tanks that lined the walls of the hangar. A chain reaction of explosions rocked the room as equipment and what remained of several ships were scattered in ruins.

When Ram finally poked his head up from behind the service vehicle he'd chosen for cover, he saw that the *Havok* had ground to a halt not too far away from Cole, who was just now getting to his feet.

Oren, on the other hand, was nowhere to be seen.

Ram winced as a burst of static blasted in his ear.

"Right then, you two, what've I missed?"

Ram could hardly believe his ears, but looking up to the *Havok*'s cockpit, there he was. "You beautiful son of a bitch!"

"Hey! That's my mother you're talking about." Sol's voice sounded pained but happy.

"I'm not wrong, though, am I?"

"Not in the slightest."

"How the hell—"

Another voice cut in over the comms. "I'd hate to break up the moment, guys," Cole said, still trying to catch his breath, "but I could use a hand."

When Ram reached him, Cole was leaning heavily against a support beam and seemed unable to hold his own weight.

"How're things over here?" Ram said, concern crossing his face.

Cole forced a smile. "I'm fine. Absolutely A-OK."

"Oh, so you'll be fine to get back to the ship on your own then? I think I tweaked my back a bit and—"

"Don't be an asshole . . ."

Ram got under Cole's shoulder and led him back to the *Havok*. "Wouldn't dream of it."

As they approached the ship, the boarding ramp lowered with a shower of sparks and Sol came limping down toward them.

"What happened there?" Ram called out.

"What *this*?" Sol replied, exaggerating his limp for effect. "You wouldn't believe it, but a ship fell on me."

Ram feigned surprise. "You don't say?"

"Yeah, hell of a thing."

"Is the ship all right?"

Sol delivered a quick right to Ram's arm, eliciting a satisfying yelp. "The old girl held up all right. Had to seal off half the ship, but she runs . . . just barely."

"How are you here?" Cole asked.

Sol got under Cole's other shoulder. "Turns out free-falling to the ground can knock some things loose. Like an escape pod."

Ram laughed. "Must have knocked something loose up top there, Sol. That was some of the worst flying I've seen out of you in years."

"It was a hell of a landing, though, wasn't it?" Sol said as he brushed some dirt off his shoulder.

"You crashed."

"All right, *crash*-landing."

"You crashed."

Sol shot Ram a hopeful look. "Would you settle for a *controlled descent?*"

Before Ram could answer, Cole chimed in. Something had caught his eye off to their right. "Sol, you said you had to seal off some of the ship?"

"Yeah, we wouldn't get off the planet otherwise."

"Is the med bay still up?"

"It is."

They had reached the ship now, and Cole shrugged off the assistance and took a few steps away from Ram and Sol. "How many pods are up?"

"One for sure, two in a pinch."

"So two pods?"

"I'd have to rejig a few things, but yeah, two pods."

"Look, Cole, I'm fine, really," Ram said.

Cole turned and looked past them out into the hangar beyond. "I need you to do something for me, and I need you to not question it."

"What do you need?" Ram asked.

"I need you to get Tobias on board and into a pod."

Sol's mouth fell open. "I'm sorry, what?"

Ram was similarly confused. "Why in the hell would we—"

Cole cut them both off. "Not now. Just, please trust me. There's no time. I'll explain everything later, but just get him in there."

Ram furrowed his brow. "Cole, what's this about? We can't just—"

"Go!" Cole shouted, and he slumped back against one of the *Havok's* landing struts.

Ram and Sol both rocked back on their heels, exchanged looks of hesitation and disbelief, and then turned and headed away from the *Havok*.

Sol cleared his throat. "Look, I'll be the one to say it . . . he's off his gourd."

Ram ignored him and continued walking to where he'd last seen Tobias, and sure enough, there he was. Whether it was under his own steam or he was thrown by an explosion, Tobias was now lying on his side.

When Ram reached down and hooked Tobias under the arms, it was clear he was unconscious or near enough as to make no difference. There was no fight left in the man.

"Grab his feet, Sol."

Instead of complying, Sol just stood there, looking back and forth between Tobias and the area of the hangar by the *Havok*. After a short while, he spoke. "He wasn't here."

"What?"

"Shithead here," Sol said, pointing at Tobias. "He wasn't here when I was shooting at him. He was . . . over there."

Ram sighed. "Right, well, that's probably because you weren't shooting at *him*."

"Then who the bloody hell *was* I shooting at?"

"Oren."

Sol's jaw went slack. "Oren? *Our* Oren?"

"He's not *my* Oren."

"I was shooting at Oren Rhey'll."

"Sure were."

"Ramses. *Why* was I shooting at Oren Rhey'll?"

"We can discuss that as much as you like when we get back to the ship, but for now, and I don't know about you, but I'd like to get away from all the *explode-y* things, so if you could kindly *grab his feet*, we can get going."

Getting the hint, Sol reached down and helped lift Tobias up. "I have clearly missed quite a lot."

"You're not the only one."

The main lights in the hangar had now gone out completely, and the room was lit only by the fires that were quickly spreading. As Cole watched Ram and Sol head back to the ship carrying Tobias, he couldn't help but feel like he was making a mistake.

Was he now really trying to save the man that tore his life to shreds?

Or, on some subconscious level, was he simply trying to save his father?

Was he even trying to *save* him?

Cole knew that it was entirely possible that Tobias wasn't his father, that Oren was just playing mind games. At the same time, though, it was just as possible that it was true.

If Tobias was truly his father, had he known? Family and legacy were the most important things to Tobias. As unstable as he was, Cole couldn't believe that he'd willingly murder members of his own family.

So maybe he didn't know. Maybe Oren really did manipulate the entire situation.

In some way, that would make Tobias a victim as well, wouldn't it?

No. Cole needed answers, plain and simple. Having Tobias alive was a means to an end.

Nothing more.

Cole shook the thought away. He couldn't afford to dwell on it. They needed to get out of there.

It wouldn't be much longer. Once they were away, there'd be plenty of time to sort everything out.

He met Ram and Sol a short distance from the ship. "He alive?"

"Just," Ram replied. Cole could see the disappointment on his face.

"All right. Get him on board."

"Look, are you sure about this? Because I'd just as happily drop this sorry piece—"

A loud scraping sound at the far end of the hangar drew the trio's attention.

Sol's mouth fell open again. "What in the nine circles of . . . ?"

A large chunk of debris—what looked to be the remains of a scouting craft—was slowly raising from the ground and drifting off to the side; in its wake, a shadow backed by flame.

Oren.

"Cole, don't," Ram said, sensing what his friend was about to do. "We can just go."

Without taking his eyes off Oren, Cole spoke. His voice was distant and calm: "He won't stop. If we leave now, he won't stop."

"Then we'll stop him," Sol offered. "*Together*. We can take another shot at this, just not now. It's—"

In the distance, the debris crashed to the ground, the sound reverberating throughout the chamber, and Oren began moving toward them.

"No," Cole said firmly, barely turning his head. "Get Tobias on board, and get the *Havok* ready to fly."

And with that, Cole broke from the group and began a slow, deliberate stride toward Oren.

Whatever protestations were thrown his way, he didn't hear them. They were just muffled noise in the background.

And so he pressed on.

The fires had begun to burn themselves out, and the low light threw shadows long across the floor.

The smell of smoke and burning fuel hung heavy in the air.

They were each battered and bleeding.

Both favored a leg as they approached each other.

Neither of them was armed.

They met in the middle of the hangar once more. They stood, unmoving, just a meter apart.

Oren breathed out deeply, breaking the long silence. "Not running?"

Cole shifted back into a ready stance. "I'm done running."

Oren chuckled. "Oh good, I don't much feel like chasing anyone at the—"

Before he'd even finished speaking, Cole launched himself at Oren. He caught him with a right to the chin, which staggered him. But only for a moment. Oren whipped back with an elbow that smashed into Cole's cheek, and Cole could feel the bone crack before he heard it.

They locked eyes, each of them knowing what was coming.

There was no elegance in what followed.

Back and forth they went. Again and again.

They didn't even bother blocking the other's moves.

Skin bruised and swelled and split.

Blood spattered.

Cole's eye had begun to close and the cut on Oren's cheek was a seeping gash.

But with each strike, the fight was leaving them. With each kick, their strength was failing.

Cole struck out with an uppercut, but his aim was wide, and Oren grabbed his wrist and wrenched it down hard. He followed by driving a knee deep into the stab wound in Cole's stomach, causing it to weep anew.

But by now, Cole was almost numb to the pain. It was just some dull sensation in his periphery. He planted both feet and pushed up as hard as he could with his shoulder, catching Oren under the chin. The force of the impact knocked both men to the ground and sent them sliding.

As they skidded to a stop, Oren rolled through and kicked with both feet, forcing the two of them apart once more.

"This ends now, Oren," Cole said.

Oren said nothing in reply. All he offered was a halfhearted smirk.

Just as he was about to re-engage and wipe that smirk off permanently, a glint of metal caught Cole's eye off to his right.

It was a hilt, Oren's.

But he'd waited too long. He knew that. He knew by now Oren would have followed his gaze and seen it too. And yet, Oren hadn't gone for it.

There was nothing else.

Cole dived for the hilt, slid for it, wrapped his hand around it, and . . .

It was gone.

Cole snapped his head to Oren, only to see the hilt fly into his hand.

As the blade extended, it seemed to shimmer with flame. And then it crackled to life.

Cole scrambled to his feet and looked around frantically for his own blade, or even Tobias's, but they were nowhere to be seen. They must have been scattered in the explosions.

The smirk on Oren's face widened to a smile.

As he approached, Cole had no choice but to back away.

Oren slashed wildly. He missed.

Cole seized the window and delivered a straight shot to Oren's midsection. He didn't even blink.

Oren pressed forward with another wayward swipe, and again Cole was able to duck under it. This time, though, Cole clamped Oren's sword hand underneath his arm, trapping it. He delivered another shot to Oren's ribs. And Oren laughed.

He laughed and then drove his forehead squarely into Cole's nose. He heard it crack, *felt* it crack, and almost instantly his vision exploded in a supernova of light.

Cole relinquished his grip on Oren's arm and staggered back, clutching at his face. His vision had returned, but it was in triplicate. He saw Oren raise the blade and bring it down.

Reflexively, all he could do was raise his arms in front of him and shield himself.

Chink.

Blood spattered onto his face as the shimmering blade bit deep into his forearms, and the sound of metal clashing with metal rang in Cole's ears. Electricity began to course through his body, freezing him in place. The framework in his arms had held, though he knew it wasn't a sustainable plan.

And he was right.

When Oren pulled the blade back for another strike, Cole was afforded a brief moment to move, and he was able to slip past the downward stroke that quickly followed. It flashed harmlessly through the air beside him, but then Oren struck up forcefully with the blade. There was no time to evade. In a clean strike, it parted flesh and bone and metal.

Cole could only watch as the lower portion of his left arm seemed to spiral away from him in slow motion, an arc of blood trailing it through the air.

I should have run.

The next strike came too fast, too swift to counter. Oren spun through the motion, maintained his momentum, and brought his blade back around in a wide slashing arc.

Cole felt his feet leave the ground, and yet he had not moved.

He began to drop forward, the floor rushing to meet him.

A powerful force halted his descent and flung his body through the air.

Moments later, he careened into the hull of the *Havok* and fell heavily to the floor below.

Still conscious, though fading in and out, Cole was able to shift onto his side. As he laid his head down on the cool metal floor, he could see Oren stalking toward him, backed by smoke and flame. He was dragging his blade behind him, the tip leaving a trail of sparks as he continued his executioner's march.

Cole's eyes were heavy, and each time they closed, Oren seemed to jump closer, like a specter.

He tried to move, to get closer to the ship, but he couldn't.

His legs didn't respond.

Now Oren stood over him. He felt a boot push him, and he rolled onto his back.

As he looked up at Oren, Cole expected to see that smug smirk spread wider than ever, and yet the face that stared back was cold, sullen, and . . . tired.

Oren exhaled slowly and placed the tip of his sword onto Cole's chest.

"Now, old friend, *now* this can end." With that, Oren began to slowly push the blade downward.

As steel pierced flesh, Cole's vision grew fuzzy and he screamed—or at least he thought he did.

. . . A heavy boot landed right by his ear. As a dark shape launched itself over his head, he realized the source of the scream . . .

Ram . . .

. . . Cole felt the blade pull away sharply and heard it clatter on the hangar floor. It was followed by a succession of thuds as Ram crashed into Oren and knocked him to the ground . . .

. . . Ram knelt over Oren, his fists going like pistons . . .

. . . Cole felt arms under his shoulders and saw Sol's face next to his as he was lifted from the ground. He felt like he was floating on air . . .

. . . Oren had gained the upper hand and had his hands around Ram's throat . . .

. . . Arcs of light began to ripple over Ram's body, and his pained screams cut through the fog of Cole's mind like a knife.

He fought against Sol's aid, such as he could.

Ram was dying.

Cole reached out to Ram with his remaining arm.

I can't let this happen.

He saw his fingers begin to tremble and then the shaking radiated like a wave down his arm.

His pulse beat loud and heavy like a drum in his ears.

Not again.

The shaking reached his vision, and at the fringes, it began to blur and fade.

The hair on the back of his neck stood on end.

Never again.

All at once he felt his strength leave him.

And the world went dark.

THIRTY

FOR A MOMENT, it was all Ram could do to just lie there and try to catch his breath. He blinked away the fuzziness from his vision and turned his head to see what he assumed was Oren lying motionless on the ground a good way across the hangar floor.

"Ram!"

The shout was distant but earnest. He followed the sound and was surprised to see just how far *he* was from the ship. Sol was attempting to lift Cole up from the boarding ramp, but he was struggling.

How did I—what the hell happened?

"Ram! You good?" Sol's voice cut through the fog once more.

Finding his voice and his feet, Ram replied: "I've felt better."

"Terrific. I'm thrilled. Now get your arse over here and help me get him on board. We need to move."

"I'll handle him," Ram shouted as he headed back toward the ship. "You just get that bucket of bolts of yours ready to fly."

Sol straightened. "My *bucket of b*—" Then he looked around at the sparking and smoking hull of the *Havok*. "Yeah, no, fair play on that one."

Ram scooped Cole up and slung him over his shoulder. It was a dead weight and his own battered body screamed at him in protest, but there was no time to waste. Bullets began to ricochet off the hull all around him as a large group of soldiers rushed into the hangar behind him, though they were soon drowned out by the roar of the engines as the *Havok* shuddered to life.

Ram cast one last glance back as the boarding ramp closed beneath him and saw Oren rising to his feet among the gathering troops.

Oren stood silently as the *Havok* wobbled into the air, turned, and scraped out of the hangar. He stood silently as the men and women he'd hired to protect the facility continued to fire into the empty air with complete futility.

He turned his back on the departing ship and was met with the sight of Captain Sharma running full tilt into the fray.

"Cease fire!" Sharma yelled. "Cease fire! What the hell are you all firing at? Stop it right now!"

Sharma stopped and stared around at the destruction before him. Fires still burned, structural beams hung limply from the ceiling, and several ships lay decimated. He was so entranced, or mortified, at the sight of it all that he didn't even notice Oren standing beside him.

"Give me your radio," Oren said flatly, holding out his hand.

Sharma jumped. "What?"

Oren grabbed the front of Sharma's tunic and pulled him close.

"Give me your—"

"Absolutely not!" Sharma shouted, clearly flustered. "I don't know who you think you are, but I'm under strict instructions to follow only Mister Navarr's orders. Now unhand me!"

Sharma attempted to pry Oren's hand away, but his grip held firm.

"And where, Tobold, do you think *his* orders come from?"

As Sharma's eyes went wide with recognition and his mouth fell open in search of words, Oren relinquished his hold.

"Oh! C-Commander Rhey'll, sir . . . I-I didn't recognize you with all the . . ." Sharma began gesturing awkwardly at Oren's injuries. "Are you all right?"

Oren's gaze threatened to burn a hole in Sharma. "*Radio.*"

"Yes. Yes, of course," Sharma said, and he sheepishly held out the radio to his commander.

Oren snatched the device and quickly dialed in a connection to his ship in orbit. "*Retribution*, this is Commander Oren Rhey'll. The *Havok* is attempting to flee. Scramble fighters. I want that ship disabled and brought on board."

Confused protestations could be heard through the static of the radio.

"You heard me! Do *not* let that ship leave the system!"

Oren ended the call and threw the radio away in disgust, inadvertently (though perhaps not) hitting one of the loitering soldiers in the back of the head.

A deep silence had formed in the wake of Oren's outburst, and it was Sharma who took the brave step of breaking it.

"Sir? What are our orders? That is . . . if you don't mind—"

Oren sighed deeply. "Clean up your mess, Tobold."

And with that, he turned and stormed from the hangar.

"Sol."

"Yeah, yeah. I see 'em."

They had just broken free of Epheria's atmosphere when a swarm of fighters began emerging from the belly of the *Retribution*.

Ram sat down heavily in the copilot's chair, his gaze fixed on the rapidly closing fighters. "How long?"

"Where we going?" Sol replied.

A flurry of rounds ricocheted off the hull as a cluster of fighters tore overhead.

"Anywhere but here, preferably."

"All right, gimme a sec," Sol said with one hand on the controls and another tapping away at a control panel. All the while, more fighters shot past the cockpit window, ripping off volleys of rounds as they went.

Ram gripped the armrests tightly. "I don't suppose you're planning on shooting back at all?"

"Would if I could, Ramses, but you see, I'm a little busy planning our escape and keeping us alive at the moment. Besides, you saw it earlier: the targeting's up the shitter."

"All right, all right, *sorry*. And here I thought you *meant* to just shoot everything in sight."

"I've still got my sidearm, so watch yourself."

The tension hung thick in the air as a warning siren began to ring out through the cockpit speakers. After a few final taps of the control panel, Sol returned both hands to the controls in time to swerve out of the way of an oncoming missile.

"OK, sixty seconds to the slip."

"The old girl gonna make it through?"

"Think of it like this," Sol replied, "if she doesn't, we sure as shit won't know anything about it."

"Well, *that's* comforting." Ram shifted uneasily in his seat, then stood up and took a long look out the front viewport at the growing silhouette of the *Retribution.* Then it dawned on him. "Oh shit . . ."

"What now?"

"Kira . . . she's still—"

"Ram, we can't." The sound of gunfire ripped across the hull of the *Havok,* and the dull thud of an explosion to the rear shook the cockpit. The lights flickered, and warnings began to flash across the displays. "We *really* can't."

Ram turned and slumped back down on a bench in the rear of the cockpit.

Sol sighed. "Look, we're not out of this yet, mate. We'll get her back."

There was no reply.

"We just need to . . . regroup and then . . . then we'll come back for her." Sol looked over his shoulder at Ram. "We'll give 'em hell."

No reply again. Ram just stared at the wall opposite him in a daze. Sol wasn't even sure he'd convinced himself, but he felt like he had to say something.

A beep from the console indicated that the calculations for the slip were just about complete.

"All right, slip in five, four, three . . ."

The lights dimmed and flickered once more as a violent shudder rolled through the cockpit and sparks shot out of several control panels. But it only lasted a moment; soon the view outside gave way to blackness as the *Havok* slipped between the cracks of space and left the *Retribution,* Epheria, and Kira far behind it.

THIRTY-ONE

THE DOOR SLID closed behind him with an almost imperceptible hiss, and for a moment, Oren Rhey'll stood enveloped in the darkness. The only sound was his own faintly wheezing breath, no doubt due to a broken rib or two.

"Welcome back, commander," an electronic voice said calmly. With it, somewhere in the black, a low hum spun up, and strips of light running along the borders of the room began to glow. They cast a sickly blue hue across the smooth metal walls and upward to the ceiling.

Oren inhaled sharply as he shrugged off his officer's jacket and dropped it at his feet. Dried, congealed blood had fixed it to a deep wound in his left bicep, and as it was pulled away, fresh blood began to trickle slowly to his fingertips.

He tossed his hilt on the large desk in the middle of the room and made his way over to a small bar. He was walking with a heavy limp, his right foot dragging on the floor behind him, and that bothered him. It bothered him that when he finally got to the bar, he had to steady himself against it as his vision temporarily blurred and his head pounded.

He was better than this.

He *knew* better.

And yet . . .

Managing with one hand, Oren poured himself a glass of a rare Thodorian spirit. It glowed a bright yellow-green in the dim light. He pushed off from the wall and ran his fingers over a small raised area on its surface. The well-concealed switch receded, and next to it, a panel slid aside to reveal a small holographic projector.

Oren took a sip from his glass, and it burned its way down as the image began to form in front of him.

Before him stood his parents, Yanis and Alaria, as he had always remembered them. It was an old recording and it had started to degrade in recent years, but Oren always marveled at how lifelike the projection was. And as always, his father's grim face stared back.

"I'm sorry, father."

He took another sip, larger this time, though it burned less.

And still his father stared back, his head turning ever so slightly over and over again. Whether it was there or not, Oren read disappointment in his eyes, over and over again.

"No, I know father. It won't happen again."

Oren's gaze shifted to his mother. Her face was just as grim, though it was pain more than disappointment that seemed to color her. A burden had weighed on her, on both of them, in the months before their deaths, and it was clear to Oren that the weight of it had weakened them.

It was a burden that, in death, had transferred itself to him. It was on him now and him alone to carry it and to show the—

Bzzt.

"Commander?" It was not the automated voice that broke the silence, but the small, self-assured one of Caroline, his ever-faithful assistant. Oren allowed himself a smile at hearing her.

"What is it?" he asked as he poured himself another glass.

"I have Misters Weaver and Rol here for you."

Oren gripped the glass tightly and said nothing.

"Sir?" Caroline prompted.

Oren exhaled deeply, wincing as he did so.

"Send them in."

The door opened silently, and they had barely entered before Oren heard the sound of a chuckle. Placing his glass calmly on his desk, Oren made his way to meet them.

"Well, you look like shit," Weaver said, still chuckling. His playful jab was met with silence and a stern look, and he began to shift uneasily on the spot. "Things go that badly?"

Oren remained silent and simply stared back at them, brow furrowed.

Weaver took a step forward. "Oren, what hap—"

"Do not assume that we are friends, Charles."

Oren's voice was forceful and without ambiguity, so Weaver stopped dead. He'd heard that tone before.

"You work for *me*, on *my* credits, of which you have been given a considerable amount for very little return thus far."

Weaver held his ground, but he was clearly flustered. Any arrogance or bravado that he'd had when he entered the room vanished. "I-I—"

"Do you know what I expect of people who work for me?" Oren held up a hand to silence Weaver before he'd barely opened his mouth to answer. "Obedience, Charles. Complete and unwavering."

"We've done everything you've asked," Weaver said, finding his voice again.

"Really?" A bemused smirk flashed on Oren's face. "Because I distinctly remember telling you to cease your pursuit of the girl."

Oren watched Weaver's eyes as he searched for an excuse, knowing full well he wouldn't find one that satisfied.

"In fairness, sir, the initial pursuit order was Federation issued and not part of our agreem—"

It was Oren now who took a deliberate step forward, and with his considerable height, he towered over Weaver. "Do you know what's most disappointing about all this, Charles?"

"I, uh—"

"Not *only* did you continue to pursue the girl, but in doing so you somehow managed, in your infinite wisdom, to get three good men killed."

Weaver cast a confused look at Jarak, who took an uneasy step forward to his captain's side in support.

"*Three*, sir?"

Oren locked Weaver with an intense stare and then suddenly, violently, lashed out to grab Jarak by the throat. His hand was bloody from the weeping cut on his arm, but it didn't affect his hold. Jarak tried to fight back, to pry away Oren's hand, but it was no good. In mere moments, Oren had crushed his throat, negating any opportunity for him to even scream.

And still Oren glared at Weaver. Unblinking. Unmoved.

He squeezed tighter and twisted, and the life went out of Jarak's body all at once. He let the moment linger to let Weaver take it in.

When Weaver finally found the courage to meet Oren's eyes again, Oren unceremoniously dropped Jarak to the floor.

"Three," Oren said calmly as he finally broke his stare and walked back to sit at his desk.

"Traske and Navarr escaped," Oren continued, his voice even and emotionless. "Barden and Dane are with them. Find them and bring them in."

Realizing he was in no position to disobey, Weaver gathered himself. "And the girl, sir?"

"She is no longer your concern."

"Yes, sir."

"Now take him and get out."

Oren picked up his glass and went to take a sip, but Weaver hadn't moved.

"What is it now, Charles?"

"I-I'll need a new team."

Oren scoffed. "If you need a new team, Charles, then find them and pay them yourself. I have done *more* than enough for you at this point."

"Of course, sir."

"Get out, Charles."

Oren watched with mild enjoyment as Weaver fumbled with dragging Jarak's body out of his quarters. After the door had shut and quiet had swept back through the room, Oren cast a glance back toward the holo portrait of his parents, their lifeless yet relentless glare still looking back at him.

He raised his glass in the air.

"Enjoy the show, Father?"

And with that, he downed the whole glass in one go.

Then he closed his eyes and let the darkness take him as it burned anew.

"All fixed?"

"Well, not *all* fixed, but yeah."

"So it's working?"

Sol leaned against a bulkhead next to Ram. "Cloak's at full, and I've powered down all other nonessential systems. We should be practically invisible. I would feel a whole lot better if we only had to power the one pod, though."

Sol looked tired, as expected. It had been several hours since their escape from Epheria, and he'd spent most of it making running repairs to a ship that was barely holding together. His limp had worsened, but he pushed through because tending to a sore leg meant they would likely all not make it.

Now they were effectively stranded in the middle of nowhere, as the slip drive had failed and the sub-lights were sputtering. All available power was being fed to the med bay and general life support.

Ram looked up at the pods in front of him. Cole was in bad shape, and he was honestly surprised when the readouts said there was a chance to save him. Preliminary tests also showed severe spinal trauma, and between the stab wounds and the missing arm, he'd lost a lot of blood.

In the pod beside him was Tobias, who wasn't in a much better state, and yet Ram could swear he still had that smug smirk plastered across his face.

"Look, I'm not gonna stop you," Ram said, "but you'd have to be the one to answer to Cole when he wakes up."

"Yeah, I know."

They sat in silence for a long while, the beeping and buzzing of the med pods gradually drifting in and out of sync.

Sol cleared his throat. "So Oren . . . he's a . . ."

"Would seem so."

"How exactly did we miss that?"

"Same way everyone else did."

Ram got up to check the readouts from Cole's pod. He was stable, for now.

"And Cole?" Sol asked.

Ram sighed. "Look, I have no idea. All I know is that Oren was on me. I heard shouting and next thing, Oren's halfway across the hangar and I'm skidding along after him . . ." Ram got up close to the pod and peered at Cole's face: cuts and abrasions, a broken eye socket gradually swelling shut. "And it didn't just *happen*."

"I can run some tests." Sol pushed away from the bulkhead and limped over to the pods. He pointed at Tobias. "Since we have to put up with this git, we might as well make him useful. Should be able to get a better idea of what's going on."

The quiet whirr of instruments inside the med pods joined the steady beeping as scheduled procedures started up. It would be many hours before either Cole or Tobias were out of the woods.

"We can't stay here, Sol."

"We can't leave either. Much as it pains me, the old girl's done. Even if I got the slip drive working, she wouldn't make it through again."

"So, what then?"

Sol turned to Ram and offered a hopeful smile, the first one the *Havok* had seen in weeks.

"Don't worry. I know a guy."

The cool of the metal floor felt nice against her face, though it did little to relieve the throbbing headache that was causing her vision to tremble with every stab of pain. Kira had been awake for some time, but it was only now that she'd taken time to properly rest.

The room was dark, but lit well enough for her eyes to adjust. A bed and general amenities lined the far wall, and that was about it, except for the force field or wall or whatever it was. She'd discovered it soon after waking as she'd gotten up and barreled straight for what she assumed was the door. However, halfway there she collided with something unseen and, from following it, learned that it ran the width of the room. There was no getting past it.

Two guards sat sentry by the door, and it turned out that the wall was soundproof as well, since they showed no response when she was screaming at them and banging on it. Kira wasn't even sure if the guards could see her. If they could, they would have also seen her repeated futile attempts to free herself of her bonds.

When she woke up, her hands were held fast in a pair of handcuffs unlike any she'd seen before, and she'd seen several in her short life. They were of solid construction, a single band of smooth white metal holding her wrists together, and there wasn't a seam or detail of note, save for a small display that showed a single meter.

Kira had become familiar with the meter.

The handcuffs were resistant to her abilities—or rather they encouraged her not to use them via an electric shock whenever the meter filled. Kira had found this out through thorough testing, hence the headache.

She didn't know how long she'd been there. It could have been hours, it could have been days. There was no way to tell.

Realizing she'd been drooling, she shifted her head out of the puddle, and as she did so, a bright light broke open across the floor from somewhere behind her.

Before she knew it, she was on her feet and at the wall.

She had to squint against the brightness, but she could see a silhouette in the doorway. Whoever it was said something to the guards that she couldn't hear, and they promptly left.

It was the first time she'd seen them move.

A few button presses later, and the door closed. As Kira's eyes adjusted, she finally saw who had come to visit her: Oren.

She was about to lunge at the wall when Oren grabbed one of the guard's chairs and began to drag it toward her. The sound of it scraping on the floor was so piercing, so deafening, it was like her ears were being exposed to sound for the first time. Clearly, whatever soundproofing was in place had been deactivated.

Oren came to a stop a few feet from the wall and sat down on the chair.

He was wearing civilian clothes, just a white shirt and pants, and he held himself with none of the confidence she had seen previously, slumping in the chair. His arms were bruised, one heavily bandaged. A split lip and more bruises and scrapes tarnished what had once been a proud and handsome face.

He looked lesser. Small even.

Kira smiled slightly as she noticed he'd left the cut she gave him on his cheek untended.

"That looks like it hurts," she said, laying on as thick a layer of sarcasm as she could muster.

For a long moment, Oren said nothing. Then he looked up at her and offered a smile, a sad smile.

"It does," he said, his gaze drifting around the room. "It all does, actually."

Kira was caught off guard by how he sounded. But however sad or broken he seemed, it didn't matter. She needed answers.

"Where's Cole? What did you do to him?"

"I don't know where he is. He and the others escaped."

"You tried to kill him!" Kira bashed her restraints hard against the wall.

Oren sat up a bit straighter and met Kira's eyes once more.

"Yes." He sighed. "I did."

"Why?"

"Kira, I will answer all of your questions in time. That one, however, will have to wait."

Oren watched as Kira began to pace back and forth behind the cell wall. If she was frustrated, she was no longer showing it. He was impressed with how she was handling this.

"So he's alive?" she asked.

"Last I saw."

Back and forth she went, deep in thought.

"And Tobias?"

"If he's not dead already, I imagine he soon will be. They took him."

Kira stopped pacing, stopped cold. "Who took him?"

He let the silence linger for just a moment too long before answering.

"Cole and the others. I saw Ramses and Solomon carry him on board."

Her eyes brightened.

"Sol's alive?"

"Yes, yes." Oren laughed. "He made *quite* the show of his return too."

Oren saw a small smile get cut short as confusion took over Kira's face.

"Why'd they take him?"

He let the question linger again and then shrugged.

"Tobias? I honestly have no idea why they'd want to, though I can't see it ending well for him."

Kira turned slightly, looking away from him. "And they're gone?"

"Yes. They escaped the system some time ago."

Now she turned fully away, hiding her face.

"They left me," she whispered.

Oren pretended not to hear, and by the time she turned back around, the smile on his face had dissipated. Her face, however, was a mask of determination. She stood firm at the wall and met his eyes with an unwavering stare.

"Let me go," Kira said. It sounded like her voice had dropped an octave.

Oren stood from the chair and walked the few steps to meet her at the wall. He looked down at her, emphasizing his considerable height advantage.

"Where would you go?"

She stared up at him, unfazed. "Anywhere but here."

He admired her spirit.

Without offering anything else in reply, Oren turned and walked back to the control console by the door. A few taps later and a panel opened up on the rear wall of the cell.

"You should eat something, Kira," he said without looking back at her. "You'll need your strength."

THIRTY-TWO

COLE AWOKE WITH a start. His heart was nearly beating out of his chest. He lifted his head slightly, but a sharp pain sent bursts of light cascading across his vision, and he quickly lowered it. It was then he realized he was no longer in bed, since when he put his head down, it was onto a pool of saliva and a cold metal floor.

Somewhere behind him, he could hear monitors beeping frantically. As his eyes began to adjust to the darkness, he saw what looked like trays of medical supplies scattered all across the floor. A chair sat within reach, but when he reached for its leg, he grabbed nothing at all. His arm just waived harmlessly past, and then he remembered: his hand was gone.

Somehow this realization caused him to feel the moment all over again—blades flashing in firelight, flesh and bone and alloy parting and breaking and rending, Oren's eyes watching it all with grim satisfaction.

He tried to roll over to get a better angle on the chair, but again, his vision exploded with light as pain shot down his spine. But the pain stopped at his lower back and lingered there. All he felt in his legs was a faint tingling sensation.

Cole gave over to the pain and tried to find some way to relax as the beeping from the monitors across the room intensified. The sound of rapidly approaching footsteps caught his attention, but he knew better now than to try and look for the source.

"Damn it, Cole."

The lights came on, and then Ram was standing over him.

"I'm OK," Cole offered, sounding as convincing as he could muster while lying face first in his own spittle.

"You know, you keep saying that, and amazingly, I still don't believe you." Ram offered a half smile as he looked at the scene and then picked Cole up and carefully sat him on the edge of the bed.

"No," Cole said as he fought weakly against Ram trying to lie him down.

"Just lie down. Doc said you're supposed to be off your feet till the implant takes."

"No more lying around, Ram. It's been weeks. I need some daylight. Please?"

Ram sighed deeply, then gave a halfhearted salute.

"Yes, sir. Daylight, coming right up."

It had been almost six weeks since their escape from Epheria. Whil T'Qar had sent a ship to collect them, and he had them secreted back to a safe house on Ferris. They were so far down that the sunlight had to be redirected with mirrors and supplemented with lighting during the day. It actually tended to be brighter at night.

It was a shame that the sun's warmth didn't quite make the journey. Still, it was nice for Cole to feel fresh air, or Ferris's nearest equivalent, on his face, rustling the fresh beard that he had grown in recovery. Cole guided his chair over to a spot by a railing that overlooked the main plaza below.

Beneath them, the hustle and bustle of everyone going about their business bubbled up. It was more than likely shady business—the surface of Ferris was a hotbed for crime families—but it was still business.

Cole could see that Ram was on edge, constantly looking around like he was just waiting for them to be spotted. "Calm down. No one knows we're here."

Ram relaxed, but only slightly, turning his back on the plaza and leaning on the guardrail. "Maybe so. But you know he has to be looking for us, right?"

"I'd expect nothing less. But if Whil's done his job, Oren's going to be looking for us everywhere *but* here."

"Yeah, because who'd be stupid enough to come back here, right?"

Cole laughed. His ribs still hurt. "Look, it'll be fine. This isn't permanent, you know. We'll be—"

The sound of sirens cut Cole short, and Ram leaped into action, his head nearly spinning off as he worked to locate the source. From across the way, a small one-man speeder tore across the plaza with several police craft in pursuit.

They passed, disappearing without incident.

"See? It's fine." Cole pointed to a nearby chair. "Now sit down."

Ram obliged, though he was still clearly on edge.

"How's Sol doing?" Cole asked.

"Poor bastard's running himself ragged, as usual."

"Any leads?"

"A few reported sightings in some of the outer systems. Nothing concrete."

"We'll find him."

For the first few weeks of their stay on Ferris, Tobias had remained unconscious in a med pod as he recovered. However, one night he woke up and had clearly taken umbrage with his captivity. He broke out and promptly vanished.

Sol had been the one on watch that night and, as such, blamed himself. He'd been working overtime with Whil to try and track him down ever since.

A strong breeze began to blow through the city corridor, cutting out most of the noise from down below.

"Do you think he knew?" Ram asked.

"Knew what?"

"That he was your . . . y'know . . ."

"My father? You can say it, Ram. No sense hiding from it now."

During their recovery, Sol had run tests on Cole's and Tobias's blood. He'd been trying to confirm Cole's status as a Conduit, which he was able to do, but he'd also found enough evidence to show that they were related. Combined with Oren's declaration on Epheria, it seemed an inescapable truth. However, since Tobias had found his pod to be less than inescapable, Cole had never had a chance to speak to him. He had no idea if he knew.

"I'd like to think that he didn't," Cole said. "But there's been a lot wrong with that man for a long time, so I don't know."

"And no doubt Oren did a number on him."

"Yeah. He's done a number on all of us."

With a final gust, the breeze dropped, and the noise from below drifted back up.

"Any change with Kira?" Cole asked.

Ram shook his head.

The *Retribution* hadn't left Epheria's orbit since their escape, and all signs showed that neither Oren nor Kira had left either. Over the last month, he'd rallied at least a dozen Federation cruisers to his location, forming an impenetrable wall around his flagship. With each passing day, the armada seemed to grow—and, inversely, the chances of rescuing Kira seemed to shrink.

But Cole wasn't going to let that stop them.

"We'll get her back. It's not going to be easy, but we—"

Several loud gunshots echoed up from below, and a silence formed among the crowd in their wake. Another flurry of shots morphed the silence into a panic, as the crowd realized what was going on and began to run.

Ram jumped to his feet. "I think that might be enough sunshine for today."

"Yeah, you're probably right."

Cole wheeled his chair away from the balcony and started to head in with Ram at his side.

"You think she'll be OK?" Ram asked as sirens began to approach in the background.

"Kira? She'll be fine. He won't hurt her."

"How can you be so sure?"

As they passed out of the light and into the relative darkness of the safe house, Cole smiled to himself.

"She won't let him."

Kira sat with her back against the side of the bed and stared down at the needle in the crook of her elbow. Her eyes followed the tube up to a bag of fluid hanging above her. And so she would sit, and had sat, while they "fed" her.

At first, she'd eaten the meals they brought, but after a few weeks, she started to refuse. While they couldn't force her to eat, they could easily sedate her and hook her up to the bag, which they did, and had done, for weeks.

She rested her head back against the mattress and squeezed her eyes tight in the hope that it would clear some of the fuzziness from her vision. Upon opening them, however, it was actually worse, though in the dim lighting there wasn't much to see by anyway.

The guards still sat at the door. The wall was still there. And every day Oren would come to talk to her. Every day the lights would go up, and every day he'd waltz in and give the guards their leave. Then he'd talk or ask questions; sometimes he'd even answer questions. Sometimes, though, he would just sit and say nothing. He'd just sit there, silently judging or maybe just observing, Kira could never be sure. She figured it didn't really matter. She was a captive audience; he could do what he liked.

And so, like clockwork, the lights in her room went up, and as she squinted against the glare, the door opened and in strode Oren Rhey'll. As always, the guards got up and left without a word—but then, something changed.

Instead of coming over to the wall, Oren lingered by the control panel.

Suddenly Kira heard a slight scraping sound and then the faintest whirring of unseen motors.

A rush of cool air flooded over her.

Fresh air. Fresh, recycled air.

The wall was down.

Her mind was screaming at her to get up and run. Every part of her wanted to, and yet she found herself pressing her back harder into the side of her bed.

"It's all right," Oren said quietly as he walked over and crouched beside her.

He took hold of the restraints around her wrists. Kira tried to push him away, but she couldn't. She flinched as Oren lifted the restraints, but soon, after a near silent hiss, the pressure on her wrists abated and the restraints fell away.

Next thing she knew, there was a sharp pinch as Oren removed the drip. He took hold of her arm and applied pressure with his thumb over the insertion point.

To Kira, it felt strangely reassuring, but she couldn't shake the uneasiness building in the back of her mind.

It was then she noticed her wrists. They were reddened and bruised, but they were free, unbound.

If she could only just . . .

So focused on her wrists was she, that Kira didn't notice Oren had released her arm and was already heading for the door.

"Coming?"

Kira looked up and saw him standing in the corridor. As she got to her feet, she stumbled and her head felt like it might spin off her shoulders. But the feeling passed, and she shuffled slowly to the door.

Her legs ached, along with her back and just about everything else.

By the time she got to the doorway, Oren was already walking away from her, down the corridor.

"What's going on?" Kira called out after him. Her voice was hoarse.

Oren stopped and turned back to face her.

"I think we can both agree you've spent more than enough time in there."

He then turned and continued on.

That was when Kira noticed the corridor itself; it was completely empty. What once was the main thoroughfare for this level of the ship was now devoid of life, save for her and Oren.

Kira began to hurry down the hall after Oren as best as she could manage, but she stopped short as she passed a large viewport.

Before her, Epheria hung silently in the blackness of space. *We haven't gone anywhere.*

By now Oren had stopped at a point farther down the corridor and was waiting for her by a large door. She lingered at the viewport for a moment longer before hurrying over to meet him.

"Why are we still here?" Kira asked, slightly out of breath. "What's going—"

Oren held up a hand to silence her.

"All in good time, Kira," he said with a smile. "But for now, get cleaned up. Once you're done, Caroline will show you where to go."

"Caroline? Who the hell is Caro . . ."

But Oren had already walked off.

Warily, she took a step toward the door, and it opened to reveal a plain-looking woman in her mid-thirties.

"Oh, you must be—"

The woman beamed, and she motioned for Kira to enter. "Caroline, yes."

Kira stepped into the room and found that it was living quarters, and they were far, far nicer than her cell.

"Commander Rhey'll trusts that you should find everything you need here. When you're ready to go, I'll be waiting outside."

And with that, Caroline turned and left, closing the door behind her.

Kira stood for a moment and took in the room. *Everything I'll need?*

As she moved through the room, she discovered that several items had been laid out on what Kira assumed was the dining table.

Kira looked at each of them in turn: a towel; fresh military fatigues, pressed and folded neatly in a pile; combat boots; a belt; a hilt—

Martiss's hilt.

Her hilt.

It felt cold in her hands. She turned it over and over again. It was definitely hers.

Kira placed the hilt back down on the table and took a step back.

It had to be a dream. Surely it had to.

She stared down at the gear laid out before her and pinched herself.

It hurt. It was no dream.

Though the mess hall was filled to near capacity, Oren sat alone at a long and empty table. Around him, Federation soldiers, *his* soldiers, were eating their final meal for the day.

On the table before him sat a small metal box, and it felt heavy as he pushed it around aimlessly.

He knew that it was a risk releasing Kira. Even more so, it was a risk releasing her with only Caroline to guard her. But this was never going to work unless she trusted him. It was a steep hill to climb, but he had every confidence they could get there.

Kira had potential unlike he'd ever seen before. He'd seen and heard the things she was capable of, and there was no doubt that it was just the very tip of her abilities. It was paramount that she come into her potential willingly.

At least at first.

Oren looked up from the table and saw, standing at the end of the row of tables, Kira with Caroline at her side.

Her short hair was out and still slightly damp, and she wore the fatigues he had left for her. She had rolled the long sleeves up to keep them away from her freshly bandaged wrists, and hanging from the small belt around her waist was her hilt.

Oren smiled and waved Kira to the table.

As she walked, Kira could feel the eyes of the soldiers around her. Many quickly disregarded her presence, but some watched her closely. By the time she reached the table, though, they'd all but lost interest.

"You came," Oren said. "Please, have a seat."

Kira remained standing. "Afraid I was going to escape?"

Oren shook his head. "Escape implies that you are still being held, Kira, which I assure you, you are not."

Kira laughed mockingly. "So I'm not being held, but I can't exactly leave, can I?"

"You're more than welcome to try."

She could tell he was only saying it in jest, but she knew there was no point. It didn't take a genius to see how carefully her "release" had been orchestrated.

Left without proper food for weeks, being shot up with who knows what along with her fluids, weakened enough so that when she was finally released, she couldn't retaliate even if she wanted to. Being led out into an empty corridor and giving her no one to go after but Oren, which she knew was a fruitless endeavor. Even leaving her alone with Caroline was smart: she was too kind and stupid for Kira to ever want to hurt.

And then finally to lead her like a tharta right into a mess hall with a few hundred soldiers?

No. She couldn't leave.

She couldn't so much as raise a finger to Oren, and he knew that.

Kira jumped a little as Caroline's arm brushed past hers and placed a tray of food on the table in front of her.

"You should eat something," Oren said, once more motioning for her to sit.

Kira knew what Oren was up to, at least in part, and she knew that she wanted no part of it. At the same time, though, her stomach was growling. She couldn't tell if it was the food itself or just that she was out of her cell, but it smelled good. So, in the end, she relented and sat down across from Oren.

It was then she noticed the small box that Oren was casually pushing around in front of him.

"What's that?" Kira asked through a full mouth of food.

With a small smile, he pushed the box over to her.

"He was given full military honors, as he deserves."

Kira swallowed and then her mouth hung open.

Gregor.

Her hands shook as she reached out for the small metal box.

As she touched it, a wall of emotion hit her and she had to fight back the tears. The box felt cold to the touch, and she didn't need to open it to know what was inside.

Oren remained silent across from her. She kept her eyes down, but she could feel his on her. He was waiting for a reaction.

Kira now knew exactly what Oren was doing—or at least what he was *trying* to do.

He was trying to be her friend.

What his motive was for doing that, though, she couldn't be sure.

What she was sure of, however, was that Oren was misreading the situation entirely.

Surely he must know what his "gift" represented.

The death of her first real friend at Tobias's hand.

A death that Oren himself had put in motion.

Kira had missed her opportunity to kill Tobias, possibly forever.

She had missed her chance for vengeance.

So, in a way, Oren *had* given her a gift.

He'd given her a second chance at vengeance, at justice for Gregor.

Kira exhaled deeply and let the tears begin to roll down her cheek.

She'd been through enough in life to know when to play along.

She'd simply wait it out, pick her moment, and then . . .

Kira met Oren's eyes with an intense stare.

After a long silence, she offered a small smile.

"Thank you."

TO BE CONTINUED . . .

ABOUT THE AUTHOR

Paul Robinson is an author, artist, and maker. He lives in Cundletown, Australia, with his cat Bubs. *Ghosts of War: Retribution* is his first novel.

You can follow him on Twitter: @robo3687.

GRAND PATRONS

Andrew Piper
Cathy Milton
Chris Robinson
Dean Robinson
Glenn Robinson
Ian C. Rogers
Jamie Robinson
Kayla Richardson
Kirsten Shanahan
Kyle Brown
Lisa Hall
Benjamin Macaluso
Lori Multer
Stacey Milton
Murray Cuell
Philip Kingsland
Riki Gardner
Samantha Seymour

INKSHARES

INKSHARES is a reader-driven publisher and producer based in Oakland, California. Our books are selected not by a group of editors, but by readers worldwide.

While we've published books by established writers like *Big Fish* author Daniel Wallace and *Star Wars: Rogue One* scribe Gary Whitta, our aim remains surfacing and developing the new author voices of tomorrow.

Previously unknown Inkshares authors have received starred reviews and been featured in the *New York Times*. Their books are on the front tables of Barnes & Noble and hundreds of independents nationwide, and many have been licensed by publishers in other major markets. They are also being adapted by Oscar-winning screenwriters at the biggest studios and networks.

Interested in making your own story a reality? Visit Inkshares.com to start your own project or find other great books.